WATCHING **THE GIRLS** GO BY

Gender and American Culture

Martha S. Jones and Mary Kelley, editors

The Gender and American Culture series, guided by feminist perspectives, examines the social construction and influence of gender and sexuality within the full range of American cultures. Books in the series explore the intersection of gender (both female and male) with such markers of difference as race, class, and region. The series presents outstanding scholarship from all areas of American studies—including history, literature, religion, folklore, ethnography, and the visual arts—that investigates in a thoroughly contextualized and lively fashion the ways in which gender works with and against these markers. In so doing, the series seeks to reveal how these complex interactions have shaped American life.

A complete list of books published in Gender and American Culture is available at https://uncpress.org/series/gender-and-american-culture.

WATCHING **THE GIRLS** GO BY

A HISTORY OF **STREET HARASSMENT** IN THE UNITED STATES

Molly M. Brookfield

THE UNIVERSITY OF NORTH CAROLINA PRESS

CHAPEL HILL

This book was published with the assistance of the Greensboro Women's Fund of the University of North Carolina Press.

Founding contributors: Linda Arnold Carlisle, Sally Schindel Cone, Anne Faircloth, Bonnie McElveen Hunter, Linda Bullard Jennings, Janice J. Kerley (in honor of Margaret Supplee Smith), Nancy Rouzer May, and Betty Hughes Nichols.

Designed by April Leidig
Set in Garamond by Copperline Book Services, Inc.
Manufactured in the United States of America

Sections of chapter 4 and the epilogue first appeared in Molly Brookfield, "The Girl Watcher: Celebrating a Man's Right to Look in the Post-War USA," *Gender & History* 37, no. 1 (2025): 315–32. https://doi.org/10.1111/1468-0424.12698.

Frontis: Detail, "Horn-Rimmed Booklugger," in Sauers, *Girl Watcher's Guide*, 56. Illustration by Eldon Dedini. Author's collection.

Cover art: *I Am Seeing Great Things* postcard, ca. 1915. (X2011.34.106). Courtesy of the Museum of the City of New York.

Library of Congress Cataloging-in-Publication Data
Names: Brookfield, Molly M., author.
Title: Watching the girls go by : a history of street harassment in the United States / Molly M. Brookfield.
Other titles: Gender & American culture.
Description: Chapel Hill : The University of North Carolina Press, [2026] | Series: Gender and American culture | Includes bibliographical references and index.
Identifiers: LCCN 2026017281 | ISBN 9781469697291 (cloth) | ISBN 9781469697307 (paperback) | ISBN 9781469692401 (epub) | ISBN 9781469697314 (pdf)
Subjects: LCSH: Street harassment—United States—History. | Sexual harassment of women—United States—History. | Urban women—United States—History. | BISAC: SOCIAL SCIENCE / Gender Studies | SOCIAL SCIENCE / Sociology / Urban
Classification: LCC HQ1237.5.U6 B76 2026
LC record available at https://lccn.loc.gov/2026017281

For product safety concerns under the European Union's General Product Safety Regulation (EU GPSR), please contact gpsr@mare-nostrum.co.uk or write to the University of North Carolina Press and Mare Nostrum Group B.V., Doelen 72, 4831 GR Breda, The Netherlands.

To Grandma June

and all the women who, like her,
never would have used the term
"street harassment" but who
experienced it nonetheless

CONTENTS

ILLUSTRATIONS

WATCHING **THE GIRLS** GO BY

INTRODUCTION

Americans who tuned their radios to a mainstream popular music station in the summer of 1956 were very likely to have heard the Four Lads singing about the pleasures of "standing on the corner . . . watching all the girls go by" at some point in the programming. The song, "Standing on the Corner," was originally penned for Frank Loesser's Broadway musical *The Most Happy Fella* and is sung from the perspective of a group of men, down on their luck and single, who get their kicks by ogling "girls." As one singer puts it, though he is broke, he feels rich whenever he heads out on the street to "review the harem parading for me there." Accompanied by a chorus of wolf whistles, the singers assure male listeners that "you can't go to jail for what you're thinking" about the women who pass by on the street.[1] "Standing on the Corner" would become one of the Four Lads' biggest hits, peaking at number three on the Billboard Hot 100.[2] The subject matter proved popular with the listening public. Dean Martin's recording of "Standing on the Corner" peaked at twenty-two on the Billboard charts that same year, and it was followed by a slew of similar songs of the 1950s and 1960s that celebrated the pastime of watching girls on the street, including the number-one hits "Hey! Baby" by Bruce Channel (1962) and "Oh, Pretty Woman" by Roy Orbison (1964).[3]

In 1956, it was at least partially true that "you can't go to jail" for watching women on the street. Certainly, the white men who sang these hit songs could safely watch, whistle at, and catcall women on the street with little fear of state intervention. At the time, such behaviors were widely accepted as normal, and relatively harmless, expressions of heterosexual desire on the part of white men. Though some women found it annoying to be watched or whistled at, white Americans rarely questioned the commonsense belief that it was natural for a virile, red-blooded American man to admire the women he encountered in his daily life. Boys, after all, will be boys.

However, not all men could feel assured they would escape reprimand if they watched women on the street. For one thing, if white Americans suspected a

Black man of watching white women, they did not celebrate him but, rather, could send him to jail or worse, as evidenced by decades of lynching.[4] Five years before "Standing on the Corner" hit the Billboard charts, Caswell County Court in North Carolina caused a national sensation when it convicted Black farmer Matt Ingram of assault by looking, what the press dubbed "eye rape." A white teenage girl, Willie Jean Boswell, had accused Ingram of watching her from a distance of seventy-five feet. Though Ingram was eventually acquitted on appeal, his initial conviction and years of court battles highlighted how a man's ability to watch girls without consequence depended a great deal on who he was and whom he was suspected of watching.[5]

And yet, even white men were not always free to ogle with impunity. In 1916, the nation was in the throes of a crusade against "mashers," men predominantly assumed to be white who accosted women in public places across the United States. In the winter of that year, the *Atlanta Constitution* reported that city councils in New York and Chicago had passed municipal ordinances to crack down on mashers. In Boston, men caught ogling, annoying, or accosting women in public could be fined up to $200 or spend up to six months in jail. "He who would ogle pretty women" should take heed, warned the *Constitution*, "and he must keep out of the eye of the law."[6]

At the height of the masher panic, over a dozen cities across the country had laws or ordinances on the books designed to criminalize accosting women in public. Because most reports of the time depicted mashers as white men who put on gentlemanly airs with the nefarious intent of sweet-talking a young woman, antimasher laws were generally intended to target white men. Several laws explicitly forbade intrusive looking, such as an ordinance that made it "Unlawful for Any Male Person to Stare, or Make What is Commonly Called 'Goo-goo Eyes'" at "Any Woman . . . Traveling Along Any of the Streets of the City of Houston."[7] At the turn of the twentieth century, even a white man could, in fact, "go to jail" for "the 'wooooo' look in [his] eye," to quote the Four Lads.[8]

What accounts for this shift in the way Americans, particularly white Americans, viewed white men's ogling, catcalling, and similar intrusive behaviors in public space? How did Americans go from trying to jail white oglers in the 1910s to celebrating them in popular songs forty years later? How did the normalization of intrusive behaviors in white men rely on the criminalization of poor or working-class men and men of color, especially Black men, and the demonization of real or imagined intrusions like Ingram's "eye rape"? What impact did intrusive looking, sexual comments, groping, and indecent exposure have on women and their ability to navigate public space? These are the questions *Watching the Girls Go By* seeks to answer.

Watching the Girls Go By examines the history of Americans' contestations over men's harassment of women in public spaces, especially urban spaces, across the country from the postbellum era to the 1980s. It charts how American social and cultural discourses normalized behaviors like catcalling and ogling—intrusive behaviors now commonly termed "street harassment"—as healthy expressions of heterosexual masculinity for middle-class white men over the course of the nineteenth and twentieth centuries. Such normalization was not inevitable. Urban reformers and women's rights activists denounced and resisted street harassment in the late nineteenth and early twentieth centuries, singling out middle-class and elite white men as some of the worst perpetrators. However, a steady stream of humorous depictions of behaviors like ogling or catcalling in American popular media trivialized middle-class white men's intrusions and established their "right" to watch, accost, and otherwise harass women in public space by the mid-1940s. To secure middle-class white men's claim to the "harem parading" down the street each day (to return to Frank Loesser's lyrics), white Americans demonized men of color and working-class men as the quintessential, and more dangerous, harassers of women in public space. In particular, white Americans' claims that men of color, especially Black men, wolf-whistled or stared at white women were excuses for public, often violent, punishment. Whether such intrusions ever took place was beside the point. In the logic of Jim Crow America, protecting middle-class white men's claim to women's bodies in public space required denying such claims to anyone not similarly privileged. Ultimately, the normalization and persistence of white men's street harassment contributed to women's discomfort and fear of sexual violence and curtailed their mobility in American public space in the nineteenth and twentieth centuries.

The impact of the historical normalization of street harassment is still felt today. For one, street harassment is extremely common. Recent studies suggest that as many as 85 percent of women in the United States have experienced street harassment in their lifetime and that more women experience sexual harassment in public space than in any other location, including the workplace.[9] Scholars of gender-based harassment more broadly have shown that many Americans continue to believe that intrusive behaviors like ogling and catcalling are mundane and trivial, despite evidence to the contrary.[10] In fact, the litany of sexual jokes, put-downs, incivility, and other typical behaviors generally associated with street harassment are far more common than the violent, serial offenses that tend to garner attention in popular media and that dominate the public imagination of sexual misconduct.

The typical forms of gendered harassment that constitute most street harassment have an outsize impact that belies their seemingly trivial nature.[11] Scholars of the phenomenon have shown that a society that treats street harassment as trivial teaches men that women do not deserve privacy or bodily autonomy in public space. For instance, women are not afforded the same right to "civil inattention" as men, to borrow Erving Goffman's term for the way strangers tend to politely ignore one another on the street, thus granting each other anonymity and privacy in public.[12] Writing not long after feminists coined the term "street harassment" in the 1970s, sociologists Cheryl Benard and Edit Schlaffer insisted that the perceived "harmlessness" of street harassment endangered women's bodily autonomy. Street harassment, they argued, "blurs the borders of women's right to personal integrity," encouraging even an otherwise nonviolent man "to engage in minor transgressions against her right to move freely" and making him "an accomplice in the more massive forms of violence against women."[13] Indeed, street harassment has been adept at forcing women to constrain or modify their movement through public space.[14] As feminist geographer Leslie Kern argues, street harassment and other forms of gendered policing uphold "male power and privilege . . . by keeping women's movements limited and their ability to access different spaces constrained."[15] Similarly, feminist philosopher Sally Scholz has provocatively described street harassment as "part of the strategy of the war within patriarchy." Intrusions like catcalls dehumanize the target, fragmenting her, reducing her to body parts (for instance, a "nice piece of ass"), and justifying future violence against her.[16] Acceptance of street harassment as mundane and harmless is a sign that a society trivializes and normalizes men's violence against women in myriad forms.[17] In a practical sense, then, the normalization of middle-class white men's street harassment has helped legitimate white supremacist patriarchal power and control over public space and the bodies that move through it.

WATCHING THE GIRLS GO BY is a multipronged story, situated in histories of urban space, gender and masculinity, and rape and sexual violence. It encapsulates over 130 years of United States history and covers a broad geographical region. The reasons for these parameters derive from the archive itself. A US historian can find examples of street harassment in every decade of the last 200 years and in rural areas, urban areas, and everything in between. Temporal breadth allows me to chart how groups of Americans—social commentators, reformers, activists, legislators, cultural producers, and individual men and women who interacted in public space—alternately protested street harassment as a form of men's violence against women or embraced those same behaviors as signs of a playful heterosexual desire. This scope illuminates how the history of street harassment is both one of change and one of continuity. It is a story of shifting definitions of street harassment, contestations over the meaning of public intrusive behaviors, and Americans' varied responses, as well as of the persistent curbing of women's unhindered access to public space.

While street harassment can exist anywhere, the earliest discussion of such behaviors began with the growth of modern American cities. *Watching the Girls Go By* thus begins in the mid-nineteenth century as the material and demographic changes that came with urbanization—increased anonymity, the development of mass public transit, and the mixing of genders, races, and classes in public space—made it possible for men to harass women they did not know in public space in significant numbers. Men stared at, touched, and inappropriately addressed white women who demanded respectable treatment in public while physically assaulting or hurling racial epithets at Black women, particularly those who claimed a right to ride public transport. In cities like New York and Philadelphia, urban reformers and women's rights activists protested the "street insults" that welcomed women as they navigated a public urban space built by and for white men. By the 1880s, these expressions of white male entitlement were so prevalent that they became the defining feature of a new category of man, the "masher." Progressive Era women reformers used this framing to advocate for state intervention to protect women in public places, leading to a slew of antimasher legislation and the introduction of women into law enforcement roles.

In these early years of grappling with street harassment, women's rights activists particularly condemned middle-class and elite white men's entitlement in public space. The men who printed stories about street insults and "mashing" in city newspapers were wont to pin such disruptive behaviors on poor, immigrant, and nonwhite men. However, women who actually experienced street harassment frequently lambasted so-called gentlemen as the worst perpetrators. Indeed, they admonished such men for failing to live up to the standards expected of their class and social status.

Nevertheless, women's work to name, define, and condemn the harm they experienced because of street harassment did not have the long-lasting impact intended. Instead, with the political victory of women's suffrage in 1920 and the revolution in sexual mores and gender norms that defined the ensuing decade, claims that men ogling or catcalling women diminished their access to public space lost their potency. Popular narratives increasingly represented catcalling, ogling, and similar behaviors as harmless, humorous, and even desirable parts of heterosexual flirtation in public space. With the advent of World War II, the United States military further encouraged enlisted men to engage in behaviors like ogling and wolf-whistling as a way to satisfy sexual needs without the danger of contracting sexually transmitted infections. As veterans returned home, Cold War anxieties that suburbia and corporate America would stifle American masculinity led to a new valorization of "girl-watching," the practice of surreptitiously assessing women's bodies in public space. Middle-class white men embraced girl-watching as a humorous way to express a virile heterosexuality without forfeiting either middle-class gentility or monogamous heterosexual marriage.

The rehabilitation of middle-class white men's public ogling as harmless, desirable, and even celebrated drew on and contributed to the racial dynamics and racist violence of Jim Crow America. White military officers, cartoonists, filmmakers, advertising executives, and businessmen elevated "girl-watching" to the status of harmless pastime primarily, if not exclusively, for middle-class white men. In order to assert the ownership over women's bodies that girl-watching implied, middle-class white men relied on the explicit and violent denial of any similar claim by men of color and, to a lesser extent, poor and working-class men. White Americans thus cast Black men as violent sexual aggressors whose wayward glances, even imagined ones, were tantamount to "eye rape" or whose alleged wolf whistles became grounds for kidnapping, torture, and murder. Popular media also emphasized that "genteel" middle-class men were surreptitious in their admiration of women on the street, suggesting that the intrusions of working-class men were ostentatious and, essentially, more intrusive. When feminists revived protests against ogling, catcalling, and wolf-whistling and demanded an end to what they called "street harassment" in the 1970s, white feminists perpetuated these same narratives. They reserved much of their sharpest criticism and vitriol for Black men, Latino men, and working-class construction workers but struggled to articulate and condemn street harassment from the middle-class white men who had been the primary targets of reformers' ire at the beginning of the century.

Watching the Girls Go By is thus a history of the way normalized violence helped maintain white supremacist patriarchy in public space.[18] By casting Black men, other men of color, and working-class men as not only the more dangerous but, in some cases, the only true harassers of women, middle-class white men legitimated their claim to women's bodies in public space. In uncovering these machinations, I show the tenuousness and fraudulence of this claim. That is, like any norm, the idea that middle-class and elite white men had an inherent right to public space and to those who occupied it was an idea that had to be constructed, reinforced, and actively policed throughout its history.[19] *Watching the Girls Go By* shows these processes in the making and the impact that policing this new norm had on the lives and bodies of anyone who was not an economically privileged white man.

From "Street Harassment" to "Men's Stranger Intrusions"

The term "street harassment" emerged in the 1970s as feminist activists and researchers sought a succinct term for one of the forms of everyday sexism that plagued them.[20] "Street harassment" beat out "street hassling," "street compliments," "verbal rape," and "street comments" to become, by the mid-1980s, the most widely used term to describe the phenomenon of men intruding on women they did not know in public places.[21] The work of feminist activists and scholars to name and condemn workplace "sexual harassment" in the same period likely gave "street harassment" additional weight, linking it to the higher-profile studies and legal cases that insisted sexual harassment was a form of sex discrimination.[22] The term remains widely used in both popular and scholarly writing.[23]

Today, "street harassment" remains such a prevalent and legible phrase that I chose to include it in the title of this book, but it is ultimately an anachronistic term and imperfect for a historian's work. First, the historical actors in these pages defined the phenomenon of men ogling, catcalling, and otherwise intruding on women in public space in myriad ways that changed over time. Each term suggested a different view of these behaviors. For instance, in 1860s New York, women complained that men who brushed up against them on the street or stared at them for an uncomfortably long time on public transportation were perpetrating a "street insult." This term highlighted the social status of the victim as much as the perpetrator's behavior. It suggested that nineteenth-century Americans believed an insult could occur only when the target was a virtuous and respectable woman, often a white woman who claimed to be a "lady," for only such a woman could be "insulted" by a man intruding on her in a public place. The association of "insult" and respectable victimhood was so strong that Black women strategically used the language of "insult" to claim respectability in public space, even when the behaviors they complained of were far more severe than those white women protested, including racial slurs and physical assault. An anachronistic term like "street harassment" cannot capture these nuances. It risks casting the problem of uninvited attention from male strangers in ways that would not have been familiar to Americans living before the 1970s.

Second, the term "street harassment" presupposes both a location and the target's perception of the action. The historical subjects featured in this book experienced uncomfortable leers and lewd comments in all sorts of public and semipublic places beyond the street, as well as in urban areas, suburbs, small towns, and even country roads. Movie theaters and public transit proved especially troublesome in the early 1900s, while beaches were popular sites for "girl-watching" in 1960s Los Angeles and Chicago. The white teenager who accused Matt Ingram of "eye rape" claimed his looks "frightened" her across seventy-five feet of rural North Carolina woods.[24] So the word "street" hardly captures the widespread nature of the phenomenon. As for the negative and even violent connotation of the term "harassment," not all women experienced ogling or catcalls as negative or unwanted. In the mid-1940s, a white woman responded to a police crackdown on ogling in Detroit by insisting that she liked when men ogled her; otherwise how could she be sure she was still attractive to them?[25] Indeed, in the racially segregated cities of the twentieth century, the same exchange or behavior might be experienced or interpreted very differently depending on where it took place—a racially segregated neighborhood or a public park in a more integrated part of the city—and on the race and class identities of the participants.[26] If street harassment was neither always on the street nor always experienced as negative, then historians need other terminology to understand the phenomenon and to recognize it in archival sources.

Instead of "street harassment," I use terminology that emphasizes the intrusiveness of the behaviors that male strangers directed at women in public places. Feminist philosopher Fiona Vera-Gray has convincingly argued for the term "men's stranger intrusions on women in public space," shortened to "men's stranger intrusions" or "men's intrusive practices," which she defines as the "deliberate act of putting oneself into a place or situation where one is uninvited, with disruptive effect."[27] Intrusions can range from ogling and uninvited "compliments" to shouted slurs, indecent exposure, following, groping, and further physical violence. The term "men's stranger intrusions" offers historians an effective conceptual tool to track how these behaviors changed over time. It emphasizes that the exchange is gendered and involves strangers; it acknowledges that the behaviors take place in many public spaces, not just the street; and it eschews the negative connotations of the word "harassment," leaving room for diverse emotional reactions to the behaviors. Thus, in these pages, I use the terms "stranger intrusions," "intrusive behaviors," and "intrusive practices"—often modified to indicate these behaviors are "men's"—to identify the behaviors that are the highlight of this study.

Intrusive Behaviors and Male Entitlement

Since feminists first theorized "street harassment" as a form of gender-based harm in public space, researchers have posited many definitions and parameters to understand the phenomenon. In the 1980s and 1990s, most research on "street harassment" understood it as a problem of male perpetrators and female victims. For example, anthropologist Micaela di Leonardo offered an early definition in 1981: "Street harassment occurs when one or more strange men accost one or more women whom they perceive as heterosexual in a public place which is not the woman's/women's worksite. Through looks, words, or gestures the man asserts his right to intrude on the woman's attention, defining her as a sexual object, and forcing her to interact with him."[28] Leonardo's definition drew on a decade of revived feminist activism against intrusive behaviors in the 1970s, most of which had discussed "street harassment" only as involving a male harasser and a female target.

In recent years, activists and researchers have increasingly heeded the lessons of intersectionality scholarship to emphasize that street harassment will look different depending on the perpetrator's and the target's identities. It does not even require a male perpetrator and female target. Anyone can be a target of intrusive behaviors in public, and anyone can perpetrate such intrusions.[29] A more expansive definition of "stranger intrusions in public places" opens up the possibility of considering gender-based or sexual intrusions alongside intrusions based on myriad other social identities. Race, age, sexuality, gender expression, ability, religion, size: All these factors, both real and perceived, can be the basis of stranger intrusions and can affect the experiences of both perpetrators and targets of intrusive behaviors, as well as the specific behaviors or remarks that constitute the harassment.[30]

Such an expansive definition can illuminate the ways people other than cis men have been perpetrators of stranger intrusions. The famous photograph of Hazel Bryan screaming insults at Elizabeth Eckford, one of the nine Black students who integrated Little Rock Central High School in Arkansas in 1957, is evidence that white women, including poor white women like Bryan, have harassed Black women in public as a way to support racial segregation and the supremacy of whiteness in their communities.[31] Women who do not engage in sex work have also been documented harassing sex workers as a way to differentiate themselves from those they perceive as transgressing boundaries of "good" womanhood.[32] Gender nonconforming, trans, and nonbinary people increasingly draw attention to the way strangers harness homophobic and transphobic epithets and threats of violence to police gender expression in public.[33] In 2011, CeCe McDonald, a Black trans woman, was charged with murdering a white man who, along with a group of bar patrons, hurled racist and transphobic verbal insults and finally a glass tumbler at McDonald as she walked to a grocery store in Minneapolis. McDonald's conviction and incarceration sparked activist campaigns that sought to highlight the everyday violence that trans people, especially trans people of color, experience in public space.[34] What these examples have in common is the way strangers can use intrusive behaviors to turn an everyday interaction into an assertion of social hierarchies and an affirmation of the supremacy of some aspect of the perpetrator's identity.

Still, using both current and historical definitions of intrusive behaviors between strangers in public, cis men are the most likely perpetrators of such intrusions, especially sexual or gender-based intrusions.[35] According to a 2014 report from the advocacy group Stop Street Harassment, most perpetrators of "street harassment" are men, and their targets are predominantly women.[36] As will become clear in the ensuing chapters, Americans have also historically understood behaviors like wolf-whistling, catcalling, and ogling as involving primarily a male actor and a female target, including when those behaviors were considered natural or complimentary.

Stranger intrusions, then, tell us something about men. For one, intrusive practices are a way of performing a specific masculinity. In a world that sees violence and aggression as masculine qualities, sociologist Simone Kolysh argues that stranger intrusions help cisgender heterosexual men assert their gender identity.[37] In her work on workplace girl-watching, legal scholar Beth Quinn argues that ogling women in groups works "as a dramatic performance played to other men, a means by which a certain type of masculinity is produced and heterosexual desire displayed."[38] Thus, when practiced in the company of other men, stranger intrusions can also bond men to one another.[39] As these examples suggest, recent scholarship has tended to associate stranger intrusions with normative or hegemonic masculinity, indicating that when men engage in intrusive practices they "improve their ranking on the masculine scale."[40] However, only some men have historically had access to stranger intrusions as a pathway to performing hegemonic masculinity, as categories like class and race shape perceptions of stranger intrusions, with poorer men and men of color consistently perceived as more frequent perpetrators of intrusive behaviors and more dangerous harassers than middle-class or white men.[41]

Sociologist R. W. Connell originally developed a theory of "hegemonic masculinity" in the 1980s.[42] Connell and her colleague James Messerschmidt define hegemonic masculinity as a "normative" ideal of masculine behavior—a "pattern of practice"—that "embodie[s] the currently most honored way of being a man" and "require[s] all other men to position themselves in relation to it."[43] Like any hegemonic discourse, hegemonic masculinity is taken for granted—as Messerschmidt puts it, it is "hidden in plain sight"—and it relies both on the compliance of those who directly benefit from its ascendancy and on the "consent and participation by the subaltern groups."[44] Hegemonic masculinity's most important feature is that it helps justify unequal gender relations, both between men and women but also between "masculinities and femininities, and among masculinities."[45] That is, a masculinity is not hegemonic unless it legitimates patriarchy. As a result, the concept of hegemonic masculinity can help make sense of the role that stranger intrusions have historically played in men's lives.

A history of men's stranger intrusions demonstrates how hegemonic masculinity has been subject to contestation, disruption, adaptation, and change. As British historian Ben Griffin argues, the concept of hegemonic masculinity offers a framework to help gender historians chart the "contests for power and influence between competing models of masculinity and the institutions implicated in those struggles."[46] Hegemonic masculinity is neither static nor transhistorical but necessarily incorporates shifts in discourse, material circumstances, and social relations in order to remain dominant. From frivolous play to condemned trespass, men's stranger intrusions in the United States are no exception.

Watching the Girls Go By documents the creation and contestation of a model of hegemonic masculinity that embraced stranger intrusions as part of its expression in public. Middle-class white men reinforced their power in public space by identifying and practicing the masculine type that embraced stranger intrusions and denying that same identification to men of color, especially Black men, and working-class men through vilification and violence. Furthermore, the actual practices of that hegemonic masculine type—the behaviors like catcalling, ogling, wolf-whistling, groping, and following—afforded middle-class white men power by denying their targets a claim to public space.

The impact that men's stranger intrusions have had on women's lives—the way men's expressions of entitlement increase women's fears of public space and curtail their freedom of movement—belies the decades-long normalization and trivialization of such behaviors that this book documents. Since the 1980s, feminist scholars have argued that women do not experience sexual violence in the hierarchized, clear-cut way that it is often described in academic research, popular media, or the legal code. Rather, acts of sexual violence reinforce one another along a continuum, where "typical" behaviors—ogling, sexual comments, wolf-whistling—can be experienced as dangerous because they serve as reminders of more extreme forms of violence or as warnings of potential danger ahead.[47] A lascivious leer may not devolve into physical violence, but cultural messages, personal experience, and even the prevalence of crime reporting in a particular area can contribute to a feeling that such "typical" behaviors could quickly escalate into something far more "serious."[48] As sociologist Liz Kelly influentially argued in 1988, this means street harassment exists along a "continuum" of sexual violence where the fear or memory of more extreme forms of sexual violence give street harassment outsize power. "It is important to remember," Kelly reminds us, "that although further violence may not be intended" in any given interaction, "women cannot know this until after the event."[49]

This blurring of typical and aberrant forms of sexual violence was well known to Americans for over a century before feminists adopted the concept of a continuum of sexual violence. In the nineteenth century, white women were expected to guard against the male gaze for its own sake but also because oglers were potential (if not actual) rapists.[50] A fear of escalation could influence a woman's decisions about how to navigate public space. For example, a New York woman walking home alone late at night in 1838 reluctantly allowed a strange man to accompany her home. She reportedly "fear[ed] he might take further advantage of her unprotected situation" and decided giving in to his demand was safer than refusing.[51] Real-life escalations could confirm such fears. When Richard Ivens murdered socialite Bessie Hollister on the streets of Chicago in 1906, coverage of the incident depicted Ivens as a meandering stranger who took the opportunity to accost an unescorted woman and then murdered her when she resisted his advances.[52] Reports linked Hollister's murder with intrusive behaviors of so-called mashers and called on law enforcement to "arrest 'mashers' and young men loitering at street corners" so that Chicago women might feel safe in public again.[53] Seven decades later in 1978, a young woman participating in a survey on sexual violence explained how, after surviving a sexual assault, "I don't move around the city as freely as I did in the past." The assault had made her more afraid of public space and "suspicious of men in new situations."[54] These examples, where interactions with strange men conjured memories or fears of rape and murder, illustrate Vera-Gray's argument that "quieter forms of intrusion . . . rely on the possibilities and realities of the louder, criminal forms, to have the particular impact they do."[55] Men's stranger intrusions both derive power from and reinforce larger societal messages about women's sexual and physical vulnerability in public space.

Apart from their connection to aberrant forms of sexual violence, stranger intrusions are also annoying, disruptive, and violent for their own sake, and they demonstrate the kinds of expectations male strangers have of women they encounter in public. Building on the work of the feminist activists who theorized "street harassment" and other forms of everyday violence in the 1970s, feminist sociologists Sue Wise and Liz Stanley suggested in 1987 that the smaller everyday burdens that men impose on women—the expectations of time, attention, and care that include stranger intrusions—are the "dripping tap" of sexism. In contrast to the "sledgehammer" of more egregious and "extreme" forms of sexual violence and discrimination, the dripping tap constitutes an endless stream of small, individual slights, put-downs, or demands on a woman's time and energy.[56] When a target experiences repeated stranger intrusions, weekly or daily and compounded over many years, she can develop a feeling of being always watched and always needing to be "on guard," or simply of being worn down in what sociologist Bianca Fileborn calls "feminist erosion."[57] One feminist writer described this very phenomenon in 1980, seven years before Wise and Stanley gave it a name: Every time a man approached her on the street, she began to worry that he might "stare at me too long or try to approach me in a more direct way." If the man passed her with no uncomfortable stares or remarks, she felt "grateful for his chivalrous mercy in sparing me, but I berate[d] myself for my 'paranoia.'"[58] In effect, the repetitive experience of intrusive behaviors teach a target to move through the world as if an intrusion is *always about* to occur, constantly bracing for the next catcall or leer.[59]

Daily stranger intrusions, then, can be thought of as a form of male entitlement. Indeed, while men's stranger intrusions can include truly frightening interactions, even the most benign intrusion can have a disruptive effect on the target.[60] A well-intentioned man wishing to pay a genuine compliment to a woman on the street still imposes himself, requesting her attention and forcing her to consider whether or how she will respond.[61] As feminist philosopher Kate Manne argues, such impositions force women into paying attention to men, into fulfilling their supposed duties as the carers and lovers of men. The nature of men's stranger intrusions—demands as seemingly benign as "Smile for me" or "What are you thinking about?"—give away the plot. A man who tells a woman to smile betrays an expectation that she should look up and focus her attention on him, not on her own thoughts, feelings, or inner life. He betrays a belief that she is there to fulfill his needs. By extension, if she ignores him, she does more than simply fail to respond. In the logic of misogyny, she abdicates her female responsibility to cater to male desires and deserves whatever punishment she gets.[62] Indeed, male aggression and even physical violence is a well-documented response to women who ignore or resist intrusive behaviors in public space.[63] The history of men's stranger intrusions shows that middle-class white men have embraced and policed the performance of entitlement inherent in intrusive behaviors, insisting that claims to women's time, attention, and bodies are theirs and theirs alone. Thus catcalls, staring, and other fleeting intrusions are sites of everyday oppression, violence, and misogyny as well as potential sites of everyday resistance.[64]

Documenting the History of Men's Stranger Intrusions

How exactly does one research the history of men's intrusive behaviors? The ephemeral nature of stranger intrusions presents a unique challenge for any scholar wishing to document their history. Catcalls and leers exist for mere seconds, evaporating into the air as quickly as they appear. I thus draw on a diverse array of primary sources to document how Americans understood men's stranger intrusions at different points in time. When activists, reformers, and city officials saw white men's intrusive behaviors as an issue of public safety, newspapers reported on individual incidents and cities passed antimashing legislation. Popular cultural products like songs, films, or novels help me trace the trivialization of men's stranger intrusions until they were seen as a normal, even humorous part of urban life by the mid-twentieth century. Finally, women who experienced behaviors like ogling and catcalling held feminist consciousness-raising groups, published manifestos, and discussed their experiences in diaries, published works, interviews, and oral histories, offering insights into how women shaped definitions of and activism against men's intrusive behaviors and how their experiences differed from or reflected mainstream cultural representations.

The archive shapes the focus of the ensuing chapters, as each time period offers different kinds of sources and requires different analytical frameworks. The first two chapters are centered in the urban North, where American cities emerged in the nineteenth century and grew at precipitous rates at the turn of the twentieth century. Here, the archive consists of newspaper reporting on insults and mashing as well as documents from urban reformers and women's rights activists who decried men's stranger intrusions in these cities and proposed solutions to the burgeoning problem. The narrative takes detours to the South to juxtapose the racial politics of men's stranger intrusions in Northern cities with Jim Crow cities.

For two reasons, the remaining chapters tell a more national story. First, increasing numbers of Americans moved to urban areas as the twentieth century progressed, with more than two-thirds of Americans living in cities by 1960.[65] In a new era of urban growth, the environments and demographics that made men's stranger intrusions commonplace spread across the country. Therefore, while the first two chapters of this book rely heavily on archives in major Northern cities like New York and Chicago, chapters 3, 4, and 5 draw on sources from a much broader range of places, especially newer urban centers in the West, Midwest, and South. Second, for periods when men's stranger intrusions were increasingly normalized, specific incidents of intrusions are much harder to find in the archive. When a behavior like ogling was considered normal or trivial, there was little incentive to document it. Thus, the kinds of antiharassment diatribes that were a staple of the early 1900s and 1910s all but disappeared in the 1930s through the 1960s. Instead, a national discourse that poked fun at stranger intrusions emerges in chapters 3 and 4. Newspapers, magazines, films, and popular music represented wolf-whistling, girl-watching, and other forms of stranger intrusions in a more abstract way, as the butt of jokes or as humorous commentary on the battle of the sexes. The fifth chapter, set in the 1970s and early 1980s, shifts the focus to active feminist groups that, like their Progressive Era forebears, worked once again to denaturalize "street harassment" and find solutions to the everyday sexism that women endured on city streets across the country. New York and Chicago reemerge as prominent cities for anti–street harassment activism, while feminist groups in Washington, DC, bring the nation's capital more fully into frame, as well.

Ultimately, this is a history of the ascendancy of a national norm, and thus it focuses predominantly (though not exclusively) on middle- and upper-class discourses, culture, and media. While there may be many different norms of masculinity within different communities, I am most interested in the norms that spread across the country through national newspapers, films, radio, and other popular media.[66] Media historians have shown how middle-class Americans created a truly national culture, reading the same newspapers and books and, especially in the twentieth century, self-consciously identifying as part of the "American middle-class."[67] The ensuing chapters will thus show how mainstream middle-class culture and public discourse have been instrumental to the creation, contestation, and dissemination of new norms for masculine behavior and to the persistence and normalization of middle-class white men's stranger intrusions in particular. While stranger intrusions emerged as a result of shifting demographic changes in growing urban centers, they persisted because newspapers, music, film, and popular print culture trivialized and normalized the behaviors. These media proliferated a "common-sense" belief that ogling or wolf-whistling, while potentially annoying, were ultimately harmless when a respectable white man was the instigator.[68] *Watching the Girls Go By* seeks to complicate this view, to reveal the violence and entitlement in the seemingly mundane and trivial. What is common sense now was not always so, nor need it remain so.

The scope of this project allows me to make two contributions to existing scholarship. First, *Watching the Girls Go By* offers a long-term model of how new masculine norms, particularly hegemonic masculinities, are created, contested, and adapted when challenged. It took time and, yes, effort to convince Americans that intrusive behaviors like catcalling or ogling, once considered aberrant and incompatible with respectable masculinity, should be considered natural and complimentary when practiced by middle-class white men. Second, this project complicates claims about how women's public presence in

American cities changed conceptions of gender, sexuality, and race. Historians of the urban United States have shown how the growth of cities offered many Americans opportunities for anonymity and social fluidity.[69] However, urbanization was a double-edged sword. The same anonymity that made the city ideal for challenging gender roles and experimenting with sexual subjectivities also allowed white male strangers to harass women in public with impunity. While the growth of American cities gave women unprecedented opportunities to exercise personal, political, and sexual autonomy, it also made possible the harassment that limited women's ability to fully exercise these newfound freedoms.[70] As legal scholar Cynthia Grant Bowman observed in her oft-cited essay on street harassment, freedom of movement is one of the most fundamental civil liberties and is required for the exercise of all other liberties and rights. Stranger intrusions thus "substantially limited" women's liberty even as that liberty expanded.[71] Freedom and its repression emerged hand in hand.

CHAPTER **ONE**

STREET INSULTS

On a fall afternoon in 1869, a public omnibus rumbled past the elegant homes along Fifth Avenue in New York City. The passengers were mostly fashionable, affluent men and women who could afford the extra fare to ride the horse-drawn omnibuses, or stages, rather than the louder, more crowded streetcars.[1] Among the passengers were two young white women riding uptown after a day in Brooklyn. At some point in their journey, one of the women felt something gently pressing against her back. At first, she "did not think anything of it," but when the feeling continued, she eventually realized it came from the well-dressed older gentleman sitting behind her. The man, who was resting his hand on the back of the woman's seat, seemed to be deliberately and repeatedly pressing his hand into her back. In recounting the story later, the young woman described how "every minute or so" she felt his hand on her back, and as time passed, "he pressed more perceptibly" against her. The young woman, "frightened" by his uninvited touching, alerted her friend to his conduct and together they decided to leave the stage before their stop. The women were then "obliged to . . . walk all the way home."[2]

Sometime later, the young woman shared her story with the *New York Times* in a letter denouncing the "outrages" that women endured on public transportation. The writer, who chose the pseudonym "A Young Lady," described the uninvited attention women received on streetcars and public stages across New York City. She claimed the worst offenders of such "insults" were "gentlemen," or at the very least, men who dressed like gentlemen. Insults could be as small as a man who brushed his dirty boots against her clean dress or, more ominously, could be the rows of staring eyes that greeted a lady whenever she boarded a streetcar or stage. This was not the first or only time A Young Lady had dealt with men's intrusive behaviors. "Every now and then," she explained, "in the Fifth Avenue stage, I am obliged to say to the man next to me, 'Please, Sir, will you move your arm off the back of my seat, that I may lean back a little?'" The only surefire way to evade this behavior on public transportation was to refrain from riding the streetcars and stages altogether. Indeed, A Young Lady asserted that she often felt "more or less unsafe" on New York's public conveyances, declaring, "I never ride when I can avoid it, only when I am going to Brooklyn." For A Young Lady, a seemingly innocuous action, like a man placing his hand on the back of her seat or watching her adjust her hat, was insulting and threatening to the point that it forced her off public transit.[3]

The "outrages" A Young Lady described would be known by many names, but the mid- to late 1800s saw the rise of the "street insult" as a unique moniker for such intrusive behaviors. Men insulted women in a variety of public and semipublic places, including shops, entertainment venues, and, of course, streets.[4] The behaviors that constituted street insults varied widely, but what they had in common was a male stranger whose actions demonstrated he did not view a "lady"—a contested category that implied respectability and a certain social status—as deserving of respect, privacy, or chivalry. In its most common form, a man engaged in street insult when he made it clear he took a sexual interest in a lady.

For a variety of reasons, street insults tended to be viewed as a problem of larger urban centers. For one, insults generally involved men and women who did not know one another, and cities were notorious for the way they flung strangers together on public transportation, on streets, and in businesses and other gathering places. As American cities grew into the tens of thousands of residents in the mid-1800s, it became normal to walk through cities like Boston and New York for an entire day without encountering a single acquaintance.[5] This urban world of strangers had the effect of cloaking urban residents in a feeling of anonymity, which could be disorienting and alienating for some and exhilarating for others.[6] Anonymity also made it easier for men to accost women in public without fear of being recognized or reprimanded, facilitating the rise in street insults.

Street insults also reflected assumptions about whom the city was for and who had the right to move through urban space unmolested. As cities grew, male politicians, city planners, economic leaders, and academics hoped to control what they saw as the disorderliness and chaos of the metropolis and viewed women as a major source of disorder. Historian Elizabeth Wilson has argued that the presence of women in the nineteenth-century city represented for men both sexual possibility (in the form of temptresses and prostitutes) and sexual danger (in the form of venereal disease). Respectable women were also at risk of reputational ruin if seduced by licentious men or tempted into an immoral lifestyle by sexually promiscuous women.[7] One way to impose greater order on the city was to divide it into separate men's and women's spaces, with women's sphere consisting of the home and domestic space and men's sphere consisting of business, politics, and public space. City centers were deemed men's spaces of productive work, while residential areas and, later, early suburbs were seen as spaces for women's reproductive work.[8] With the city so resolutely associated with men, writes Wilson, women became "an irruption in the city, a symptom of disorder, a problem."[9]

The nineteenth-century American city was thus a "city of men," for it was (and still is, as urban geographer Leslie Kern argues) constructed by and for men.[10] In practice, this meant middle-class and elite white men expected to be able to move through urban space freely, while women who occupied public space were automatically suspect. Prostitution was seen as the great social evil of the nineteenth-century city, and affluent Americans believed policing all women's movements was necessary to limit the damage that sex work could have on the populace. Thus, women who walked the streets without a male escort, especially after dark, were generally assumed to be sexually available, if not sex workers per se, and could be arrested under suspicion of vagrancy or prostitution.[11] The association between sex work and public space was so strong that a common euphemism for a prostitute was a "public woman."[12]

It is on this terrain that street insults became sites of contestation for working out the shifting power dynamics and hierarchies of gender, class, and race in urban space. Americans debated what constituted a street insult, who were likely to be the victims of such an insult, and who were the primary offenders. First, a woman who labeled a behavior an "insult" asserted her respectability and right to exist in public space. The term itself suggested a case of mistaken identity. A man "insulted" a respectable woman when his behavior betrayed an assumption that she was actually a "public woman," that is, open to an acquaintance—and, by implication, a more intimate relationship—with a stranger. For a woman to protest a street insult, then, was to claim a status as a virtuous woman, a "lady," who would feel only humiliation at men's leers, lewd remarks, or uninvited touching, all actions that implied she was sexually available. Unsurprisingly, in the white press the term "street insult" was thus generally reserved for incidents involving middle-class, elite, or respectable working white women, who could more easily claim a virtuous or pure nature according to assumptions of white womanhood at the time. Because dominant racist and classist stereotypes tended to depict poor women, Black women and other women of color, and sex workers as inherently disreputable and sexually promiscuous, white men who bothered or threatened such women were understood to be exercising their prerogative over vulnerable women's bodies, not "insulting" them. However, Black women used the term "insult" to describe the violent enforcement of racial segregation, including behaviors as extreme as a white conductor forcibly removing a Black woman from a train while white passengers cheered. Decrying insult, then, became a way for Black women, as well as white women, to claim identities as "ladies" who deserved respectful and deferential treatment in public space. Black and white women tended to point the finger at middle-class and elite white men, or gentlemen, and in the process asserted their rights to navigate public space as freely as these men.

Ultimately, discourses of "street insults" bolstered and reinscribed middle-class and elite white men's access to and power over public space in the latter half of the nineteenth century. Though Black and white women protested insults and tried to pin them on affluent white men, the white male journalists, authors, and urban reformers who denounced street insults shifted the blame to poor or working-class white men. In moralistic diatribes against "corner loafers," they attributed street insults to men who loitered on public thoroughfares and insulted passing ladies.[13] Significantly, men of color, and Black men in particular, were rarely accused of street insults. Racial ideology ensured that any intrusive behaviors they exhibited toward white women were considered far worse than mere "insult." Gender and class norms also dictated that middle-class and elite white men would use their social positions and freedom in urban space to defend ladies from insult and injury. The defense of "respectable women" was a vital part of demonstrating their genteel masculinity. Thus, far from being perpetrators of insults, middle-class and elite white male commentators suggested that their racial and class peers were actually the key to eliminating street insults, at least for white women. By casting insults as the uncontrollable impulses of poorly bred working-class loafers, affluent white men absolved themselves of guilt and portrayed themselves as white women's natural protectors. Middle-class and elite white men thus threatened women's safety in public space while simultaneously stepping forward to "save" those they deemed most deserving. Whether acting as the protectors of white ladies or as the men who insulted and humiliated women in public, affluent white men's entitlement over public space—the "city of men"—remained intact in the face of contestation.

The Street as Picture Gallery

American newspapers reported incidents of men accosting women in public from the earliest moments of urbanization. In 1803, for instance, Philadelphia newspapers accused young men of annoying Quaker women by waiting at meetinghouse doors and approaching female worshippers as they left.[14] Eight years later, New Yorkers complained the city was beset with "bloods" and "rakes" who accosted women with cries of "Dam'd fine girl, by g——d!" and "Where do you lodge, my dear?"[15] As cities grew in the nineteenth century, the geography and relationships between urbanites shifted, too. Cities went from places where homes and businesses occupied the same spaces and residents often walked as their primary mode of transportation to metropolises where homes and businesses occupied separate areas or neighborhoods. Public transportation facilitated movement between the reproductive and productive parts of the city and allowed people from many different backgrounds and neighborhoods to converge in public space.[16]

The anonymity that large urban areas afforded to nineteenth-century Americans was, at turns, exhilarating, frightening, and sensual. In the daytime, strangers brushed past each other, jostling one another, shouting and laughing, or rushing by without a word. At night, dark streets could harbor pickpockets, drunks, or other disreputable characters. Urban commentators encouraged nineteenth-century Americans to be skeptical of strangers, as any seeming gentleman or lady met in public might be a confidence trickster or prostitute, hiding their true nature behind an artful facade of fine clothing or a genteel manner. Etiquette manuals warned against approaching strangers, while popular fiction and melodramatic city guides depicted the possible dangers that awaited those who entangled themselves with deceitful urbanites. In this urban world of strangers, where one might spend a whole day surrounded by people whose true character and intentions remained undiscovered, Americans struggled to delineate rules for navigating city streets and engaging with people they did not know.[17]

For affluent white men, encountering strangers in public space offered an exhilarating opportunity to consume the city with their gaze. The gentleman urban explorer, or the *flaneur*, permeated cultural representations of the city in the mid-nineteenth century. In his most well-known form, the flaneur was a well-to-do white man with an adventurous, romantic edge whose gender, racial, and class privilege allowed him to wander the city streets undetected, marveling at the great cacophony and spectacle of urban life. These men were supposed to "[take] visual possession of the city," as their privilege protected them from notice and from censure, especially when the primary objects of their observation were the working classes.[18] The flaneur was an ideal figure, but writers like Walt Whitman and Charles Dickens wrote of their own wanderings through the modern city and solidified the flaneur as an influential trope of urban masculine privilege and curiosity.[19] The flaneur and similar representations asserted affluent white men's ownership of urban space, whether or not such men could actually observe strangers as freely in practice as the flaneur did in literature.

The presence of women on city streets was part of what made urban spaces exciting to explore. In representations of the male gaze, and particularly that of the flaneur, women were visually consumed as "a part of the spectacle" of urban life.[20] Oliver Wendell Holmes Sr. described how looking at women on the street was one of the pleasures of urban life in his widely read *Atlantic Monthly* column.[21] In June 1858, Holmes's column featured a fictional boarder at a New England boardinghouse who expounded on "the law of the road with regard to handsome faces." That unwritten law, the boarder opined humorously, allows "all males the right of at least two distinct looks at every comely female countenance, without any infraction of the rules of courtesy or sentiment of respect." As the boarder explained, the first glance ensures the viewer does not bump into an approaching woman, while the second is "an appreciating homage of the eyes." The boarder bemoaned the "vulgar beauties" who are "morbidly sensitive" to these looks from male strangers. "When a *lady* walks the streets," the boarder insisted, "she leaves her virtuous-indignation countenance at home; she knows well enough that the street is a picture-gallery, where pretty faces framed in pretty bonnets are meant to be seen, and everybody has a right to see them."[22] Though it is doubtful that when Holmes's boarder referred to "everybody" he really meant that anyone—prostitutes, pickpockets, Black men, con artists—had a right to admire the "pretty faces" on the street, the depiction of the street as a "picture-gallery" exemplified the way that many descriptions of urban space celebrated the opportunities the city street offered for watching women.

Men's observation of women on city streets was understood to be commonplace enough that it was sometimes the subject of illustrated scenes meant to depict everyday urban life. For instance, in an 1874 lithograph from a popular illustrated newspaper, a fashionable young woman is shown walking down a

FIGURE 1.1. Commentators often used the language of a "gauntlet" to describe the intimidating rows of staring eyes that women were forced to endure on city streets. J. N. Hyde, "Running the Gauntlet—A Scene in Front of a Popular Hotel in New York City at Five O'Clock P.M.," *Frank Leslie's Illustrated Newspaper*, May 16, 1874. Courtesy of Syracuse University Art Museum / Bridgeman Images.

city street as a crowd of men watch her pass (fig. 1.1). The men stand in a disorderly line, two or three people deep, on the front step of a "popular hotel in New York City." Their stances suggest they have been watching the crowds for some time, as they languidly lean on pillars, smoking pipes and cigars, hands shoved casually in pockets. According to the caption in the newspaper, it is "five o'clock," and thus a particularly busy time of the day when the great diversity of the urban populace is likely to be hurrying up and down the street.[23] The object of the men's observation is a pale-looking white woman in a ruffled gown and hat. She is some ways from the men on the hotel steps, in little danger of touching them but still well within their line of sight. She stares straight ahead, ignoring the many pairs of eyes fixed on her, a distant look that etiquette manuals claimed was necessary to protect her from insult.[24] The accompanying article describes the scene as one of "profound silence" as the men fixate on the passing lady, who advances with a "slight palpitating tremor" and "a blush" as she feels the many eyes upon her.[25] Tellingly, the image is labeled "Running the Gauntlet," an expression derived from a style of punishment in the military in which an accused man would run between two rows of men while they whipped him with sticks or rope.[26] Newspapers and magazines regularly used the phrase to describe the looks and stares women endured along urban thoroughfares.[27] Thus, even this slightly playful depiction of the male gaze acknowledged that the experience might not be pleasing to a passing lady.

The titillation of watching fashionable ladies passing on the street was made more intense by the presence of her antithesis, the urban prostitute, an enticing and anxiety-inducing fixture of nineteenth-century urban life. The sense that women of vastly different reputations mixed in urban spaces led social commentators and moral crusaders to worry that distinctions between "respectable" ladies and sex workers might blur.[28] Middle-class Americans balked that "street-walkers"—sex workers who sought clients on the streets rather than in brothels—could be found even on the most fashionable thoroughfares, mingling with the monied elite in theater and entertainment districts.[29] Wealthy and poor areas of the city might also butt up against each other, giving one New Yorker the impression that "fine ladies" could lean out their windows and look down on their "unfortunate sisters" in the street below.[30] Thus, middle-class white women who moved through working-class neighborhoods "risk[ed] their status as 'ladies,'" as if poverty, and the depravity that supposedly accompanied it, might rub off on anyone who came in contact with it.[31]

Middle-class urbanites feared that the presence of brothels and sex workers in affluent neighborhoods especially put respectable women at risk of insult, or worse. For instance, residents in New York City complained that "houses of ill fame" brought unwanted people into their neighborhoods. In one 1826 court case, male residents and homeowners pointed out that brothels encouraged people to "[collect] together" on the street. Brothel patrons then "molested and disturbed" residents to the point that "our wives and daughters cannot go out in the evening to the grocery or church without being insulted or crowded off the walk by the frequenters of these abominable houses of iniquity."[32] Another resident complained that the mere presence of "prostitutes and other persons of ill name and fame" in the streets made it "unsafe for respectable females to pass . . . after nine o'clock at night."[33] Thus, the physical presence of prostitutes and brothels in certain neighborhoods convinced many city dwellers that the streets were unsafe for respectable ladies, whether or not male strangers actually mistook them for sex workers or disreputable women. Such a "mistake" came to define the nineteenth-century street insult.

Defining Street Insults

The concept of the street insult initially grew out of the middle-class fear that ladies might be mistaken for sexually available women, highlighting the slipperiness of determining a woman's respectability in urban spaces where people of many classes and reputations mixed. As white Americans defined it, a street insult took place when a male stranger let a middle-class, affluent, or respectable working woman know that he found her sexually appealing, considered her sexually available, or wished to make her acquaintance in a way that suggested improper intentions. The behaviors that constituted a street insult were often opaque. Newspaper reports tended to leave the specifics of insulting behavior up to the reader's imagination, simply stating that a man had insulted a woman "by words and action" or "by looks and manner."[34] When a local police superintendent wrote to the New Orleans *Times-Picayune* about the outrages women endured on that city's streetcars, he relied on his readers' prior knowledge of public insults, suggesting, "You can readily perceive how a drunken brute, in the form of a man, may insult a lady and firmly convince her by tone and manner of a horrible motive or design upon her, a tone and manner impossible of description."[35]

Nevertheless, some reports of street insults offered examples of the "manner" that women found bothersome. Men might insult women with implicit or spoken overtures or greetings directed at women with whom they were not already acquainted. Such insults could be as simple as addressing a group of women with a "Good evening, ladies," implying a level of familiarity and intimacy between strangers that bordered on the improper.[36] Newspapers were especially troubled by reports of young men who approached female strangers and offered to walk them home. A Massachusetts newspaper described how a New York man accosted a woman at night, "[taking] advantage of the darkness and her unprotected state to insult her with his base importunities to accompany her home."[37] Disguised as acts of chivalry, these offers offended middle-class white Americans because they implied that the woman thus addressed was open to new acquaintances and, potentially, sexual offers. A young man could also insult a woman without uttering a word. Some touched women without their consent, like the man who pressed his hand against A Young Lady's back in the Fifth Avenue stage.[38] Others tried to make acquaintances surreptitiously, like the doctor in St. Louis who silently passed his card to a young white woman on a streetcar. Her brothers whipped him in retaliation.[39]

Ogling was considered especially suspect and rude, not least because etiquette rules forbade middle-class and elite white men from staring at "respectable" women for fear the lascivious look impinged on another man's property—that is, the woman herself.[40] Nevertheless, reports of street insults often commented on the leers women endured and the discomfort they felt when men stared at them.[41] In her descriptions of insults on New York public transit, A Young Lady alleged if a woman on "an omnibus puts her hand to her head to arrange her veil or hat, every man's eye is on her and kept on her until she returns her hand again to its place; and some men are not yet satisfied, but keep on staring until the lady, sometimes feeling indignant, will give a haughty return glance."[42] Returning a glance could be risky, however, and the *New York Times* warned that ladies who "happen to glance . . . momentarily" at a man might find he had mistakenly taken their looks for romantic interest.[43]

In its simplest form, street insults were infractions of public etiquette, and as such, social commentators tended to view uninvited speech, looks, and touching as evidence of a man's poor breeding and ungentlemanly status. According to middle-class etiquette, the primary method of protecting oneself from censure and embarrassment when going out in public, and affording strangers the same protections, was to make oneself invisible and to treat everyone else on the street as if they were invisible, too. Direct eye contact between strangers was frowned upon. Nineteenth-century Americans understood that one's gaze could be as evocative and meaningful as speech, requiring censorship in public places.[44] One etiquette writer warned, "It is not allowable to leer, to wink, or to say anything with the eyes which it would not be entirely proper to say in so many plain words." The easiest way to avoid improper or embarrassing looks was simply to physically avoid all strangers. The same etiquette writer explained, "Around every person there is a certain sphere of repulsion, into which no one ought to intrude."[45] Defining how to direct one's attention and how to deal with impertinent overtures from others was thus a primary occupation for Americans wishing to appear respectable in public.

Because gentlemen were understood as the archetypical watchers in urban space, etiquette writers warned them of the power of their gaze and their ability to embarrass, expose, or harm others if they stared. Middle-class white men were supposed to contain their gaze like they did their emotions, keeping overt displays of interest or observation hidden so as not to embarrass others. One etiquette writer acknowledged, "It is a great temptation, I am perfectly aware, on a wet day, to turn and look at a pretty ankle." However, a well-bred gentleman must resist and should not see, "or, if that is impossible, [should not] seem to see, or to have seen, anything that another person would choose to have concealed."[46] The wording of this rule is telling: To look was not inherently bad; only "seeming to see" was forbidden. Etiquette dictated that a gentleman must conceal his gaze, affording strangers a veneer of privacy and invisibility, however contrived.

If maintaining a "sphere of repulsion" around strangers was key to proper etiquette, manuals insisted it was "still more imperative" when a gentleman encountered a lady in public.[47] Etiquette writers were adamant that gentlemen must show the utmost respect to ladies. "A man who will annoy or insult a woman in the street," wrote one etiquette expert, "lowers himself to a brute, no matter whether he offends by look, word, or gesture."[48] To avoid insulting a lady in public, etiquette manuals dictated that ladies should control the extent of any interaction, especially with men, and thus gentlemen were expected to take their cues from a lady's demeanor.[49] As etiquette writer Robert De Valcourt put it, "It is [a lady's] right to bow to [a gentleman] in the street . . . . It is her right to offer to shake hands, and not his. It is her right to dismiss him."[50] A lady thus dictated how much interaction to have with gentlemen in public, and if a gentleman respected this right, she was ostensibly protected from unwanted or unpleasant interactions. If a gentleman confronted a lady he did not know in public space and demonstrated his interest in her, he was, by definition, guilty of a serious infraction, namely, of insult.

Gentlemen, in fact, were often perpetrators of insult. When women complained about individual incidents of insult, they often pinned street insults on men they identified as "gentlemen" and white men in positions of authority. The offending men's clothing and appearance provided clues: More often than not, women reported that the worst street insults came from men who dressed "genteelly." A Young Lady went so far as to insist that she preferred riding New York streetcars to public stagecoaches because the "poorer class" of clientele on streetcars "are generally better behaved."[51] Women also complained that men in positions of authority—including police officers, soldiers, and streetcar conductors—abused their power by insulting women.[52]

However, rather than acknowledge that gentlemen could be guilty of insult, middle-class white male commentators often blamed street insults on poor upbringing and moral deficiency, insisting that men who insulted could not possibly be gentlemen in breeding or social class. When newspapers and magazines reported on the general phenomenon of the street insult, they often attributed harassment to young, belligerent white men who were coded as working-class or poor. Reports used terms like "corner loafer," "street loafer," and "Broadway statue" to imply that these men were likely unemployed and had nothing better to do than loiter in public places and insult women who passed.[53] At other times, newspapers depicted harassers almost as if they were their own species. One newspaper diatribe against the "outrages" women faced on streetcars described male harassers as "base-minded creatures . . . who have a sort of instinct for insulting every woman they meet."[54] Similarly, in response to a letter from a reader about a "dastardly scamp" who was bothering ladies in a Baltimore neighborhood, editors of the Baltimore *Sun* insisted one could tell a gentleman apart from a "dirty fellow" liable to insult "by the brazen stare with which [he] regard[s] every passing female."[55] According to this writer, something as simple as a taboo ogle betrayed a man as lacking the manners of a proper middle-class gentleman. Men who leered and insulted women in public thus demonstrated an ignorance of middle-class etiquette and supposedly exposed themselves as deadbeats who had nothing better to do than to ogle and insult women.

When accounts of street insults made their way into newspapers, male commentators often suggested that any appearance of a harasser's gentlemanly status was a disguise that poorly hid his true nature. Thus, "fellows in the garb of gentlemen" approached schoolgirls in the streets, and a man "dressed in a peculiar fashion, half gentleman, half groom," was known to impose "his insulting gallantry" on young ladies he passed.[56] On other occasions, newspapers mocked harassers' clothing as inappropriately fussy or over-the-top. A young man accused of insulting women might be described as "foppishly dressed" or as a "pretty fellow," while the *New York Herald* warned that the city's streets were teeming with "well-dressed loafers."[57] According to such accounts, men who insulted women were not true gentlemen; they only appeared as such. Their clothing and comportment allowed them to pass as respectable gentlemen until their actions betrayed their true characters. As a result, while women continued to report that middle-class and affluent white men regularly accosted them in public places, public discourses upheld the narrative that the worst offenders were lazy, working-class loafers.

Conversely, white commentators, both men and women, rarely accused Black men of street insults. Such an omission derived not from Black men's perceived sexually benignity but from the perception that they were especially sexually dangerous, particularly to white women. Since the colonial period, white enslavers and lawmakers criminalized sexual relationships between Black men and white women and reserved the harshest punishment for Black men. Interracial relationships between Black men and white women threatened to upset a racial and gendered order that gave white men legal ownership over the white women in their families and justified white men's unfettered sexual access to Black women, especially enslaved women. In cities with visible free Black communities, fears of interracial sex often justified anti-Black violence and attacks on Black businesses, infrastructure, and other symbols of Black autonomy. When in 1838 a white mob burned down Pennsylvania Hall, an antislavery meeting space in the free Black community of Philadelphia, white people justified the attack in part on "the fraternal commingling of the races and the sexes in and around" the hall.[58] In the latter half of the nineteenth century, the rape of white women by Black men became a primary justification for lynchings, regardless of whether such rapes actually took place.[59] A Black man who expressed—or was perceived or accused of expressing—his sexual interest in a white woman in the nineteenth century committed an offense deemed far worse than insult. In a way, then, to be accused of insult for ogling a woman or asking to walk her home was a privilege reserved for white men.

An 1840 account of a Black man accused of street insult serves as an exception that proves the rule. When the Baltimore *Sun* reported that a Black man followed a white woman to her door one evening, the paper brushed off the insult as an example of how enslaved men copied their "masters' vices." These vices included imitating European manners and fashion and the practice of taking "a night cruize [*sic*] about the streets in search of an opportunity of insulting unprotected females." The *Sun* portrayed the Black man as comical and harmless, stripping him of agency and placing the blame for his behavior at the feet of his "master and his master's associates" who had failed to teach him good manners. "It is nothing more than can be expected," lamented the *Sun*, "from the example set him by those who are presumed to be his betters, but who are in reality on par with him in gentlemanly behaviour."[60] According to this account, the enslaved man's potentially insulting conduct was neutralized because, incapable of acting on his own, he was simply copying the white men he saw around him. That is, Black men might be accused of street insult, but only when they were perceived as subservient, nonthreatening, and devoid of agency. Had he been perceived as behaving of his own accord, the enslaved man's offense would likely have been interpreted as far more serious and garnered a response far more extreme and violent than a slightly amused write-up in the *Sun*.

The paucity of examples of Black men accused of street insults was thus not a sign of a lack of anxiety about racial mixing or Black male sexuality. On the contrary, it was white men's racial and gender privilege that protected them from the violence directed at Black men who were perceived to have made sexual overtures to white women. The relatively tame moniker of "street insult" was reserved for behaviors that were deemed distressing and bothersome when perpetrated primarily by white men but were understood as grounds for murder when Black men were accused of the same conduct.

Accounts of street insults thus bolstered middle-class and upper-class white men's power over urban space. While women tended to accuse middle- and upper-class white men of street insults, these men were also the primary interpreters of intrusive behaviors. As the owners of city newspapers and the frequent authors of etiquette manuals and city guides, professional white men in particular had significant power to decide when an insult had taken place. Their depictions of insult scapegoated working-class white men for the intrusive behaviors of gentlemen, who then continued to bother women in public places.

Protesting Street Insult

While many Americans agreed that street insults were violations of public etiquette, women contested the meaning of street insults, including who were the worst perpetrators, how targets could reasonably respond to insulting behaviors, and which women could claim the status of "lady" victim. Two examples of women contesting dominant narratives of street insult help to illustrate the battles over the meaning of street insults in the mid-nineteenth century. First, an 1869 debate in the pages of the *New York Times* highlights the way affluent white women insisted that "gentlemen" were the worst perpetrators of insult, not least because affluent men felt the most entitled to women's bodies in public space. Second, Black women used the term "insult" to describe the physically violent enforcement of racial segregation on streetcar lines and other public transportation. In doing so, Black women demanded they be seen as "ladies" and that white men treat them as such. Thus, women's counternarratives of street insult depicted the problem as one of white male entitlement and violence.

NEW YORK CITY, 1869

One of the clearest examples of white women contesting narratives of street insult centered around the treatment of "ladies" in streetcars in 1860s New York City. Streetcars and similar public conveyances proved especially troubling urban spaces, not least for the opportunities they provided for observing and engaging with strangers in public. Streetcars were cramped public spaces where strangers pressed together in closer proximity and for longer periods of time than did passersby on the street.[61] As the cheapest form of transportation in many cities, streetcars also attracted a diverse ridership, from middle-class women shoppers to laborers to businessmen.[62] Sex workers were known to ride certain routes and solicit clients.[63] An 1865 essay in *Godey's Lady's Book* reveled in the thrill of watching strangers as their paths briefly crossed on public streetcars, advising readers, "It is as well to look around you in your trips . . . and read a page from human nature in the daily journey of life."[64]

It was this opportunity to observe strangers in streetcars that, according to many news reports, made them spaces where insults went unchecked.[65] The problem of insulting behaviors on public streetcars erupted onto the pages of the *New York Times* in 1869 when the paper's well-to-do readers disagreed over what kinds of men were to blame for street insults and what should be done to punish them. The debate began in early October when the *Times* reported the arrest of Alexander J. Hamilton, a sixty-year-old businessman who had bothered a young female passenger on a Third Avenue streetcar. The arresting police officer, Detective George Elder, claimed Hamilton used a newspaper to obscure his hands from view, allowing him to "take improper liberties" with the young woman. When the officer "snatched the paper" away, he found Hamilton's "hands . . . upon the lady." Hamilton protested that he had been wrongfully accused, claiming he was a "respectable citizen" who had simply been reading his newspaper "with both hands."[66]

Despite his protestations, the incident matched what many women claimed was their experience of street insults. For one, the offender was an older professional white man who wielded authority and clout as a result of his social class.[67] Hamilton's actions also appeared to confirm reports that men who insulted women often used surreptitious actions intended to be easily dismissed as harmless. Indeed, in defending his decision to arrest Hamilton, Detective Elder and his supporters argued, "It was a common practice in cars, stages and other crammed places for men to take unwarrantable liberties with the persons of females in the crowd, and it was done in such a manner that the women themselves would scarcely notice it; and further, it was almost invariably old men who were engaged in this bestial business."[68] In this context, Hamilton's actions appeared neither unusual nor surprising.

Perhaps because of its archetypical features, the Hamilton case caught the public's eye. Two weeks after the initial reports, the *New York Times* published excerpts from letters from several female readers who complained about the frequency with which they encountered men "who habitually use public vehicles in order that they may insult defenceless women." Over the course of the next few weeks, readers wrote in to respond to the allegations that women were "treat[ed] . . . as if they were cattle" on New York streetcars and stages.[69]

This monthlong exchange in the pages of the *New York Times* offers a microcosm of the debates and negotiations about the nature of street insults that were taking place across the country among middle-class and affluent white Americans. Readers debated what constituted an insult, who were the worst offenders, and what were the appropriate responses to insult. Some wrote in to support women's claims, some wrote in to refute them, and still others implored women to speak up more often if they were bothered, or else the daily insults would continue.

Wrapped up in these debates were ideas about the proper behavior and place of ladies and gentlemen in public space. First, white women harnessed their culturally imposed roles as moral arbiters to castigate affluent white men for inadequately performing gentlemanly behavior.[70] Women letter-writers claimed that white men too often failed to respect ladies or protect them from insult, humiliation, and harm. A reader who identified herself as "A Mother" accused "men dressed in the garb of gentlemen" of routinely insulting women in public. Her choice of words suggested that the offenders performed gentlemanly respectability in their appearance, but their treatment of ladies fell short of the ideal. A Mother lamented that the insults were so bad they "would make a man of honor and principle blush for his sex," further indicating that any true gentleman would not stand for such behavior.[71] Similarly, a reader calling herself "Another Young Lady" pointed out that "half of the so-called men," far from defending ladies, were "mere tailors' blocks," that is, they stood motionless like a mannequin. Instead, the writer challenged men to "imagine that in protecting any defenceless woman, he [was] paying respect to his own sister."[72] The *New York Times* agreed, stating, "It is a safe rule to act toward a woman upon the supposition that she is honest and respectable."[73]

Indeed, the *New York Times* initially took a sympathetic stance toward the women complainants. The editors argued that accusations of insulting behavior were usually backed up with "only too much foundation" and warned that "ladies" were "liable to more annoyances now in our streets than at almost any previous time."[74] But the *Times*' sympathy was not solely reserved for middle-class or affluent white women who might claim the moniker "lady." Garnering particular sympathy were the several women correspondents who the *Times* explained were trying to "earn a respectable livelihood" and rode public transportation "on their way to business." Such respectable working women were, according to the *New York Times*, "in a position which of itself appeals to every chivalrous sentiment" a gentleman ought to have. And yet the working women found themselves "the objects of the loathsome attention of gray-headed profligates," gentlemen who should have known better and embarrassed both themselves and the women they insulted with their behavior. The consequences of this ungentlemanly behavior were all too clear to the *Times*. If it was allowed to continue, New York's "honorable reputation for the freedom with which ladies could go about the streets" would soon evaporate, and the city would be little better than "London or Paris" where "a woman can scarcely ever stir abroad without being dogged by men, or otherwise insulted." For the editors of the *Times*, insults against ladies in public threatened the very fabric of a democratic and free American metropolis and foretold a degradation of the bodily freedom enjoyed by "American girls."[75]

The insults that took center stage in these exposés were often nonverbal and sometimes nonphysical. One female reader complained of a common move where a man would lean back and stretch his arms across the back of the streetcar seats so that he could "insult" women sitting next to him without them noticing.[76] The reader calling herself "A Young Lady" singled out uninvited looking as an intrusive practice. She peppered her letter to the *Times* with references to men who watched her on public transit and complained of the discomfort it caused her.[77] The *Times* confirmed her experience and argued that too many men took a casual, unintended glance from a woman as an open invitation to engage. Furthermore, streetcar conductors "corroborated" the women's complaints. Conductors both witnessed and heard about insulting behavior and were "sometimes strongly tempted to take the law into their own hands."[78] Such depictions of nonverbal intrusions made clear that street insults were not in the same category as, say, physical or sexual assault. Nevertheless, many readers agreed they still represented a reprehensible breach of public etiquette, and they embarrassed women who were trying to go about their day unmolested.

Condemnation of street insults was not universal, however, and descriptions of nonverbal and nonphysical insults left space for ambiguity and reinterpretation. By the end of October 1869, the *Times*' male readers had begun to defend themselves. They balked at the implication that insults were the fault of men who failed to behave as gentlemen. Instead, several readers blamed street insults on women who failed to act as ladies by dressing provocatively, inviting attention, or approaching men in public. Male letter-writers protested they could not look away from the women who dressed and comported themselves as immodestly as those on New York streetcars.

Male New Yorkers' defenses drew on established etiquette rules that encouraged women to be unnoticeable in public space so as to avoid insult. Etiquette manuals advised genteel women to don inconspicuous clothing, including veils that shielded their eyes, and to walk with male escorts whenever possible. Even a woman's gait was supposed to be carefully calibrated to be unassuming and graceful.[79] Ladies were also expected to ignore all molestation or ogling. They were certainly never to return a gaze. The exception that proved the rule was the urban prostitute, who was believed to advertise herself by her flamboyant dress and bold, inviting stare. A woman's gaze threatened to expose her as sexually immoral or available if she offered it too liberally to others.[80] Thus, a woman's conduct influenced whether she could convincingly protest a street insult. Etiquette manuals warned middle-class women that failure to follow the rules of public comportment would open them up to scrutiny and censure. As one manual put it, a lady's "dress, carriage, walk, will all be exposed to notice; every passer-by will look at her, if it is only for one glance; every unlady-like action will be marked."[81] Etiquette manuals promised to protect middle-class white women from these dangers, but, by the same token, if men targeted her with insults, a woman could be accused of failing to communicate her middle-class gentility convincingly.

The *New York Times* echoed the idea that women welcomed insult with their comportment when, just one week after defending lady streetcar riders, the paper suggested that women themselves were to blame for streetcar insults. Supposedly, the improper comportment of a few uncouth women ruined streetcar rides for more respectable ladies. An unnamed *Times* author argued, "The insults respectable women receive often originate in the shameless behavior of the depraved members of their sex."[82] That is, ladies themselves might not be to blame, but their less respectable counterparts encouraged men to behave badly. In fact, a letter-writer going by the initials F. S. D. explained that, in his experience, women insulted men rather than the other way around. Whenever he boarded an omnibus or streetcar, he claimed, women "will commence casting side glances at me—putting on roguish smiles, and all that sort of thing—which to a bashful person (such as myself) is anything but pleasant, for it causes the color to mount my cheek, and is apt to give people in general an impression that I am the guilty one."[83] One reader pointed out that some women even rode public transportation "for the express purpose of forming an acquaintance," alluding perhaps to sex workers who met clients on streetcars.[84]

Men's defensive maneuvers met with mixed results. While few disputed the fact that men might encounter disreputable women in public space, New Yorkers were not always convinced that men were absolved of guilt when it came to insulting lady riders. For instance, on the one hand, the reader calling herself "Another Young Lady" bemoaned the conduct of some women, recounting, "I have seen disgusting behavior on the part of some—of course, they were 'ladies!'—in our stages, and on such occasions I do not wonder that the men forget to be gentlemen." Still, this reader was skeptical of the argument that a few bad behaviors "on the part of some" excused men of all insults. She wondered how male riders could confuse real ladies with imposters, asking, "Where are your perceptions, that you cannot tell wheat from tares"?[85]Similarly, the *New York Times* acknowledged that "dissolute females" often rode public transportation, but editors also suggested that "men are not often deceived in these matters, although it may suit them to pretend to be. The depraved woman soon betrays her character."[86]

The debates over who was to blame for intrusive behaviors illuminate how ladies and gentlemen had to reinforce their respectable status regularly. When, as the *New York Times* pointed out, it was "impossible to place an official at the door [of a public conveyance] to demand a certificate of moral character," men and women had to prove their respectability in other ways.[87]

One way that women could distinguish themselves as "ladies" was through their responses to intrusive behaviors from men, but New Yorkers disagreed on what constituted a ladylike response. Some men asked, if women disliked being ogled or touched so much, why not protest in the moment? "Virtue is said to be bold and fearless, and vice, mean and cowardly," wrote one male reader, so why "do not the ladies when insulted in stages and cars speak out, so that all eyes may be turned upon the offender"? Respectable women, he insisted, "themselves have the most effectual remedy for the evil complained of."[88] Another reader admitted he had seen "silly men" insult women from time to time but insisted, "I have never seen the 'ladies' resent, or even show disapprobation of, these acts." In fact, he argued, the women were themselves to blame, for until they "deport themselves modestly" they cannot "complain of 'insults,' of which there are fewer than is supposed."[89] Reader F. S. D. implored ladies to speak up so that men might learn "better manners."[90]

However, women made it clear that speaking up was not always an option for them. As one letter-writer explained, she would never call out an offending man or go to law enforcement for help. "We shrink from any such notoriety as the attempt [to alert police] would give us," she wrote, adding that such an action "would be met, of course, by a strict denial of any intention to annoy, so we can only find relief for our wounded and insulted feelings in the sympathy of our friends."[91] Here, the letter-writer hints that protests against street insult would not likely hold up to a gentleman's flat denial, a kind of psychological gaslighting that would exacerbate the harm done. Indeed, the *Times* noted that men could more easily escape embarrassing situations than their female counterparts, noting, "Even in the worst case, a man can easily protect himself, while . . . [ladies] are obliged to submit quietly to indignities which they cannot effectually resent and are unable to punish."[92]

Women who were frustrated by insults on public transit found themselves in a no-win situation. If women did not speak up, they could be perceived as wanting the attention or at least tolerating it. If women reprimanded men who insulted them, they risked more unwanted attention, this time from authorities, and might even be accused themselves of inviting the insult. This double standard left at least one letter-writer, A Young Lady, feeling helpless. She commented, "No matter how quietly a lady sits in a stage, she is liable to insult."[93] White women insisted, then, that even proper ladylike comportment would not save them from street insults or from incredulity should they accuse a man of insult.

RACIAL VIOLENCE AS INSULT

White women like A Young Lady may have recognized that their comportment could not protect them from insult, but their whiteness gave them greater access to the moniker of "lady"—and the right to respectful treatment in public space that it implied—than women of color had, especially Black women. Black women also fought to claim the status of "lady" and demand protection from insult, but their experiences of insult differed significantly from those of white women. For one, Black activists took particular aim at segregated public transportation, which threatened to significantly limit their access to public space in urban areas. Campaigns to desegregate public transit used the language of "insult" to describe the indignities that white passengers and conductors inflicted on Black women, but the behaviors implied by the term "insult" were likely to be physically violent and racially motivated. In cities like New York,

Philadelphia, and Washington, DC, insults against Black women included racial slurs and physical attacks, such as white conductors forcibly dragging Black women off segregated public conveyances. By using the term "insult" to refer to these experiences and emphasizing their respectability as "ladies," Black women claimed their right to occupy public space and demanded they be treated with the same deference as their white counterparts.

Black women fought an uphill battle as they struggled to be recognized as victims of insult in the eyes of white Americans. White Americans portrayed white women as the primary victims of street insult in both newspaper reports and fictionalized accounts. In city guides and melodramas about the dangers of city life, urban reformers and religious moralists emphasized the whiteness of their heroines as proof of their virtuousness. One city guide dwelled on the central character's "large blue eyes, golden hair and figure" and the "great tears [that] ran down her blushing cheeks" when her way was barred by a group of men.[94] Newspapers similarly harped on white women's supposedly inherent innocence in the face of harassers. Insults were said to bring a "blush to the cheek of the modest and virtuous," a phrase that did dual work to emphasize the whiteness of the victims and the humiliation they felt when they received uninvited attention.[95] As the Baltimore *Sun* put it, the street "insult is an offence against the majesty of virtue and purity of female innocence." While the *Sun* also claimed that "those spiritual essences are the same in all conditions" and thus a woman's "rank . . . can make no difference" to how much she was insulted, the fact that the *Sun* defended only white women from insult in its pages exposes the limits of that claim.[96]

Black women rarely appeared in the mainstream white press as victims of street insults. Racist myths of Black women's hypersexuality had been used to justify white men's rape and sexual assault of Black women for centuries.[97] In Northern cities, "derogatory narratives of Black womanhood" made it unlikely that white people would cast Black women as victims of sexual violence or insult. Free Black women who moved visibly through urban spaces, especially those who presented themselves as respectable or middle-class, instead risked public censure from white commentators. As art historian Jasmine Nichole Cobb has argued of antebellum Philadelphia, a city with a thriving free Black community, white citizens in the North were threatened by the visibility of Black freedom and especially the potential for a "Black gaze" that could be turned on them in public. For instance, when white illustrator Edward Williams Clay published a series of Black caricatures in 1828, he mocked the perceived self-importance of free Black Philadelphians and lampooned Black women's attempts to exhibit respectability by dressing and comporting themselves as ladies.[98] Black women who tried to lay claim to the status of lady—and all the protections that came with it—thus threatened dominant racial and gender hierarchies and risked ridicule in the press as well as in public.

Black women endured threatening and humiliating actions from men in public places—actions that were often both racially and sexually motivated—and they pinpointed public transit as one of the most problematic urban spaces for such insults. Segregated public transportation was a common fixture in Northern cities in the antebellum period. As free Black communities grew in cities like New York and Philadelphia, white-owned transit companies attempted to control the mixing of white and Black passengers in their public conveyances.[99] As historian Elizabeth Stordeur Pryor has argued, white Americans used "a combination of social customs, racial codes, and popular culture" to "construct a system that surveilled, curtailed, and discouraged black mobility," with public transportation emerging as "one of the most notorious spaces for antiblack aggression."[100] White Americans who supported segregated public transportation saw integration as the start of a slippery slope that would lead to interracial relationships beyond the streetcar. In 1864, for instance, Ohio Democratic congressman Samuel Sullivan Cox warned that "black suffrage" and "African equality in street cars" would lead "steadily forward to perfect social equality of black and white, and can only end in this detestable doctrine of—Miscegenation!"[101] Ironically, while Cox's alarmist tone and conflation of desegregated streetcars with miscegenation were intended to frighten white Americans into voting Democrat, he was correct that desegregated, and safer, public transportation would give Black citizens greater mobility and freedom, especially in urban areas.

When African Americans in the North began to protest segregation on public transportation in the mid-1800s, Black women were often at the forefront of such activism. Historian Blair L. M. Kelley has argued that the very existence of Black women disrupted the logic of segregated transportation. If, as many argued, racially segregated streetcars and railcars were designed to protect white women from supposedly predatory Black men, then segregation should not extend to Black women. The fact that Black women were nevertheless not only denied entry to segregated public transportation but often attacked and beaten if they tried to ride in whites-only cars belied the logic of segregation and revealed it was "about not separation and protection but violence and stigma."

Black women thus became some of the "most effective leaders and protesters" in the fight to desegregate public transportation across the country.[102] In Philadelphia, for instance, some of the most compelling evidence of the injustice and violence of segregation came from stories of Black laundresses, elderly Black women, and other Black women who claimed respectable status but were forcibly expelled from streetcars. For instance, two Black women who boarded a streetcar in Philadelphia in 1865 were subjected to dangerous speeds and "the most insulting language" until one of them jumped from the careening car. Their experience became part of the Black community's rallying cry to end the "shameful" practice of racial segregation on public transportation.[103]

Fifteen years before the *New York Times'* readers debated the insults that white women endured on streetcars, a young Black schoolteacher and organist named Elizabeth Jennings sued New York's Third Avenue Railway for the treatment she received on one of its streetcars. On July 16, 1854, the twenty-five-year-old Jennings tried to board a Third Avenue streetcar on her way to a church meeting, but the white conductor stopped her. At the time, the company's policy dictated that Black passengers had to ride on the outside platforms, rather than inside the cars, unless no white passengers objected. The company also ran a number of special cars open only to Black passengers. The conductor who stopped Jennings insisted that she wait for the next car, which he said would have "[her] people in it."[104] When she refused to leave the car, arguing that none of the white passengers objected to her presence, the conductor grabbed her and tried to force her off the car. As *Frederick Douglass' Paper* reported, the conductor "got her down to the platform, jammed her bonnet, soiled her dress, and injured her person," but she resisted and remained onboard.[105] The conductor then solicited the help of a passing white policeman, and together they succeeded in dragging Jennings from the car by her feet.

Like her white counterparts, Jennings asserted her respectability and status as a lady to decry such an "insult" and argue for respectful treatment on public transportation. Jennings claimed the conductor asked her to leave the car, and she "told him [she] was a respectable person, born and raised in New York." "I had never been insulted before while going to church," she told the conductor and accused him of being "a good for nothing impudent fellow for insulting decent persons."[106] The Black newspapers that reported the incident likewise emphasized Jennings's respectability and piety but also her parentage, as she was descended from a prominent free Black family in New York. This strategy had some success in the court system, even if it did not convince the conductor in the heat of the moment. Jennings's suit against the Third Avenue Railway made it to the New York State Supreme Court, which awarded her $500 in damages plus court costs. The judge in the case ruled that the conductor had used unnecessary force against Jennings. He further suggested that Black New Yorkers should have the same rights as white citizens, provided they conduct themselves, like Jennings, in a respectful and peaceful manner.[107]

In a strikingly similar incident ten years later, a white conductor ousted the famous Black orator and abolitionist Sojourner Truth from a Washington, DC, streetcar. As Truth tried to board the streetcar in the fall of 1865, another passenger challenged her right to ride, drawing the attention of the conductor. The conductor tried to forcibly remove Truth from the car, grabbing the eighty-year-old woman by the arm. As Truth told it, the conductor "slammed me against the door." Truth enlisted the help of white philanthropist Laura S. Haviland, a fellow passenger, and threatened to report the conductor to his employer. At this, the conductor left Truth alone. When Truth lodged an official complaint, the conductor lost his job and faced charges of assault and battery. Before his trial concluded, Truth remembered that "the inside of the cars looked like pepper and salt" and conductors were addressing Black women passengers as "ladies." For Truth, this marked "a great change" in the treatment of Black women on public transit in DC. For Black women to be identified as "ladies" was to be afforded some of the protections and respect that white women took for granted.[108] The change, however, would be neither widespread nor permanent. Indeed, another famous Black activist, Ida B. Wells, suffered similar treatment on the Chesapeake and Ohio Railroad in 1883. When Wells attempted to ride in the "Ladies Only" car, she was forcibly dragged from the car by the conductor, to cheers from the white passengers.[109]

Racially and sexually motivated attacks and insults against Black women were not limited to public transportation. When pro-slavery advocates rioted in Detroit in 1863, the *Liberator* argued that such violence was the result of a white culture that indoctrinated white people with hatred for Black Americans from infancy. White children were taught "by word and example, that the negro is to be hooted and kicked by all respectable people." To prove the point, the *Liberator* told the story of a young Black woman who was "accosted and insulted" on the street. A "red-faced, whisky-bloated fellow" yelled at her as he left a saloon, asking her, "Have you heard from your father Abe, lately?," referring to President Abraham Lincoln. The insult questioned the legitimacy of the woman's birth and implied that she was the product of an interracial relationship, thus targeting both her race and her sexual reputation. While the insult was likely intended to embarrass or frighten the young woman, or at least to assert the dominance of the white assailant, the Black "servant girl" countered with her own rejoinder. "Yes," she responded, she had heard from Abe and "he wants somebody to black his boots, and would like to give you the job." The man "beat a sudden retreat" back into the saloon, apparently embarrassed at being outwitted by a young Black working-class woman.[110] Nevertheless, the racial and sexual overtones of his remark demonstrate the way that Black women endured dually racist and sexist "insults," in sharp contrast to the glances A Young Lady protested.

White people's harassment of Black women demonstrates the chasm between what counted as "insulting" to white women versus Black women in dominant narratives of street insult; the bar was far higher for the latter than the former. Black women were even less likely than their white counterparts to garner sympathy or protection from intrusive and even physically violent behaviors. Indeed, even when Black activists won key legal victories in the battle to make public transportation safer for African Americans, this did little to change everyday experiences of Black women and men on public transportation. For instance, while lawsuits against discriminatory policies on Philadelphia streetcars and railroads were often successful, especially when women were the plaintiffs, they did little to actually change streetcar company policies in that city.[111] When Black women tried to assert their rights as respectable women and ladies, primarily by demonstrating their "ability to deal politely with inhumane treatment," abolitionist and Black newspapers defended them, but this rarely translated into better treatment in the everyday spaces of the street or streetcar.[112] As later chapters will show, Black women continued to endure insulting behavior and physical violence at the hands of white men on public transit long after women like Elizabeth Jennings and Sojourner Truth had won legal victories against their assailants. Furthermore, Black women and girls would continue to use the term "insult" to describe embarrassing, frightening, and physically violent harassment from white strangers into at least the 1930s.[113]

Female Vulnerability, Male Protectors?

As Black and white women protested that affluent white men or men in positions of authority were the worst perpetrators of insult—and white women particularly admonished gentlemen harassers for failing to respect ladies as they should—white male–owned newspapers continued to depict middle-class and elite white men as the best defense against insult, and particularly as the protectors of white women. These reports did not dispute that men insulted women in public, but they insisted that respectable men could never be guilty of insulting a lady. Editorials on the street insult problem emphasized that any true gentleman would be called to action if he saw a lady insulted in public.[114] Newspapers often described how brothers, fathers, or benevolent male strangers stepped in to protect the honor of white women accosted in public places. Indeed, when white men did not protect white women from insult, newspapers noted their complacency. One New York father lamented that the man who insulted his daughter had "crronious [*sic*] ideas on the divine right of gentlemen to insult those whose duty it is to protect from insult."[115] Similarly, when three men boarded a streetcar in New Orleans and insulted a white woman passenger, the *Times-Picayune* disclosed that two male passengers had "witnessed this scene" but had failed to protect the woman.[116] Middle- and upper-class white men who insulted or failed to defend white women were thus seen to fail in their obligation to protect white women's purity and virtuousness. If a true gentleman saw a woman being insulted, common sense dictated that he was within his rights to act as "one of *nature's police officers*, if not judge and executioner at the same time."[117]

Newspaper reports particularly excused violence on the part of male relatives, justifying men's desire to mete out justice when their female relatives were targeted. White male relatives in fact had a vested interest in protecting the women in their families as they were protecting their own property. For instance, under the legal classification of coverture, married women did not have legal autonomy separate from their husbands. An insult, sexual overture, or sexual assault aimed at a married woman was understood "as a harm done to her husband."[118] So, when a reader calling himself "A. Brother" wrote to the Baltimore *Sun* for help identifying a man who had been insulting ladies, the *Sun* sympathized with his struggle: "If any thing can justify a man in taking the law into his own hands, it is in a case like this, where a dastard indecently accosts an unprotected female and outrages every feeling of delicacy by language and behavior endured by none but the most abandoned."[119] This remark did dual duty, affirming white men's right to protect their women from insult and betraying the assumption that any woman who "endured" insult must be "abandoned," that is, without male relatives to defend her.

The expectation that gentlemen would act as "nature's police officers" to keep the peace may also have persisted because official law enforcement, such as it was, proved ineffective at reducing street insults. Policemen were still relative newcomers to urban space. New York City had established its police department in 1845, barely two decades before the *New York Times* debate over streetcar insults.[120] Still, some urban residents expected enough from police departments to be disappointed with their responses to street insult. In 1874, for instance, a Trenton, New Jersey, shopkeeper feared his business would suffer because of the "crowd of loafers" that gathered on the sidewalk outside his store every night and "insult[ed] my lady customers and my sales-ladies." He went on to complain that local police refused to help him. In fact, rather than enforcing the city ordinance against congregating on the sidewalk, policemen actually joined the "crowd" of loafers. The police told the shopkeeper the loiterers had the right to congregate wherever they pleased.[121] In some cases, law enforcement maintained they could not get involved with street insults. Police commissioners in New York explained that "an actual breach of the peace" had to take place for police to step in, and in their estimation street insults were rarely severe enough.[122]

As the New Jersey shopkeeper's complaint suggests, policemen were sometimes themselves the offending parties, drunkenly insulting women on streetcars or joining in when other men leered or made comments about women. A Minneapolis woman complained in 1876 that, though she endured "ill-treatment" from men on the streets, she could not rely on law enforcement to protect her as policemen had "taken a hand in the disturbance."[123] In New Orleans, the city's police superintendent apologized to residents for the behavior of one of his officers who, rather than arresting the drunk US soldier who was bothering two women on a streetcar, had instead joined the soldier in "grossly and wantonly" insulting the women.[124] Even when law enforcement was willing to get involved on behalf of victims of street insult, women often did not want the attention that came with criminal proceedings. In 1870, for instance, the *New York Times* lamented that a "scoundrel" grabbed a woman by the waist on a New York stage but was allowed to escape because the ladies feared their names appearing in "a disagreeable Police-court's news-item."[125]

In addition to the ineffectiveness of law enforcement, narratives that presented street insults as the domain of vulgar ne'er-do-wells also reinforced the argument that gentlemen were not the perpetrators of insult but rather ladies' protectors. Both newspaper reporting and fictionalized city guides depicted street insults as a tactic that only rakes and criminals employed to entrap pure, unsuspecting white women. In these narratives, a lascivious leer easily turned into an uncouth remark, which in turn could become an unwelcome touch, culminating in seduction, destitution, a turn to sex work, and even murder. Newspaper exposés explicitly warned women that street insults from unsavory characters could escalate into violence. When the *New York Herald* ran a piece denouncing the "corner loafer nuisance," referring to working-class men who blocked thoroughfares and "subjected [ladies] to insult," the paper suggested that this seemingly trivial inconvenience was a symptom of a much greater threat to ladies. It warned that in "the less reputable streets the loafer is not only a nuisance, but a danger," adding that he "[is] not infrequently a thief" and sometimes even a "murderer." Because of loafers' violent reputation, "respectable citizens often suffer insult and outrage without daring to offer resistance."[126] Such narratives depicted men who insulted ladies on the street as, at best, ill-bred working-class loafers and, at worst, akin to thieves, rapists, and murderers.

In 1871, the murder of Avery D. Putnam, a rider on a streetcar who defended two lady passengers from insult, confirmed fears that seemingly harmless intrusions could devolve into violence. On the evening of April 26, Putnam was traveling uptown on a Broadway streetcar in New York. A Madame Duval and her daughter were also on board. The younger Duval had stuck her head out of the car window to admire some passing buildings when she was "insulted by the driver" and an off-duty conductor, William Foster. Foster had reportedly "leered insultingly at the ladies" and then opened the door of the carriage so he could stare at them longer. Putnam, observing this, claimed the women were with him and asked Foster not to "annoy the ladies." Foster proceeded to sit down next to the women anyway and threatened Putnam with violence. Putnam and the two women decided to leave by the back door, only to have Foster follow close behind. Foster grabbed an "iron hook" from the driver and hit Putnam in the head with the "heavy implement." Putnam died three days later.[127]

For some, the incident was proof of the dangers of city life. Days after Putnam's murder, the *New York Times* declared "ruffianism" a persistent problem in New York City and lamented that "nobody who has any experience of the night-cars will be greatly astonished" at Putnam's violent end.[128] When *Harper's Weekly* reported on Foster's indictment for murder, the piece included an illustration of "a car crowded with rowdies and thieves," which the magazine claimed "is a sight to be witnessed every day on almost every line in New York" (fig. 1.2). The image, which the magazine captioned "Beauties of Street-Car Travel in New York," depicts a woman and a young girl, presumably meant to represent Madame Duval and her daughter, ascending the steps of a streetcar.

FIGURE 1.2. This depiction of the dangers awaiting a woman and young girl on a busy streetcar illustrated a report of the murder of Avery Putnam, the man who tried to defend Madame Duval and her daughter from insult in New York City. "The Street-Car Murder," *Harper's Weekly*, May 20, 1871. Courtesy of HathiTrust.

At the front of the car, a slogan reads "All Hope Abandon Ye Who Enter Here," a misquotation of the inscription on the gates of Hell from Dante's *Inferno*. The car's conductor stands in a commanding position at the top of the stairs, while male passengers—including what appears to be an intoxicated man and a gentleman in a shiny top hat—peer out the window at the mother and the girl. Across the top of the streetcar, signs warn of the "murderers" and "pickpockets" to be found aboard.[129] Stories and illustrations like this reinforced the idea that public places, especially the confined and semiprivate spaces of public transit, were rife with unsavory characters who might begin an interaction by ogling and end it with murder.[130]

Whether or not street insults were truly perpetrated only by loafers, rakes, and criminals, there were few clear ways to distinguish such men from supposedly respectable gentlemen. Women thus learned to be wary of seemingly benign overtures from all male strangers and to expect that even a wayward glance or a friendly greeting could devolve into seduction, rape, or murder.[131] A lascivious look became not just a look but the potential beginning of a moral and sexual downfall. At the same time, as women continued to insist that middle- and upper-class white men were not protectors but some of the worst perpetrators of insult, they began to take their protection into their own hands.

The fear of insult convinced many women to self-impose curfews, monitor their own behavior in public, or curtail their movement throughout the city. Women chose alternate routes, avoided parts of town or going out at certain times of the day, or chose their transportation options based on their likelihood of encountering insult. For example, "loafers" apparently blocked "chief thoroughfares" in New York City, creating a hostile environment that women tried to avoid.[132] Public transportation proved especially tricky as it was essential to navigating large cities safely and efficiently, yet women found that certain streetcar lines or certain times of the day were more problematic than others. One lady streetcar rider explained that women sometimes had to disembark before their destinations to escape insulting conduct; if the conduct persisted over multiple rides, it could "prevent her taking that course" and she might seek other means of transport or forfeit trips that required riding problematic streetcar lines.[133] The surest protection from harm, however, was simply to avoid public space altogether. At least five different etiquette manuals suggested it was indelicate for their lady readers to go out alone at night. Instead, they offered this identical advice: "After twilight, a young lady would not be conducting herself in a becoming manner, by walking alone."[134] If all else failed, staying home might feel like a woman's only option to stay safe.

Yet some women had no choice but to navigate public space alone and at undesirable times. Women who held professions that kept them out late developed codes of conduct intended to keep them safe. Actress Clara Morris, who walked the boards in New York City in the 1870s, recalled in her memoir that "one of the most unpleasant experiences in the life of a young actress" was the "frightened lonely rush through the city streets at twelve o'clock at night to her boarding-house." After dark, Morris explained, men became dangers to young women in ways they were not during the day. "The kindest old drake of the farm-pond," she lamented, "becomes a vulture beneath the midnight street-light." To protect herself from unwanted attention, Morris developed a set of rules to follow that she called the "Clara Code." Morris's rules urged women to navigate city streets vigilantly, leaving plenty of physical space between themselves and any potential danger. To that end, Morris instructed young women to avoid passing "between two advancing men . . . lest they might seize hold of and so frighten [them] to death." The rest of the rules continued in a similar manner: Never walk on the inside of the pavement when meeting a stranger; always put the entire length of the pavement between oneself and a dark alley. In some cases, Morris advised walking in the "street itself" rather than too close to an unknown man. "When in doubt," she intoned, "take to the centre of the street." Morris shared her code with her fellow actresses and claimed it saved many of them from harm.[135]

Black women, who had far fewer avenues than white women to seek justice for street insults and who were more likely to endure physically violent attacks, might take even more extreme measures to protect themselves. Eliza Potter, a successful hairdresser and a freeborn Black woman, carried a gun in her purse to protect herself from the dangers she encountered on a regular basis in Cincinnati, Ohio. Rather than rely on white men to defend her womanhood, as some white women might have felt was their prerogative, Potter knew that she would need to protect herself in public. In her autobiography, she described the kind of violence she feared as a Black woman in the 1850s. In one incident, a group of men followed and threatened her while she was on her way to dress hair for an evening party. As she walked down the street, "several persons" were "hallooing and hooping," and she heard one say, "Let us frighten her to death." Potter took courage from the gun, her "good protector," in her basket and continued on. At the party, she dressed the "ladies'" hair and enjoyed watching the festivities, staying "rather later than I intended." As she walked home from the party, Potter encountered "two men standing on [a] corner." One began following her down the street, not speaking. Suddenly, the man stopped in front of Potter. She took a step back and, referencing her firearm, "told him if he took another step he would fall at my feet." Taken aback, the man insisted he had not been following her but rather looking for a nearby doctor's office. Potter watched as he pretended to ring the bell of the doctor's office and then "ran away as fast as he could" as soon as he thought she could not see him. For Potter, this was proof that "any man who will attack a woman on the street is an arrant coward, and a woman can frighten him to death." All the same, after the incident, Potter resolved not to attend any more late-night parties that required walks home in the dark.[136] Her experience speaks to both the degree of violence Potter feared and the lengths she felt she needed to go in order to protect herself. As a Black woman, she did not expect any "gentlemen" to come to her aid, nor could she rely on her social position to protect her. Her life was in her own hands.

Intrusive behaviors, then, had a real and observable effect on women's freedom of movement in urban space. Men's stranger intrusions could be unpleasant in and of themselves, but stories of ne'er-do-wells attacking ladies and their male defenders could mean women perceived street insults as omens of violence to come. Street insults did not force women from the streets entirely, but women incorporated the existence of stranger intrusions into their conceptions of the city and adjusted their actions accordingly. They self-monitored their comportment to ensure they could not be accused of attracting attention. They avoided parts of the city or public transportation lines where they believed they were likely to encounter insult. Some may have stayed home when they would rather have gone out, especially if it was after dark or they did not have a male escort.[137] The fact that middle- and upper-class white men were perpetrators of insults—and were also supposedly the ideal protectors against such behaviors—suggests that street insults and the narratives that gave them meaning helped middle- and upper-class white men exert and reassert their power over public space, just as the increased presence of women threatened to diminish it.

THE DEBATES over street insults in the mid-nineteenth century mark the beginning of an ongoing discursive struggle between women targets of intrusive behaviors and the male perpetrators and reporters who often had the power to interpret those behaviors for public consumption. White and Black women consistently pointed out that "gentlemen" and white men in authority positions were frequent perpetrators of insult. Their insults were, indeed, all the more egregious because such men failed to live up to the women's expectations of—or, in the case of Black women, demands for—respectful and chivalrous treatment that was supposed to be a hallmark of gentlemanly comportment. At the same time, white male–owned newspapers continually downplayed the social position of men accused of street insult, choosing to suggest these men merely *looked* like gentlemen or were simply a few bad apples. Middle- and upper-class white men who insulted women could deploy their class positions as a way to protect themselves from accusations and even claimed to be (white) women's primary protectors themselves. They argued that "corner loafers" and other ne'er-do-wells were the more likely perpetrators of insult. Women's early protests against street insult, then, mark a period when women tended to see insult as something upper- and middle-class white men did, while those same men worked to shift the blame onto working-class men.

The emergence of the "street insult" as a category offered an opportunity for women to demand respectful treatment in public space. However, it also marked the beginning of a decades-long crusade by middle- and upper-class white men to enforce their claim to women's bodies in public space, not least by casting stranger intrusions as the purview of men outside their class, racial, or ethnic peer group. In the mid-nineteenth century, this meant pinning insults on working-class men. However, as men's stranger intrusions persisted and cities became home to more immigrants and people of color, the scapegoats changed. Women's responses also changed as their cries for the eradication of men's intrusive behaviors went largely unanswered. While women in the mid-nineteenth century often did not trust law enforcement or state institutions to protect them from men's stranger intrusions, by the turn of the twentieth century the political terrain had shifted. Women increasingly called on police, city officials, and men in positions of authority to finally do something about the scourge of insult that followed them wherever they went. In the Progressive Era, men's stranger intrusions acquired new meanings—and evoked new responses.

What can be done to rid the
Palmer House
of
Mashers
The Kind of Man Who Mashes and How He Insults His Victims
CHIEF COLLINS ON THE MASHER.
icago Women Tell How Mas
Walk on State Street a Fea

FIGURE 2.1. A two-page illustration depicts the "gantlet [*sic*] of staring looks" women encountered on city streets in turn-of-the-twentieth-century Chicago. "What Can Be Done to Rid the Palmer House Block of Mashers," *Chicago Daily Tribune*, February 4, 1906. Courtesy of Newspapers.com.

CHAPTER **TWO**

THE MASHER

On the morning of Sunday, February 4, 1906, the *Chicago Daily Tribune* posed an urgent question to its readers: "What can be done to rid the Palmer House block of Mashers"? The headline, scrawled across two pages, was accentuated with an illustration that dominated the top half of the section (fig. 2.1). The drawing depicted a young white woman walking down a Chicago street while a group of well-dressed white men, ten in all, stood in a line and watched her pass. These men were the "mashers" of the headline, men who leered at, spoke to, followed, and otherwise bothered women they did not know in public places.[1]

According to the *Tribune*, Chicago's city streets were teeming with mashers who "smirk and leer at every pretty woman who passes the corner without a male escort." Prominent local clubwomen explained that mashers "infested" Chicago and that women were "growing tired of running the gantlet [*sic*] of staring looks" wherever they went. The *Tribune* reported that mashing was particularly prevalent in the popular shopping districts of downtown Chicago: "Thousands of women [were] insulted between the hours of 10 a.m. and 11 p.m. each day" at the corner of Monroe and State Streets, where the elegant Palmer House hotel stood (and still stands today). White clubwomen described how mashers followed them down the street, accosted them in movie theaters, and pressed up against them on public transportation. Lucy A. Boone Carpenter, president of the Chicago Woman's Club, highlighted the masher's leering looks as especially insulting. She declared "ogling" was "as disgusting and offensive to a good woman . . . as any other mode of attack." Still, lest *Tribune* readers mistake mashing for an annoying but essentially harmless pastime, Evelyn Allen Frake, president of the Illinois Federation of Women's Clubs, contended that the "masher and the murderer . . . belong to the same species. It is positively dangerous for a woman to go on the streets nowadays."[2] Frake and Carpenter, cognizant that earlier calls for a law enforcement crackdown had failed, demanded a stronger response to mashing. Carpenter insisted that "detectives should be sent out to arrest every man who makes a business of mashing." Once convicted, clubwomen suggested mashers should be subjected to "the whipping post," "the horse whip," "torture," and "a month in the bridewell at hard labor."[3]

The problem of the masher was not unique to Chicago. When the *Tribune* published its exposé on the Palmer House block masher, the nation was in the throes of what some newspapers were calling the "crusades" against mashers.[4] Local and national press took notice of the masher from his first inception in the 1880s, but coverage of mashing skyrocketed in the first years of the twentieth century, peaking in the mid-1910s.[5] By the late 1890s and into the next decade, mashing was a subject of public debate and outrage across the country, from Boston, Massachusetts, to Portland, Oregon, and from St. Paul, Minnesota, to Dallas, Texas, though it was most prevalent in the teeming Northern metropolises.[6] Though one Wisconsin paper described the masher as "an evil belonging to larger cities," medium- and small-sized towns were by no means immune to mashing.[7] Towns as small as Mount Vernon, Iowa (population 1,532 in 1910), had a masher problem large enough to warrant consideration of an antimashing ordinance.[8] Headlines across the country described how "vile-tongued mashers" "scare[d] poor, timid girls" and "lured" them into "unforeseen dangers" with their "insulting tricks."[9] It seemed no place was safe from the masher.

Americans reserved the moniker of "masher" primarily, if not exclusively, for white men, making the antimasher crusades a significant, if short-lived, challenge to white men's dominance in public space. Women's rights activists were particularly forceful in their critiques of mashing, pointing out that white men who mashed betrayed a sense of entitlement over women's bodies. White women insisted that mashing made a laughingstock of the idea that white men were their natural protectors. White men were the primary perpetrators of intrusive behaviors, they argued, so how could they rely on those same men to defend them from sexual violence in public? Instead, white women's rights activists called on the state to intervene on their behalf and, when the state failed, encouraged women to learn to defend themselves against white men's intrusive behaviors. At the same time, Black women and men were able to harness the mainstream outrage at white men's intrusive behaviors to demand an end to the public insults, sexual propositioning, and violence that had been a fixture of Black women's urban experience for decades. Black commentators and reformers reprimanded white mashers for assuming Black women were sexually available and cautioned Black men to set a positive example by treating Black women with respect.[10] In tandem, Black and white activists' efforts sought to curtail white men's sexual and political power in American public space.

The Progressive Era debates over the masher also highlighted how many Americans—Black and white; middle-class, working-class, and elite; women and men—saw intrusive behaviors as incompatible with the masculine ideals of the time. As scholars of Progressive Era masculinity have shown, the practices and identities that constituted the era's hegemonic masculinity were in flux. At the end of the nineteenth century, white Americans emphasized self-restraint and temperance as ideal qualities of "civilized" white "manliness," while progressives like Theodore Roosevelt increasingly emphasized athleticism, militarism, and ruggedness as the key to saving middle- and upper-class white men from effeminacy and weakness.[11] The masher embodied neither of these competing masculine models. Rather, he represented much that was potentially harmful or ridiculous about uncontrolled white masculinity. The masher was lascivious and unrestrained, even effeminate, more interested in appeasing his vanity and following his sexual desires than practicing either the cool self-control or rugged self-sufficiency that many white Americans saw as essential elements of masculinity.

Thus, the masher posed a threat not only to women's ability to navigate public space but also to the supposed superiority of white American manhood. Newspapers across the country chastised mashers in gendered terms, suggesting they were overly feminine, brutish, or weak. The specifics of the critiques differed depending on who was making them. For instance, working-class white women often criticized so-called gentlemen of middle- or upper-class status for being particularly entitled, while newspapers aimed at the business elite tended to depict mashers as working-class fools masquerading as gentlemen. But what these critiques had in common was an understanding that bothering or embarrassing women in public was unacceptable behavior for men hoping to identify with the hegemonic masculinity of the period. At the center of these critiques, and of efforts to curb mashing, was an awareness that intrusive behaviors impeded women's freedom of mobility. Women insisted they could not reap the benefits of their increased access to public urban space until they could navigate the city unmolested.[12]

Antimashing Campaigns and Women's Activism

It is no coincidence that the mashing crisis coalesced as an influx of single women, of many racial and ethnic identities, moved to Northern cities in unprecedented numbers at the turn of the twentieth century. These women found work and filled city streets, movie theaters, department stores, dance halls, soda shops, public streetcars, and omnibuses.[13] Male philosophers, anthropologists, urban reformers, government officials, and journalists grappled with the dual anxiety and excitement aroused by women's presence in public space. The visibility of women in urban space represented both the sexual possibilities of the city (particularly for white women and men) and the danger and potential sexual degradation that threatened female virtue.[14]

White women reformers sought to protect single working-class white and immigrant women, especially those moving to cities for the first time.[15] New arrivals, they argued, could fall victim to confidence men and rakes who accosted women on trains or at stations, impeding their access to public space and leading them down a path of sexual ruin.[16] White women's rights activists argued that so-called fallen women were victims of male sexual privilege, not their own moral deficiency. They set up groups like the Travelers Aid Association, which promised to help the thousands of "young girls" who arrived in big cities "with no idea of the dangers in their paths."[17] Activists also demanded that the state protect women from entitled male seducers, namely by raising the age of consent for women and girls and arresting and punishing men who "ruined" women with sexual intercourse, including sexual assault.[18] Supporters of new statutory rape laws sometimes explicitly invoked the masher as the target of such legislation.[19]

Female activists' efforts succeeded in reshaping the legal landscape in the 1880s and 1890s and offered new mechanisms for protecting women from sexual dangers. As Mary Odem has argued, however, enforcement was uneven and influenced by gender, class, and racial tensions of the time. The male police officers, judges, and other state actors who enforced new age-of-consent laws had little interest in reformers' wider goals of dismantling male sexual privilege. Rather, policies originally designed to protect women from men became tools for controlling female sexuality. As reformers, including female social workers and women's rights activists, increasingly "acknowledged the sexual agency of young women" in the 1910s, they called on the state to regulate women as much as their male partners (if not more so), especially young working-class women "who violated dominant codes of female respectability."[20]

Antimasher activism fit neatly into the existing priorities and campaigns of many women's rights activists and urban reformers. For one, activists and reformers worried that mashers were among the sinister and calculating men who might lure unsuspecting young women into immorality. Indeed, mashers themselves admitted they deliberately tried to "trick" women into conversation. As an overture, a masher might brush up against a woman, cough loudly, or offer a woman an umbrella in poor weather.[21] One New York masher claimed he ensnared his targets with reading material that he knew would be "likely to attract a woman." Whenever he boarded the train, he made sure to have "Harper's Bazaar, or some pictorial" paper that he would "rattle" loudly in front of a woman to catch her eye. The "ruse generally succeeds," he told a newspaper correspondent, and once he locked eyes with the woman, he offered her the paper and struck up a conversation with her.[22] Many urban reformers feared such interactions would end in a woman's sexual downfall. Fiction could bolster such suspicions. In Theodore Dreiser's influential novel *Sister Carrie*, the eponymous heroine descends into immorality after a masher engages her in seemingly innocent conversation on a train to Chicago. Though the masher introduces himself with banal commentary on the weather, he slowly builds up compliments and familiarities until he and Carrie are well enough acquainted that he is able to renew the interaction anytime he likes. This innocuous beginning sets Carrie on a path of moral ruin as she engages in two illicit affairs, including with the original masher, and seeks fame on the stage.[23] Stories like these placed the masher in the same category as other kinds of male seducers who entrapped or abducted young white women on the street and forced them into prostitution, or "white slavery."

Women who decried mashing emphasized how intrusive behaviors limited their ability to navigate public space freely. Affluent white clubwomen were among the loudest proponents for state intervention to curb mashing, and they often framed the masher as part of the larger problem of male sexual privilege that shaped women's vulnerability in urban space. A female reporter in Chicago lamented that the "result" of mashing was "that I'm afraid to go out alone here at night and disgusted when I walk the streets by day."[24] White working women had similar critiques as their monied counterparts, and their experiences often highlighted how male economic privilege exacerbated the problem.

As one working woman argued, low wages and extended periods of unemployment made it all too easy for working-class women and girls to "yield to the temptations held out to them by flirts, mashers, white slavers, and others, who seek their prey among this class of girls."[25]

As the language of "white slavery" suggests, efforts to protect women from sexual violence in the Progressive Era were also deeply divided along racial lines. White female reformers saw victims of male predation as primarily, if not exclusively, white. They rarely worked on behalf of Black women, who often faced far greater dangers and more extreme forms of white men's sexual violence than white women. As Hazel Carby has argued, far from igniting a protective urge in white Americans, the movement of Black women into Northern cities in the early twentieth century set off a "series of moral panics" as Black women's "everyday behavior in public areas of the city . . . was watched carefully and monitored for propriety."[26] Black reformers and women's clubs worked to combat white people's racist assumptions that Black women were naturally sexually promiscuous and thus a danger to respectable white urban residents.[27] Largely excluded from white women's clubs, Black women formed their own clubs and interrogated the role of racism in exacerbating problems affecting women and children in the Black community.[28] Black women's clubs also sometimes employed a politics of respectability. They argued that middle-class Black women must uplift their less fortunate sisters—mainly working-class and rural Black migrants—and ensure they conformed to middle-class moral standards, which were often shaped by white expectations.[29] Nevertheless, as the crusade against white mashers progressed, the Black press took advantage of the growing indignation against white men's entitlement in public space and insisted that Black women deserved treatment as respectful as that given to white women. Together, Black women's rights activists and Black newspapers argued that to oppose mashing was to combat not only white men's sexual entitlement but also their racial privilege in public space.

Defining the Masher

Efforts to eradicate mashing grew and changed alongside the shifting definitions of this new category of man. When the masher first emerged in the 1880s, descriptions of this type of man played on the broader fears of male strangers endangering young women, particularly white women, in America's growing cities. However, mashers were known for behaviors and types of interactions that marked them as distinct. The list of behaviors attributed to the masher ran the gamut, from staring to touching to physical assault or threats of violence. Mashers sidled up to women on the subway, on streetcars, or in darkened movie theaters and surreptitiously rubbed against women's arms or legs.[30] Mashers followed women down the street, sometimes silently and sometimes yelling epithets or pet names, including from moving vehicles.[31] At least one man labeled as a masher accosted women with "an exposure of person."[32] What unified these actions was that they broke social etiquette without veering explicitly into the criminal (until the onset of antimasher legislation, that is).[33] Thus, mashing constituted behaviors that embarrassed or frightened women but were rarely deemed as egregious or aberrant as rape, assault, or murder. Of course, mashing could lead to such physical and sexual violence, or a masher could turn out to be a "white slaver" who kidnapped young white women and forced them into prostitution. However, mashing's defining feature was its ordinariness and ubiquity. If mashing was anything, it was seen as common and widespread.

Nowhere was the insidious nature of mashing more obvious than in the behavior for which he became most known: ogling. Intrusive looks went by a variety of monikers in the masher era, including "stare," "glance," "goo-goo eyes," "smile," "making eyes," and "lustful gaze," but "ogling" was the most common term.[34] Mashing was associated so strongly with ogling that newspaper reports often used the term "ogler" interchangeably with "masher," even when the man in question had engaged in behaviors other than looking.[35] Intrusive looking exemplified the relative mildness and ubiquity of mashing. It was annoying to those who endured it and could feel threatening under the right circumstances, but it was also the quietest of the masher's behaviors, and it was close to impossible to catch him in the act. As one woman put it, mashers worked hard to "convey the impression that they are rather shy" as a feint so they could ogle "without detection."[36] Unlike reports of "street insults," which did not disproportionately mention looking, intrusive looking appeared in about one-third of mashing reports, coming second only to verbal overtures (also about one-third of mashing reports) as mashers' most common intrusive behavior. Looking eclipsed other behaviors like following (about 15 percent of reports) or whistling (less than 1 percent of reports).[37]

Reports of mashing pointed out how ogling made women feel appraised, suggesting that intrusive looking was discomfiting in part because it revealed the entitlement that men felt to evaluate women in public space. For instance, when a "throng of idlers" parked themselves on the steps of the post office in downtown Detroit in 1910, a local paper reported they subjected "every woman who passes . . . to scrutinizing attention." Working women showed "signs of vexation and even anger when subjected to the [mashers'] appraising scrutiny."[38] In a 1914 essay in the *Chicago Daily Tribune*, a New Yorker visiting Chicago explained she did not have room to document all the "leers and 'size-ups'" she endured "from the insulting eyes of men standing before cigar shops, on car platforms, on street corners, or from those who, having walked past me, grinned or merely stared into my face as they passed."[39] Such appraisal could force a woman to alter her plans for the day. As one woman described, when a man sitting opposite her on a New York City subway car tried to "draw my attention by moving his eyes," she became so "embarrassed" that she disembarked at the next opportunity.[40]

Ogling proved a troubling intrusion in part because, while women complained that mashers looked at them in ways that were inappropriate or threatening, urbanites understood that looking was also one of the great pleasures of city living. At the turn of the twentieth century, advertisers and business owners increasingly expected women to partake in pleasurable looking in public. Department stores designed elaborate window displays and movie theaters plastered enticing film posters across their facades, often aimed explicitly at women consumers who obliged by window shopping and buying movie tickets in ever larger numbers.[41] Popular media of the time also depicted looking, even sexualized looking, as characteristic of heterosexual interactions on city streets. Representations of women in urban space from the period cast them as objects to be admired, lusted after, or romanticized—but above all, observed. Looking at women on the street was, then, not seen as wholly bad. A man could ogle without being labeled a masher.[42]

Paintings, newspaper reports, films, and fiction especially portrayed white women as natural focal points for white men's sexual desire in urban space. For instance, cartoonists and postcard printers produced images of women as titillating sights on the streets of urban America. A representative postcard from New York City depicts a young white man in a suit and hat admiring the ankles of a young white woman as she holds up her skirts to cross the street (fig. 2.2). The famous Flatiron Building looms in the background, and the caption informs the postcard's recipient, "I am seeing great things."[43] The postcard's caption and image made it clear that the "great things" one could view in New York City included both famous architectural landmarks and the bodies of young women. Seen from another perspective, however, the postcard presents

FIGURE 2.2.
This postcard suggested that women's bodies were among the attractions male tourists could admire while visiting New York City, muddying the waters of what constituted proper and improper looking in the age of the masher. *I Am Seeing Great Things* postcard, ca. 1915. (X2011.34.106). Courtesy of the Museum of the City of New York.

a classic mashing scene. In the early years of the twentieth century, the corner of Twenty-Third Street and Broadway, where the Flatiron Building still stands today, was notorious as a spot where the placement of buildings produced a wind tunnel. Men were known to stand on the corner waiting for a gust of air to blow women's skirts up, revealing their legs.[44] The high numbers of "shop girls" who "pour[ed] out of the big stores and wholesale houses" made the corner a "Masher's Mecca."[45] Depending on the perspective, the same New York corner could be either a prime spot to admire the female form or a spot where "seedy middle-aged men" chased down young working women.[46] As these competing depictions of the male gaze show, intrusive behaviors alone were thus not enough to label a man a masher. Instead, Americans concerned with eradicating mashers argued that men who mashed were particularly deviant or failed to live up to expectations of respectable masculinity.

During the antimasher crusades, the masher came to constitute a separate category of man. Mainstream reporting first depicted him as a ridiculous, even subhuman, creature but then gradually began to view him as an ordinary white man who had failed to conform to idealized norms of white masculinity. The category of the masher marked a shift from the nineteenth-century diatribes against "street insults," which fixated primarily on intrusive behaviors—that is, on the "insults" themselves. Progressive Era debates about men's stranger intrusions, on the other hand, constructed the masher as a specific kind of man, one who might engage in any number of intrusive behaviors but who was fundamentally different in character from nonmashers.

At first, depictions of the masher were humorous in tone and tended to emphasize, in pseudoscientific language, the characteristics that distinguished him as a separate category of man. In 1879, Mrs. Hugh L. Brinkley laid out many of these characteristics in one of the earliest definitions of the masher. In her monograph, *A Woman's Thoughts About Men*, Brinkley purported to act as a "naturalist" who would describe man "as he is." In her definition of the masher, Brinkley presented the "pest" in terms and descriptors that would endure for decades in denunciations of the masher and his antics. She began by insisting that "every woman has at one time or another" encountered a masher and "suffered" his annoying behavior. The breadth of his influence was unsurprising to her given that a "male menagerie . . . infests" major thoroughfares in places like New York. She acknowledged that the masher had "generally a good looking face" that he combined with an "everlasting smirk" to entice women into conversation. The smirk hinted at his conceited sense of his own attractiveness, as he "fancies there is enough in his tolerable countenance and intolerable impudence to cause a woman to forget alike, modesty, etiquette and common sense, and to form his street acquaintance." Brinkley implied the masher was lazy, describing how he "stands for hours" at "the club and hotel windows . . . staring with all his might at every woman who passes." When it came to the masher's actions toward women, Brinkley focused almost exclusively on his propensity to stare. She explained he "sees every curve of a woman's foot, every glance of a woman's eye as she passes," and "if she be a modest woman he seeks to stare her out of countenance." All the markers of the typical mashing diatribe are here in this early example: Brinkley likened the masher to a different species of animal with words like "pest," "male menagerie," and "infests"; she emphasized his appearance and use of good looks and clothing to entrap his victims; she scoffed at his inflated ego and misplaced confidence in his ability to woo women; and she fixated on the way his ogling stare discomfited women.[47]

Other early descriptions of the masher also played up the sense that he was a new category of man, even using faux anthropological or zoological language to depict him as a separate species. In 1880, the Chicago *Daily Inter Ocean* claimed to have employed a "naturalist" who placed the masher in the same class as either the "earth-worm" or the "order *Blatta*, class *Orientalis*," that is, the cockroach.[48] Detractors of the masher referred to him as a "creature" or as the "genus masher" and described his presence on city streets as an "infestation" or an "epidemic." This kind of language drew on phrenological and scientific racist discourse that delineated different categories of humans and placed them in a hierarchy. Describing the masher as a new species of man marked him as "other" and as less than human: a "homo insignificanticur," as one newspaper put it, literally an insignificant human.[49] The masher was thus more than just a man who had misbehaved. He was a new kind of man, barely human, who failed to live up to the expectations of civilized white manhood.

At a time when immigration from Europe was on the rise, some representations of the masher drew on an existing visual culture that depicted ethnic whites as subhuman. An 1882 cartoon in the humorous *Puck* magazine, titled "A Curious Creature at Coney Island," shows a masher who has "crawl[ed] up out of the sea" and accosted two white women strolling along a beach (fig. 2.3). In comparison with the delicate features of the two women, the masher is drawn with cartoonish dimensions: an oversize head, a broad chest and a short jacket that emphasizes his tiny waist, a bowler hat far too small for his head, slicked back hair and a mustache. He appears grotesque and ridiculous beside the slight feminine bodies. The "creature's" features, his arrival "out of the sea," and the "strange motions and noises" he makes, as if speaking in an unknown language, all echo late-nineteenth-century xenophobic depictions of recent immigrants, especially those from Italy and southern Europe. The creature is soon thwarted by a tall white man in a top hat who hits the masher with his cane. The gentleman rescuer, in contrast with the masher, is drawn with a perfectly proportioned body and suit, highlighting his white, and probably Anglo, manliness. In this early caricature, the masher is a distinctly othered "creature" that cannot compare with the respectability and composure of the white Anglo rescuer.[50]

FIGURE 2.3. This cartoon depicts the masher as a "creature," drawing on visual imagery that recalls stereotypical portrayals of southern Europeans of the period. "A Curious Creature at Coney Island," *Puck*, July 19, 1882. Courtesy of HathiTrust.

While depictions of the masher as a creature or ridiculous species of man would persist throughout the masher's heyday, by the early 1910s such men were increasingly overshadowed by antimasher diatribes that decried the masher as a criminal rather than a caricature. As it became clear that the masher was not just a humorous subject for tongue-in-cheek cartoons and denunciations but a physical man who actually bothered women in public places, discussions of his antics increasingly read as crime reporting focused on individual men and their victims. As mashing's ubiquity and impact became ever more apparent, the category of "masher" morphed into a descriptor for white men whose intrusive behaviors marked their masculinity as deviant and threatening, especially to "respectable" white women.

The sheer number of mashers who seemed to lurk on every city street made the phenomenon impossible to ignore. At the turn of the twentieth century, newspapers and magazines increasingly adopted a panicked tone, describing how mashers lay in wait around every corner. A typical piece in the *Detroit Free Press* described the "army of men" who congregate "in commanding positions on the downtown thoroughfares and about public places, where they smile and smirk at every prepossessing girl or woman who passes." Accompanying illustrations depicted the masher engaged in his signature activities, including giving a young woman a ride on his motorcycle and buying her a drink in a roadhouse. The main illustration pictured a dandily dressed white man smiling at two white women passing on the street and bore the caption "The Masher Is Ever Present" (fig. 2.4).[51] The masher was no longer a babbling, grotesque monster but increasingly presented as an ordinary-looking white man who betrayed his depravity with his intrusive behaviors.

As it became clear that the masher was a living, breathing threat to women in public, newspapers spilled much ink trying to predict which men were likely to be mashers. The picture of the masher that emerged in the early twentieth century was of a native-born white man who failed to conform to idealized conceptions of white masculinity. In the white mainstream press, the typical masher was usually quite well-dressed (or, at least, considered himself to be so) and often coded working-class, though there is plenty of evidence that men of all classes and many occupations harassed women on the street. A masher could be any age, and reports variously claimed that either young ruffians, middle-aged married types, or lecherous old men were the worst offenders, though in general elderly mashers were particularly reviled as they were supposed to know better.[52] Most important, middle-class (and especially male) commentators insisted that

FIGURE 2.4. Activists and urban reformers worried that mashers could entice women into dangerous or promiscuous relationships by luring them with innocuous conversation or seemingly harmless glances. This masher appears to be testing the waters by directing a friendly glance toward two young women on the street. "What to Do with the Masher," *Detroit Free Press*, October 15, 1911. Courtesy of Newspapers.com.

mashers were not "gentlemen." If mashers appeared to be middle- or upper-class by their dress or occupation, the fact that they mashed supposedly negated the social capital their class status afforded them. Thus, while there were exceptions to this typical picture of the masher, middle-class Americans generally saw intrusive behaviors and normative masculinity as incompatible in the masher's heyday. Men who mashed were not considered "real men."

While mashing was generally seen as a problem of white men, the few exceptions highlight Americans' disagreements over how to understand the mashing problem. In places with an influx of recent immigrants, Anglo newspapers and native-born white residents alike were wont to pin intrusive practices on foreign-born men, particularly immigrants from eastern and southern Europe. In New York in 1912, a local correspondent claimed that while most mashers "devote a great deal of time to personal adornment, many of the most persistent annoyers of women and girls are day laborers, generally men who have been in this country only a short time. Their grimy appearance does not prevent them from ogling women or addressing remarks to them." This description pitted presumably white male mashers who cared about "personal adornment" against "grimy" recent arrivals and insisted that while the former might be most common, the latter was more annoying.[53] People in interracial relationships might also get caught up in attempts to crack down on mashing. Thus, police used an "anti-mashing" ordinance to arrest a white woman and an "Americanized Japanese" man in Portland, Oregon, when they were caught "flirting" in a public park. The woman had apparently traveled from Oregon City to visit her boyfriend.[54] White residents who sought protection from harassment on the street also harnessed racist and xenophobic stereotypes to strengthen their complaints. For instance, Abram Hewitt, New York City mayor, received a slew of letters in the 1880s from white residents who complained that "Italian bootblacks" were obstructing sidewalks with their vending carts, throwing garbage on the streets, and accosting women and girls.[55] A number of complaints focused on the ages of the women and girls, claiming that "little girls from 10 years up to 16" were especially vulnerable to disrespectful "insinuations" from Italian men.[56] However, these incidents were the exception: Of the 568 newspaper reports of mashing consulted for this project, only 12 explicitly pinned mashing on foreign-born men.

Significantly, African American men were also unlikely to be labeled as mashers. In the white press, the title of "masher" was primarily reserved for men whose race and gender privilege protected them from the violence and public outcry that could accompany an accusation of sexual impropriety leveled at a Black man. As Estelle Freedman has argued of mashing, a Black man who "looked a white woman directly in the eye . . . could be construed as a sexual assailant, not merely a flirt."[57] African American mashers do appear in white newspapers on occasion, and more so in the South than in the North, but their treatment differed significantly from that of white mashers. For instance, in Atlanta, a Black man was tried in court for waving a white handkerchief at several white women in Inman Park, the city's first planned suburb.[58] A white policeman had staked out the neighborhood at residents' request and claimed he saw the Black man "pull a white handkerchief from his pocket and begin to wave it in the direction of [a] young lady." The scene so enraged the policeman that he admitted he was "tempted to pull his pistol and empty the contents immediately."[59] Instead, he arrested the masher, who was eventually fined twenty-five dollars, but the policeman's murder threat was indicative of the ferocity of the vitriol leveled against Black men accused of mashing. White newspapers were also more likely to emphasize physically violent behaviors from Black men than from white men. Thus, white readers in St. Louis and San Jose learned of Black "mashers" who grabbed women in the street, while Louisville apparently endured an hours-long "reign of terror" in 1916 when a Black "masher" was accused of trying to kidnap three separate women in one night.[60]

Coverage of mashing in the Black press tended to include a much wider array of players than in the white press. Early in the mashing crisis, Black newspapers depicted both Black and white men as mashers and identified both Black and white women as victims of mashing.[61] When Black newspapers reprimanded Black men for mashing Black women, they often employed a politics of respectability. This philosophy encouraged African Americans to conform to white middle-class appearance, taste, and comportment in public in the hopes that such displays of "respectability" would bolster Black Americans' claims to full civil rights. For instance, an 1888 newspaper report in Washington, DC, reprimanded local Black business owners for letting "boisterous crowds of idle men" gather in their stores or restaurants. The reporter suggested DC needed Black businesses with a more refined atmosphere and clientele, places where "ladies . . . will be free from the gaze of ogling and brainless dudes, who stand in front of our churches, pool rooms and bar rooms and barber shops and make insulting remarks of women."[62] A reporter for the *Freeman*, the prominent Indianapolis Black newspaper, similarly lamented in 1903 that Indiana Avenue in that city was filled with "'Jim Crow' Negroes" who spent their time "ogling the women and getting off cheap, flippant remarks as they pass." The *Freeman* drew a distinction between respectable Black men and the "exodus Negro, the newcomer," that is, a recent migrant from the South whose lack of good breeding was supposedly on full display in his treatment of ladies in public.[63] Reports like these argued that Black mashers were a problem because their behavior reflected poorly on African Americans in general. The Black press feared Black mashing undermined arguments that Black Americans were as respectable as white Americans and thus as worthy of civil rights and autonomy.[64]

From the mid-1910s, the Black press reported on Black mashers less and less and were instead increasingly indignant at white men who accosted Black women in public.[65] As the *Chicago Defender* decried, one masher believed "that because he was white and well dressed he could command the favorable attention of any pretty girl not white with whom he was not acquainted."[66] Such indignation echoed the denunciations from prominent Black activist Ida B. Wells, who, in her famous antilynching tract *A Red Record*, had argued that "colored women have always had far more reason to complain of white men" when it came to sexual assault and rape "than ever white women have had of Negroes."[67] Thus, reports of white male mashers accosting Black women mirrored Black activists' larger campaigns to debunk the myth that Black men posed a sexual threat to white women while white men were the natural protectors of womanhood. On the contrary, sometimes reports of white mashers depicted Black men as protectors of Black womanhood. For instance, when a white man "made insulting remarks" toward a Black woman in Atlanta in 1916, her husband, a Black man working nearby, responded by crushing the white man's head with a piece of ballast from a construction site.[68] Twelve years later, another Black man stabbed a white sailor after the sailor had flirted with "several girls."[69]

White men's sense of entitlement over Black women's bodies was so great that they often accosted, harassed, and humiliated Black women in the women's own neighborhoods.[70] The late 1910s and 1920s saw what Anne Gray Fischer describes as an "inundation of white men into Black neighborhoods" as law enforcement relocated red-light districts into Black areas of many major cities and allowed sex workers' white male clients to run rampant.[71] A Black woman living in Chicago wrote to the mayor to complain of this phenomenon, describing how white men wandered the Black neighborhoods of the city, soliciting any Black women they encountered.[72] In a particularly striking example from 1928, two white men "attempted to flirt" with two Black women as they were "driving peacefully" down Central Avenue, the main thoroughfare in the Los

Angeles Black community. Mrs. Clyde Howell and Grace Garth "ignored" the "two white men" who pulled up alongside them. Resenting this reaction, the men "soon became quite insulting" and forced Howell and Garth to pull over to the curb. Seeing that Garth was "very fair," one of the men commented, "You are out of place down here; I bet you are some society girl on a lark." The man's reaction demonstrates his knowledge of the area—he expected to find only African Americans in the segregated neighborhood—but it also suggests he had chosen to harass the two women with the assumption that they were Black. The two women proceeded to "give their tormentors a sound thrashing" and were soon joined by a male friend.[73] This incident took place at a moment when white newspapers were less and less likely to report on men's stranger intrusions involving white women and men.[74] However, Black newspapers continued to denounce white mashers into the 1930s and 1940s, well after the white press had lost interest, a phenomenon explored further in the next chapter.

Though the Black press focused increasingly on white mashers over Black mashers in the 1910s and 1920s, that does not necessarily mean that Black men never mashed. It is quite likely that Black men accosted, ogled, catcalled, or otherwise harassed Black women in public space in those decades.[75] Perhaps Black women and the Black press were reluctant to publicize these incidents as the antimasher crusades gained steam in the white press. Historians Wendy Rouse and Estelle Freedman have posited that the relative silence of the Black press on Black mashers after 1910 may have been the result of anxieties about feeding into anti-Black stereotypes of dangerous Black male sexuality. To accuse a Black man of mashing would be to risk confirming such stereotypes in the minds of white people. As Freedman argues, Black women "may have felt constrained from reporting insults lest they fail to express solidarity with men of their race." The Black press may have had similar motivations, in addition to a "broader press strategy of exposing white men's sexual crimes as part of the anti-lynching effort to deconflate rape and race."[76] Significantly, Black women's reports of intrusive behaviors from Black men increased again in the 1930s and 1940s, so the momentary silence of the 1920s and 1930s likely does not reflect an absence of Black men's stranger intrusions.

While race played a significant role in the way newspapers, middle-class reformers, and law enforcement identified mashers, social class proved a muddier category for distinguishing mashers from nonmashers. There was a great deal of ambiguity about the class position of mashers, with some commentators suggesting that all white men were equally likely to be mashers, while others insisted that mashers were either predominantly working class or predominantly upper class. As one New Yorker explained in 1912, the masher "is in all classes. He sits outside of fire houses and car barns as well as in the windows of Fifth avenue clubs."[77] Newspaper accounts of mashing give some indication of the variety of jobs that mashers held. Men accused of mashing were office workers and clerks, store managers, businessmen who frequented members-only clubs, actors, ticket collectors on trains, policemen (one officer was discharged from the service after he was caught mashing), professors, sheet metal workers, conductors on streetcars, and "wealthy" stockbrokers.[78] An employee of the War Department was accused of mashing two women on a streetcar in Washington, DC.[79] Such diversity of occupations suggested that neither a man's social position nor his perceived respectability guaranteed he would not "mash" a woman if given the opportunity.

The ambiguity of mashers' class affiliation left room for some commentators to suggest that any masher who appeared to be middle- or upper-class was likely employing deception. Newspapers lamented that the masher "has, unfortunately, the outward semblance of a gentleman" or warned he was "a man of elegance in dress" who "comes fresh from the barber—clean, sleek, fanciful."[80] The Chicago *Daily Inter Ocean*, a newspaper catering to businessmen, held particular scorn for the masher's appearance, labeling him a "curled and plastered darling, with glossy boots, the latest agony in hats, irreproachable shirt, stunning cravat, etc." Yet beneath his well-dressed exterior, the paper argued, the masher was "on a level with the less dressy but equally salacious boor of the lower walks of life."[81] Such reports acknowledged that mashers often looked like middle- or upper-class men because of their attire but insisted that this belied their true breeding and their lowly social and class positions. As the *Inter Ocean* put it a few months later, the masher's fine clothes were the only thing that protected him from being mistaken for a "loafer of the worst type."[82] While these examples represent the earliest moments of the masher era, similar ideas persisted throughout the masher's tenure, as in 1921 when a newspaper in New Iberia, Louisiana, warned, "The greatest rogues are, as a rule, to all appearances, the most polished gentlemen, and good clothes too frequently cover hearts not of the same quality."[83] With rhetoric like this, middle- and upper-class gentlemen could maintain the narrative that they were never mashers themselves; any masher who looked like a gentleman was merely wearing a costume.

While much reporting on "gentlemen" mashers purported to prove that gentlemanly clothing was a disguise, there is evidence that many mashers were, in fact, affluent white men who might otherwise have been perceived as gentlemen. In addition to the stockbrokers, members of exclusive clubs, and professors who made the paper for mashing, there are multiple examples where newspapers or women targets described the masher generally as a "gentleman" or an elite or especially affluent man. For instance, St. Louis passed an ordinance against "that elegant gentleman known as the masher" in 1883, while the following year Holley Williams, a "gentlemanly young fellow," was fined $2.50 for flirting with students at a local women's college in Washington, DC.[84] In New York, "working girls" complained that the "masher with good clothes and evidence of money seems to feel he has a right to ogle and insult" women on their way to work, suggesting that affluent men felt the most entitled to mash because of their social status.[85]

Some "gentlemen" accused of mashing saw no incongruity between their intrusive behaviors and the high social status they claimed, foreshadowing the way stranger intrusions would become part of middle-class masculine performance by midcentury. In 1901, an unnamed young Chicagoan described the frustration she felt that the same men who made "comments on [a woman's] dress" or told a woman "whether or not [she is] good looking" also thought those behaviors were perfectly respectable. The "funny part of it all," she told the *Chicago Daily Tribune*, "is that many of them consider themselves gentlemen."[86] Some accused mashers resented being mischaracterized as working-class and insisted on their respectability. For example, when a Chicago man insulted a masher by calling him a peanut seller, the masher exclaimed, "I'm a gentleman."[87] The Black newspaper the *Washington Bee* reported that a cheeky young woman intentionally treated a masher as a loafer in order to publicly shame him. An unnamed New York nurse, who is depicted as a white woman in an illustration, found herself without an umbrella on a rainy day. When a "well-dressed" man with "the air of a decidedly well-to-do person" began following her, offering his umbrella, she ignored him. When he refused to leave her alone, she finally opened her purse, took out one cent, and handed it to the man. Affronted, the masher asked, "What do you take me for?" "A beggar," she reportedly replied with "triumph."[88]

Middle-class Americans who refused to believe that mashers could be gentlemen often associated mashing with working-class culture more broadly. Many Progressive Era social workers and reformers viewed working-class public leisure spots like movie theaters and dance halls as sexually suspect and, not coincidentally, as breeding grounds for mashing.[89] These fears were not entirely unfounded. Men were aware that semipublic places allowed them to approach women in ways they would not be able to on the street. As one man told a sociologist at a Chicago dance hall, "When you see a cute looking girl in the street you can't go up and talk to her but at a dance hall you can."[90] Public attractions popular with working-class Americans like cabarets, fairs, and public parks were all reported hotspots of mashing.[91] Movie theaters frequented by couples looking for privacy were also notorious masher hunting grounds.[92] The problem was so bad in 1914 that the Chicago chief of police suggested instituting gender-segregated seating to deter movie theater mashing.[93] Public transportation also proved problematic. If approached by a masher at a streetcar stop, a working-class or poor woman was essentially a sitting duck, forced to wait with no other means to navigate the city.[94] Once on a streetcar or train, strangers were sardined together, putting riders at risk of intrusive behaviors. One Chicagoan described how "the crowded condition of the street cars during the rush hours" gave the masher "a great field for his nefarious exploits."[95] The jostling of a full train could mask all manner of touching.[96]

Even if women escaped mashing on public transportation or in public leisure spaces, middle-class reformers viewed working-class and immigrant neighborhoods themselves as hotbeds of mashing. For instance, settlement workers interviewing residents in the working-class immigrant neighborhoods of Chicago noted that young girls and working women endured intrusive behaviors from men in their neighborhoods. As one settlement worker explained, "On every corner crowds of boys gather and, to quote the girls, 'pass remarks' upon all who pass." This behavior, according to the interviewer, "of course leads to conversation of a vulgar nature" and "rough housing" among the boys.[97] Thus, despite women's frequent accusations that middle- and upper-class white men mashed, disbelieving reformers or reporters easily scapegoated working-class white men (or, in this case, boys) as the most obvious mashers.[98]

The contestations over the masher's identity, particularly his class status, highlight how Americans struggled to make sense of seemingly respectable men who engaged in stranger intrusions in public places. Intrusive behaviors represented a breach of public etiquette and a failure to perform the era's normative masculinity, namely, the expectations of affluent white masculinity. Scholars have described the period of the masher's ascendancy as a "crisis of masculinity," when older models of "manliness" that emphasized restraint, learnedness, and the ability to resist sexual temptation gave way to a model of "masculinity" that emphasized action, ruggedness, and the embrace of a "strenuous life."[99]

The *Dallas Morning News* hinted at this crisis of manhood in 1913, lamenting that society needed to "infus[e] in men higher standards of manhood, higher ideals of gallantry than those that are now conventional."[100] The masher was an easy target for anyone criticizing white men's failure to live up to the standards of either the older model of a civilized white manliness or the newer model of rugged masculinity.

If, for instance, it was impossible to ignore evidence that an affluent man was a masher, critics could deny the masher's claims to gentlemanly status by labeling him as too vain, too concerned with the opinion of others, or too weak and effeminate. An 1895 diatribe against the masher described him as "dressed in the latest togs, begloved and beflowered" and "strut[ting] up and down" the street to attract the attention of women. This "asinine vanity" marked the masher as feminized, for while women were expected to be interested in supposedly trivial concerns like clothing and appearance, gender norms dictated that men were supposed to be too consumed with business, politics, or athleticism to be concerned with fashion.[101] Working-class publications like Chicago's *Day Book* especially ridiculed the masher and similar characters who cared about their appearance, describing the "male flirt" as a "whimpering kid" whose narcissism marked him, and not women, as the true "weak sex."[102] The same paper published a short joke in 1913 where a masher rushes into a restaurant and asks, in affected speech, "Aw, say, can a man get a dwink here?" "Yes. Fetch your man in," retorts the waiter, "dryly."[103] As late as 1929, syndicated columnist Doris Blake was advising young women to stare past a masher or male flirt "as if he were not there." After all, she argued, such men were "just vain nitwits and a blow to their vanity is the kindest thing that can be awarded them."[104] Mashers thus supposedly betrayed their deviant masculinity not only through their intrusive behaviors but also by exhibiting too much interest in clothing and flirtation, preoccupations associated more closely with women.

As Americans sorted out the boundaries of the masher category, it became clear he embodied an aberrant masculinity that served as a foil to the hegemonic masculinity of the period. In one revealing example, a 1911 article in the *Los Angeles Times* explicitly linked mashing with other marginalized masculinities defined by their rowdiness or lasciviousness. According to the article, mashers were "pink Willie-boys," "senile Lotharios," "Loutish Larrikins," or "any male thing that attempts to inflict odious attentions on unwilling maidens." Such men were "stamped at once as belonging to the class of undesirables."[105] Mashers' apparent inability to hide their lascivious desires suggested they lacked the self-control necessary to claim respectable status. Since mashing was deemed incompatible with gentlemanly behavior, it was easy to conclude that most mashers had never been gentlemen at all. Mashers, rather, were their own "class" of men.

Enduring Mashing, Smashing Mashing

As Americans debated how to identify mashers, mashing's impact on women's access to urban space grew ever clearer. Women described how experiences of mashing had convinced them to limit their own mobility to avoid annoying or frightening intrusions. Women changed their planned routes or were compelled to disembark from public transit, all to avoid the "gantlet of insult" that seemed to follow them wherever they went.[106] In Indianapolis, both Black and white women made "it a study to avoid the objectionable places" where mashers congregated, while women in Chicago would "cross to the other side of the street" to avoid "notorious" street corners.[107] Department store saleswomen in New York were known to leave stores in groups to protect one another from the advances of mashers who loitered outside, while others quit their jobs altogether because they were scared to leave work after dark.[108] Nighttime was considered particularly frightening and dangerous, and women often made a point to describe how dark and deserted streets made them feel unsafe.[109] If they did not curtail their own mobility, concerned family members might forbid young women and girls from visiting certain parts of the city or from going out at night. Settlement workers in Chicago noted that "decent" working-class girls were "not safe from insult on the street," and their mothers often insisted girls stay indoors after nightfall, while Sadie T. Wald and Evelyn Allen Frake, two prominent clubwomen, both forbade their daughters from going out in the city after dark.[110]

Mashing revealed the lie behind the supposedly equal access to public space enjoyed by white men and women in the United States. Women's rights activist (and creator of the Kewpie cartoons and dolls) Rose O'Neill suggested in 1916 that her experiences of the city streets differed significantly from men's. "A man walks along the street without a sense of being watched or commented upon as he goes," she wrote. "I sometimes wonder if he could maintain that vigorous and conquering stride if he were aware of laughter in his rear; if he had to pass the gauntlet of quaint and contemptuous comment with which a woman is assailed."[111] In this light, to protest mashing was to assert a woman's right to navigate public space unmolested. An Oakland woman, in explaining why she attacked the man who followed and then grabbed her on the street, made such an assertion: "No man has a right to seize my arm and attempt to detain me on the street and I am sure every fair-minded person will uphold me in my action."[112] Chicago's *Day Book*, which catered to a working-class readership including many working women, was especially adamant on this point. Actress Ethel Intrapodi advocated self-defense for *Day Book*'s women readers, explaining that to feel "safe on the streets . . . is a great deal to a woman who has to make her way in the world."[113]

While complaints of "street insults" in the mid- to late nineteenth century had rarely manifested in an organized response to intrusive behaviors, the Progressive Era crusades against mashing harnessed a growing infrastructure of reform that included women's clubs, municipal governments, law enforcement, and athletic clubs to crack down on mashing. White and Black women's clubs advocated for those they perceived as the most vulnerable victims of mashing and demanded a tougher legal response from the city officials and police where they resided. Municipal governments and law enforcement, hearing women's cry and perhaps seeing an opportunity to expand police power, drafted a range of ordinances meant to eliminate mashing and other "undesirable" behaviors on city streets. Some police departments hired women as decoys or as bona fide police officers to aid in their masher crackdowns. Proponents of women's athletics offered classes in jiujitsu and other forms of self-defense designed especially to arm working-class white and immigrant women against mashing.[114] The organized and highly publicized nature of these antimashing tactics highlights how many middle-class Americans saw intrusive behaviors not only as an inappropriate manifestation of white masculine entitlement but also as criminal acts deserving of legal and even violent response.

White women's clubs were among the strongest supporters of antimashing legislation, and they often called on law enforcement to arrest mashers. Alice I. Sterling of the Protective Agency for Women and Children voiced a typical demand in 1903, calling on Chicago's chief of police to "send a squad of policemen to State street and arrest every masher on sight."[115] At times, these calls were aimed at protecting middle-class and monied white women like club members themselves, especially in fashionable shopping districts where mashers bothered female customers.[116] However, clubwomen also linked their antimashing campaigns to their other work on behalf of working-class white women. The Denver Business Woman's Club, for instance, vowed to patrol the streets near the shops and offices where women worked and report mashers to the police, saving victims the embarrassment of having to testify in court themselves.[117] Once police arrested mashers, clubwomen suggested they deserved punishment in the form of public shaming rituals. As Chicago Woman's Club member Katherine Knowles Robbins put it, "Those vain individuals who wear the clothes of men should be held up to public scorn and ridicule." One suggestion? To "douse" mashers "with water in the public streets."[118]

The legal response to mashing began as early as the 1880s when zealous police officers started arresting mashers in places like Chicago and St. Louis using existing disturbance of the peace ordinances.[119] At least twenty-five municipalities went on to consider new antimashing laws, to revise laws to include mashing behaviors, or to direct courts and law enforcement to reinterpret existing ordinances in order to arrest mashers. Houston was the first major city to implement a stand-alone antimashing ordinance when the city council passed a ban on "goo goo eyes" in 1905.[120] Soon after, the mastermind of the Houston ordinance, T. H. Stone, was advising other cities on how to develop their own antimashing ordinances.[121] By 1921, at least fifteen towns and cities had officially passed new or revised ordinances designed to combat mashing.[122] Such ordinances, as the *Detroit Free Press* put it, were designed to give police the "utmost power" in arresting mashers.[123]

Antimashing ordinances and crackdowns were a response to critiques from urban reformers, women's rights activists, and Progressive politicians of the time who couched the mashing crisis in the context of their larger reform efforts. For instance, Chicago's Juvenile Protective Agency suggested that strengthening laws against rape and seduction, a key goal of many women's rights activists, would also protect women from mashers' random assaults on the street.[124] In places where school-age girls were targets of intrusive behaviors, some boards of education suggested using new age-of-consent laws to prosecute the men who hung around schools and waited to accost young girls who emerged at the end of the day.[125] Other places, like New York City, tackled mashing by expanding vagrancy or "move-on" ordinances that were designed to clear the streets of anyone deemed undesirable or unsightly.[126] However, arrests under vagrancy laws were vulnerable to dismissal in court, leading Theodore Roosevelt, noted Progressive and then-governor of New York, to call on the state legislature to explicitly ban mashing in 1900.[127]

While antimashing laws and police crackdowns appeased activists, they did not guarantee that mashers were arrested, prosecuted, and sentenced smoothly or to constituents' satisfaction. Despite the groundswell of support for tougher responses to mashing, when police began arresting white men for mashing and courts began fining them, they were sometimes met with resistance. In an early example from 1887, a justice in the New York police court who had fined a man ten dollars for "insulting and annoying School Girls" found himself on the receiving end of criticism from local reporters. He defended his decision to Mayor Abram Hewitt by asserting, "I will mete out such punishment as I think the case warrants, even should I displease the Reporter of the 'World.'"[128] On the other hand, if residents complained about troublesome sections of town or thoroughfares that were popular with mashers, there was no guarantee that the police would take these complaints seriously. For instance, a New York resident reported to local law enforcement that a particular Harlem bridge was often lined with "tramps, drunken loafers, and ribald young men" that made crossing unpleasant. According to the resident, "Women and young girls make its passage only at the expense of lewd glances, insulting words, and indecent jostlings."[129] When a police officer investigated, he found this description to be "utterly untrue" and took no action.[130]

White citizens also used disorderly conduct and antimashing sentiment to try to clear the streets of anyone but themselves and thus to assert their dominance over public spaces. For example, an anonymous New York resident asked the police to clear his neighborhood of "alot of colored would be dudes who congregate in this block." These men blocked the sidewalks, he alleged, and "there is no white lady passing through there that is not insulted."[131] This attempt to rile up New York City law enforcement fell flat. The local police captain who investigated the complaint reported that "147 colored families" lived in the neighborhood and acknowledged that these Black families were "nearly if not quite all respectable and . . . entitled to some privileges on the street and sidewalks where they live."[132] However, complaints like this, which appealed to white supremacist beliefs about the inherent innocence of white womanhood and the inherent brutality of Black masculinity, were a major reason why Black Americans and Black women's clubs rarely supported the expansion of police power to crack down on sexual violence, fearing new laws would be used to target Black men and protect only white women.[133]

When law enforcement and judges chose to crack down on mashing, they soon encountered another problem: the reluctance of women to report and testify against mashers. In 1901, Chicago Chief of Police Francis O'Neill practically begged women to come forward with charges against mashers. "While of course I know that the masher is more or less annoying to women, no complaints have been made to me," he explained to the *Chicago Daily Tribune*. "I do not see how we can do much unless complaints are handed in."[134] City officials' frustrations led some to blame women for the mashing problem. W. L. Bodine, a superintendent in the Chicago public school system, argued the city "would be ridden of mashers if women would be brave enough" to alert the police and testify in court. "The entire question of checking mashers," Bodine insisted, "is up to Chicago womanhood."[135]

Women had good reason to fear the notoriety that could come with testifying against mashers. Women who accused men of mashing regularly found themselves blamed for the men's behaviors. Some judges went so far as to suggest that women accused mashers to get their "names and pictures in the newspapers."[136] In other cases, women found themselves on trial for their conduct. A New York woman confronted a display of white male solidarity when she tried to turn a masher in to the police. When asked to account for his actions, the masher had asked the policeman, "You can dope what she is, can't you? Why, she gimme the lamp!" To translate, the masher accused the woman of looking at him and, thus, encouraging him. The white police officer sided with the masher and told the woman to "beat it."[137] Similarly, near the end of the antimashing crusades, a woman brought a case against a man who she said pinched her leg in a movie theater. By the end of the court proceedings, the accused had been freed and his accuser had herself been charged with disorderly conduct. The man claimed she had been the one who rubbed his leg, not the other way around.[138]

Black women may have been especially nervous that such a fate might befall them. The relative paucity of Black women's accounts of mashing in Progressive Era newspapers may be in part the result of their anxieties about being labeled sexually immoral if they came forward with stories of sexual violence.[139] Indeed, the white press often portrayed white women accusers as sexually suspect or immoral—suggesting that white women's fashions were too "extreme" or their glances too inviting—so it would not be surprising if Black women feared the same and worse.[140]

Still, there are examples of Black women demanding legal and state protection from white mashers. In 1924, the *Chicago Defender* reported that Estelle Richardson, "a musician and a young woman of culture," confronted a white masher on a New York subway car. The man, John Elliot, "attempted to flirt" with Richardson on the subway and made "insulting remarks." When she rebuffed his advances, Elliot threatened, "If you were in Georgia, I would have you strung up." Richardson quickly left the train and managed to grab Elliot, with the help of a white female passenger, and held him until police came to arrest him. Elliot was sentenced to the workhouse, and the judge who oversaw the sentencing congratulated Richardson on her "pluck."[141] Despite the positive feedback from the court, Elliot's reaction to Richardson's rebuke highlights the cost Black women faced if they reported white mashers. Elliot's choice of words alluded to lynching, reflecting the way white men's sexual insinuations in public were also racialized when they targeted Black women. Reports of Elliot's violent threats could have convinced other Black women it was better to ignore insults from white men than reprimand them publicly.

As it became clear that white men, whether policemen or strangers on the street, could not be relied on to protect white women, let alone women of color, women began to argue for taking matters into their own hands. Prominent clubwomen in some cities called on law enforcement to enlist women to help catch and arrest mashers. Cities like Chicago, Los Angeles, and Pittsburgh hired women as decoys to entrap mashers on the street.[142] By 1915, several cities had hired or were considering hiring women as official police officers with the ability to arrest mashers on the spot.[143] While most of the first women police officers were white, Black communities in the urban North also called on police departments to employ Black women as police officers in hopes they could better protect African American women from urban dangers. As the *Chicago Defender* explained in 1914, Black women police officers would be able to "mingle with the crowds on the street, in the cars, in the public and private parks and places of amusement to protect the women of the race from those who go beyond 'mashing' and insult the girls and women of the race."[144] By the late 1920s, Black policewomen were reportedly helping to investigate vice in dance halls in New York, patrolling the West Park district of Chicago in an attempt to eradicate mashers, and arresting white men who bothered Black women on streetcars in Washington, DC.[145]

When all else failed, women turned to self-defense tactics to protect themselves from mashers and assaults on the street. Historian Wendy Rouse suggests self-defense became "a means for white women to empower themselves against their alleged natural protectors—white men."[146] As one Los Angeles woman put it after she attacked a would-be masher, "I didn't see anyone to protect me, so I protected myself."[147] White male–owned newspapers did not always take their efforts seriously, gleefully reporting how women stuck mashers with hatpins, hit them with umbrellas, and even used their fists or martial arts like jiujitsu.[148] Still, working-class women particularly embraced self-defense to combat mashers. For instance, Chicago's *Day Book* celebrated the strength, bravery, and quick-wittedness of working women who physically fought off unwanted advances.[149] As one young telephone operator argued, she had no qualms about "smashing her handbag" over a masher's head and "pummeling him with her fists."[150] Black women also sometimes found that only they could save themselves from white mashers. In 1928, as the antimashing crusades had all but disappeared, the *Chicago Defender* cheered Helen Waters, who "battered" a white masher's "face and body" when he touched her knee in an insulting gesture.[151] While these piecemeal, individual responses to mashing may not have had long-lasting effects on mashing's prominence, they do confirm the numbers and varieties of women who denounced mashing as an inappropriate display of masculine entitlement.

While none of the tactics for eradicating the masher's intrusive behaviors proved entirely successful, the nationwide organized response to mashing was unique to the Progressive Era. At no time in the United States before or since has there been such a widespread condemnation of men's stranger intrusions or such a robust set of legal and extralegal frameworks for addressing those behaviors. Clearly, the antimasher crusades benefited from the larger reform movements of the Progressive Era. To combat mashing, activists and reformers harnessed the existing infrastructure and political clout of organizations like women's clubs, the growing strength of municipal police forces, and the faith in state solutions to social problems typical of the era.[152] However, none of these responses would have seemed necessary if middle-class commentators and reformers had not viewed the masher's leering looks, indecent remarks, and supposed obsessions with fashion and flirting as a deviant masculine performance that required policing. The fact that antimashing legislation, self-defense classes, both the Black and white press, and even antimashing policing predominantly targeted white mashers suggests that Americans overwhelmingly viewed intrusive behaviors as incompatible with the era's expectations of idealized white masculinity. The strength of the response to the masher, then, was indeed emblematic of progressives' larger concerns for social welfare but was also evidence of the way middle-class Americans in positions of power viewed the masher's intrusive behaviors as nonnormative and deserving of official censure.

THE ANTIMASHER CRUSADES marked a new moment in Americans' understanding of intrusive behaviors. After the initial outcry over street insults in the mid-nineteenth century, women's clubs, urban reformers, and journalists began to articulate intrusive behaviors as the antics of a particular kind of man:

the masher, a man almost always depicted as a white man with indecent intentions. The category of "masher" allowed commentators to link men's stranger intrusions with a man's character. The masher could be many things—vain, predatory, effeminate, dangerous, annoying—but he was never considered normal, never considered an ideal of manhood. A man who "mashed" proved he was deficient. He was too interested in the attentions and affections of women; he was too concerned with his appearance; he annoyed and frightened (white) women instead of protecting them. Because mashers were largely understood to be white men, the masher became known as a category of white masculinity that was deviant or marginalized, a category to which one ought not to aspire. Thus, for a time, many Americans denounced white men's stranger intrusions as mashing and sought help from state actors to crack down on the behaviors.

At the same time, popular representations of the masher and his victim in white-owned media left an indelible mark on the way Americans would articulate and understand stranger intrusions in the coming decades. The fact that white-owned mainstream media portrayed both the category of the masher and his victim as white suggested that many white women were suspicious of their white male counterparts and understood that white men could not be relied upon to protect them, a belief bolstered by other campaigns to curtail male sexual privilege in the Progressive Era. However, those same discourses limited who could claim the status of a masher's victim and the albeit limited protections that came with it. White women, especially middle- and upper-class white women, were the "ideal" victims of stranger intrusions in white-produced media and thus could claim protections more readily and with fewer grievances. Women of color, on the other hand, were less likely to be viewed as victims or as requiring help against mashers unless they experienced especially severe attacks, including threats of violence and murder. Indeed, their experiences rarely featured in white press coverage of mashing and would all but disappear from the white press by the 1930s. Instead, mass and popular media would begin to portray intrusive behaviors not as the unique violence of white men but as the natural right of white men and would cast white women as the natural object of white men's desire. The masher had broken the rules of social engagement between strangers, but by the 1940s, a new set of rules emerged.

CHAPTER **THREE**

WHISTLING WOLVES AND OGLING SAILORS

DETROIT WAS coming down from a summer heatwave on Tuesday, July 23, 1946. Temperatures had peaked at one hundred degrees four days earlier but were finally cooling off.[1] At three on the morning of the twenty-third, Detroit police officer Earl Johnson was patrolling in the Canfield district, a neighborhood about two miles northwest of downtown Detroit.[2] Also on the street at that time was William T. Jansen, a white Detroit resident. It is impossible to know why Jansen was out in Canfield at three a.m. on a Tuesday. Perhaps he had a late shift, or a very early shift, at the automobile factory where he worked.[3] Perhaps he had spent the evening with a friend and was walking home in the dark early morning hours. It is also unclear what about Jansen's behavior caught Officer Johnson's attention. Jansen might have been flirting with a woman on the street, or perhaps he let out a whistle as a woman passed him, or perhaps Officer Johnson was suspicious of the way Jansen looked. Whatever the case, the Detroit newspapers reported later that morning that Officer Johnson had cited Jansen for "ogling" and issued an ordinance violation ticket.[4]

The ordinance in question was the "anti-ogling" ordinance that the city council had updated in 1910 to crack down on mashers. However, rather than applaud the police officer's efforts to eradicate ogling on the street, as they might have done in 1910, local newspapers were bemused that a man could be fined for something as innocuous as ogling. The *Detroit News* claimed that Jansen was "the first citizen charged with ogling," as if the preceding thirty-six years—and decades of antimasher crusades—had never happened.[5] While the ordinance was likely spottily enforced from its inception, the same newspaper had reported previous ogling and mashing charges as late as 1929, while the *Detroit Free Press* reported police had arrested a "telephone masher" just a month before Jansen was cited.[6] The idea that ogling and similar forms of mashing could be punishable offenses was thus not so novel as the *Detroit News* suggested. Yet in response to his arrest, Jansen's family protested and claimed not to know what "ogling" meant. The *News* reported even the police could not define the term and were forced to look it up in an "unabridged dictionary."[7] Despite these protestations, Lieutenant Charles Witherite, the supervising officer who had ordered his men to target oglers, explained he was just following the law.[8] In defending his "anti-ogling drive," Witherite did not reference a scourge of mashing or women's complaints of stranger intrusions. He declared simply, "It's right there in the compiled ordinances. You can look it up. Ogling is against the law."[9]

The day after Jansen was cited, the Associated Press picked up the story. Newspapers from Lewiston, Maine, to Los Angeles, California, ran near-identical stories about the "ancient law" that was wreaking havoc for oglers in Detroit. The article cast Officer Johnson and Lieutenant Witherite as prudish men enforcing an outdated decree. It called Detroit's anti-ogling ordinance "ancient" and "recently unearthed," suggesting it had lain dormant in the municipal code for centuries. The Associated Press interviewed Dale Belmont, a twenty-two-year-old white woman described as a "curvaceous showgirl" and "pinup favorite of overseas veterans." Belmont made it clear that no campaign against ogling had her blessing. "I think it's a crazy ordinance," she said. "I think it's a wonderful thing that men turn around and stare at girls. If they didn't ogle me I'd think I was slipping." Nineteen-year-old Dorothy Mahon, a student at "a local finishing school for young ladies," echoed Belmont's take. She explained, "It seems silly in this day and age to have an ordinance like this. Why most girls want boys to whistle at them."[10] Next to the testimony of these young women, forty-two-year-old Lieutenant Witherite appeared uptight and out of touch as he insisted that ogling would no longer "go unchallenged" in his district.[11]

The nationwide ridicule of Detroit's drive against oglers stood in contrast to the denunciations of mashing in national and local press a few decades before. The responses to Jansen's citation exemplify how shifting discourses trivialized and normalized men's stranger intrusions in the 1930s and 1940s. The cries of "smash the masher" that had permeated discussion of intrusive behaviors in the Progressive Era gave way to the insistence that these same behaviors, when practiced by white men, were now not only acceptable and benign but what women wanted. Public commentators increasingly cast intrusive behaviors as natural for heterosexual white men and as an expected and unremarkable part of urban life. Newspaper reports mocked anti-ogling campaigns, and films and popular culture cast intrusive behaviors as humorous flirtation. Women, even middle-class white women, expressed a desire for flirtatious interactions in public places and suggested that their self-worth derived in part from how many men they attracted on the street. In this new cultural context, stranger intrusions were nothing to worry about but were to be celebrated and enjoyed as part of a more sexually liberated society.

Crucially, the idea that men's stranger intrusions were a harmless, even enjoyable, part of urban life applied only when white men were the instigators. When white men ogled, wolf-whistled, or remarked on a woman's appearance in public space, their behaviors were cast as the natural expressions of healthy male sexuality. In some cases, newspapers and commentators suggested these behaviors were one way to find a romantic partner, perhaps even a wife. In contrast, Black men who whistled at, spoke to, or even looked at white women were likely to be cast as sexual predators or rapists. In the eyes of white Americans, the mere perception that Black men had engaged in these behaviors was often enough to justify violence and lynching.[12] Rumors that Black men had raped white women were a common excuse for white anti-Black violence throughout the twentieth century, including a concentration of race riots in the 1940s.[13]

One of those riots took place in Detroit in the summer of 1943, just three years before Detroit police cited William T. Jansen for ogling. The city was transitioning to wartime manufacturing, experiencing an influx of Southern migrant workers (both Black and white) and dealing with the housing shortage that ensued. Interracial violence erupted on June 20, 1943, with skirmishes between Black and white youths at Belle Isle in the Detroit River. The conflicts quickly escalated and spread across the city, lasting four days. While many factors contributed to the tensions and antagonism between white and Black Detroiters in the 1940s, at least two rumors about interracial gender or sexual violence also fueled the mobs. One rumor claimed that a white mob had thrown a Black woman and her child into the Detroit River. This story confirmed for many Black residents what they already suspected: that white Detroiters had no regard for the lives of Black Detroiters. On the other hand, white residents justified their violence in part by spreading a rumor that a Black man had raped a white woman at Belle Isle. Neither of these rumors was ever confirmed, but they demonstrate the power of residents' anxieties about interracial gender and sexual violence. White residents feared Black male sexuality as especially violent and targeting white women, while Black residents feared that Black women were vulnerable to white men's sexual and physical attacks. In the end, the rumors fueled violence that resulted in thirty-five deaths and over 700 injuries, the vast majority affecting Black Detroiters.[14]

Intrusive behaviors like ogling, catcalling, or wolf-whistling were not, therefore, deemed universally harmless or trivial. When Dale Belmont and Dorothy Mahon told the Associated Press that they enjoyed being ogled or whistled at, they were almost certainly referring to white men's ogling or whistling. If they had been in Detroit in 1943 or had read about any of the other riots that took place in the mid-1940s, it seems unlikely they would have forgotten the lessons such riots seemed to offer about the dangers of interracial sexual relationships and sexual violence. Rather, in the twenty-five years following the antimasher crusades, white Americans steadily incorporated intrusive behaviors into hegemonic ideals of masculinity, normalizing such behaviors as the purview of white men. While Americans had denounced behaviors like ogling, catcalling, and the like as incompatible with normative conceptions of white masculinity in the Progressive Era, they increasingly became part of the expected performance of white heterosexual masculinity in the 1930s and 1940s.

To understand the normalization of white men's stranger intrusions in this period, one must turn to the national arena. As concerns over mashing waned and sexual attitudes and practices shifted in the 1920s and 1930s, Americans documented individual experiences of stranger intrusions less and less. New expectations for "modern" heterosexual relationships emphasized women's newfound freedoms—and responsibilities—in such relationships. Americans increasingly viewed women as powerful, or at least equal, players in heterosexual interactions who could choose to rebuff, ridicule, or accept men's advances at their pleasure. Mainstream white newspapers no longer considered reports of intrusive behaviors to be newsworthy. Instead, depictions of men's intrusive behaviors relocated to popular culture, especially motion pictures, popular songs, and humor writing that spread across the country in magazines and other mass media.[15] While Americans openly contested representations of intrusive behaviors, especially at the local level, national media increasingly depicted stranger intrusions as quotidian, humorous, and natural for white men. Those with a vested interest in the maintenance of patriarchy contributed to the normalization of stranger intrusions in a way that legitimated the dominance of masculinity, whiteness, and heterosexuality in public space. For one, mass culture—especially visual culture in the form of films, cartoons, and advertising—poked fun at behaviors like catcalling and ogling in the 1930s and early 1940s, furthering their trivialization. With the onset of the Second World War, the US military advanced the normalization of stranger intrusions by proliferating images and discourses that depicted servicemen's consumption of women's bodies as a vital part of boosting troops' morale. White women bolstered these narratives, describing how intrusive behaviors affirmed their attractiveness, in a bid to align themselves with the shifting boundaries of hegemonic masculinity.

However, the discourses that normalized intrusive behaviors were by no means universal. The Black press offered a significant counternarrative that shared more in common with Progressive Era antimasher discourses than with the mainstream white press of the 1930s and 1940s. Thus, Black women and men interpreted stranger intrusions differently from white people, and the Black press did not always see stranger intrusions as signs of sexual liberation or natural sexual expression.

The 1930s and 1940s, then, represented a period of contestation and retrenchment when it came to men's stranger intrusions. If the Progressive Era saw the construction of the "masher" as a bugbear upon whom social reformers, women's groups, law enforcement, and individual women could heap their criticism, the interwar and immediate postwar period saw the rehabilitation of intrusive behaviors as part of the supposedly natural rights afforded to middle-class white American men.

The Modern Woman and Stranger Intrusions

The sexual landscape that produced the backlash against Detroit's anti-ogling campaign differed significantly from the context that welcomed the antimasher crusades of the Progressive Era. For one, women won the vote in 1920, near the end of the antimasher crusades. With that new civic right, they gained the power to demand and effect change through the legal and electoral system, at least in principle. Notably, Southern Black women still faced significant barriers to exercising suffrage.[16] At the same time, the concept of separate feminine and masculine spheres that had characterized middle-class white ideology of the Victorian era was crumbling. Middle-class American youth mingled more and more in heterosocial spaces and groups, dating without their parents' supervision. The increasing affordability of cars gave many young people semiprivate spaces to engage in "necking" or "petting." Indeed, young women soon found that not engaging in this kind of sexual activity could earn them the label of prude.[17] In light of these changing expectations for heterosexual relationships, the *Chicago Daily Tribune* noted in 1929 that the "modern woman" now boasted a "much advertised ability to take care of any situation," and she "makes a straight bee line" as soon as she "sees her man." Sexual assertiveness was no longer the sole domain of men.[18]

Thus, when *Vogue* assistant editor Marjorie Hillis published her best-selling advice book for single women, *Live Alone and Like It,* in 1936, she knew her readers had come a long way from their turn-of-the-century counterparts. They needed frank, modern advice for a new age. This was especially true when it came to sex. Hillis devoted an entire chapter to the decision of whether or not to have premarital sex with a man. In it, she conceded, "It would be foolish to pretend that things are as they used to be." While there was a time when a "Woman's Honor" was "mentioned with bated breath and protected by her father, her brother, and the community," the decision to have sex was "now her own affair." According to Hillis, a modern American woman "can be a lot more aggressive now than [she] could have been a few years ago." Hillis attributed this change partly to the Great Depression. As young men struggled financially and could no longer foot the bill on dates, "it began to be quite usual for the girls to pay for practically everything" and, consequently, to dictate more of the terms of the relationship. Hillis was not the first to note a change in the American sexual landscape, but the success of her book—which sold over 100,000 copies in its first five months—made it clear that her insights into life as a single white woman of the 1930s resonated with many Americans.[19]

In this context of liberalizing sexual mores and expansion of women's rights, there came a new acceptance of, and even desire for, interactions between female and male strangers in public. The kinds of middle-class white women who might have organized against mashers in the Progressive Era now often described intrusive behaviors as harmless and even romantic and desirable. As unchaperoned dating and heterosexual socializing were more widely accepted, men and women alike began to see brief encounters in public places as potential romantic overtures. An ogle might still be unwanted from time to time, but it could also be a nonthreatening opening to a romantic encounter. Indeed, in her advice book, Hillis encouraged women to approach men in public and to seek out interesting conversation and acquaintances. "This was once considered a Grave Danger," Hillis noted, but in 1936, "any modern girl" knew how to approach a stranger for some harmless flirtation.[20]

As women's desires became ever more apparent and women began to assert themselves more forcefully in sexual relationships, their newfound agency came at a price. While social mores were shifting to acknowledge and even accept that men and women could both pursue sexual relationships outside of marriage, women were far more likely to shoulder the blame if something went wrong. The rhetoric of turn-of-the-century social reformers and women's advocates may have cast women, especially working-class women, as helpless and in need of guidance from their "betters," but it also afforded them a degree of protection. Historian Julie Berebitsky argues that as Americans began to become more aware of and accept women's sexual desires, white women in particular "lost the limited degree of protection that had existed when a large segment of the population believed they were inherently innocent."[21] By the 1940s, a sexual double standard had replaced an older ideal of universal sexual self-restraint.[22] Studies of high school students conducted in the 1930s, 1940s, and 1950s demonstrated that they held different expectations of sexual experience and permissiveness for boys and girls and that girls were expected to be both open to sex with their male partners and also responsible for not letting it go too far.[23] Women and girls who were too enthusiastic about the potential for sexual intimacy risked being thought of as "easy" or disreputable. The sexual double standard sifted into ideas about intrusive behaviors and public flirtations. Women had to tread a fine line between being open to sexual advances from men in public places and being too eager for sexual interactions. One young man who liked to go out and "flirt" with women in the early 1930s thus admitted that he felt "better" when women "snub[bed]" him. He explained, "When I meet a girl [by flirting with her in public] I don't think much of her."[24]

Even those tasked with helping vulnerable women less frequently saw them as innocent victims. For instance, social workers who assisted young women after 1920 continued to worry about the slippery slope from a wolf whistle to a "pick-up" to extramarital sex, but the grammar had changed. One settlement house worker noted as early as 1924 that police officers picked up one of her female clients "in company with a young fellow with whom she flirted," thus emphasizing the young woman's agency in the relationship. The settlement house worker worried that her client was "flippant—flirts with passersby."[25] Twenty years later, one young woman named Muriel linked early experiences of men's stranger intrusions with her later sexual activity, confirming social workers' fears about the effects of intrusive behaviors on women. She told a Travelers Aid worker that "men were always trying to pick her up" when she was a girl and she "could not walk down the street without being whistled at." These stranger intrusions convinced Muriel that she might be able to use her sexual desirability to her advantage, and she soon began going out with men and having "sexual relations."[26] During the antimasher crusades, such clients would likely have been cast as victims who fell afoul of conniving mashers. By the late 1940s, though, women were likely to be held equally responsible as men for indiscreet flirtation, if not more so.[27] As a result, women who wanted to combat men's stranger intrusions found fewer avenues for protest or sympathetic ears.

The shift in Americans' attitudes to men's stranger intrusions was evident in the backlash against antimashing policing. Though the Detroit anti-ogling ordinance received the most widespread condemnation in 1946, garnering editorials in national papers, the backlash began as early as 1931 when John Alcock, Chicago's acting police commissioner, vowed to crack down on "sheiks and hoodlums hanging around street corners" who try "to flirt with unescorted young women and girls who pass by." The *Chicago Daily Tribune* scoffed at Alcock's "old fashioned edict" and questioned the relevancy of the antiflirt drive. After all, as the paper implied, the "old and new fashioned pastime of flirting" was going nowhere. The paper even claimed that the "last occasion" for an antiflirt drive was "in the days of yore when 'O, you kid' was considered quite a daring remark when addressed to long haired girls in long dresses."[28] Though the *Tribune* may have had an ulterior motive in criticizing Alcock—he had been appointed by corrupt, and recently defeated, Mayor William Hale Thompson—the allusions to outdated fashions and slang cast the antiflirt campaign as belonging to a bygone time, and thus as an inappropriate response to flirtation in the 1930s. The *Tribune*'s reporting appeared on the paper's front page and established a tone of mocking contempt for the police's seemingly prudish responses to flirting.

Despite the *Tribune*'s suggestion to the contrary, attempts to crack down on intrusive behaviors had gone relatively unquestioned, if not lauded, as little as three years previously. In July 1928, police arrested seventeen men in the Woodlawn neighborhood of Chicago on charges related to "automobile mash[ing]." The *Tribune* greeted the arrests with relief, reporting, "Residents smiled as they learned the anti-flirt campaign was on again."[29] Even in the midst of criticizing the antiflirt drive three years later, the *Tribune* acknowledged that Alcock was responding to residents' complaints that district stations had received "for some time."[30] Alcock's crackdown on intrusive behaviors was thus not the result of an autocratic decree from law enforcement bent on eradicating ogling at all costs. It was, rather, evidence that, for some, men's stranger intrusions were still objectionable and unwanted. Contrary to the *Tribune*'s characterization, antiflirt drives were not a hangover from "days of yore" but a long-established and resident-supported response to intrusive behaviors. The contempt for antiflirt policing and embrace of white men's stranger intrusions that bubbled up in the early 1930s thus remained contested at the time, but the normalization of white men's intrusive behaviors would grow and intensify in the ensuing years.

Men's Desires and Women's Agency in Popular Culture

Just as the cultural, political, and sexual changes of the 1920s and 1930s influenced Americans' perceptions of men's stranger intrusions, the growing objectification and sexualization of women in popular and mass media intensified the change. Technological innovations and revolutions in marketing fueled the growth of mass media and advertising in the interwar period and, with them, the use of the female body as an erotic object.[31] Advertising and Hollywood films, not to mention pinup drawings and girlie magazines, all highlighted the physical attributes and passivity of models and actresses. With the rise of consumerism in the 1920s, merchandisers and advertisers began to rely on the "implied sexuality" of the female body—particularly the white Anglo-Saxon body—to sell products. As one model photographer said of his subject in 1930, "She sells the stuff by making it desirable."[32] Meanwhile, during the rise and dominance of classical Hollywood cinema in the 1930s and 1940s, "Hollywood style" films bolstered what feminist theorist Laura Mulvey has described as patriarchal "ways of looking" that reduced women to sexual objects for the pleasure of implied male viewers. Hollywood producers cast women as passive erotic objects for both male characters and audiences to visually consume, encouraging a way of looking that reduced women to sensually lit body parts.[33] In the two decades following the antimasher crusades, ogling women became an everyday practice.[34] Americans could ogle (mostly white) women in the unremarkable moments of daily life, while flipping through magazines at the dentist's office or walking past a movie theater on the way to work. The normalization of the "male gaze," as Mulvey termed it, in American popular culture significantly influenced representations of men's stranger intrusions in national media.

Ogling was, in a sense, becoming central to American cultural and consumer industries. In the 1930s, advertisements, films, popular songs, and other cultural products increasingly depicted men's intrusive behaviors in normalized and humorous ways, and by the end of World War II, Hollywood films depicted intrusive behaviors liberally and flippantly.[35] An entire film might be organized around chasing women, such as 1949's *On the Town*, an adaptation of the hit 1944 Broadway musical about three sailors who roam New York looking for dates. In the film, sailors let loose whistles, dog howls, and cries of "Get a load of that!" at women on the street. One musical number features dancer Vera-Ellen posing for Gene Kelly as he whistles and sings,

> There's the corner where
> The boys hang out
> As each girl goes by
> They rate her
> Whistle and try
> To date her later.

On the other hand, stranger intrusions might appear as incidental backdrop, such as in the 1946 film *The Stranger*, where a group of high school boys, in the middle of a conversation with their teacher, played by Orson Welles, catcall a passing woman. The interaction lasts all of two seconds and neither is played to comedic effect nor becomes relevant later in the film. It functions simply to mark the catcalling teenagers as young and rambunctious—in the way that was expected of high school boys at the time (and still today).[36]

Because they were designed to appeal to an audience of many ages and class levels, animated films provide a particularly useful lens for charting changing attitudes to men's stranger intrusions in mainstream culture. Each time moviegoers bought a ticket to the cinema in the 1930s and 1940s, they were treated to a variety of offerings in addition to the feature film: Animated cartoons, newsreels, and short serial films were all included with the ticket. In an attempt to make their animated offerings broadly appealing to both adult audiences and children, Hollywood cartoons often included sexual themes, if not explicitly sexual scenes.[37] For example, the popular flapper-style songstress Betty Boop frequently put up with men ogling and wolf-whistling or flirting with her on buses, streets, and other public places.[38] Double entendres and innuendo were particularly popular after 1930, when Hollywood adopted the Motion Picture Production Code, or Hays Code, in response to public outcry over moral bankruptcy in the film industry. Overt sexuality all but disappeared from feature films, while cartoons doubled down on their use of innuendo to suggest sex.[39] In response to the code, Betty Boop sported longer skirts and less obvious cleavage, but she still dealt with flirts on the regular.[40]

Men's stranger intrusions were well suited to the winking approach to depicting sexuality that the Hays Code required. Films and cartoons that featured ogling, wolf-whistling, and similar behaviors could take a lighthearted and humorous tone but still garner knowing laughs from adult viewers. Two Tex Avery cartoons—*Little Red Walking Hood*, from 1937, and *Red Hot Riding Hood*, made six years later—help mark the shift from depicting intrusive behaviors as annoying to fun and sexy.[41] Avery produced some of the most recognizable and popular cartoons of the 1930s and 1940s, including legendary characters like Bugs Bunny, Daffy Duck, and Porky Pig. His Little Red Riding Hood cartoons are modern retellings of the classic fairy tale, all featuring a girl or young woman and a licentious wolf on the hunt.[42]

Little Red Riding Hood was an obvious choice for a spoof if a cartoonist was looking for opportunities for double entendres. The original fairy tale is freighted with undertones of sexual danger, but even more suggestive was the option to play off the term "wolf."[43] While Little Red Riding Hood is traditionally stalked by a real-life wolf, in the 1930s and 1940s the term "wolf" referred to certain kinds of sexually aggressive men. As historian George Chauncey has shown, "wolf" was initially used within the gay male community to describe men who "abided by the conventions of masculinity" but preferred male sexual partners.[44] While this definition of the term dates to the first three decades of the twentieth century, by the late 1930s and 1940s the term had entered more mainstream parlance. Articles in prominent newspapers used "wolf" to describe men who unabashedly flirted with and chased women, including in public places.[45] Unsurprisingly, both definitions of the term emphasize the sexually predatory behavior of the "wolf." A human wolf, like the animal, was understood to be powerful and aggressive. Depicting a sexual aggressor as a cartoon wolf would have been an obvious choice for Avery.

Avery's retellings of Little Red Riding Hood represent starkly different ideas about the power of female sexuality and women's agency in heterosexual relationships. In *Little Red Walking Hood*, released in 1937 while Avery was at Warner Brothers, the fairy tale story is retold in a generic urban setting, but the gender dynamics of a powerful masculine character seducing a girl are intact. In the cartoon, a "Mean Old Wolf" is "lurking in a pool hall," where he catches sight of a young girl with blonde curls, a frilly dress, and a telltale hooded red cloak. As she passes by the pool hall, the Wolf sticks his head through the doorway and lets out a long wolf whistle. He rushes to his car and begins slowly trailing the girl down the street. His car is outfitted with mechanical devices that augment his flirtation, including a button that can make his taillights "wink." "Hello, pretty girl," he croons. "Going my way, babe?" The rest of the story proceeds predictably, with the Wolf sweet-talking Little Red Riding Hood while she gives him the cold shoulder.[46] Finally, he speeds ahead to Grandma's house, goes through the requisite disguise and reveal with Little Red Riding Hood, and is finally defeated when a diminutive man, who has been following the couple throughout the cartoon, pulls out a mallet and hits the Wolf over the head, saving the little girl.

Throughout, Little Red Riding Hood is depicted as a slightly snooty, refined young girl who is visibly exasperated with the Wolf and does her best to keep him at bay. The Wolf's antics are neither surprising nor new to her. As she laments, "Really, in this modern age of flaming youth, a girl has to put up with such embarrassing situations." She suggests that her experiences will be familiar to the women in the audience, remarking, "Two-thirds of you girls out there have gone through just what I'm going through now. You know how it is, don't you, girls?" Though she successfully puts off the Wolf's flirtation for a time, his trick to dress up in her grandmother's clothing works, and he chases Little Red Riding Hood around Grandma's cabin. She is saved only when the other male character in the cartoon attacks the Wolf. Her ultimate helplessness both amplifies the danger of the Wolf's advances and maintains a gender hierarchy where masculinity is expected to save vulnerable femininity.

Six years later, Avery's second retelling of Little Red Riding Hood depicts a more "modern" heroine. *Red Hot Riding Hood* begins with a revolt, as the characters break the fourth wall and refuse to reenact a traditional version of the fairy tale. "I'm fed up with that sissy stuff," complains the Wolf. To appease the characters, the cartoon begins again, this time at the corner of Hollywood and Vine, the Los Angeles intersection known for its concentration of film and recording businesses. Rather than stalking the woods looking for Little Red Riding Hood, the Wolf drives a black limousine, wears a top hat, and wolf-whistles and howls at a pair of disembodied feminine legs passing by. This Wolf is better-dressed than his 1937 iteration and does not lurk in a pool hall but instead heads to an exclusive nightclub. There he encounters Red, a grown-up version of Little Red Riding Hood, who eschews the cloak and hood for a red minidress and croons a lounge song from the stage. The Wolf responds with the exaggerated gestures that made this cartoon famous: He jumps out of his seat with a "boing!," his eyes bug out of his head, his tongue rolls out of his mouth and onto the table, and he bangs on the table and stamps his feet. When her song finishes, the Wolf tries to seduce Red, to no avail, and then rushes to Grandma's house, now a penthouse apartment above a nightclub.

Here, the traditional story is turned on its head. Grandma is a sexually aggressive madam character modeled on Hollywood actress Mae West, and she soon chases the Wolf around the apartment, trying to kiss him.[47] The Wolf finally escapes and ends up back at Red's nightclub, where he swears off all women. Within seconds, however, Red is back onstage, and rather than succumb to her temptations again, the Wolf shoots himself in the head. His ghost proceeds to whistle at Red and make catcalls from the audience, and the film ends. Tellingly, there is no male hero who comes to the rescue. In this iteration of the story, the Wolf is soundly defeated by Grandma and Red. Far from being the vulnerable girl of *Little Red Walking Hood*, Red is a full-grown woman who can hold her own with the Wolf. She tactfully rebuffs his advances in the nightclub, and in the end her sex appeal drives him to suicide. The Wolf is entirely at the mercy of her charms.

Audiences went wild for *Red Hot Riding Hood* when it premiered. It has since been spoofed multiple times, and animation professionals voted it the seventh greatest cartoon of all time in 1998.[48] The resonance of Avery's Little Red Riding Hood films speaks to their cultural relevance and the way they drew upon mainstream, yet changing, ideas about heterosexuality. As Little Red Riding Hood herself contends in 1937's *Little Red Walking Hood*, the women in the audience would have recognized the Wolf's unwelcome advances as the kind of intrusive behaviors that occurred on the street all the time, albeit from a human "wolf." When *Red Hot Riding Hood* premiered in 1943, a different sexual dynamic reigned. The Wolf was overtaken by desire at the sight of Red, and his uncontrollable lust resulted in his death and her triumph. As Avery scholar Pierre Floquet has argued, Avery's cartoons did not necessarily reflect social norms and trends, but they "modif[ied] and play[ed] with them." Thus, in the earlier *Little Red Walking Hood*, Avery played with "the moral standards" of the 1930s, when "a ladies' man was not a good thing." By the time he made *Red Hot Riding Hood*, those moral standards had shifted, and a "ladies' man," while not exactly a desirable quality, was at least now harmless, even amusing.[49] American audiences who saw *Red Hot Riding Hood* would have come away with a sense that women could hold their own against flirtatious men. A wolf whistle or an eye-popping ogle were simply humorous manifestations of a natural masculine sexual urge.

Servicemen's State-Sponsored Ogling

Between the release of 1937's *Little Red Walking Hood* and 1943's *Red Hot Riding Hood*, the United States entered World War II and the federal government enlisted millions of citizens in the war effort at home and abroad. The shifting depictions of sexuality in Avery's cartoons and the US entry into war are more closely connected than first meets the eye. Film historian Eric Smoodin has argued that the advent of World War II and the need to boost troops' morale provided filmmakers with an excuse to include more sexually explicit material in their productions, especially depictions of the female body. The Hays Code, which ostensibly forbade explicit displays of sexuality, could be "flexible enough to tolerate what might be considered sexier films if . . . they could be deemed to be beneficial to the war effort."[50] A cartoon like *Red Hot Riding Hood* could get away with sexual situations, especially representations of female sexuality, because it entertained America's fighting men. Indeed, while Tex Avery recalled censors cutting the more risqué scenes from *Red Hot Riding Hood* for a general audience, he claimed the US military asked to screen an uncut version for enlisted men. This version, according to Avery, "went great overseas."[51] Avery's depiction of Red as a sexually provocative, pinup-style songstress who elicited hoots and hollers from watching wolves (and servicemen) was thus not only sanctioned by the US military but arguably made possible by a belief that raunchy entertainment supported American troops' morale and thus the larger war effort. During World War II, then, the US military was instrumental in supporting and, in some cases, driving the changing depictions and attitudes toward men's stranger intrusions.

World War II had a profound impact on the meanings of heterosexual relationships and displays of male sexuality in the United States. Wartime mobilization created new social contexts in American cities as millions of young men and women signed up for military service or wartime jobs and left the familiarity of their hometowns for urban areas. Released from the expectations and watchful gaze of relatives, neighbors, and childhood peer groups, many young people began to experiment with new forms of sexual expression or new kinds of sexual relationships. Premarital sex was more available and less stigmatized.[52] The circumstances of wartime, in which young people spent much of their time in sex-segregated working and living spaces, also made same-sex relationships accessible in ways they had not been during peacetime.[53] As historian John

D'Emilio has described it, World War II "created something of a nationwide coming out experience."[54]

The opportunities for sexual exploration facilitated by wartime mobilization concerned the United States military. On the one hand, as millions of men joined the armed forces and the men-only spaces of the mess hall, barracks, or battleship, the military worried that troops might engage in same-sex relationships when no women were available. The federal government hoped to eliminate "homosexual tendencies" from the military and began to crack down on those they perceived as "homosexuals."[55] To counteract the potentially erotic same-sex environment of the military, the federal government invested in programs and messaging that encouraged troops to channel their sexual urges toward female USO workers, overseas entertainers, military personnel, or women they encountered on leave (not to mention local women in overseas war zones), rather than toward other male troops. The military also called on American women to boost troops' morale by focusing on their physical appearance and flirting with servicemen. Women who practiced such "sensual patriotism," as historian Marilyn Hegarty terms it, attended dances or clubs frequented by servicemen. They offered conversation and the allure of sex, if not the actual practice of sex.[56] Thus, the military encouraged men's heterosexual desire as a deterrent against both homosexuality and low morale.

On the other hand, the specter of venereal disease hung over heterosexual relationships. Military administrators feared that the same spaces and activities that offered servicemen a chance to relax and flirt with women might also promote promiscuity. They worried that venereal disease lurked in both sex workers and women who believed it was their patriotic duty to bring comfort and pleasure to the troops. Venereal disease had the potential to put thousands of servicemen out of commission, depleting manpower at a time when a strong military was crucial to victory. To prevent such an outcome, the military cracked down on sex work, encouraged men to use prophylactics, and warned servicemen against "Victory Girls" or "patriotutes"—a portmanteau of "patriot" and "prostitute"—who promised a night of pleasure but might also pass on diseases. The United States thus enlisted female bodies and female sexuality for the war effort while cracking down on the versions of female sexuality thought to pose the greatest threat to servicemen.[57]

In this context, ogling, whistling, and other intrusive behaviors became a way for servicemen to tap into heterosexual desires and display an aggressive masculinity without making themselves vulnerable to venereal disease. Endorsing troops' right to assess and flirt with women at a distance—a kind of "look but don't touch" expression of sexuality—proved the safest and most effective way of promoting heterosexual desire within the military without sanctioning potentially dangerous sexual behaviors. In practice, this meant the United States government was both a proponent and manufacturer of discourses that naturalized and encouraged men's intrusive behaviors. Such efforts dovetailed with the retrenchment of patriarchal concepts of masculinity that often comes with wartime. Military institutions try to convince men to volunteer for service by promising them an opportunity to demonstrate their manliness through aggression and domination.[58] Historian Aaron Hiltner has argued that violence, including "carousing in bars, cornering and chasing women, and beating up the guy not in uniform," became a way for American troops to distinguish themselves as soldiers and embody a wartime masculinity.[59]

To encourage enlisted men to let off sexual steam with nonphysical flirtation, the US military distributed literature that sanctioned all kinds of intrusive behaviors. The Naval Training Station in San Diego, for example, published a guidebook that implicitly encouraged servicemen to enjoy American womanhood before they left for overseas combat. The pamphlet suggested a variety of wholesome activities for sailors who found themselves with free time in the city. Attractions included the San Diego Zoo and local golf courses, ice rinks, and movie palaces. However, the guide made it clear that the women of San Diego were also part of the city's charm.[60] Tellingly, the text itself said little about how to find dates or where to pick up women in San Diego—perhaps navy administrators knew that would be taking the encouragement too far—but cartoonish images scattered throughout the guide depicted sailors in titillating entanglements with women. Illustrations show sailors going to the movies, dancing the jitterbug, and roller-skating arm in arm with women, often to humorous effect. Sailors are also portrayed engaging in intrusive behaviors, ogling women and trying to pick up dates in public places. For example, in a plug for the local USO clubs, the guide depicts a sailor watching a young woman walk by (fig. 3.1). Her long legs, short skirt, and sharp cheekbones have distracted him from the game of checkers he is playing with an older woman in Victorian-style dress. Cartoon motion lines indicate the speed with which he has whipped his head around to watch the young woman, suggesting his reaction is reflexive and automatic.[61]

Cartoonish images of servicemen ogling and trying to pick up women on the street conceded that such behaviors were amusingly predictable. They depicted

FIGURE 3.1. In a travel guide for enlisted men on leave in San Diego, illustrations like this one suggested that sailors would encounter young women throughout the city and might ogle them as part of their leisure activities. *Ashore in San Diego* (Welfare Department of the Naval Training Station, 1942), entry 44, box 1, Record Group 215, National Archives at College Park, MD.

troops as no different from the average, virile white American male in their sexual appetites and exemplified the military's expectation for a certain amount of sexual boisterousness and eagerness among enlisted men.[62] As Marilyn Hegarty has argued, the armed forces harbored a quiet but "official acceptance of... men's need for sex" and hoped to control and direct that need rather than suppress it altogether.[63] A doctor tasked with evaluating the military's recreation programs espoused this belief when he insisted on men's "normal desire for feminine companionship." The doctor worried that recreation programs that employed older women as motherly figures for homesick troops would not fulfill servicemen's needs. If the military did not put enlisted men in contact with young, attractive women, the doctor warned, servicemen might seek such feminine charms in less safe conditions. Better to let them flirt with military-approved women than end up in brothels.[64]

The celebration of American masculinity at wartime also served to normalize and forgive behaviors that might have been unacceptable or worrying in other periods. After all, how could anyone deny troops a last flirtation before they were shipped off to combat zones? Film critic Pauline Kael, who was in her twenties during the war, remembered that troops internalized this expectation and even "used the techniques they saw in the movies" to flirt with women on the street. "If you were walking down the street and a guy in a uniform tried to stop you and you weren't interested," Kael recalled, the serviceman might remind a woman, pointedly, "That's what we're fighting for, that's what we're giving our lives for. They tried to make you feel guilty for not wanting to go to bed with them."[65] Indeed, Aaron Hiltner has found that Americans often expected "street harassment and rape" from troops stationed in their cities, treating such intrusions and violence "as if it was a normal, obvious part of their wartime lives." Women who lived in port cities recalled how servicemen would linger "in high-traffic areas, like busy street crossings, bus stops, and subway stations, assessing the women and girls passing by." One woman, using language reminiscent of the antimasher crusades, even described trying to avoid "a kind of GI gauntlet" in Times Square.[66]

At the same time that servicemen's (hetero)sexual antics were fodder for knowing chuckles, military administrators continued to emphasize that such antics should ultimately remain chaste. The federal government identified sexual relationships between strangers or acquaintances as especially dangerous to servicemen.[67] So-called pick-ups—women whom servicemen met in public places but who were not sex workers—accounted for more venereal disease diagnoses than "paid prostitutes," according to one government pamphlet.[68] The military's admonition against sexual dalliances between strangers drew on decades-old anxieties about sex work, the difficulty of telling "respectable" women apart from prostitutes, and the dangers that might lurk behind the friendly face of a stranger.

Government warnings to servicemen often echoed Progressive Era diatribes against mashers who lurked in public places, but now the military viewed women rather than men as the dangerous element. Government officials even worried that men would succumb to "pick-ups" in the same kinds of places where women once fell prey to mashers. For instance, a field representative for the Massachusetts Society for Social Hygiene declared that "girls are flocking to public parks and places of commercial amusement where they meet soldiers and sailors."[69] One government tract warned that a flirtation with one of these women "may start with a cold drink and dancing. But when it ends in a trip to the nearby fields, a car, or a hotel room, look out for trouble!"[70] To drive the point home, one army advice manual compared female strangers with weapons of war. The manual cautioned servicemen that "girls who make a habit of hanging around railroad and bus stations and juke-joints, waiting to be picked up, are to be especially avoided—just as you would avoid any other Booby Trap." An accompanying illustration depicted a white woman, dressed in a pink shirtdress and pink hair bow, with the words "BOOBY TRAP" stamped across the image in large, bold type.[71] The illustration echoed the oft-repeated warning to servicemen that a woman's good looks, pleasant dress, or appearance of cleanliness could not guarantee that she was free from venereal disease.[72]

By the 1940s, then, policymakers and government officials viewed sexual or flirtatious interactions between strangers quite differently than they had in the Progressive Era. In 1911, if a white man approached a woman in the street with flirtatious remarks and she was not a sex worker, he risked a citation for accosting, ogling, or molesting her. He might get a write-up in a local newspaper as an example of the mashers who infested downtown streets. In 1943, the roles were reversed. If the man was a white serviceman, he needed to watch out for respectable-looking women who might lead him into temptation and infect him.[73] Because military officials bought into the assumption that enlisted men could not wholly suppress their sexual desires, they telegraphed the expectation that servicemen would flirt with women as needed but would stop short of sexual intercourse. The United States government thus implicitly, and occasionally explicitly, sanctioned military men's intrusive behaviors as a way for them to let off steam with female strangers without risking contracting venereal disease.

The end of World War II only served to intensify the growing belief that American servicemen were entitled to ogle, whistle at, and even touch American women in public places. When conflict ceased, the immediate need for a strong military force eased, and with it the anxieties about venereal disease and troops' sexual relations. Government officials, psychologists, and national media encouraged returning veterans to celebrate victory and begin the peacetime process of finding wives and starting families.[74]

Some of the most enduring images of the nation's victory parties depict the newly lackadaisical attitude to servicemen's sexual activities. Alfred Eisenstaedt's famous photograph of a sailor kissing a woman on V-J Day in Times

FIGURE 3.2. Alfred Eisenstaedt's famous photograph of V-J Day in Times Square suggests that spontaneously grabbing and kissing strangers was a humorous and expected manifestation of servicemen's celebration of victory. Courtesy of Alfred Eisenstaedt / The LIFE Picture Collection / Shutterstock.

Square exemplifies the conflation of celebration with white heterosexual desire (fig. 3.2). The woman—often mischaracterized as a nurse but actually a dental hygienist—wears a white uniform that contrasts sharply with the man's dark sailor's uniform. The iconic neon signs of Times Square and the festive crowds frame their embrace. As the original caption in *Life* magazine reads, the woman "clutches her purse and skirt as an uninhibited sailor plants his lips squarely on her." This kind of "uninhibited" sexuality had been of great concern to the federal government during wartime, but in August 1945 the image earned a full-page spread in *Life*. It was a representation of the joyous outpouring of pent-up sexuality that came with the end of the war.[75] Eisenstaedt's image was symbolic of both the anxieties about and hopes for veterans' reintegration into civilian life. In addition to Eisenstaedt's photograph, the spread ran similar images of servicemen kissing women in Kansas City, Miami, Hollywood, and Washington, DC, as well as photographs of women skinny-dipping in San Francisco, members of the navy's women's auxiliary having a pillow fight, and sailors stealing alcohol from liquor stores to fuel their revelry. All the young people featured were white. The message was clear: Now that the war had been won, Americans—and white veterans in particular—were entitled to a little fun.[76]

However, even in times of celebration, there was a dark undercurrent to some of these images. The *Life* feature recounted how "the men of war" engaged in a "coast-to-coast frenzy of kissing" that included the occasional "mob-assault" on a single woman. "Some servicemen," reported the magazine, "just made it a practice to buss everyone in skirts that happened along, regardless of age, looks or inclination." Perhaps most ominously, the caption for the image of sailors looting a liquor store told how the "revel turned into a riot" as servicemen destroyed public property and "attacked girls" across San Francisco.[77] Even Eisenstaedt's famous photograph has been reassessed in recent years as scholars and feminist critics note the way it depicts a potentially nonconsensual sexual encounter.[78] Eisenstaedt himself described how he noticed the sailor "grabbing every female he could find and kissing them all—young girls and old ladies alike."[79] More pointedly, the woman in the photograph, Greta Zimmer Friedman, recalled, "It wasn't my choice to be kissed. The guy just came over and kissed or grabbed."[80] These examples suggest that supposedly enthusiastic, joyous embraces were not always expected, consensual, or desired by all parties. Rather, many were likely examples of intrusive behaviors and sexual violence from male strangers that came to symbolize an unbridled sexual enthusiasm that spilled out onto city streets across the country.

In the immediate postwar years, depictions of servicemen and veterans ogling women in public spaces continued to normalize stranger intrusions as the purview of these veterans, particularly white veterans. As Brooke Blower notes in her analysis of Eisenstaedt's photograph, race and sexual object choice are crucial to this view of postwar male sexuality. After all, had Eisenstaedt's subjects been a Black man and a white woman or two men kissing, the reaction to the photograph would have been condemnation and violence, not glorification and immortalization.[81] Popular culture representations of veterans delighting in flirtations with women reinforced the messages of Eisenstaedt's

FIGURE 3.3. The *Chicago Daily Tribune* playfully titled this photograph "Phone Calls Can Wait When There's Ogling to Do." The caption suggested the sailors, who were in New York City on Navy Day, had paused to "review the passing parade." "Sailors Watching Women Pass By," October 25, 1945. Bettmann via Getty Images.

photograph. Depictions ranged from cinematic portrayals, like the sailors of *On the Town* running around New York in search of female companionship, to humorous and tongue-in-cheek images and human-interest pieces in newspapers. For example, in October 1945, just a few months after Eisenstaedt took his iconic photograph, an Associated Press wirephoto presented three white sailors "ogling" women in public (fig. 3.3). In the photograph, the sailors are sitting in phone booths, receivers to their ears. They have all turned their heads in the same direction to watch two women, backs to the camera, walk by on Navy Day in New York City. According to the *Chicago Daily Tribune*'s caption of the image, the sailors were "review[ing] the passing parade," suggesting that the real spectacle on Navy Day was not the sailors but the women in the city. The photograph's caption reads, "Phone Calls Can Wait When There's Ogling to Do," playfully portrayed ogling as pressing business that required a man's full attention.[82] Here, white American servicemen, perhaps newly returned from fighting in the Pacific, were transitioning to normalcy by establishing and exercising their right to ogle American women's bodies. The passing women did their part by not resisting.

Freed from the restrictions and government control that came with wartime, white heterosexual veterans readied themselves to rejoin civilian life and enjoy American women as part of the deal. As GIs returned home, state and cultural institutions encouraged men to transition from the homosocial world of the military to what Margot Canaday has called the "heterosexual and familial imperatives of postwar America."[83] Legislators worried that the country faced potential unrest if veterans were not given outlets for the pent-up energy they brought home after serving in combat zones. Federal legislation like the GI Bill attempted to direct veterans' energies into education, productive employment, and domestic pursuits. Marriage and fatherhood were the ultimate goal as the stability of the American family was increasingly seen as crucial to national stability. The investment in the nuclear family as the protector of American ideals only intensified as the United States entered the Cold War.[84]

Establishing white men's right to ogle and whistle at American women fit neatly into the project of rehabilitating and domesticating veterans. On the simplest level, white American veterans were encouraged to see sexual and romantic relationships with women as part of their reward for serving their country.[85] After the war was over, the military continued to stage USO-style shows featuring young female performers as entertainment for servicemen. For instance, in 1946, the army put on a beauty contest for troops at Fort Meade. Soldiers chose the contest winner by "whistling, stamping of feet, and choruses of wolf calls." The Associated Press covered the beauty contest as a foil to Detroit's anti-ogling ordinance, warning that if servicemen exhibited such behavior in Detroit, they might find themselves under arrest.[86] By pitting the hollering soldiers against the Detroit police cracking down on ogling, the Associated Press article highlighted the shift in normative conceptions of white masculinity that had taken place over the preceding two decades. While Progressive Era campaigns against mashers had cast intrusive behaviors as incompatible with respectable masculinity, by the postwar period an institution as venerable as the United States Army was endorsing sexually suggestive whistles and caterwauling as part of its official programming for servicemen. While these tensions would persist into the early 1950s, the normalization of intrusive behaviors as part of hegemonic masculinity would steadily overwhelm most attempts to condemn such behaviors.

Affirming and Contesting the Normalization of Men's Stranger Intrusions

Eleven months after *Life* featured Alfred Eisenstaedt's photograph of the kissing sailor in a full-page spread, the national press was debating the meaning of such stranger intrusions in the wake of Detroit's crackdown on ogling. The case of the 1946 enforcement of Detroit's anti-ogling ordinance serves as a microcosm of the debates and shifts that were happening across the country. On the one hand, the backlash against the ordinance demonstrated how much white Americans' opinions about men's stranger intrusions, especially ogling, had changed since the antimasher campaigns. On the other hand, Americans were by no means monolithic in their mockery of the ordinance or of Detroit's efforts to crack down on intrusive behaviors. Some white women expressed ambivalence about men's intrusive behaviors, though their reservations or complaints failed to garner much sympathy. Others insisted that ogling and wolf whistles were not only expected and normal but also desirable. Both reactions suggested that white women did not view white men's intrusive behaviors as worthy of public outcry any longer. Meanwhile, the Black press rarely bought into the normalization of intrusive behaviors and instead continued to denounce white men's entitlement to Black women's bodies and report on the far more violent—indeed, deadly—threats many Black women faced in American cities. Black newspapers offered the strongest counternarrative to the idea that white men's stranger intrusions were a harmless expression of heterosexual desire.

When Detroit police officer Earl Johnson cited William Jansen for ogling in 1946, the backlash from the white mainstream American press was swift and emphatic. The Associated Press reporting on the arrest spread from coast to coast, supplying Americans across the country with amusing stories about the puritanical sensibilities of Detroit's police. The story became a humorous foil with which to measure the relative prudery of various police departments. In response to the news out of Detroit, Newark police announced they would not arrest men for "ogling" unless it was "accompanied by sound, such as wolf calls or remarks." Police Chief Philip Sebold explained that they simply couldn't criminalize ogling in Newark because enforcing the law would overwhelm the police. "I'm afraid that if ogling were against the law," Sebold said, "we would have to lock up a lot of women in addition to men."[87] The *Chicago Daily News* mocked the Detroit anti-ogling crackdown by suggesting that only a man who had been dormant or secluded in the "Michigan woods" for decades and missed the changes in women's fashions would stare at women "in a manner disturbing to the public peace."[88]

Meanwhile, Detroit residents themselves grappled with the meaning of the anti-ogling ordinance and debated whether it remained relevant in their city thirty-six years after its passage. Responses ranged from confusion about what ogling meant—the *Detroit Free Press* assured readers that no ogling charge could stick because "not even a great eye specialist can tell when a man looks at a woman whether it is a wanton ogle or just a gander"—to suggestions that ogling encouraged women to dress inappropriately and act foolishly in public to grab men's attention.[89] Misinformation proliferated as several reports dated the passage of the anti-ogling ordinance to 1870, rather than 1910, and one newspaper column even claimed that it had been passed to protect men from "certain brazen hussies who walked up and down Woodward avenue and openly flirted with the innocent male citizens."[90] Given these attitudes, it is unlikely that any court convicted a white man cited for ogling from the mid-1940s onward, including Jansen. Many probably dismissed any such charges. In fact, not even a month after Jansen's citation, four men accused of ogling were let off when the two women they ogled did not appear in court. The judge in that case argued that ogling was permissible and legal if no woman objected.[91] This ruling reflected the contemporary attitude to women's sexual agency, suggesting that women might enjoy being ogled or, at the very least, were not inherently in need of protection.

Several reports on Detroit's anti-ogling law implied that ogling was either necessary for forming heterosexual relationships or so commonplace that it was hardly worth discussing. Veterans in Detroit were particularly concerned that a crackdown on ogling would limit their chances at matchmaking.[92] As one Detroit man complained, "I, like many other fellows, spent two years in the South Pacific and when I got back all the nice girls were married. Now how are we going to find a girl friend if we don't ogle?"[93] The editors of the *Chicago Daily News*, on the other hand, suggested that men rarely ogled in a way that disturbed women. Most city-dwelling men, they argued, were so "accustomed" to seeing women display their limbs in public that they either took no notice or knew how to assess a woman surreptitiously. Indeed, as the *Daily News* put it, "Those who are looked at"—that is, the women themselves—"must be thoroughly habituated to the experience." Such language implied that white men's ogling had become an expected part of urban life and neither men nor women thought twice about the occasional intrusive look of a stranger.[94]

The narratives that cast men's stranger intrusions as normal, trivial, or necessary for heterosexual partnering drew on assumptions about men's "natural" inclination to ogle and women's desire to be ogled. The most vocal disseminator of these assumptions in Detroit was the *Detroit Free Press*'s managing editor, Malcolm W. Bingay. Bingay wrote several columns addressing the resurfaced anti-ogling ordinance, and each reiterated that men were destined to ogle and women to enjoy it. Bingay argued that it was part of a woman's "instinct" to enjoy being looked at on the street. "I am quite sure," he asserted, "that if nobody looked at her, after she had gone to all the trouble to make herself appear beautiful, that she would be very much discouraged and disappointed."[95] He trotted out a fake anthropologist to argue that women have dressed for men's attention since "the time of Adam and Eve" and emphasized the naturalness of such behaviors. Detroit police, he argued, "can't arrest a man for looking at a good looking girl any more than they can forbid him looking at the glories of the heavens." Women liked being ogled, Bingay claimed, adding that he had "never yet found a good looking woman who did not enjoy being admired—even when she pretends the opposite."[96]

Some Detroit residents agreed with Bingay's interpretation. Letters to the editor in the months following the anti-ogling arrests were peppered with allusions to the naturalness of ogling. A reader calling himself Ogler 1/C insisted, "The good Lord gave us eyes to look at beautiful things and why should man take it upon himself to give his fellowmen a ticket for using his eyes to the best advantage[?]" Indeed, Ogler 1/C contended, if men could be arrested for ogling, soon all the men of Detroit would be behind bars and all the women would have "died old maids."[97] Michigan resident Arvo Wain declared he was "staying out of Detroit" as long as ogling was against the law. After all, "who among us," he asked, "unless he or she be an old prude or prune, is not guilty" of ogling now and again?[98]

As it became more common to perceive intrusive behaviors like whistling or ogling as normal expressions of white male sexuality, social commentators and cultural arbiters enlisted white women to legitimize the normalization of such intrusions. Many women obliged, describing how they derived enjoyment or validation from male strangers' attentions. Others expressed ambivalence, suggesting that their feelings about men's intrusive behaviors differed depending on circumstances. However, few white women denounced ogling or similar intrusions as they had three decades earlier, perhaps sensing that such protestations no longer held water. The way white women reacted to intrusive behaviors in the 1940s suggests not only that such behaviors were seen as benign by middle-class white Americans but that this belief changed white women's feelings about men's stranger intrusions as well.

Detroit's 1946 crackdown on ogling again offers examples of how some white women perceived male stranger intrusions in a positive light, or at least saw them as harmless. In several cases, reporters appear to have specifically interviewed white women for their supposed expertise on gender relations. When "curvaceous showgirl" Dale Belmont and finishing school student Dorothy Mahon told the Associated Press they thought it was "wonderful" that men ogled and the anti-ogling law was "silly," the women's identities granted their endorsements more power. Belmont's purported standing as a "pinup favorite of overseas veterans" suggested that, because she made her living appealing to former US servicemen, she was both patriotic and qualified to comment on male heterosexual desire. In case Belmont's occupation as a showgirl turned off readers, Mahon's status as a student at a lady's finishing school marked her as a representative for an affluent white femininity laden with connotations of respectability and prudence. Her theory that "most girls want boys to whistle at them" derived credibility from her social status and helped legitimize the notion that men's stranger intrusions were something to be coveted.[99]

Soon after the Associated Press lambasted Detroit's anti-ogling ordinance, the *Detroit Free Press* ran a special article on local women who defended ogling. The interviewees argued that women had an evolutionary need to attract male mates with their physical appearance and that men were naturally inclined to admire women's efforts. Virginia B. Barnett, the manager of a charm school in Detroit, reportedly wondered what was offensive about an "admiring glance at some slick chick who has dressed to the teeth just so she will be noticed?" She claimed, "Every woman wants to be ogled." The head of a modeling agency, Ann Evans, echoed Barnett's dismay when she asked, "Why do you think women spend hard-earned money for those low cut and form-fitting dresses? Certainly not to please fuddy-duddies in City government." Dorothy Cloudman, the fashion director at a Detroit advertising agency, chimed in, "Ogling is a natural reaction."[100]

Significantly, Belmont, Evans, and Cloudman all benefited materially from a cultural paradigm in which men ogled and assessed women's bodies as part of their consumption habits. A showgirl, the head of a modeling agency, the fashion director at an advertising firm: These women's livelihoods depended on the visual consumption of women's bodies, often, if not exclusively, by men.

Where would Belmont be without her admiring audiences of overseas veterans? How would Evans find work for her models if advertisers like Cloudman did not believe that sex—and women's bodies—sold all manner of products?

The women who professed to enjoy the odd ogle or wolf whistle also derived social benefits for allying themselves with the emerging hegemonic masculinity that embraced men's intrusive behaviors.[101] Women could align themselves with the power and prestige of hegemonic masculinity by demonstrating their willingness to permit stranger intrusions. White women in particular, who already held more social and cultural power than women of color by virtue of their race, could bolster their power by acquiescing to a gender order that rewarded them based on their perceived sexual attractiveness. When Dale Belmont explained that stares from male strangers assured her that she wasn't "slipping," she acknowledged that her attractiveness to men was a part of her social value, something to be guarded and maintained. The fact that her ability to pay her bills depended on men's desire to see her perform as a showgirl only reinforced the social value of her attractiveness and her acceptance of men's sexual attentions.

However, white women did not universally agree that stranger intrusions were harmless or desirable. Some expressed ambivalence, suggesting they expected men to engage in intrusive behaviors, but that did not mean they had to like it. A 1945 column in the *Chicago Daily Tribune* offers a rare glimpse at the myriad reactions women had to stranger intrusions. That summer, the paper's "Inquiring Camera Girl" asked six Chicago women what they did "when a strange man whistle[d] at" them.[102] Some women welcomed such behaviors without hesitation. Lorraine Michaels, a sales manager, said she thought it was "kind of cute when men whistle." "They don't mean anything by it," she explained, and admitted that sometimes she whistled back. Mrs. Robert Reed, a housewife, conceded, "It's flattering to me to have a man whistle" and insisted, "It doesn't annoy me in the least." Other responses were more ambivalent. Inez Taylor, a key puncher, suggested that it depended "upon the surrounding circumstances," explaining that when she was "alone at night and someone whistle[d]" she would "ignore it." Ruth Selig, an office worker, argued that the man's physical attractiveness played a role in whether or not she welcomed a whistle. "If he's good looking I put my glasses back on and take another look," she quipped.[103] In rare cases, women had unequivocally negative reactions to men's stranger intrusions. In 1944, student Shirley Chlebowski told the *Tribune*'s Inquiring Camera Girl that it was "embarrassing to walk down the street and have strange men say, 'Hi, Babe' or 'Hey, Mabel'—and then whistle or howl." Such remarks made her feel "self-conscious," and she lamented that there was "no reply that fits the comment."[104] With this remark, Chlebowski acknowledged both consternation and a feeling of helplessness in the face of men's intrusions.

White women's responses to intrusive behaviors in the 1940s may have been conditional and ambivalent, but they were a far cry from Chicago clubwomen's vitriolic outrage in the early years of the 1900s. Without the framework of a larger social movement against stranger intrusions and with the proliferation of popular media that turned wolf whistles and ogling into comedy, white women who disliked intrusive behaviors could not denounce them without appearing out of step with the larger culture. White women who complained about the odd ogle risked being perceived as delusional, problematic, or naive. Denunciations of ogling or catcalling made less sense and held less power in a new context in which the danger of stranger intrusions was no longer assumed. Little wonder, then, that women began to make sense of their experiences differently and to view stranger intrusions as normal or even desirable: Would anyone have believed them if they said otherwise?

When white women discussed men's stranger intrusions, there was an unspoken implication that they were talking primarily, if not exclusively, about white men's stranger intrusions. For intrusive behaviors to be defined as desirable or flirtatious, or at worst as annoying and embarrassing, was a privilege afforded primarily to white men. The same could not be said of an intrusive look from a Black man. As civil rights leader Aaron Henry recalled of his boyhood in 1930s Mississippi, he learned at an early age to be vigilant when interacting with white women. Though the rules of Jim Crow segregation in the South were not explicitly laid out to him, he knew "that Negroes were lynched" for "violations of the code, such as speaking an alleged obscenity to a white lady or even looking at her the wrong way."[105] Henry's fears were confirmed in cities across the country when white people's fears of interracial sex—in particular, Black men's supposed lust for white women—fueled violent attacks from lynchings to race riots in the same period when white women were expressing desire for ogling and wolf whistles.

The double standard that cast white men's intrusive looks as normal expressions of heterosexual desire and Black men's looks as violence was not lost on Black Americans. The Black press, in particular, remained a forceful voice against white men's stranger intrusions at the same time that white America had begun seeing intrusive behaviors as natural expressions of white men's heterosexual desire. For decades, prominent Black activists and commentators had noted the hypocrisy of lynching Black men accused of the smallest infractions against white women while white men raped Black women with impunity. Given this history, it is not surprising that some of the most vehement opposition to stranger intrusions in the 1930s and 1940s came from African American newspapers. Black reporters and commentators saw little change in the way white men treated Black women in public since the Progressive Era, and they even occasionally used "masher" to describe harassers, a term that white newspapers had all but jettisoned by the 1930s.

A counternarrative against men's stranger intrusions persisted with particular force in Black newspapers in places like Chicago, New York, and Baltimore that denounced white men's victimization of Black women. Many stories described how white men insulted Black women by treating them as sexually available, or even as sex workers. Policing patterns bolstered these assumptions as law enforcement increasingly criminalized Black women in public space.[106] For instance, a 1936 report in the *Afro-American* described the arrest of twenty-three-year-old Loretta Brown, a Black woman, and David Carmen, a thirty-year-old white man, in Baltimore. Police ostensibly arrested the duo for soliciting and selling sex on the street, but Brown insisted that she was "on route home" when Carmen "accosted her." Carmen "made an indecent proposal" and then tried to "grab" Brown by the arm "as the officer approached." Though both Brown and Carmen were arrested, Brown must have been convincing because the *Afro-American* reported a five-dollar fine for Carmen but no punishment for Brown.[107] In a similar incident two years later, two white men accosted a Black woman in her home, demanding "intimacy" in exchange for cash. In that case, the police released the men with a warning.[108] These examples emphasize the way that both white passersby and white police officers assumed Black women were sexually available or suspect and acted accordingly.

Reported incidents of white men accosting Black women tended to be significantly more violent than reported incidents of white men wolf-whistling at or ogling white women. If a Black woman dared to resist a white man's advances, she was particularly susceptible to his violent ire. Twenty-two-year-old Marjorie Trent found this out when she responded to a white man's lewd comments in Boston in 1932. As she and another Black woman walked down Tremont Street, two white men began making sexual remarks about them. When Trent resented the insult, the two men attacked her. When her friend ran to Trent's aid, three white men in a nearby store ran out and began beating and kicking her as well.[109] According to the Boston Black press, the two women became "martyrs for a righteous cause—the right of women to walk the streets unmolested by young ruffians." Trent and her friend had fought back on behalf of the many women who "patiently submit to this treatment in our streets."[110] The white men who had attacked Trent tried to pay them off once the police arrived, but the women refused to be appeased.

Black newspapers noted how the realities of a white supremacist society made it nearly impossible to crack down on white men who harassed Black women. Apart from the dangers Black women faced if they resented white men's intrusions, Black men who confronted white harassers also risked violence at the hands of white bystanders, white law enforcement, or the harassers themselves. Even Black police officers had to deal with violent resistance from white men who challenged the authority of Black men to arrest white people.[111] Black women could not rely on the police, particularly white policemen, to come to their aid. Historians Danielle McGuire and LaKisha Michelle Simmons have shown how police not only did not take Black women's complaints of harassment and assault seriously but were frequently perpetrators of such violence. Ferdie Walker, who grew up in Fort Worth, Texas, in the 1930s and 1940s, remembered the white police officer who regularly exposed himself to her on the street. She was just eleven years old at the time.[112] Similarly, in 1930s New Orleans, white policemen were known for accosting Black women and girls on the street and insulting them with suggestive remarks or slurs.[113] As Simmons argues, such experiences convinced Black women and girls that "white violence was outside the bounds of the law."[114]

The lack of a state response to the harassment of Black women in part explains why a "crowd" of Black Baltimoreans took justice into their own hands when a white "auto masher" drove through their neighborhood in 1933. The masher was driving down Presstman Street in the heart of the Black community at one in the morning when he "grasped a young woman by the arm" and tried to force her into his car.[115] Two men who saw the incident stopped the car, dragged the driver into the street, and began to beat him. They were soon surrounded by a large crowd, some of whom joined in. At one point, a man in the crowd tried to run the driver over with his own car. The Baltimore *Afro-American* reported that a passing woman called the police only because she thought that all the men, including the driver, were "colored," and so the "ofay flirt" escaped "being lynched." The *Afro-American* noted that such "approaches by white men" were common in the "northwestern" Black neighborhoods of

Baltimore, though they rarely took such a "serious turn." In the end, the police did not charge the white masher and instead went in search of the Black men who had beat him, lending credence to the belief that the Black community needed to take Black women's safety into their own hands.[116]

Frustrated with the reality that white men felt entitled to ogle and objectify Black women, the *Afro-American* imagined an alternative future in which Black men could protect Black women from white male sexual aggression. In early 1946, the paper ran a speculative short story set five years in the future at a time when "our girls can walk around without being molested by white would-be mashers." In the story, the narrator recounts how Black women and men complained to the police commissioner that Black women "couldn't walk a block without being accosted or tooted by those pests." But to no avail. As the narrator muses, "You know how white cops are about colored people being molested by whites. We should have saved our breath and our stamps." Instead, a local veteran, Ben Robins, organized a group of local Black men to distribute bricks to every Black household. That way, whenever white mashers followed Black women, residents could drive them away with a barrage of bricks. In response, the police sent officers to suppress the resistance. The narrator snidely remarks that this was what the community was after all along, "only just the other way around." In the story, the increased police presence works in the Black community's favor, and it "became less and less necessary" for the "little group of vigilantes" to confront white mashers. Thus, in this imagined future, Black women could now "walk up and down our street freely, without being bothered by anything more than a few whistles from the corner wolves."[117]

The story is a fantasy. The author, Albert Jefferson, does not entertain the idea that an increased police presence would disproportionately target Black residents but imagines a world in which Black vigilantes and white law enforcement could work together toward the overall safety of the Black community. He positions Black women as a valuable part of the Black community who deserve protection from, and respect from, white men. Tellingly, he also suggests that equality between Black and white Americans would mean equal opportunity wolf-whistling. In the imagined future of the story, Black men can now "whistle at the sisters of corner wolves" without fear of "a sudden lynching," a clear marker of the campaign's success.[118] In this alternative reality, white men faced consequences for molesting Black women, and Black men could whistle at white women without fear of violence. Even in a utopia, the *Afro-American* did not dare to imagine that stranger intrusions disappeared, simply that they carried less potential for violence against Black women and men. In the fictional world of the story and the real world of 1946, stranger intrusions were an expected part of the urban landscape.

Despite the emphasis on entitled white men in the Black press, Black men were not exempt from Black Americans' denunciation of stranger intrusions. While it was often easier for the Black press to attack white mashers, Black women complained that both white and Black men accosted them in public places. However, even in reports of Black men bothering Black women, the trivializing rhetoric of the mainstream white discourses was largely absent in Black conversations about stranger intrusions in the 1930s and 1940s. For instance, while the term "masher" had all but fallen away from dominant white discourses of intrusive behaviors, Black newspapers continued to report on mashers and mashing into the 1960s.[119] When the Baltimore *Afro-American* solicited stories of "wolfs" and mashers from women readers in 1956, the results looked strikingly similar to the stories that defined the mashing era. Men "press[ed] against" women in subway cars or stopped women in the street to ask directions as a way to initiate a date invitation. Women rebuffed such advances with an "icy stare" or stabs of their "8-inch hat pin[s]."[120] Such stories suggested that African Americans continued to see men's stranger intrusions as social problems.

Indeed, just four months after Detroiters had laughed at the idea that ogling could incur a fine, the *Afro-American* published an exposé on the "sex-crazed males" who lurked in the New York City subway. Reporter Alvin White warned readers, "If you've never been in one of Harlem's cavernous subway stations late at night—when they are practically deserted—you've never experienced the dread of running smack into terror at the next turn of the corridor." He went on to describe how a young Black woman named Ethel Blank had to walk the frightening, deserted streets from the subway station to her Harlem home at one every morning after finishing her "job downtown." Three nights in a row she noticed a Black man who "star[ed] at [her] intently" on the train and disembarked whenever she did. One night, employing a technique that may be recognizable to women today, Blank tried to trick the ogler by pretending to get off at an earlier stop. The man started to disembark but then stayed on the train when he realized Blank was not leaving. When Blank reached her true stop, she sought help from a white man who agreed to escort her to the next level, where he planned to change trains. Stuck in the subway station, Blank was "tempted to stay in the station all night" as she knew "the wolf was lurking around the exit, waiting for me to make a move in that direction." Finally, her husband, who had grown concerned that she had not returned home, went in search of her and found her at the station.[121]

The timing of the *Afro-American*'s exposé suggests that Black Americans had not embraced intrusive behaviors as part of what it meant to be a Black heterosexual man, even as white Americans increasingly saw ogling, wolf-whistling, and the like as natural for white men. While the mainstream white press had eschewed the antimasher rhetoric of the turn of the century, prominent Black newspapers continued to denounce intrusive behaviors from both white and Black men. In contrast, far from denouncing such behaviors, white male reporters defended their white male ogler counterparts, insisting that such behaviors, at best, derived from natural urges and should be interpreted as compliments or, at worst, were merely silly.

The differing reactions to intrusive behaviors in the Black and white press solidified men's stranger intrusions as normal primarily for white men. For, while Black Americans reprimanded both Black and white men for bothering women in public spaces, white Americans celebrated, normalized, or trivialized only white men's intrusions. Thus, the mainstream, white-dominated discussions of men's stranger intrusions confirmed that white normative masculinity included the natural inclination to whistle at and ogle women in public.

While the Black press offered an important counternarrative to the normalization of white men's stranger intrusions, at other times it was clear that Black women had much more to fear on city streets than the odd ogle. When white Detroiters' indignation over the anti-ogling ordinance raced through national newspapers in 1946, the Detroit Black press—which was often the most vehement denouncer of stranger intrusions in other cities—did not comment on the resurfacing of the anti-ogling ordinance. Rather, in the weeks following William Jansen's citation for ogling in downtown Detroit, the city's Black newspaper, the *Michigan Chronicle*, was investigating the rapes and murders of two Black women, Frances Harris Smith and Ruby Kay Wobington. The crimes had taken place within two weeks of each other in late July and early August 1946. Police suspected both women had been attacked while "they walked the streets in the late evening or early morning hour."[122] The *Chronicle* linked their deaths to other complaints from women who said they had been followed or attacked on Detroit streets in recent weeks. The police fielded call after call from Black women who felt unsafe in public spaces, including multiple accounts of men who had offered rides to women and then tried to assault them.[123] Next to these harrowing reports, white Detroiters' debates over ogling appear inconsequential. The *Chronicle* was far more concerned that Black women were being raped and murdered on the city's streets with what appeared to be alarming regularity. Little wonder that the white middle-class uproar over ogling garnered little to no comment from the Black press at the time.

ON JULY 27, 1946, Malcolm W. Bingay, the *Detroit Free Press*'s editor, published his first blistering attack on the Detroit anti-ogling ordinance. In it, he employed humor and faux legalese to argue that ogling was constitutionally protected. History was full of venerable oglers, he argued, citing former associate justice of the Supreme Court Oliver Wendell Holmes Jr.[124] The revered justice had apparently ogled girls on the street with some regularity. The Detroit ordinance thus set "a heavy price for a look" and ought to be revoked. However, Bingay was careful to distinguish between ways of looking. He acknowledged that there was a difference between "ogling" and "looking 'em over" and that the former might indeed be worthy of punishment. To ogle, he argued, meant to "stare amorously," while to "look 'em over" was merely to admire from afar. "Ogling" obscured a nefarious intent—whether to seduce a woman or simply to make her squirm—while "looking 'em over" was "purely academic." The difference, according to Bingay, distinguished a lascivious, disturbing action from a harmless diversion.[125] Distinctions like this, which cast certain kinds of looking not only as normal but as a hobby that required skill and sophistication, would lead to the blossoming of a new category of white heterosexual man: the "girl watcher," the subject of the next chapter.

But Bingay's remarks also tapped into a new cultural zeitgeist. Detroit's anti-ogling ordinance reflected the social and sexual mores of another time, when most Americans had agreed that ogling and similar behaviors were not compatible with hegemonic masculinity. In Bingay's world, some thirty years after the ordinance's passage, such interactions were natural expressions of white men's heterosexual desire. With advances in women's rights and an increasingly liberal acceptance of extramarital sex, it was ridiculous to think that a mere look could harm a sexually liberated woman of the 1940s. Popular culture reinforced the idea that ogling, wolf-whistling, and catcalling were part of the amusing game of flirtation and seduction, expected and even enjoyed by both men and women. In practice, many white women still held ambivalent feelings about white men's stranger intrusions, while Black Americans decried white men's entitlement over Black women's bodies in public space. Soon, however, it would become clear that the racialization of men's stranger intrusions was increasingly bifurcated as white men identified themselves with a hegemonic masculinity that embraced ogling and catcalling while Black men's looks, whistles, and similar behaviors were grounds for high-profile arrests and murders in the 1950s.

CHAPTER **FOUR**

GIRL-WATCHING AND "EYE RAPE"

IN THE SUMMER of 1951, a slew of headlines, all similar in tone, screamed forth from African American newspapers, as well as the Communist Party's *Daily Worker*: "Negro Jailed Because White Woman Saw Him."[1] "Convict Man for Assault 75 Ft. Away."[2] "Gets 2 Years for 'Looking' at Girl!"[3] The authors of these articles were outraged that the Caswell County Recorder's Court in North Carolina had convicted forty-four-year-old Matt Ingram, a Black farmer and county resident, on the charge of assault with intent to rape in June of that year.[4] What had Ingram done to warrant this charge? According to the prosecution, he had looked at a white teenage girl from a distance of between fifty and seventy-five feet.[5]

The "eye rape" case, as it was commonly known, became an international scandal. After Ingram's initial conviction, the National Association for the Advancement of Colored People sent in its lawyers. Newspapers from North Carolina to England watched the progress of the appeals. Ingram's defenders in the courtroom and the press balked at the prosecution's admission that Ingram had never been close enough to touch his accuser, let alone rape her. An Associated Negro Press reporter spoke for many when he insisted that Ingram was the real "victim" in the case, subject as he was to a "strange interpretation of rape."[6] The case became a symbol of the white supremacy baked into the justice system in the American South and, for many, was proof of a double standard that cast Black men's looks as akin to rape while white men not only looked at but assaulted Black women with impunity.[7] As if to prove the point, in January of the year Ingram was first convicted, a white lawyer in Houston, Texas, admitted to violating the city's masher-era ordinance against making "goo-goo eyes." His ogling, however, garnered little more than a fifty-dollar fine and a few humorous write-ups in the newspapers.[8] Ingram was eventually acquitted on appeal in February 1953, but he would never recover from the loss to his finances and reputation.[9]

On November 3, 1954, just under two years after Ingram's case concluded, New York advertising executive Donald J. Sauers published a new book on the "delightful hobby" of "girl watching."[10] Sauers explained *The Girl Watcher's Guide* was modeled on bird-watching manuals, but this guide promised to teach its readers how to surreptitiously watch women in public places across the country. Just as a bird-watching manual might include tips for successful birding, *The Girl Watcher's Guide* offered techniques for effective girl-watching, including suggestions for how to remain hidden so as not to frighten quarry.

Girl-watching took off quickly, especially in urban centers in the North and California. By 1962, *The Girl Watcher's Guide* had reportedly sold 32,500 copies and been translated into German and Japanese.[11] From 1954 to the early 1970s, the girl-watcher took hold as a widespread cultural trope, appearing in national periodicals, television commercials, films, books, and popular music. He appeared in magazines helping to sell nylons, liquor, and airline tickets and was the subject of hundreds of humorous human-interest pieces in local and national press. *The Girl Watcher's Guide* inspired girl-watching societies and a copycat pamphlet, *The Official Girl Watchers Manual*.[12] Those seeking more titillating entertainment could pick up a copy of *Girl Watcher* magazine, which featured black-and-white photographs of scantily clad women and humorous advice on how to secretly girl-watch by hiding behind trash cans or peering from behind newspapers.[13] Rock musicians had hits with songs about girl-watching, most notably North Carolina pop group the O'Kaysions' 1968 top ten hit, "Girl Watcher."[14] Local DJs and businesses hosted pageants where men rated women on their "watchability," an idea that especially took off in places with beaches, such as the coast of California or the shores of Lake Michigan in Chicago.[15] Girl-watching went international when Montreal, Canada, advertised girl-watching opportunities as one reason to visit the International and Universal Exposition in 1967.[16] Even teenagers participated. Publications like *Seventeen* magazine warned adolescent girls that they were always "being watched" and proffered advice for how to increase one's "girl-watchability."[17]

Eye rape and girl-watching: These two terms lay bare the extreme poles of Americans' understandings of men's intrusive looking in the postwar period. While middle-class white men who looked at women on the street were "girl watchers," Black men—especially in the South—were guilty of eye rape if white

FIGURE 4.1. Radio announcer Gary Owens awards actress Eileen O'Neill the title of "Miss Most Watchable," as bestowed by the San Fernando Valley chapter of the International Society of Girl Watchers. Owens is showing off his girl-watcher lapel pin featuring two staring eyes. April 18, 1964. Courtesy of Valley Times Collection / Los Angeles Public Library.

people so much as accused them of engaging in the same kinds of looking. In fact, the two definitions of looking shaped one another. Girl-watching drew power and specificity when juxtaposed with other categories of looking. Girl-watchers defined their version of looking as self-consciously not ogling, leering, or any other kind of disruptive or conspicuous looking, and certainly not eye rape. So-called experts agreed the key to successful girl-watching was found in furtive, surreptitious glances. As *The Girl Watcher's Guide* put it, "A girl watcher never leers, nor does he utter a sound which might betray his joy. His reaction is secret. His pleasure is warm, quiet, internal."[18] Advocates insisted that girl-watching was a "genteel sport," "a matter of subtleties," practiced only by the most reverent and "congenial" men "who appreciate women."[19] Girl-watchers thus coded their favorite form of looking as a refined, middle-class pursuit, and girl-watchers regarded themselves as gentlemen. The infamous descriptor of "eye rape" was, in this context, a useful foil against which to define girl-watching as trivial. The concept of "eye rape" as a marginal, dangerous way of looking helped to normalize the supposedly harmless way of looking that became known as "girl-watching."

Girl-watching's heyday marked a new level of Americans' acceptance of middle-class white men's intrusive behaviors and the solidification of the normalization that had come to prominence in the 1930s and 1940s. For the first time since the emergence of the "street insults" of the nineteenth century, middle-class white Americans largely embraced a specific, defined practice of intrusive looking and categorized it as the purview of respectable white men. By condemning leering or ogling as "vulgar," girl-watchers distinguished these forms of intrusive looking as uncouth or dangerous, practiced by laborers, construction workers, teenage hoodlums, and others marked as working-class. By adopting the moniker "girl-watcher," a middle-class white man made two claims: that his form of ogling was part of a respectable masculine performance and that he had the right to assess any woman's body he encountered in public space.

In the years leading up to the publication of *The Girl Watcher's Guide*, Americans used the 1951 case of Matt Ingram to begin to outline the different kinds of looking that men did in public and to distinguish respectful looking from threatening or insulting looks. Strangely, though Ingram's arrest and conviction were clearly a product of the white supremacist legal system that criminalized Black men for simply existing in white spaces, the case appeared to strike a nerve with white men who enjoyed ogling. As the case took hold in national newspapers, middle-class white men—including Ingram's lawyers—pointed to Ingram's conviction as proof that *all* men's right to look at women in public places was under attack.

With their attempts to define proper and improper looking and enlist Matt Ingram as a mascot for all oglers, the white men who came to Ingram's defense implicitly confirmed that they, and not Black men, held the power to decide whose looking would be perceived as a threat in the midcentury United States. Thus, some thirty-five years after middle-class white Americans had condemned white men for "mashing" and "ogling," those same classes of Americans now celebrated the intrusive behaviors that had once been seen as insulting and harmful. The ascendance of the girl-watcher represented a widespread delineation, acceptance, and celebration of a specific kind of looking as the right of middle-class white men.

When Watching a Girl Is "Eye Rape"

Matt Ingram's troubles began on June 4, 1951, when he went in search of a trailer to haul hay. He drove his 1936 Chevrolet to the farm of W. L. Boswell, a white man who had helped him in the past.[20] Ingram hoped to borrow Boswell's trailer for a few hours that day. He drove slowly through the small farming community where Boswell lived, stopping at a stop sign and then coasting his way toward Boswell's farm before parking and getting out of his car to walk the rest of the way. These are the facts of the case, relatively undisputed, as Matt Ingram and his lawyers told them. What happened next was the subject of heated debate both in and out of the courtroom.

Ingram said he looked around Mr. Boswell's farm and, seeing no one but a few young boys working off in the distance, decided to leave and find a trailer elsewhere. The State of North Carolina and Caswell County resident Willie Jean Boswell, Mr. Boswell's seventeen-year-old granddaughter, told a different story. On June 4, Willie Jean awoke after her father and younger brothers had left their house. She dressed in overalls and a turtle shell hat and headed out to the cornfields between her father's house and her grandfather's house to help her brothers as they worked. According to Miss Boswell, she noticed Ingram driving down the highway that went through her community. She saw him stop at the stop sign, but then, she claimed, Ingram "came up the highway and he kept watching me." As she turned toward a wooded area to get off the road, Ingram pulled up and stopped his car on the side of the road. This frightened Miss Boswell, who quickened her pace, but Ingram "kept on coming" until, she claimed, he "stopped and stood and watched" her. When she finally reached her brothers in the cornfield, Miss Boswell said she told them what she had seen. They ran to tell their father, who called the police, and two weeks later Matt Ingram stood before the Caswell County Recorder's Court on the charge of criminal assault with intent to rape.[21]

In her testimony about the incident, Willie Jean Boswell described Ingram watching her but nothing else. Not a word was uttered between them, and Ingram had not followed Boswell, though witnesses for the prosecution argued that Ingram's path on June 4 indicated he was trying to "cut [Boswell] off."[22] Boswell testified that Ingram only ever came within seventy-five, perhaps sixty, feet of her in the entire time of the incident. Nevertheless, on June 18, 1951, Ingram was sentenced to two years in the county jail and assigned to work on road projects for the county. By mid-July, NAACP lawyer W. Frank Brower was investigating the incident and the NAACP had published a pamphlet, *Assault . . . at 75 Feet*, to raise funds for Ingram's legal fees.[23]

With the NAACP now in charge of Ingram's defense, his case traveled through the North Carolina court system on appeal after appeal. His first appeal ended in a mistrial, but a new jury convicted Ingram in the North Carolina Superior Court in November 1952.[24] In subsequent appeals, Ingram's lawyers argued that discriminatory jury selection practices had stripped Ingram of his constitutional right to a jury of his peers.[25] The state attorney general agreed with Ingram's lawyers during the final appeal to the North Carolina Supreme Court, which voided Ingram's conviction on February 25, 1953, almost two years after Willie Jean Boswell's initial accusation.[26]

In the three years before Sauers published *The Girl Watcher's Guide*, the Ingram case raised questions about when a look was just a look and when, if ever, it could be considered tantamount to sexual assault. Each time Ingram went before the court, it created a new furor among Ingram's defenders and sympathizers. The case had received little coverage in local or national press at first. However, thanks to the national NAACP fundraising campaign—as well as some rabble-rousing from a local member of the Communist Party who sent exposés to European newspapers—reporters all over the world were soon covering Ingram's case.[27] The press dubbed it the "eye rape" case or the "assault from seventy-five feet."[28] Most press coverage depicted the case as, at best, foolish and, at worst, a shocking example of the racism of the Southern American criminal justice system. In response, English housewives wrote to the mayor of Yanceyville, the county seat of Caswell County, and demanded justice for Ingram. American newspapers hotly debated the particulars of the case, quoting lengthy passages from court testimony and worrying that such a miscarriage of justice would provide fodder for the Soviet Union's anti-US propaganda.[29] At the heart of these debates was the question of whether it was reasonable for Willie Jean Boswell to have feared Ingram's looks and whether such looks could constitute rape.

For their part, Boswell's legal team tried to prove that a look—or a leer—was enough to charge someone with assault. Boswell's fear was central to her attorneys' argument that Ingram's actions should be considered threatening. Boswell told the recorder's court that Ingram "was going real slow and had his head turned watching me the whole distance." She said she began running from Ingram at some point, not because he had changed his behavior in any way but "because I was scared. If it had been anyone else, I wouldn't have run, but he kept watching me, and when I went to the woods, he pulled up to the side of the road and stopped."[30] In later testimony, Boswell used the term "leer" to describe Ingram's look, and one of her attorneys tried to imitate the leer in the courtroom to demonstrate how it had frightened her and was thus a legitimate threat.[31]

When the case went before the North Carolina Superior Court, Judge J. A. Rousseau ruled there was insufficient evidence to try Ingram on the charge of intent to rape, yet he maintained it was possible to find Ingram guilty of assault on a female. Rousseau encouraged the jury in that trial to think expansively about the charge of assault. "It is not always necessary for one to be guilty of assault that there be some physical contact with the person alleged to have been assaulted," Rousseau told the jury. Indeed, looking at someone in a "leering manner" might be sufficient grounds for a guilty verdict if the defendant "causes another to reasonably apprehend imminent danger."[32] Rousseau's comments, and the state's evidence, must not have been convincing enough, however, because the first appeal ended in a mistrial, with two Black jurors refusing to vote guilty.[33] Judge Rousseau, disappointed with the lack of decision, admitted he at least thought there was evidence of a "display of violence—evidence that the defendant chased the girl."[34]

Ingram's defense team, unsurprisingly, strongly disagreed with the interpretation that Ingram was guilty of assault simply because Willie Jean Boswell feared that was his intent. In written objections to Rousseau's rulings, Ingram's lawyers argued Ingram was a victim of Boswell's "suspicion and unbridled imagination." In the absence of evidence that Ingram did anything other than look at Boswell, it was "thus abundantly clear," the lawyers argued, that "the fright of the prosecutrix should be attributed to her imagination rather than to any overt, intentional, or unlawful act of the defendant." Boswell, they said, could not even define a "leer" when pressed, so how could she argue that Ingram had leered? If the court found Ingram guilty, his lawyers warned, "all men regardless of color and irrespective of intent may be summarily brought into Court and criminal sanctions imposed against them upon the mere whim or caprice of a young, immature, and perhaps unstable girl."[35]

The idea that Boswell's complaint was a figment of her imagination drew on decades of similar arguments used to discredit women's rape accusations, against both Black and white men. A deep mistrust of female accusers—whom legal scholars and psychiatrists often constructed as liars or fantasists—permeated legal literature and consensus from the seventeenth century onward and would persist after the Ingram case, proving fodder for feminist antirape activism in the 1970s.[36] However, the circumstances of Ingram's case were also familiar to antiracist activists in the South who had been denouncing the rape double standard since Ida B. Wells's forceful editorials. Indeed, twenty years before Boswell accused Ingram of "eye rape," two white women riding the rails in rural Alabama had accused nine Black youths of rape. The nine teenagers were convicted at the county seat of Scottsboro, with eight of them sentenced to death. The plight of the Scottsboro Boys, as they came to be known, garnered national attention and became "synonymous with racial injustice."[37] The fact that one of the white female accusers admitted she had lied to avoid getting into any trouble herself cemented both the idea that women lied about rape and that white women would willingly send Black men to their deaths to save their own reputations.

The Scottsboro case, which also went through a round of appeals with an NAACP defense team, may have been on Ingram's lawyers' minds as they drafted objections to the rulings and testimony presented in the case. As one of Ingram's NAACP attorneys, Martin A. Martin, told *Jet* magazine in 1952, "It is unfortunate that a lot of young white girls feel that every time they see a Negro man, he wants to rape them."[38] In fact, as Lisa Lindquist Dorr has argued, the Scottsboro case was exceptional, not least because judges in the case questioned the character and intentions of the white female accusers, much as Ingram's lawyers would question Boswell's mental stability. Even in 1931, then, white Southerners did not universally believe all white women accusers, even when they accused Black men of rape.[39] By the 1950s, courts were less and less likely to uphold rape convictions against Black men who had done "little more than scare white women." Courts often opted instead for lesser morals violations as a way to punish Black men who broke "taboos against interracial interaction in public."[40] Still, the long history of both state and extralegal violence against Black men accused of raping white women continued to hang over allegations like those leveled at Ingram.

Ingram's arrest and initial conviction were thus confirmation for many that a Black man's wayward glance at a white woman, even when imagined, continued to garner disproportionate punishment in Southern courts. Fred Upchurch Jr., the local Caswell County attorney who was the first to defend Ingram in court, summed up the sentiments of many Northern and African American newspapers when he told reporters, "My home county and not Mack Ingram is on trial here."[41] In an *Afro-American* editorial published soon after the first appellate court upheld Ingram's conviction, columnist Cliff Mackay pointed out that a double standard continued to apply to sexual violence in the South. While Ingram "drew two years" for looking "at a white girl from a distance of 75 yards [*sic*]," just four months later, three white men convicted of the "brutal mass rape of 19-year-old Mrs. Lula Artes," a Black teenager, "got only 16 months."[42] Ingram's conviction was proof that white Americans had the power to decide that postwar rhetoric trivializing and normalizing white men's ogling did not apply to Black men.

Thanks to national publicity and a team of NAACP lawyers, Ingram walked a free man in 1953, but there was no guarantee he would have escaped conviction without significant help, resources, and public attention. Ingram's acquittal was an exception to the racist norms of the Jim Crow legal system and the widespread use of extralegal violence to maintain white supremacy in the South. Indeed, the much more famous lynching of Emmett Till suggests how horrifically Ingram's situation might have turned out under different circumstances. Just one year after the publication of *The Girl Watcher's Guide*, two white men murdered Emmett Till, a fourteen-year-old Black teenager, following accusations that he had flirted with a white woman in Money, Mississippi. Till's murder became an important rallying point for civil rights organizers and revealed the lie behind the idea that stranger intrusions were harmless fun. Had Till been white, his young age and his alleged offense—which varied from whistling to flirting verbally with a twenty-one-year-old white woman, Carolyn Bryant, in her husband's store—would likely have solicited knowing chuckles and acknowledgments that "boys will be boys." But because Till was Black, Bryant's male relatives saw Till as a dangerous sexual assailant and viewed the actions of which he was accused (accusations that were at least partly, if not entirely, fabricated) as a sexual overture, if not a threat of sexual violence.[43] The white men who tortured and murdered Till understood that intrusive behaviors could be powerful and dangerous, but they had the power to define who would be viewed as a sexual threat and under what circumstances.

Noting the double standard that resulted in the disproportionate response to Ingram's supposed offense, Ingram's defenders used the postwar trivialization of men's intrusive looks to their advantage, insisting that merely looking at a woman was every man's right. Ingram's lawyers had explicitly warned the North Carolina Superior Court that to uphold Ingram's conviction would be to open up "all men regardless of color" to legal repercussions if a woman thought a man had looked at her funny.[44] They thus argued that Ingram's fate was wrapped up in the fate of not just all Black men but all men, period. Men naturally looked at women on the street, they admitted, even with lustful or "carnal" intent, but that was not grounds for criminal conviction.

The *New York Post* went a step further in late 1952. While Ingram's defense team was understandably reluctant to admit that Ingram had even seen Willie Jean Boswell, let alone watched her with any hint of sexual desire, the *Post* argued that even if Ingram had watched Boswell, that was no reason to charge him with assault. The Ingram case, the *Post* maintained, "provides grotesque material for the human comedy. For if men can be hauled into court for allegedly thinking carnal thoughts about women whom they see from an automobile window, one of democracy's most precious freedoms is lost."[45] This facetious comment echoed the Detroit residents who, in 1946, insisted that the city's anti-ogling ordinance infringed on the right of every man to admire feminine figures. However, while the pro-ogling rhetoric of the 1940s in most cases omitted any mention of race in a way that assumed white men as the quintessentially harmless oglers, here the *Post* took the example of a racially charged court case—where most commentators agreed Ingram's race was the primary reason for his arrest and conviction—and deliberately expunged its racial stakes. The *Post* instead depicted the case as a prudish attack on "men," not just a Black man, and on the "precious freedom" of "thinking carnal thoughts" about women supposedly afforded to all men.[46]

White commentators seized on the counterintuitive claim that Ingram's conviction was unjust, not simply because of the racial double standard but because it endangered men of all races who enjoyed looking at women in public. United Feature Syndicate columnist Robert Ruark epitomized the argument in a December 1952 editorial, three weeks after Ingram had lost his first appeal. Ruark interrogated the difference between an insulting leer and a complimentary glance in an effort to understand the stakes of Ingram's conviction. Ruark was born and raised in North Carolina, and he wrote his editorial from South Carolina, so he could hardly be unaware of the racial implications of Ingram's case.[47] Still, Ruark opened his column with a nod to "a guy" who "went to book in Yanceyville," without so much as mentioning Ingram by name, and then explained he would "ignore the racism" of the case and instead "progress to the purely scientific aspects of when a smile deserves a slap and when an ogle becomes an insult."[48]

What followed was Ruark's delineation of the different types of looking in a tongue-in-cheek editorial that anticipated the humorous tone, the metaphors, and even the "rules" that would soon permeate discussions of girl-watching. Acknowledging that if "any man" was "potentially guilty of assault by leer, I am this man," Ruark insisted that it was possible to distinguish between dangerous or intrusive looking and harmless looking. For instance, Ruark admitted that any "God-fearing girl will tell you an eyebrow raiser is up to no good." Such a man was wont to look at women in a way that made them feel naked or, as Ruark put it, in "the absence of pantalettes." Ruark described a true ogler, on the other hand, as a man who does not seek to "approve, disapprove or lust after. To look at is enough." Ogling, Ruark explained, was a "spectator sport" that was a "heap more fun than tennis" and thus had no end goal in mind other than admiring beauty. "The true rule of ogling," Ruark finished, "is that the starer just wishes to appraise. . . . And in the interest of justice, I might append the fact that no ogle, leer, frown or stare is deadly unless the subject has an overdeveloped sensibility to public appearance. Not even on a clear day at 75 yards."[49]

The speed with which Ruark jumped from Ingram's conviction for "ocular assault" to a satirical discussion of the proper way to ogle downplayed the racist realities of the case in service of reinforcing the discourses that cast ogling as natural and harmless. But whatever Ruark argued, Ingram's case was not an attack on all men's ogling; it was an attack on a poor Black farmer whose presence in a white farming community was interpreted as a sexual threat. The fact that Ruark, a white man, did not meaningfully engage with race or white supremacy meant that, far from serving as a defense of all men's right to ogle, Ruark's editorial became a defense primarily of ogling on the part of men like him. Ruark described himself as an avid ogler and argued that European men were the best oglers of all. "To the European," he wrote, "ogling is the literal breath of existence." Thus his defense of the proper ogle only referenced white men as practitioners of this style of looking.[50]

Ruark's column, and arguments like it, foreshadowed the way girl-watching would reinforce middle-class white men's right to look without explicitly discussing race. By failing to comment on what, exactly, was racist about Ingram's conviction, Ruark instead fell back on the existing postwar rhetoric that cast white men's intrusive looking as natural. Ruark also insisted that the "true ogle is not practiced at the corner drugstore or fronting the poolhalls of the nation," hinting not only that ogling was primarily a white man's pastime but that working-class men were not respectful oglers either.[51] Later discussions of girl-watching would similarly confirm girl-watchers' racial and class privilege through omission. As historian Georgina Hickey puts it, the "whiteness of girl watching was unmistakable, though precisely because of the privilege of whiteness, it did not need to be explicitly made so."[52] It was self-evident to Americans that ogling was dangerous for Black men and harmless for white men. Ingram's conviction for eye rape only confirmed the standard while also offering an entry point for white American men to defend their own right to ogle.

Matt Ingram's case shows how the normalization of intrusive behaviors was so commonplace by 1952 that Americans used the belief in the trivial nature of ogling to defend men from accusations of assault and harassment. Crucially, it also demonstrates the power that white men had to dictate who could watch women in public space and to claim that their looks were harmless. Ingram, as a poor Black farmer living in the South, was an inadequate avatar for white men seeking to bolster their own claim to watch women in public. Yet white men bent over backwards to do just that. Ingram's white defenders were able to ignore the glaring white supremacist assumptions that underpinned Ingram's conviction and use him as the symbol of all men's right to ogle. One year after Ingram's case was finally dismissed, *The Girl Watcher's Guide* would stake a claim that the most harmless looking of all was the furtive, polite looking practiced by middle-class white girl-watchers. In the wake of the "eye rape" case, the girl-watcher's insistence on unobtrusive looking and his assumed status as a middle-class, professional white man made him the perfect cultural trope to advocate for white men's right to ogle and assuage fears that such a right was under attack.

Furtive Looking:
The Masculine Restraint of Girl-Watching

A year after Ingram's acquittal, the publication of *The Girl Watcher's Guide* tapped into a growing national uneasiness over the state of white masculinity. Returning veterans of the Second World War faced disillusionment with the drudgeries of domestic life and nine-to-five jobs. The rise of the middle-class suburbs and white-collar professionalism fed a postwar anxiety that white American men, especially middle-aged married men, risked feminization if they spent too much time kowtowing to their wives in cookie-cutter homes or to their bosses in soul-sucking corporate workplaces.[53] The fear of a weakening American masculinity only intensified as Cold War rhetoric identified homosexuality as a threat to the fabric of society. Psychologists and government officials worried that gays and lesbians could pass as straight and infiltrate any part of American life where they became targets for Russian agents looking to blackmail American citizens into turning against their country. In the logic of Cold War containment, the security of the United States depended on the elimination of "the homosexual" from public life and the maintenance of traditional gender roles.[54] According to historian Elizabeth Fraterrigo, the "prolonged, commitment-free bachelorhood" promoted by Hugh Hefner and *Playboy* magazine offered one antidote to the perceived problem of flagging masculine heterosexuality in the 1950s.[55] Girl-watching offered another.

Girl-watching gave middle-class white American men a way to demonstrate their heterosexual masculinity through the consumption of the female form in public. Given the larger Cold War anxiety about the stunted masculinity of middle-class professional men, it is little surprise that, from its inception, girl-watching was most often depicted as the pastime of white-collar men, often middle-aged and often married. By the mid-1960s, such men were the most visible and vocal girl-watchers in the press. Though teenagers and single men also claimed the girl-watcher moniker from time to time, middle-aged married men celebrated the pastime as a sign that they retained their interest in heterosexual, extramarital desire (if not sex), without threatening their marriages.[56] Wives sometimes played along. Martha Sauers, whose husband Donald wrote *The Girl Watcher's Guide*, defended the practice to the press, claiming girl-watching was a natural expression of masculinity. "I know what men are," she told the *Boston Globe* in 1955, asserting that all men liked to watch women, whether they were married or not. According to Mrs. Sauers, it was better to know that your husband watched girls than for him to keep it a secret.[57]

The characterization of the girl-watcher as a married urban professional makes sense given its origin story. The author of *The Girl Watcher's Guide* (and husband of Martha), Donald J. Sauers, worked as a copywriter with New York advertising firm Sullivan, Stauffer, Colwell and Bayles.[58] According to the *New York Times*, Sauers got the idea to found an American Society of Girl Watchers and write a guide to girl-watching during an "informal Madison Avenue luncheon" with "a handful of advertising men."[59] In Sauers's *Girl Watcher's Guide*, illustrations portrayed girl-watchers almost exclusively in business attire, except when they were shown participating in leisure activities like fishing, lounging on the beach, or playing tennis. Cartoons depicted bosses admiring their secretaries, library patrons turning to gaze at female bookworms, and white tourists watching native women in the Pacific islands through binoculars. A few men were shown in other types of jobs—the deli worker serving coffee to a

FIGURE 4.2. Girl-watching was intended to be compatible with white-collar office work. These girl-watchers are practicing watching women on a break from their jobs in a large city. "First Field Trip," in Sauers, *Girl Watcher's Guide*, 26. Illustration by Eldon Dedini. Author's collection.

girl-watcher, the cowboys branding a bull as a woman walks by in tight jeans—but they were few or, in the case of the cowboys, their hypermasculinity neutralized the manual and working-class connotations of their labor.[60] Beyond the guide itself, the press generally described girl-watchers as white and white-collar: ad-men, college professors, stockbrokers, and the like. As one journalist put it, girl-watching societies were largely run by "attornies, CPA's, salesmen, insurancemen and bankers."[61]

Girl-watching was also designed to slot easily into white-collar workers' daily routines. For instance, because "thousands of girl watchers [were] employed in nine-to-five careers" in city centers, *The Girl Watcher's Guide* suggested taking up girl-watching over the lunch hour. During this prime time, the guide pointed out, thousands of watchers and the girls they liked to watch spilled out onto city streets. A helpful illustration in the guide depicted two men in suits walking down the street, surrounded by skyscrapers and throngs of women (fig. 4.2).[62] These men were presumably employed in the city, and their neat attire and refined demeanor—their noses are tilted slightly in the air and they are careful not to ogle or leer too obviously—suggested the sophistication and gentility of a girl watcher.

Girl-watching media also often depicted men watching women together in a kind of group bonding experience.[63] For instance, the "girlie" magazine *Girl Watcher* pictured groups of men clustered around café tables looking at female patrons or following a blonde woman down a quiet street.[64] *The Girl Watcher's Guide* similarly encouraged men to watch girls together. If a group of watchers took a lunch break together, the guide instructed them to name a spotter who would keep a lookout for watchable women and signal the group when one drew near. A nudge might be sufficient, but if there was a large group, the spotter could use auditory signals like a cough, a shout of "Tallyho," or an "unusual word such as 'wickiup.'"[65] With such redirection, men could comfortably engage in girl-watching, reinforcing one another's heterosexual desires in a group activity without being discovered.

Most articles, advertisements, and descriptions of girl-watching depicted white women as the object of the girl-watcher's gaze, but girl-watching was ultimately about asserting middle-class white men's claim to appraise all women's bodies in public, including women of different nationalities, ethnicities, and races. For one, girl-watchers argued that traveling was an ideal way to find women worthy of being watched. While much advice suggested visiting European capitals like Rome, London, and Paris, some advice had a whiff of exoticism. For instance, *The Girl Watcher's Guide* explained that, just as a bird-watcher would travel to the "South Seas" if he wished to see a "South Sea Island bird," so a girl-watcher should travel to see "rare, South Sea Island girls." An accompanying image depicts two white men, dressed in suits, watching a woman who appears to be completely naked save for a see-through grass skirt, a beaded necklace, and a bird perched on her shoulder that strategically covers her breasts with its tail. She has long dark hair and eyes so dark there appears to be no whites.[66] A similar piece in a 1963 issue of the *Chicago Tribune* suggested that American men visiting Jamaica would benefit from the island's excellent girl-watching. The "local girl" was the most desirable object of the girl-watcher's gaze, according to author Richard Joseph, because unlike "tourist girls" they were not "leery of the tropical sun" and did not "cover up." Joseph specifically went into the racial and ethnic makeup of "local girls," describing the "Jamaican people" as "a melange of African, Chinese, European, and East Indian." He noted, "Whenever you see an outstanding beauty—which is often—chances are strong that she's of at least partly Chinese descent."[67]

The image of an exotic woman of an island nation turning the heads of white American men was not new. For decades, American popular media, from Herman Melville to classical Hollywood cinema, had popularized the idea that women in foreign lands, especially nonwhite women, were sexually exciting, dangerous, or promiscuous. The "South Seas" in particular were supposed to be "a sensuous Arcadia where, unrestrained by western social mores, Islanders engaged freely in sexual relations within and outside the bounds of marriage."[68] These ideas persisted into World War II, when American servicemen stationed in the South Pacific often exoticized the local women they met and the military propagated the idea that local cultures were sexually permissive. The image of the South Sea island girl in *The Girl Watcher's Guide* may have brought to mind such images, or perhaps the popular Broadway musical *South Pacific*, which had won the Pulitzer Prize and multiple Tony awards in 1950.[69] In any case, *The Girl Watcher's Guide* made it clear that girl-watching was about asserting middle-class white men's right to ogle all women's bodies.

No matter the object of their gaze, girl-watchers insisted that their style of looking was surreptitious and undetectable such that they could watch women anywhere. Self-control, discipline, and, above all, furtiveness were all important qualities to the true girl-watcher because, unlike the readers of "girlie" magazines, he admired the female form in the wild.[70] *The Girl Watcher's Guide* featured an entire section, called "Types to Look For," featuring drawings of the myriad "specimen[s]" a girl-watcher might encounter in public places. Faux ornithological names accompanied the images, suggesting a girl-watcher should be on the lookout for the Hatboxtoter, the Clock-Watching Bossducker, the Horn-Rimmed Booklugger (fig. 4.3), and the Quarterback-Collecting Sweatersweet.[71] The guide's illustrator, Eldon Dedini, a cartoonist for the men's magazine *Esquire* and a soon-to-be regular contributor to *Playboy*, supplied exaggerated caricatures of each female subspecies, all pouty lips, minuscule waists, and ample bosoms.[72] Like the bird-watchers the *Girl Watcher's Guide* spoofed, girl-watchers were supposed to be quiet and unnoticed in their observation.

Newspaper and magazine articles about girl-watchers overwhelmingly agreed that such men avoided ostentatious looking, suggesting that undetectability made this form of voyeurism acceptable. The proper way to girl-watch, according to girl-watching's proponents, was out of the corner of one's eye, using one's peripheral vision as much as possible. Humorists and journalists claimed that turning the head to watch a girl pass or, worse, doubling back and following a girl down the street were amateur moves and not condoned by "real"

FIGURE 4.3. Illustrations in *The Girl Watcher's Guide* purported to show different "types" of women one could watch, using terms intended to mimic the names of bird species. "Horn-Rimmed Booklugger," in Sauers, *Girl Watcher's Guide*, 56. Illustration by Eldon Dedini. Author's collection.

girl-watchers. A glance or a quick once-over was enough to take in a girl without the watcher needing to move his head at all.[73] If all else failed, sunglasses could hide the watcher's eyes, so long as it was summer and sunglasses did not look out of place.[74] Ray Bauer, president of the American Society of Girl Watchers, warned succinctly in 1965, "Never get caught watching girls."[75]

To avoid detection, veteran girl-watchers encouraged their less-experienced comrades to practice "eyeball dexterity" and suggested helpful techniques and exercises.[76] For example, *The Girl Watcher's Guide* offered the "Triangle Test" as a way to practice watching two girls at once without either noticing. In this test, the "student" would choose two pictures of watchable girls and place them ten feet apart. He then stood ten feet from the pictures, making an equilateral triangle, and practiced looking at one picture and then the other without moving his head. Another exercise helped a girl-watcher master the "once-over." Here, the "aspirant" would stand six feet away from a coatrack and practice scanning the length of the rack from bottom to top, without moving his head.

The exercise promised to help girl-watchers who wished to admire a woman's entire body without raising her suspicions.[77]

Girl-watchers justified the need for furtiveness in three ways. First, sources suggested the girl-watcher's subtle tactics shielded women from concealed lascivious thoughts. "Furtive glances and shy smiles hide what lurks in the mind," ominously noted the *Los Angeles Times*.[78] Second, girl-watchers claimed they did not want to scare away the objects of their gaze. The frequent comparisons between bird-watching and girl-watching helped to articulate this fear. Donald Sauers told a Reuters reporter in 1967, "Girls like to be watched, but if the watcher is flagrant the girl, like a bird, gets frightened."[79] The last thing a girl-watcher wanted was to lose the object of his gaze because she was disturbed. Finally, girl-watchers did not want to become the target of a woman's ire. *The Girl Watcher's Guide* warned its readers, "Beautiful girls . . . are instinctively suspicious," and a man who raised those suspicions might be in danger of a firm dressing down.[80] Such admissions suggest that girl-watchers knew women did not always enjoy being watched and might take offense if they caught a man looking. As Sauers explained in 1962, enjoying women "quietly" allowed girl-watchers to practice their favorite pastime "without censure."[81]

All this insistence on restraint was part of an effort to distinguish girl-watchers from playboys or oglers whose lascivious leers besmirched more civilized watchers. Furtiveness was supposed to be evidence of a girl-watcher's sophistication and social status, and girl-watching advocates went to great lengths to distinguish what they did from more objectionable forms of looking or flirting. *The Girl Watcher's Guide* took pains to warn readers against behavior that could be construed as unrefined. A "knowing glance or nudge . . . should be considered vulgar," so Sauers implored his readers to maintain "self-control" and to refrain from "undisciplined displays of emotion." Girl-watchers were meant to be "honorable" men who practiced their art with "dignity and personal discipline."[82] In particular, girl-watchers emphasized that their sport rarely had an endgame. The point, according to girl-watching's representatives, was never to solicit dates from women but merely to watch them from afar.[83] Regardless of whether a "girl" liked to be "watched," *The Girl Watcher's Guide* insisted a girl-watcher cared about the object of his gaze and did not wish to disturb her. A girl-watcher who spoke to a girl or, worse, "ask[ed] for name and telephone number [was] like a bird watcher who [stole] eggs."[84] In a (funhouse) mirror of the Progressive Era laws against ogling, girl-watchers in the Century City shopping district of Los Angeles even said they wanted to regulate proper forms of looking. During the shopping area's annual "Girl Watching Week" in 1972, event organizers recruited "a corps of local secretaries and models" to ticket "offenders" who did not abide by girl-watching etiquette. "We abhor improper watching," claimed Joe Beagin of the International Society of Girl Watchers. "Being obvious and ungentlemanly about it spoils the pastime for everyone."[85]

Women also reinforced the idea that girl-watching was uniquely respectable. For one, women often reported on girl-watching, penning at least twenty-five articles on the practice between 1951 and 1974. While not every female author defended girl-watching or girl-watchers, the vast majority were neutral or contributed to the growing consensus that girl-watching was harmless. In one noteworthy example, a young woman wrote to her local paper to ask how she should deal with the annoying leers, whistles, and sexual remarks she received from men on the street. The advice columnist, Jane Lee, responded that "we girls would never want boys to stop looking" but admitted that not all men looked at women in a respectful way. Lee interviewed several self-proclaimed girl-watchers who insisted they never engaged in the kinds of behaviors that upset the letter writer. "Being whistled and yelled at is a nuisance," one girl-watcher conceded. "Remember, though, that the men who do this are in the minority. . . . Just looking . . . never harms anybody, unless it's made too obvious." Another maintained that as "a man of refinement and good taste," he never whistled or called out to women on the streets. "But as a longtime admirer of the feminine gender," he went on, "I must confess to a little discreet leering now and then. I've never seen anything wrong with just looking (by either sex)."[86] In giving girl-watchers a platform, Lee aided their efforts to differentiate the supposedly innocent and unobtrusive practice of girl-watching from behaviors perceived as inappropriate, upsetting, and disruptive, such as verbalizing, whistling, or looking that was "too obvious."

Ultimately, like many a cultural category, girl-watching was defined at least in part by what it was not. It was not lascivious; it was not leering; it was not an insult but a sign of respect; it was not dangerous. It was also not a pastime of working-class men, gay men, or racial minorities. If these men engaged in the furtive glances of the girl-watcher—clandestinely watching strangers out of the corner of the eye—they would be labeled at best as uncouth oglers and at worst as dangerous sexual predators. The "eye rape" conviction of Matt Ingram, a poor Black farmer in a pre-integration Southern state, is just one of the more famous examples of this racist double standard. On the other hand, whiteness, middle-class status, and sexuality or marital status shielded girl-watchers from accusations of impropriety. Instead, they claimed the surreptitious ogle as a respectable and natural manifestation of their masculinity and, by implication, also claimed the right to assess any woman's body in public space.

Normalizing Girl-Watching Through Consumerism and Humor

The 1954 publication of *The Girl Watcher's Guide* spawned a rich trove of girl-watching reporting, commentary, and media representations. American newspapers from New York to Los Angeles as well as international publications as far away as Dublin and Jerusalem reported on the "new" type of man known as the girl-watcher and the pastime of girl-watching.[87] Early pieces relied heavily on *The Girl Watcher's Guide* and often featured excerpts or interviews with author Donald J. Sauers. As the term gained traction, however, girl-watching increasingly became part of common parlance and turned up in all sorts of stories. An air hostess strike threatened to curtail mile-high girl-watching; a summertime photo essay identified Chicago's best spots to watch girls; a woman blamed her husband's parking fine on the fact that he was too busy girl-watching to remember to plug the meter; girl-watching advocates called for the need to preserve "female beauty" as an important "natural resource" in the nation's cities.[88]

Girl-watching quickly gained popularity in large part because it fit seamlessly into postwar consumer culture. At a time when cultural commentators, economists, and politicians identified Americans' participation in mass consumption as one of the primary ways to ensure the strength of American capitalist society during the Cold War, advertisers seized on the commercial potential of girl-watching.[89] Consumer culture touched nearly every facet of American life during the postwar era, including the sexual. In particular, the use of the sexualized female body in advertising reached new heights in the 1950s and 1960s. Advertisements encouraged women and girls to remove body hair, address facial blemishes, and buy underclothing intended to emphasize waists and breasts, all suggesting that women should expect near-constant scrutiny of their bodies.[90] Men could also turn to consumption as a means of bolstering their masculinity. Men's magazines like *Playboy* and *Esquire* presented what Elizabeth Fraterrigo calls an "upscale, masculine identity based on tasteful consumption and sexual pleasure."[91] *Playboy* encouraged men to live "the good life" through their choice of consumer goods, from plush apartments to high-end cocktail accessories. As a reward for their consumption, the men of the *Playboy* world could be assured that "playmates" would flock to their sophisticated bachelor pads.[92]

Advertisements and the centerfolds of *Playboy* had in common an emphasis on looking as the means of transmitting sexual messages. Indeed, when consumption is touted as the central conduit for participating in society, looking—or what feminist theorist Rosemarie Garland-Thomson describes as the "consumer vision"—becomes "the primary means of apprehending the world the modern individual must negotiate."[93] Cultural historian Michael Denning argues that 1950s popular culture of all kinds was steeped in "the voyeuristic eye." Everything from lipstick advertisements to James Bond novels drew on a "narrative structured around the look," with men in the role of the subject, or viewer, and women as the object of the look. Even the pornography of *Playboy*, Denning argues, is perhaps better defined as a representation of voyeurism than of sexuality: The pornography of the 1950s, that is, did not so much depict "sexual activities" as it depicted "women's bodies in various states of undress."[94] As such, girlie magazines of the 1950s were just one part of what feminist media scholar Annette Kuhn has described as "a continuum of representations of women," with pornography occupying one end of the continuum and "such commonly available and highly socially visible representations as advertisements" at the other end.[95] Girl-watching advertisements and products sat firmly on this continuum and reinforced male looking and female objectification as defining features of postwar consumer and popular culture.

Girl-watching's implications for advertising were immediately apparent to some. Soon after the publication of *The Girl Watcher's Guide*, the American Tobacco Company partnered with Sauers to create a series of ad campaigns featuring illustrations and excerpts from his book. The ads ran in 205 college newspapers, and 200,000 college students reportedly joined Sauers's American Society of Girl Watchers in response.[96] Just six months after the publication of *The Girl Watcher's Guide*, noted mannequin designer and window display artist Lester Gaba suggested using girl-watching as the basis for store displays to sell sweaters. Girl-watching was "sweeping the country," he told *Women's Wear Daily* readers in May 1955, and store managers could capitalize on the phenomenon by reminding shoppers that "girls who are watched the most are girls in sweaters." Gaba recommended framing store windows with "cut-out painted eyes" and putting up signs that encouraged women shoppers to "Dress for the Girl-Watchers in Your Life!" Stores could even directly tie into the publication of *The Girl Watcher's Guide* by showing "sweaters on mannequins labeled as some of the sweater-girl types in the book" or offering copies of the guide alongside the clothing.[97]

Girl-watchers reinforced the connection between girl-watching and advertising by openly commenting on women's looks and fashion as part of their practice. By 1965, the International Society of Girl Watchers expected its members to have an "awareness of fashion and style" and to judge women based on how well their outfits were put together.[98] This relatively neutral stance quickly gave way to strong opinions with the introduction of the miniskirt. Girl-watchers loved and hated the new fashion item. They variously condemned the miniskirt for taking the fun out of girl-watching or declared their intentions of fighting any attempts from the fashion industry to repopularize long skirts. Sometimes, girl-watchers shared both these stances in quick succession. In 1967, Donald Sauers declared he hoped to form a "subsidiary" to his American Society of Girl Watchers that would specifically advocate for "the prevention of longer skirts."[99] Two years later, however, Sauers was adamant that "TRUE GIRL watchers, like bird watchers, are happiest only when the subject is alive and moving and well clothed."[100] Similarly, local Detroit newspaper columnist Bob Talbert lamented that revealing fashions took the "sport" and technique out of girl-watching, removing the need for finesse or "style."[101]

The idea that girl-watchers were not only watching women but assessing their bodies, makeup, and clothing made its way into fashion advertising. One fashion writer suggested that girl-watchers were good for the fashion business because they "[praised] women who avoid the conformity of slovenliness," thus raising the standards of dress for women in general.[102] Advertisers encouraged women to look their best for girl-watchers by investing in the "gamut of girl-watcher colors" from Revlon lipstick or the "Girl Watcher panty" from Warner's, designed to be worn with ever-shortening skirts.[103] Hosiery company J. P. Stevens claimed, "Every United Air Lines Stewardess wears Finesse" stockings because they could "stand up to a full flight of ogling."[104] Within the fashion industry, male designers and executives might use girl-watching as evidence of their expertise. The improbably named bra designer Larry Van Tassel submitted his credentials as a girl-watcher as proof of his knowledge of cutting-edge fashion trends: "If a man happens to be a girl watcher as I am, you know that the American woman couldn't give up the bra," he intoned in a 1968 issue of *Women's Wear Daily*.[105]

Some ads not only warned women they were always on display but also suggested that women might actually want to be watched. In an echo of Lester Gaba's advice to "Dress for the Girl-Watchers in Your Life," Diet Pepsi developed a popular print and television advertising campaign in 1966 that implied women should aspire to attract girl-watchers (fig. 4.4). One twenty-second television commercial featured a woman in a bikini walking through a marina, the sun shining and her towel and gauzy headscarf blowing in the breeze. A man

FIGURE 4.4. A billboard suggests that women who wanted to catch the attention of girl-watchers should drink Diet Pepsi. Photo by Werner W. Lenggenhager, April 1967. Courtesy of The Seattle Public Library [spl_wl_bil_00019].

lounging in an inner tube and another in full scuba gear smiled admiringly at her as jaunty Tijuana Brass–style music played in the background. The narrator announced, "The girls girl watchers watch drink Diet Pepsi Cola with only one calorie. Diet Pepsi: try it! Someone will be watching."[106] PepsiCo considered the campaign to be one of its most successful of the era. In annual reports, the company boasted that the commercials "recorded the highest consumer awareness ever scored," and the jingle, titled "Music to Watch Girls By," was "a popular record" after a cover by Bob Crewe climbed the charts.[107] Donald Sauers took note, and the second edition of *The Girl Watcher's Guide* featured a Diet Pepsi ad on the back cover.[108] What stands out in the Diet Pepsi campaign, however, was the suggestion that women actually wanted to *be* the "girls girl watchers watch" and would adjust their diets accordingly. Drinking Diet Pepsi supposedly ensured that a woman would be desired and admired wherever she went. Advertisers thus harnessed the promise that men were always watching in order to entice women to buy products that would have them looking their best, while simultaneously perpetuating the idea that women enjoyed being watched. Girl-watching became part of the explicit justification for consumption.

In addition to traditional advertising, brands organized girl-watching events, pageants, and contests as publicity stunts. For instance, the First International Girl-Watching Pageant, held in 1962 at the Freedomland amusement park in the Bronx, New York, crowned "The Most Watchable Girl in the World" from twenty-five entrants. Donald Sauers's American Society of Girl Watchers endorsed the event, and Trans World Airlines conducted the voting for the competition. Voters cast ballots at boxes that Trans World placed at its ticket counters across the country. Prior to the competition, Sauers told a *New York Times* reporter that he hoped the event would be a "Miss Rheingold contest on a nation-wide scale," referring to the long-running advertising ploy from Rheingold brewery that asked customers to choose a "Miss Rheingold" from six contestants.[109] On a smaller scale, Joe Beagin's International Society of Girl Watchers hosted a "Most Watchable Golfer" contest to promote local San Diego golf courses, while Los Angeles's Century City shopping mall hosted a Girl Watching Week every year from 1970 to 1974 to encourage shopping during the presumably slow days of late September.[110]

While most girl-watching events crowned girls deemed most watchable, girl-watchers could also win recognition for their skills. Addison, Illinois, native Rick Braun, for instance, was chosen as a judge for the 1972 Miss USA Pageant after winning a girl-watching contest hosted by a local radio DJ. (It is unclear what Braun had to do to win this honor.)[111] In 1964, a girl-watching contest designed to promote the film *Under the Yum Yum Tree* was simply a raffle. Only men could participate, and the winner walked away with a chest filled with $350 worth of jewelry to give to the "gal" he "like[d] to watch the most."[112] These contests harnessed the popularity of girl-watching, both as an activity and as a cultural trope, to aid commercial ends.

As the rhetoric used in girl-watching campaigns suggests, girl-watching was meant to be funny. Throughout the height of girl-watching's cultural relevancy, girl-watchers discussed and described girl-watching in a lighthearted, humorous tone that made it clear they viewed their favorite pastime as a playful joke. The cartoonish illustrations in *The Girl Watcher's Guide*, over-the-top recommendations for girl-watching techniques, and marketing of gag gifts like girl-watching sunglasses all confirmed that the activity was not meant to be taken too seriously.[113] The fact that girl-watching articles or advertisements often read like a long, suggestive wink gives the sense that girl-watchers felt they were getting away with something.[114] Girl-watchers spoke like they were proud to have found a way to ogle women in public without risking accusations of impropriety, and they could not wait to share the trick with others.

The "joke" of girl-watching was also what gave the trope its cultural power. The playfulness and silliness of girl-watching made the practice seem harmless and trivial. The impact of girl-watching's comicality mirrors the effect of jokes about rape and intimate partner violence, both of which flourished during girl-watching's heyday: Such jokes trivialize gendered violence and the sexual objectification of women.[115] In 1978, journalist and communications scholar George Gerbner would lament that rape had become so normalized in American popular culture, it had "even been made a topic of humour."[116] Girl-watching contributed to the normalization and trivialization of sexual violence some twenty years earlier. Humorous girl-watching narratives were especially effective tools of normalization because girl-watching itself was easily dismissed as not only nonviolent but nonphysical, nonverbal, and even unnoticeable. As historian Georgina Hickey has argued of girl-watching, "humor . . . softened the violence" of the practice, particularly the way it depicted men as predators and women as prey, "but it did not diminish the message to men and women about who controlled" public space or who "held the social power."[117] That message was simply couched in the hundreds of articles, songs, and advertisements that depicted girl-watching as little more than an amusing manifestation of the seemingly natural sexual impulses of white heterosexual men.

Nowhere was the humor of girl-watching more apparent than in the way girl-watchers imbued the practice with the language of a club sport. After all, what could be more harmless than a friendly game, especially a noncompetitive one? The use of sporting metaphors to describe girl-watching in the popular press also lent it a sense of leisure and gentility, marking it as a middle-class pursuit. Girl-watching was repeatedly dubbed a "fine sport," a "genteel sport," a "superb sport." It was also a "masculine spectator sport" or an "individual, free-style sport."[118] CBS Radio commentator (and soon-to-be TV sheriff of Mayberry, North Carolina) Andy Griffith went so far as to describe girl-watching as a healthy hobby. "It gets you into the open," he told the *Los Angeles Tribune* in 1959, "and that's a good thing."[119] The attempts to equate girl-watching with bird-watching aided its claims to respectability: While girl-watching was supposed to be far superior to bird-watching in terms of the entertainment it could provide, *The Girl Watcher's Guide* insisted, "These two hobbies do share one important feature. They are both *genteel*."[120] Sporting metaphors also linked girl-watching with decades of discourse that emphasized gentlemanly sportsmanship—and the "strength, vigor, and physical assertiveness" that sports supposedly encouraged—as a key facet of American idealized masculinities.[121] In a midcentury context where many Americans believed the monotony of office jobs threatened masculine virility and independence, girl-watching-as-sport was one way for middle-class, white-collar men to prove the robustness of their heterosexual masculinity and the self-discipline with which they exercised it.[122]

As girl-watching took root, humorous newspaper coverage began to describe girl-watching's transition from an amateur "sport" into something more organized and professional. Journalists interviewed girl-watchers like field experts, asking them to elaborate on proper technique. Girl-watchers assumed this mantle gladly, providing "lectures on proper girl spying" at girl-watching events and offering advice to aspiring girl-watchers.[123] With the introduction of girl-watching societies, enthusiasts could become "card carrying members" whose own watching styles might be judged by the society's constitution or official manual.[124] Donald Sauers's own American Society of Girl Watchers claimed 2,500 members after its first mail campaign in 1954, as many as 200,000 in 1962, and still boasted 50,000 members by 1970.[125] Sauers's main competitor was educational film producer Joe Beagin, who made headlines in 1963 when his *Official Girl Watchers Manual* appeared on a list of available program instruction materials at the Department of Health, Education, and Welfare.[126] Beagin founded the rival International Society of Girl Watchers in San Diego in 1960. According to Beagin, the idea came to him when he wanted to show his appreciation to a flight attendant on a trip to Denver. Beagin handed her a small card on which he had written the words, "You have been observed by a member of the International Society of Girl Watchers." Soon after, Beagin began printing similar cards that other men could hand to the women they watched. The cards featured a list of "compliments" that a girl-watcher could check off, thus informing the women they watched of their most attractive features. Each member of the International Society of Girl Watchers received a stack of these cards in the "Girl Watchers kit" that came with their ten-dollar annual membership fee.[127]

Like the rules of girl-watching itself, part of the popularity of girl-watching clubs and merchandise was no doubt the opportunity they offered for men to engage in homosocial bonding. One can imagine friends buying each other *The Girl Watcher's Guide* or a membership to a local girl-watching club for a humorous birthday gift. These activities, not to mention the act of girl-watching itself, gave men a way to proclaim their heterosexuality to their peers and reinforce relationships with other men. As such, girl-watching continued a legacy of men using women as a tool to build and strengthen relationships with one another.[128] Participating in girl-watching clubs or buying girl-watching merchandise, which

FIGURE 4.5.
Gag gifts, like this iron-on transfer depicting a girl-watcher, had replaced most official girl-watching society merchandise by the late 1960s. Author's collection.

did not even require a woman to be present, was one way for a man to use the objectification of women to strengthen his relationship with other men. The usefulness of objectification as a means for connecting men is likely one reason why girl-watching as a practice long outlived the girl-watching clubs and novelty items that proliferated in the 1950s and 1960s.

For indeed, the various girl-watching societies and ad campaigns dissipated in the late 1960s. By 1969, no one was answering the phone at Sauers's American Society of Girl Watchers.[129] Pepsi abandoned its girl-watching-themed Diet Pepsi campaign in 1970.[130] With the demise of the two biggest girl-watching societies, joke gift manufacturers took over where those societies left off and began selling products with girl-watching themes. If one wished to show off his propensity for furtive looking, for example, he could buy an iron-on transfer featuring a bug-eyed man in a "Girl Watcher" shirt and decorate his own clothing with the image (fig. 4.5). (This jokey monetizing of girl-watching persists to this day. Consider the widely available T-shirts emblazoned with phrases like

"I'm not a gynecologist . . . but I'll take a look!" or "FBI: Female Body Inspector."[131] What are such products if not twenty-first-century echoes of a lapel pin or iron-on transfer that proudly proclaimed the wearer to be a girl watcher?) For a time in the 1950s and 1960s, however, advertisers and girl-watching societies, both together and separately, disseminated discourses that celebrated girl-watching and girl-watchers. Advertising campaigns, pageants, and novelty girl-watching products trivialized the sexualized looking of girl-watching, turning it into a humorous pastime or a natural expression of white heterosexual masculinity and casting women as willing objects of the girl-watcher's gaze.

Girl-Watching on the Wane

Sixteen years after Donald Sauers's *Girl Watcher's Guide* popularized the practice for millions of Americans, girl-watching had its last great hurrah. In July 1970, the chamber of commerce for the Century City district of Los Angeles announced it was hosting Girl Watching Week, a new annual event intended to "commemorate one of Century City's outstanding natural phenomena," its women. The event was due to run September 21–26, 1970, and promised to give "careful attention to the preservation of girl-watching," a venture that the *Los Angeles Times* reported "has been noted as vital to national morale."[132] From 1970 to 1974, the Century City Chamber of Commerce ran Girl Watching Week every fall, garnering press coverage in local and national newspapers throughout its run.[133] The event was intended to draw consumers to Century City's shopping center, and some press coverage obligingly advertised deals and highlighted the event's sponsors alongside tips for proper "girl-watching etiquette."[134] In some years, the week culminated with the crowning of Century City's Most Watchable Girl. The 1973 winner officiated at Century City events for one year and walked away with $1,000 worth of prizes, including a weekend getaway at Century Plaza Hotel and a "soft drink known for its girl-watching advertising campaign," undoubtedly Diet Pepsi. The Century City Civic Council executive director, Steve Lantz, perhaps aware that the event sounded ludicrous, told the *Los Angeles Times* in 1973 that Girl Watching Week was "not . . . like an onerous beauty pageant. It almost comes off as a spoof."[135]

From its inception, Century City's Girl Watching Week sparked mixed reactions, including protests and letters to the editor from "women's libbers" and their supporters. In 1971, local resident Bruce W. Farcau chastised the organizers for endorsing "blatant staring accompanied by suggestive looks."

Farcau forcefully denounced the week as an "organization of . . . mental rape" and explained that girl-watching was "at best embarrassing and at worst highly degrading for the hapless young lady." Farcau emphasized it was particularly unfair to subject women employees to girl-watching, as they could not choose to avoid Century City during the week.[136] The following year, the Los Angeles chapter of the National Organization for Women (or NOW) released a similar statement denouncing Girl Watching Week "because it invades the privacy of women who work or shop in Century City . . . forcing them either to remain indoors for a week, or to submit meekly to the unwanted, leering scrutiny of girl watchers."[137]

In response, subsequent reporting on the event highlighted comments from women who enjoyed being watched, as if to counter feminist protests. In 1973, women told a *Los Angeles Times* reporter that they were "flattered" at being watched and even that they wished men were more "aggressive" and actually approached women. That year, event organizers expected "little problem" from organizations like NOW and commented that feminist protests had actually raised the profile of the event and brought more "oglers" to Century City.[138] Despite such grandstanding, Girl Watching Week's days were numbered. Whether because of changing cultural norms, the influence of the feminist movement, or disorganization and lack of leadership on the Century City Civic Council, the event petered out without much fanfare by the mid-1970s.

The protests of Century City's Girl Watching Week were indicative of a wider backlash against girl-watching as an organized activity, especially from the "girls" themselves. As the feminist movement gathered steam in the late 1960s, both girl-watching in particular and men's intrusive behaviors more generally faced more and louder opposition. For one thing, despite girl-watchers' insistence that their pastime was furtive and undetectable, women were far from oblivious to the practice. As one woman told the Associated Press in 1972, "I can tell when somebody turns around to look at me. You know, it's like you can tell when someone's staring at you."[139] All the way in Ann Arbor, Michigan, *Ann Arbor News* staff writer Liz Elling responded to the Century City event by labeling girl-watching an "age-old problem women face" and an "invasion of our privacy." Elling claimed she would rather get a "bomb in the mail" than have a man wolf-whistle at her.[140]

Other reactions were more ambivalent, however, and some women continued to help reinforce the distinction between supposedly genteel girl-watching and forms of looking coded as more dangerous. When interviewed about the

Century City Girl Watching Week, one married Los Angeles woman claimed she liked it when men in that part of town watched her. "I feel flattered being watched by men in Century City," she explained. But when men watched her in "other areas," she clarified, "I feel DOWNGRADED."[141] This distinction, which highlights the way women absorbed the rhetoric of girl-watching as genteel—that is, white and middle-class—would color analyses of intrusive behaviors in the 1970s. Still, by the mid-1970s, articles about "women's libber" reactions to girl-watching, while not necessarily sympathetic to feminism, were becoming more frequent, and the tongue-in-cheek articles about girl-watching as a sport were dissipating.[142]

Despite continued ambivalence from the "girls girl watchers watch," the popularity of organized girl-watching continued to wane in the 1970s, and with it, girl-watching as a cultural trope began to lose its potency. From the mid-1970s onward, the term "girl-watching" became detached from the societies, manuals, and prescribed rules that had given the pastime a more specific meaning and currency in the 1950s and 1960s.[143] Early articles on the girl-watcher had sketched out the contours of the girl-watcher as a category of man. As the term gained traction, however, girl-watching increasingly entered common parlance and was no longer a subject for a full exposé. Girl-watching slowly became synonymous with ogling and myriad forms of looking that men directed at women.

The flattening of girl-watching was particularly evident in its latter-day application to Black men. Initially, Black men were rarely if ever described as girl-watchers. Though some white people had come to Matt Ingram's defense after he was charged with "eye rape" in 1951, they stopped short of celebrating Ingram specifically or Black men generally as girl-watchers. Any celebration of the right to watch women was applied to "all men," a rhetorical leap that erased the specificity of Black men's experience.[144] Most mainstream depictions of girl-watching continued to depict girl-watchers as white men through the mid-1960s, not least because persistent racist stereotypes about Black men's dangerous hypersexuality essentially necessitated that "genteel" girl-watchers be white men, particularly when watching white women.

Still, the Black press periodically reprinted girl-watching pieces from white newspapers in the 1960s, spreading stories about girl-watching to Black readers.[145] These girl-watching pieces—produced by white journalists and published in Black newspapers—suggest that the discourse of girl-watching was a part of the way Black media and readers made sense of heterosexual desire, relationships, and intrusive behaviors. The white-produced girl-watching articles published in Black newspapers rarely depicted specific women or men, letting readers fill in the details and thus allowing for the possibility that Black men could be girl-watchers and Black women could be the ones whom girl-watchers watched.[146] But, even Black newspapers would not depict Black girl-watchers until the pastime's popularity among white Americans had waned.

In the late 1960s, Black journalists began to report more explicitly on Black girl-watchers. Photo essays about summertime vacationing, a popular context for girl-watching in both the Black and white press, might feature Black women in bikinis and a Black man admiring the view. The *Afro-American*, for instance, advertised the vacationing opportunities in Atlantic City with a spread on the women one could encounter on the beach. An accompanying photograph featured a row of eight Black women, all in swimsuits, standing arm in arm in a line. A Black man in swimming trunks and a beach hat sits casually in a beach chair in the foreground, a "grin on his face." The piece repeated some of the rules and reprimands that proliferated in white reports of girl-watching, tongue firmly in cheek. The unnamed author, for instance, lamented that the man in the photograph was an example of an "oggler," the "amature" leerers who were replacing the "bonafide girl watchers."[147] However, this was no antimasher tirade against leering men on street corners but rather a jokey reprimand leveled at men who were too outwardly admiring of women. Indeed, far from censuring Black men for ogling Black women, there is an undercurrent of fun and celebration in the piece. Everyone in the photographs is smiling. The women pose with one leg slightly in front of the other, to show off their figures for the camera. The men may not have been part of what the paper described as the "vanishing breed" of girl-watchers, but they certainly were not "eye rapists" either.[148]

Significantly, the Black press described Black men as girl-watchers primarily when they looked at Black women. Thus, a 1968 fashion spread in the *Milwaukee Star* advertised "Girl Watcher Fall Fashions" with Black models in the latest styles of dresses and slacks.[149] A spread in the *Afro-American* the next year drew even more heavily on girl-watching tropes. The feature showcased three "professional models" and college students sporting swimwear and flares. As the paper explained, all three models—Trina Taylor, Frances Ladimirault, and Rosalyn Smith—were "rare and precious" examples of the "species" "Gloriso Corinitus," as defined by "The Girl Watchers' Manual" (possibly an erroneous reference to Sauers's book). "It is suggested," opined the *Afro-American*, "that all novice Girl Watchers study them carefully." The article, titled "For Girl Watchers Only," lacked any references to brand or store names to lure shoppers, indicating it was intended primarily to titillate male readers.[150] Black men also explicitly embraced the girl-watcher moniker for themselves in the late 1960s. When the *Milwaukee Star* profiled local teen Kenneth Coulter Jr. in 1969, for instance, he listed his hobbies as "reading Black History, writing, playing football, and girl watching."[151] Two years later, boxer George Foreman bore the title of "Champion Girl Watcher" when he posed with a Black *Playboy* bunny in a photo in the *Los Angeles Sentinel*.[152]

The adoption of the girl-watching trope in the Black press in the late 1960s, even in the few examples here, suggests that Black men had begun to view the rhetoric of girl-watching as a tool for asserting their masculinity.[153] It is no coincidence that in 1968, just as the Black press was highlighting Black girl-watchers, striking Black sanitation workers in Memphis, Tennessee, carried signs declaring "I *AM* a Man," highlighting their demands for dignity from white Memphians. The slogan, as historian Steve Estes has argued, challenged "white men's paternalism and power in Memphis" and the "monolithic (and monochromatic) model of masculinity" that defined manhood only on white men's terms.[154] Black men's embrace of girl-watching, then, may have been part of a more widespread demand for recognition and respect of Black men's manhood, on Black men's terms.[155]

The increased tolerance for Black girl-watching represents a departure from previous decades when the Black press often reprimanded Black men who molested Black women, supposedly casting the entire race in a poor light. Girl-watching's reputation as a respectable, natural pastime offered cover for behaviors that might have garnered censure twenty years earlier. It is possible that such an acceptance also meant that Black women would have faced more resistance to complaints of intraracial stranger intrusions than they might have in earlier decades. While specific examples of stranger intrusions are difficult to find in general for this period, and especially for Black women, a researcher for the University of Minnesota collected interviews with thirty-some Black teenage girls in California in the mid-1970s that speak to the prevalence of stranger intrusions in their lives. Conducted half a decade after the publication of most of the girl-watching pieces above, these interviews describe the daily intrusions Black teenage girls experienced as they walked down the street. Twenty-two of the thirty-three girls interviewed said they had experienced a "boy" or "man" making "a pass at" them in a public space. Their reactions ranged from embarrassment to validation to disgust, but not one seemed to think such behaviors were anything other than normal and expected.[156]

Black men's ogling had seemingly come a long way from the days of "eye rape." However, the relative lateness of these examples suggests that the moniker "girl-watcher" was applied to Black men only once it lost its specificity and then only when Black men watched Black women. It is not coincidental that, just as Black men embraced the trope, girl-watching was no longer associated so closely with Sauers's *Girl Watcher's Guide*. It might still have a whiff of tongue-in-cheek "gentility," but the imagery, strict "rules," and clubs of Sauers's brand of girl-watching were largely obsolete by the end of the 1970s. As the twentieth century came to a close, girl-watching became something mentioned in passing, without explanation, as if it were the most natural thing in the world. Girl-watching had become part of the American lexicon, and girl-watchers no longer needed to fit the mold of middle-class white men.

THOUGH GIRL-WATCHING would not last as a defined practice with specific rules and membership requirements, its eventual conflation with other forms of looking speaks to how successfully girl-watching changed Americans' attitudes toward intrusive looking. The humor with which girl-watchers and their chroniclers described girl-watching so effectively trivialized uninvited looking for white men that it silenced any protest that remained from the debates over ogling in the 1930s and 1940s. The postwar girl-watching craze thus represents a moment when behaviors that had been considered insulting and dangerous in the early twentieth century, including when enacted by white men, were instead treated as a natural manifestation of middle-class white masculinity, that is, of hegemonic masculinity. In casting the girl-watcher's favored pastime as a genteel, unobtrusive show of admiration, girl-watchers normalized observation of female strangers as the prerogative of middle-class white men in particular. While the mostly white mashers of the early twentieth century had risked censure and even arrest for ogling women on the street, girl-watchers created their own clubs and guides without protest. The widespread depiction of girl-watching as a harmless, even amusing, pastime in newspapers, magazine articles, popular music, and a slew of advertising campaigns is evidence of its acceptance in American postwar society and popular culture.

By emphasizing their furtiveness and respectability, girl-watchers marked their style of watching as respectful, setting themselves apart from uncouth oglers or sexual predators. Indeed, the girl-watching of middle-class white professional men contrasted starkly with the charge of "eye rape" leveled at black farmer Matt Ingram. Though Ingram's lawyers would try to argue that men had a natural impulse to look at women, and thus Ingram's conviction would endanger all men who enjoyed looking at women, it was clear from his arrest and trial that Black men's looks carried a different meaning for white people than white men's looks. The lynching of Emmett Till only solidified the double standard that cast white men's looks as "girl-watching" and Black men's looks (or whistles) as akin to rape. During girl-watching's heyday, Black men could not claim the moniker of "girl-watcher" nor the respectability it implied. In this period, as Steve Estes argues, Black men had to "cloak their sexuality and mask their manhood for fear of trespassing on the race and gender prerogatives of white men."[157] The fact that some Black men embraced the moniker of girl-watcher by the late 1960s suggests that, as girl-watching as a term became detached from the rules and middle-class white associations of Donald Sauers's *Girl Watcher's Guide*, Black men began to embrace girl-watching as a way to assert their masculinity in a new era of Black activist militancy.

As girl-watching's cultural power waned, ogling, leering, and other kinds of intrusive looking did not disappear. Rather, the normalization of girl-watching as the harmless pastime of middle-class white men continued to influence the way Americans understood men's intrusive looks in later years, even if the term itself had lost its specificity. In the 1970s, as feminist theorists and activists denounced the phenomenon they increasingly called "street harassment," many feminists, especially middle-class white feminists, more easily denounced working-class men and men of color for catcalling or ogling but struggled to define middle-class white men as street harassers. White feminist activists and theorists instead often described a vague unease and frustration with such middle-class white men without a vocabulary to identify and call out the behaviors that bothered them. Professional or middle-class white men thus tended to escape feminists' accusations of street harassment, instead blending into the urbanscape, just as *The Girl Watcher's Guide* hoped he would.

CHAPTER **FIVE**

DEFINING STREET HARASSMENT

FRANCINE GOTTFRIED was a twenty-one-year-old computer operator for Chemical Bank New York Trust Company in New York City when she made international headlines in September 1968. That fall, a crowd of onlookers congregated around the subway station near the New York Stock Exchange where Gottfried emerged every morning. Men working in the area had noticed Gottfried's figure ("Wall Street's New Statistics: 43–25–37," noted one newspaper headline), discovered what time Gottfried usually arrived at the subway station, and waited for her at the entrance. According to the *New York Times*, the crowd was so large that it stopped traffic and police had to escort Gottfried to her work. Bemused, Gottfried told the *Times*, "I think they're all crazy. What are they doing this for?" Newspapers broadcast Gottfried's story around the world and followed up with a string of similar stories in 1968 and 1969, all featuring "busty" women who drew crowds and stopped traffic on Wall Street.[1]

Gottfried's story and the subsequent spate of girl-watching episodes caught the eye of Karla Jay, at the time an active member of the Redstockings feminist group in New York City. Reflecting on the incident in 2014, Jay described Gottfried's experience as the "most egregious example" of street harassment she had seen. Disturbed by the newspaper reports about groups of men accosting women in the street, Jay decided to stage an "Ogle-In," a piece of comic theater where feminist activists "turn[ed] the tables on the men on Wall Street." Jay and a group of fellow feminists wandered up and down Wall Street one day in the early spring of 1970, catcalling and ogling businessmen on their way to work. As Jay recalled, "When the men emerged from . . . the subway station, we called them names, we made whistling noises, we sucked our mouths at them, we made the gestures that they made. . . . The men's jaws fell and they ran. They started running down the street. They didn't know what to do."[2]

Inspired by the counterculture activist street theater she had encountered in the late 1960s, Jay's Ogle-In was designed to attract the attention of the press. She contacted local television stations in New York, and at least one, ABC, showed up to document the protest. ABC producer Marlene Sanders included the footage in her documentary on women's liberation, which aired in May 1970. Jay featured prominently, in a floppy knitted hat and a cheeky grin. In the footage she walks down the street, a sign in her hand, and turns to the camera to say, "Oh they're so beautiful, all of them. Oh, those men, those sex objects! What a nice tie. Look at the legs on that one! I'm so turned on!" About a dozen other women join Jay, joking, pointing, and making kissing noises. One holds a sign that reads, "OGLE DAY." Another young woman hugs an older man in glasses as Jay shouts, "Oh, I love gray hair! Makes men so sexy!" The protesters stop in the middle of the street to give interviews, surrounded on all sides by onlookers. One woman explains, "We're trying to point out . . . what it feels like being whistled at, put down constantly sexually every time we walk down the street." She makes kissing noises to illustrate her point, and some of her companions cheer in agreement. "We're supposed to dig it," she goes on, "because we're supposed to dig that we're sexual objects, and we don't want to be sexual objects anymore."[3]

A few days later, Jay and some of her fellow activists gave an interview on a local New York City radio station to further raise awareness of the scourge of harassment in the city. The women tried to describe the obscenities they endured on city streets but struggled to do so within the confines of the Federal Communications Commission censorship rules. Jay became frustrated with the male radio host who, she recalled, "just really didn't seem to be getting it, because he was a guy and he was probably doing it, too." However, the spot hit a nerve with female listeners. Hundreds wrote to Jay thanking her for shedding light on an experience that was so ubiquitous to them. "They understood what was happening to us," Jay recalled. "Most of them said, 'Yes, this has happened to me, too.'"[4]

The women's liberation movement of the 1970s marked a watershed moment for Americans' understanding of men's stranger intrusions. As feminists like Jay gained confidence from their shared grievances, they pushed back against the previous four decades of rhetoric that cast white men's stranger intrusions—girl-watching being the most prominent iteration—as trivial, harmless, and natural. Feminist activists and theorists began to see catcalling, wolf-whistling, and other intrusive behaviors as part of a larger infrastructure of gender oppression that kept women in a position of vulnerability and subservience to men. As Robin Morgan wrote in the introduction to *Sisterhood Is Powerful*, an early anthology of radical feminist writing, the "verbal assault on the street" joined a litany of other indignities and humiliations, from sexist jokes to unequal pay to "rock-song lyrics" that "barrage your aching brain." In such an environment, Morgan concluded, "you begin to see how all-pervasive a thing is sexism."[5]

In the 1970s and 1980s, feminists worked to define and denaturalize men's stranger intrusions and succeeded in changing mainstream conversations about these behaviors. In an echo of the activists who aimed to transform Americans' understandings of intrusive behaviors with the new category of "masher" at the beginning of the century, 1970s feminists created the new language of "street harassment" to argue that men's stranger intrusions existed on a continuum of men's violence against women, with rape and sexual assault at the extreme end. Like their Progressive Era counterparts, who worried that mashing could quickly lead to more extreme violence, feminists some sixty years later suggested that behaviors like wolf whistles or "street comments" served as reminders of women's vulnerability to rape and could lead to sexual assault. Even if a catcall did not end with physical violence, feminists argued that stranger intrusions curtailed women's physical and mental autonomy, infringing on women's privacy in public space and forcing them to modify their behaviors to avoid demeaning comments or objectifying stares. In language that recalled groups of mashers lining city streets, feminist writer Ann Sheldon argued, "Women will not be free as long as walking down the street, with eyes straight ahead, stomach contracted, is like running the gauntlet."[6] This analysis rang true for many women who, through consciousness-raising, found a way to describe why seemingly small, trivial behaviors like catcalls or whistling had such an enormous impact on their sense of autonomy and safety in public space. Little did they know that women's rights activists had made similar claims in the first decades of the twentieth century.

However, while Progressive Era feminists pinned mashing primarily on white men and viewed affluent white men as among the most entitled, middle-class white feminist activists in the 1970s were inclined to link street harassment to marginalized masculinities. Widespread beliefs that rape primarily took place on urban streets and at the hands of a stranger bolstered existing racist stereotypes that men of color, especially Black and brown men, were more sexually predatory than white men. White feminists, who already tended to view gender as the primary vector of oppression for all women, adopted many of these assumptions in their analysis of street harassment and often depicted Black and brown men as the archetypical harassers. In response, women of color and antiracist feminists challenged many white feminists' fixation on sex to the exclusion of other social categories, arguing it foreclosed a fuller understanding of the way racism obscured Black women's experiences and scapegoated men of color for intrusive behaviors. At the same time, middle-class feminists tended to see working-class white men, especially construction workers, as particularly obnoxious harassers and struggled to articulate the "everyday sexism" of men of their own race and class. This meant, as feminists worked to denaturalize stranger intrusions, that middle-class white men remained largely safe from accusations of "street harassment." Men's intrusive behaviors, especially the more surreptitious behaviors like ogling, thus remained part of the formulation of hegemonic masculinity, while men who embodied marginalized masculinities were cast as the prototypical catcallers.

"Little Rapes": Denaturalizing Men's Stranger Intrusions

The renewed critiques of men's stranger intrusions emerged out of the women's liberation movement of the 1960s and 1970s, particularly from the young, radical feminists who had cut their activist teeth in leftist, antiwar, and antiracist movements of the 1960s. Noting the persistent sexism that plagued these other anti-oppression movements, women began to form groups of varying levels of formality. They participated in "consciousness-raising," where women shared their everyday experiences of sexism as a way of building political identities as feminists.[7] Consciousness-raising became a key methodology of the feminist movement that included writing personal memoirs, participating in informal group conversations, and organizing structured speak-outs as a means of unearthing the nature of sexism. Participants in consciousness-raising often described having a "click moment" when a conversation suddenly revealed how patriarchy operated in even quotidian, seemingly trivial events or issues.[8] Feminists began to argue that "the personal is political," that is, women's concerns about gender roles, domestic duties, unequal pay, and sex were not just personal concerns but the basis for political struggle in a society dominated by men.[9] Through these conversations, many feminists, especially middle-class white feminists, developed a political framework that saw gender (or sex, to use the terminology of the time) as the primary factor in the oppression of all women.[10]

Consciousness-raising's focus on everyday experiences of sexism lent itself well to analyses of men's intrusive behaviors, especially when women began to talk about how the threat of sexual violence showed up in their daily lives. Conversations about rape and sexual violence easily led to—or sometimes began with—discussion of men's stranger intrusions. Guides for organizing consciousness-raising groups might explicitly name "street hassling" as a topic that would prompt women to talk about how fears of sexual violence constricted their lives.[11] In one 1970 consciousness-raising session broadcast on New York radio, a participant described how men constantly ogled or whistled at her as she traversed the city in her job as a messenger. Her story prompted other group members to reflect on how the fear of sexual violence curtailed their mobility. Another respondent explained that she felt "outraged" at "the fact that the streets are owned by men."[12]

Rage was a common response to having one's consciousness raised, especially around issues of men's violence against women. Susi Kaplow, a member of the New York Radical Feminists, cataloged the rising anger she saw spilling forth in the wake of women's feminist awakenings. Street harassment could trigger such anger, Kaplow notes, as women became "furious" at "the men on the street who visit their daily indignities" on their bodies. Kaplow warned such men that they might find themselves on the receiving end of a sharp "fuck off" or, if the woman was "brave, a knee in the right place." Kaplow encouraged women to use their rage as fuel for consciousness-raising, as anger was "the emotion which accompanies the first steps toward liberation."[13]

As men's stranger intrusions consistently came up in consciousness-raising conversations about rape and sexual violence, feminists began to intentionally link them. By connecting men's intrusive behaviors to other forms of sexual violence, feminists sought to make three interlocking arguments that would help to denaturalize intrusions. First, feminists viewed behaviors like catcalling and wolf-whistling as existing on a continuum of sexual violence that included sexual assault and rape.[14] Street harassment, as feminists defined it, was not necessarily as extreme a behavior as sexual assault, but it served as a threatening reminder of women's constant vulnerability to rape. Second, feminists insisted that street harassment curtailed their physical and psychological autonomy, not only because it conjured fears of rape but also because the behaviors were disruptive and intrusive in their own right. Feminists described how men's catcalls, wolf whistles, and physical intimidation or touch robbed women of the privacy and freedom that men enjoyed in public space. Third, feminists argued that intrusive behaviors normalized more extreme forms of sexual violence. They suggested that persistent exposure to sexual comments and objectification in small doses inured women to sexual violence more broadly and taught men they did not need to respect women. By arguing that catcalling, ogling, and groping were part of a larger continuum of sexual violence that kept women living in fear, feminists could insist that men's stranger intrusions were not natural expressions of heterosexual masculinity. Far from being the funny, trivialized behaviors celebrated in girl-watching, street harassment formed one part of the sexist, misogynist scaffolding that maintained patriarchy and male supremacy in society.

From the earliest feminist theorizing of street harassment, feminists connected less extreme and nonphysical behaviors like catcalling or indecent exposure to more extreme, physically harmful forms of sexual violence. Even the early terminology that feminists used to talk about stranger intrusions demonstrates the way they analytically linked those intrusions to rape. In the early 1970s, as women's liberationists began to consider their own experiences of men's stranger intrusions, they used terms like "verbal rape" or "little rape" to describe what would later be known as "street harassment."[15] The use of the term "rape," modified to signify its nonphysical manifestation, was a shorthand for the larger feminist argument that men's stranger intrusions felt like a violation of one's bodily autonomy. Notably, this language bears a striking resemblance to the "eye rape" turn of phrase that was similarly meant to denaturalize Matt Ingram's alleged looks, transforming them into sexual assault under the law. But if feminists ever encountered Ingram's story or the charge of "eye rape," it does not appear to have dissuaded them from adopting similar language to denaturalize the stranger intrusions they encountered on the street every day. Rather, feminists argued that a "verbal rape" or "little rape" rightfully depicted stranger intrusions as cousins to "forcible rape," the legal category that, in the 1970s, described "unlawful carnal knowledge of a woman by force and without her consent."[16] Many feminists thus saw intrusive behaviors as forms of sexual violence that existed in the same family as assault and rape.

Before "street harassment" emerged as its own category of analysis, feminists began to write about how behaviors like catcalling functioned as reminders of their vulnerability to rape. Feminists argued that women lived with the pervasive sense that rape could happen to anyone at any time. Every interaction with a man on the street was potentially dangerous. As feminist writer Meredith Tax explained in her 1970 essay *Woman and Her Mind*, "Women are hyper-aware of their surroundings. We have to be. Walk down a city street without being tuned in and you're in real danger; our society is one in which men rape, mug, and murder women whom they don't even know every day." Tax's essay, which became a classic of early women's liberation writing, demonstrates the way that fear of assault influenced how women moved through public space. Tax describes the need to be aware, to "keep track of what car is slowing down" and of who "is walking up behind you," even to adjust one's face, to mollify potential attackers. Tax's advice mirrored the instructions women grew up hearing across the country, like the San Francisco Bay Area woman who remembered her mother warning her to "stay away" from "boys on [the] street" and to never "stop when men talked" to her.[17] To avoid harm, Tax wrote, women "must be prepared to return the right kind of smile to passing Prince Charmings," implying that a smile was not a harmless interaction but an overture that required the correct response to avoid escalation or violence.[18]

Though feminists connected rape and men's stranger intrusions, they also saw intrusive behaviors as their own burden. Ann Sheldon, whose article "Rape: A Solution" appeared on reading lists for courses on feminist rape prevention, suggested that rape was just the most obvious way that women's freedoms were limited in a patriarchal society. Women, Sheldon argued, would never enjoy true freedom "as long as they are subjected to 'verbal rape'—the coarse proposals, the lip smackings, the touches and pinches."[19] A woman responding to a researcher's survey on rape echoed Sheldon's diagnosis when she reflected on the childhood messages she received about sexual assault, lamenting that she experienced "constant hasseling [*sic*]" as a young girl. Teenage girls, she recalled, had "no real physical freedom," frustrated as they were by overtures and molestation from "guys in movies or guys cornering you at bus stops." The constant intrusions of men taught this woman that her body was not her own and that she could expect "hasseling," or worse, wherever she went.[20] Thus, men's stranger intrusions, and the precautions women took to avoid them, were "part of the problem of rape," as Sheldon put it.[21]

Antirape feminist activists sometimes saw rape and intrusive behaviors as so intertwined that their solutions were intended to address both. For instance, Detroit-based antirape organization Women Against Rape advocated for instituting "anti-rape squads," groups of women who went out into public space together to ensure safety in numbers. As members explained in 1971, "Women have lost a basic civil liberty—the right to be on the street—going to a neighbor's, to the store, or just for a walk." Antirape squads, they argued, would protect women not only from rape but also from stranger intrusions. "Groups of women (4–8) are not hassled by men on the streets," they asserted. "The man who calls 'chick' or 'babe' to a woman alone hurries by a group of women. Rape most commonly occurs when a woman is alone and the male knows he can overpower her."[22] The quick jump from the "man who calls 'chick'" to rape in this passage suggests the group understood catcalls and rape as deeply intertwined, as versions of the same kind of sexist oppression. In many feminists' eyes, the catcaller and the rapist were the same kind of man, prone to objectify and sexualize women, and the eradication of one would aid in the elimination of the other.

As feminists saw it, because stranger intrusions reminded women of the constant threat of sexual violence, street harassment impinged on women's autonomy in public space. As one antipornography pamphlet screamed from its pages, "IT IS NO LONGER EVEN DEBATABLE THAT WOMEN LIVE UNDER A SEXUAL REIGN OF TERROR. . . . We live as though we are soldiers in combat, dividing our cities into 'safe' and 'unsafe' zones. . . . We spend our lives watching out."[23] New Yorker Gloria Schuh described in 1970 how even nonverbal and nonphysical interactions with men affected her ability to feel safe in public. She noted that men had a habit of "imposing" themselves on women simply by standing over them "ominously" on the subway. The point, Schuh surmised, was to make the woman "aware that [he's] there and [he has] the power to do something." Schuh sensed "vibrations" from these interactions that were so disturbing they physically affected her. "You're suddenly rearranging yourself," she explained, "and you're checking to see that nothing's showing and you're really upset and uncomfortable. And eventually maybe you'll even get up and move your seat."[24] A man did not even need to say anything for a woman like Schuh to feel afraid and try to protect herself.

As Schuh's experience suggests, many feminists insisted that behaviors like catcalling, ogling, or indecent exposure curtailed not only their physical freedom but, as writer Ingrid Bengis put it, their "psychic freedom," too.[25] Meredith Tax described how men who "use [a woman's] body with their eyes" or "comment on her defects" effectively "make her a participant in their fantasies without asking if she is willing." Such men, wrote Tax, "demand that [a woman's] thoughts be focused on them."[26] Bengis echoed this complaint, writing in her memoir that every time she went out in New York City, "I have to take into consideration that my desire to be alone won't be acknowledged by the men who haunt the streets, that if I want to think, I'd better do my thinking at home."[27] One unnamed New York feminist, directly addressing men who made "oppressive comments to women on the street," described how such men "interrupt our conversations with each other or our train of thought when we are walking alone." These disruptions, she argued, demonstrated that men thought their commentary on women's bodies was more important than what women had to say to one another. "You wouldn't interrupt the conversation of two men on the street," she pointed out. "Our conversations are important too."[28]

For some, the anticipation of men's stranger intrusions could be as much of a mental burden as the experience of the intrusions themselves. For instance, a *Ms.* magazine reader explained that she had experienced so many "whistles," "obscenities," and "hassles from men" beginning at age twelve that by age twenty-three she was "alert" and expecting them every time she went out. The expectation of stranger intrusions, she complained, made it "hard to think about being yourself" or go "for walks spontaneously or just grocery shopping without feeling uncomfortable and jumpy by any passerby."[29] Journalist Gwenda Linda Blair similarly argued in 1974 that "one of the most oppressive aspects" of "street hassles" was the "tension I have to endure when I see a man or group of men." She explained, "I have to spend the next minute or two dreading possible hassling and deciding what, if anything, I'll do: cross the street, ignore them, yell back." She described the mental energy required to make these decisions, both in the moment but also before even leaving the house. Blair had to "calculate" what to wear when she went out, hoping that she could control the number of "hassles" she received based on the clothing she chose.[30] The mere anticipation of an intrusive behavior was enough to consume a woman's mind and compel her to physically alter her outward presentation.

In feminist media and sexual violence research, women described the kind of sixth sense they developed to navigate the city safely.[31] In 1978, for example, sexual violence scholar Diana Russell and a team of researchers interviewed women in the San Francisco Bay Area about the precautions they took to avoid sexual violence, including intrusive behaviors, in public. Respondents described how they never went out alone, especially at night, and avoided isolated places like parks or movie theaters. When they did go out, Russell's interviewees explained that they would walk in a hurry, "walk close to the street" to avoid anyone lurking in doorways or alleys, or "ignore men in general on the street." One respondent dressed "matronly, unobtrusively," certainly "not sexy or attractive." Some women carried items intended to keep them safe, such as a whistle, a loaded gun, or a knife. As one woman put it, the fear of sexual violence "does control what [you] can [and] can't do. It curtails [your] activity greatly."[32]

The need to protect oneself from unwanted intrusions could be dehumanizing. Catcalls, whistles, and the like made Blair "feel like shutting everything down, eliminating all interchange" with strangers. But "human interchange," Blair wrote, "is vital to the maintenance of . . . dignity in my life": To fear interactions with strangers was to eliminate a key connection to one's humanity.[33] In "Rape: A Solution," Ann Sheldon suggested that diminished humanity was part of the "real chains" that bound women in a society that normalized rape. The threat of rape taught women to be suspicious of all men and to avoid sharing an "open friendly glance into a man's face on the street or even smile, as one human being to another."[34] When Diana Russell interviewed women about the impact of rape in their lives, many confirmed that stranger intrusions alienated them from others in public. One of Russell's respondents described how she was "not friendly anymore," lamenting, "I'm always interested—but now when someone approaches me I look them over to see if he's the type to assault me." Another interviewee described how an experience of sexual violence "affected how I respond to people" and that she became "suspicious of men in new situations. I jump to conclusions now I never would have in the past."[35] These women approached the world always on guard, with their eyes peeled and their bodies ready to respond to any affront on the street.

Meredith Tax argued that men's stranger intrusions alienated women not only from other people but also from their own bodies. Catcalls and the like created "a split between mind and body, between one self and another." Either a woman must hate her body and "consider the mind the real 'self,'" or she must "glorify the body," embracing it as "an instrument to satisfy the desires of others." In the latter case, Tax argued the body becomes "a thing, and the mind a puppeteer to manipulate it."[36] Both the precautions women took to avoid intrusive behaviors and the behaviors themselves thus alienated women from their bodies, their sense of self, and their humanity. The amount of mental and emotional energy women expended on anticipating, avoiding, and responding to men's stranger intrusions suggests that intrusions curtailed not only women's physical freedom but also, as feminist theorists argued, their mental health and psychological autonomy.[37]

Once feminists linked street harassment with rape and sexual assault, they began to view the seemingly small daily intrusions men imposed on women as a patriarchal tool that helped normalize rape. Feminists argued that catcalling, ogling, and other sexualizing behaviors from male strangers conditioned all genders to see women as solely sexual objects, existing for men. In this formulation, the ostensibly trivial nature of girl-watching, catcalling, and the like was precisely what made these behaviors so dangerous. A woman might experience many intrusions throughout one day, but if none of them led to physical violence, she might eventually see them as a normal part of life. Once those behaviors were normalized, more and more extreme behaviors might subsequently appear normal until a woman's defenses had disintegrated.

Sexual violence theorists Andra Medea and Kathleen Thompson put forward this argument in their 1974 rape survival manual, *Against Rape*. In a sign of how much feminists were connecting street intrusions with rape, they devoted the entire fifth chapter of their book to the "little rapes" women endured on the street every day. In an opening vignette, the authors described how a woman walking home must dodge multiple groups of men and teenage boys to avoid "staring" and "comments." The authors asked the reader to imagine herself in this position: They described how "your body tenses" and "your face burns with embarrassment" as you navigate these "incidents." While the vignette concludes with the imagined woman arriving home safe, without any further violence, Medea and Thompson warned that "acceptance" of stranger intrusions "as normal is dangerous." Normalizing such behaviors, they cautioned, "is one of the ways in which women are *prepared* to be victims."[38]

Part of the way such intrusions were normalized, argued Medea and Thompson, was through sheer volume and repetition. To illustrate this point, they recreated the barrage of comments men hurled at women on the street every day, listing them in an intimidating block of text:

> Hey, baby, where ya goin', whatcha doin', what's happenin'? Ya lookin' good, sugar. Nice ass. Looka them legs. Wanna give me some? Mama. Hey, look at those. Where's your bra, honey? Don't they get cold that way? I'll keep 'em warm. What have you got *there*? What a nice piece. Wanna drink? Where ya goin' so fast? Can I come too? Ha, ha, ha. Ain't ya goin' ta talk to us? Ain't ya even gonna smile? Whatsa matter with you? You stuck up, or something? Think you're too good, huh? Ugly bitch anyway, fat legs . . . Hey, wanna come up ta my house? Show ya a really good time. You got real nice legs, honey. Got anything between 'em for me? . . . Hey, look at that one. What a pig . . . Hey, you. Your blouse is undone. Whoooeeee.

> Ain't ya gonna give me a peek? Bouncy, bouncy, bouncy. Doin' anythin' tonight? How much? Huh? How much for it? Ten bucks? Five? Hey, whatsa matter with you? I'm just trying to be friendly.[39]

Here, the reader is confronted with the alarming ease with which seemingly harmless, even friendly, greetings could turn into outright aggression. For Medea and Thompson, to be "subjected" to these "little rapes" on a daily basis causes "a gradual erosion . . . of your self-respect and privacy."[40] This loss of self-respect made women vulnerable to sexual violence, suggested Medea and Thompson, for women became convinced that they were not worthy of privacy or autonomy in public.

Medea and Thompson contended that even the way women were socialized to respond to stranger intrusions contributed to their victimization. Women, they maintained, were taught to "please others," so they often felt the need to be "pleasant to the man in the street who approaches" them. Of course, women had good reason to appease men in such circumstances. To refrain from doing so could risk a violent response, from shouted epithets like those Medea and Thompson offered in their litany of "little rapes" to violent attacks. Ironically, when women responded to intrusions with pleasantries or ego-stroking, however disingenuous, they might inadvertently encourage men to push for further sexual contact. This, lamented the authors, "sets women up to be raped."[41]

Feminists seized on this idea that street harassment conditioned women to be victims of rape. In a 1974 consciousness-raising session with the National Congress of Neighborhood Women, a network of grassroots organizers aimed at empowering poor and working-class women, a young attendee argued that feminists' response to rape has to include "every time a man whistles at us on the street or pinches our ass." When feminists coupled these small infractions with more extreme forms of sexual violence, the attendee argued, "you really begin to see how our whole lives are geared toward perceiving ourselves, in reality, as victims of men accosting us in some way or another."[42] In a 1971 *Woman's World* essay, Catherine Henry observed that "girl-children are very early taught to associate affection with physical violation," including from the men who "leer like hideous gargoyles at us on the streets." These "innumerable compounded" intrusions on a woman's body "ultimately culminate in the rape act itself," wrote Henry, suggesting not only that men's stranger intrusions lie on a continuum of sexual violence but that they actually lead to further, more extreme acts.[43] This idea would persist for at least a decade: In the mid-1980s, feminist street assertiveness training suggested that a potential attacker might use street harassment as a way to "gauge a woman's vulnerability to rape."[44] Seen in this light, stranger intrusions served as a kind of grooming that taught men how to objectify and taught women to expect to be objects.

In the face of the psychic harm and objectification of street harassment, some feminists struggled to know how to respond. An unnamed writer for an anticapitalist newsletter in the early 1970s argued that, though "a lot" of women were "thinking of how to change things," action was difficult when women spent so much of their time processing men's stranger intrusions. The author went on, "If a woman is walking down the street and guys are saying 'Hi ya babe—Oh, you're looking good today.' And they're looking your body up and down, and you got to be conscious of your breasts and rear all the time. It's hard to think of things to change the world when everybody's looking at you like a piece of meat."[45] Nevertheless, as feminists continuously honed their theories of stranger intrusions, some turned to public actions and art projects to engage an audience beyond feminist circles and raise awareness of the effect of intrusive behaviors on women's lives.[46]

Guerrilla theater, protests, and direct engagement with men who harassed women were among the most popular collective responses to stranger intrusions. Karla Jay's 1970 Ogle-In is perhaps the most famous example, not least because of its appearance in a 2014 documentary film, but it was not even the only action of its kind to take place that year.[47] In her memoir, lesbian feminist author Rita Mae Brown described a similar event at Yale University in February 1970, likely a month or two before Jay's Ogle-In. Three Vassar women, she recalled, created the so-called Operation Hassle as a way to give Yale men "a little sample of the street chatter we women hear every day of our lives," including smacking them on the rear end. Male students responded with such hostility that Brown concluded, "Being treated as a woman is the worst thing that can happen to a man."[48] Similarly, in June 1970 another New York feminist group known as Bitches ("not an acronym," assured the *Village Voice*) put on the "First Official Ladies Floating High Tea, Picnic Lunch, and Ogle." Participants stood at Fifty-Seventh Street and Park Avenue in Midtown Manhattan and acted out scenarios of catcalling. Swarms of media showed up, prompting the *Village Voice* to describe the event as a "street circus." As a television producer reportedly went in search of a "good-looking" woman who could speak in opposition to the event, event participants argued that what some viewed as "street 'compliments'" were really "put-downs." Such harassment, they argued, was illegal under state penal code, but no one seemed to know or care enough to follow the law.[49]

Some feminists used more anonymous forms of art activism to denaturalize men's stranger intrusions, particularly as a way to engage directly with men who bothered them on the street. In 1971, New Yorker Marigold Arnold wrote a "Street Harassment Statement" that she mimeographed and handed out whenever a man harassed her. "Brother," it began, "I feel insulted and oppressed by your comment. You and men like you make it unpleasant and difficult for all of us women, including your mothers, sisters, and daughters, to leave our houses alone. Why are you constantly harassing us on the street?" Arnold asked men to consider how they might feel if they received comments such as, "I like your legs," "What, no jock strap?" or "My, what an interesting penis." At eighteen sentences, it is hard to imagine how the statement could have fit onto a card one could easily hand out on the street, but a feminist group published the text in its newsletter as an option for how to respond to men's stranger intrusions.[50]

Indeed, women were hungry to learn retorts they could use to rebuff intrusive behaviors. Feminist organizations and conferences frequently hosted workshops about street harassment, offering tips for how to respond to unwanted advances.[51] A 1971 workshop on the "verbal rapist" suggested women confront oglers by "staring at their crotch" or embarrass flashers by remarking on their small genitalia.[52] At a 1972 conference on prostitution, participants shared their responses to street harassment, including spitting on assailants, shouting "Fuck off Fatty (or Baldy or whatever suits)," telling men to "fuck each other like you'd really like to," or shooting a water pistol at a harasser's crotch. Others warned that such tactics might elicit violent responses from harassers.[53]

As these examples suggest, some anti–street harassment activism turned the tables on men who intruded on women in public space. Feminists threw catcalls back at men on the street, using the same kinds of coarse language they heard from men. In some cases, women's responses were intended to insult men for their perceived failings, rather than sexualize them, while still others were overtly physical. All these responses were designed to point out the negative impact of intrusions, especially the way they made women feel insulted, objectified, and angry. Sexual remarks, wolf whistles, and intrusive stares were not harmless compliments, these responses insisted. They were harmful harassment. Street-level activism thus extended the work of feminist writers who tried to present intrusive behaviors as unnatural and violent. By forcing street harassers to feel uncomfortable or insulted, activists pointed out that dealing with sexual or aggressive behavior from strangers on the street was disruptive and distressing.

The Stranger in the Street: Race in Feminists' Analysis of Stranger Intrusions

While connecting typical intrusive behaviors to rape helped feminists denaturalize street harassment as a form of sexual violence, it also limited the scope of that analysis. Like the mainstream antirape movement, which often put the issue of gender oppression at the center of a feminist understanding of rape to the exclusion of other identity categories, the largely middle-class white feminists who were most focused on street harassment privileged gender as their primary category of analysis.[54] Radical feminists' discussions of men's stranger intrusions, as well as sexual violence more broadly, often cast all men as oppressors and all women as oppressed, regardless of race, class, or other social categories. For example, journalist Gwenda Linda Blair described catcalls or ogling as a "common ground of experience" that brought women together and reminded them of their shared vulnerability to gender and sexual violence, without acknowledging that women's experiences of stranger intrusions might differ depending on their and the perpetrators' other social identities.[55] At the same time, middle-class white feminists' race and class prejudices often shaped which men they were most likely to view as harassers. Their inattention to what theorists now call intersectionality would prove contentious as their discussions of intrusive behaviors began to solidify around stereotypes of street harassers as primarily shadowy, "urban" strangers—often a dog whistle for Black and Latino men—or white construction workers.

A national conversation about rising urban crime, unsafe streets, and the danger of stranger rape influenced how feminists interpreted intrusions on the street and who they viewed as the likeliest harassers. In the late 1960s and 1970s, many Americans feared that cities were growing increasingly dangerous. Several nationally destabilizing race rebellions in the late 1960s led many white Americans to view cities as hotbeds of violence, crime, drugs, and poverty, which they equated with people of color, especially Black and brown Americans.[56] At the same time, many urban centers saw an uptick in sexual industries, as theaters showing pornographic films, peep shows, and adult bookstores took up visibly prominent storefronts and marquees in places like Times Square.[57] This shifting urban landscape led some feminists to view cities as hostile spaces for women, especially middle-class white women. Everywhere they went, it seemed, white women risked mugging on the street or public transit and were targets for harassment from the patrons who frequented porn theaters and adult bookstores.

In this period, many Americans believed that rape and other forms of sexual assault were primarily crimes that men committed against women they did not know in public places, especially urban streets and alleyways. A rape crisis center worker voiced this assumption when she told the feminist newspaper *Majority Report*, "Rape is a threat common to all women. Any woman can walk down the street and be assaulted."[58] Another antirape pamphlet warned, "The rapist needs and counts" on his "anonymity: The probability that he will not be known or recognized."[59] What little statistical research that existed on rape and sexual assault seemed to confirm the ubiquity of stranger rape. In 1972, for example, *Women: A Journal of Liberation* reported that almost half of rape victims were attacked "on the street," and 60 percent were "attacked by a stranger."[60] At the same time, mainstream conversations about rape rarely, if ever, acknowledged that women might be at risk of sexual violence from men they knew or loved. Indeed, a 1977 survey of Americans' perceptions of crime found that a whopping 87 percent of the 1,536 respondents believed rapists were "sick and perverted males," or put another way, aberrant rather than "normal."[61] The association of rape with abnormality reinforced assumptions that rape was a crime that deviant men committed against strangers, not against intimate partners or family members.[62]

Rape prevention and self-defense literature also reinforced the assumption that rape took place primarily in public places and at the hands of strangers. Both feminist groups and law enforcement advised women that they could protect themselves from sexual assault by walking with purpose down the street, avoiding dark alleyways and parks, carrying impromptu weapons (such as keys), looking out for suspicious strangers, walking only on well-lit streets, or refraining from going out alone at night altogether.[63] While some feminists disseminated this style of avoidance advice, others critiqued it for encouraging women to view public space as inherently dangerous.[64] Many feminists had learned to distrust the state, noting that law enforcement and courts believed rape victims only when it suited them and rarely prosecuted sexual violence crimes effectively.[65] As one feminist writer put it, when it came to rape, "the police solution, (like Daddy's solution)," was to "stay indoors, stay off the streets, don't act free because that might be provocative."[66] Feminists similarly lampooned any suggestion that men might be able to protect women from sexual violence. New York Radical Feminist members Mary Ann Manhart, Joan Mathews, and Florence Rush described the threat of rape as "a way of keeping women in their homes and in the company of men, their 'protectors.'"[67] But, as feminist sociologist Kathleen Barry pointed out, "the role of protector of women . . . only implies another kind of violence. Men protect women from the violence of men."[68]

Even as feminist activists and sexual violence researchers pointed out the hypocrisy of common rape safety advice and increasingly argued that rapists were "normal" men who often knew their victims, the potential menace of the stranger rapist lurking in the shadowy city street proved difficult to dispel.[69] For instance, when the women's erotic magazine *Viva* surveyed readers about rape in 1975, just 15 percent of respondents reported experiencing "street, all[e]y and park rapes." However, in interpreting the data, sexual violence researcher Pauline Bart wrote that this category of rape remained "usually the most frightening."[70] The association between urban space and sexual violence was so strong that the Northern Virginia chapter of the National Organization for Women told the *Washington Post* in 1972 that suburban women, while concerned about rape in a general sense, "just don't feel as threatened" by the specter of rape as women who lived in urban areas.[71]

Because white Americans and policymakers equated urban crime with Black and brown residents, the fear of stranger rape was most often translated to a fear of racialized rapists. White feminists sometimes reinforced these stereotypes in their analyses of sexual violence. Sometimes, the connection between rape and racialized others was implied. In 1977, when feminists in Dallas started a campaign to raise awareness of the ongoing threat of rape in women's lives, they named their venture the Kitty Genovese Women's Project after the twenty-eight-year-old Italian American bartender who was raped and stabbed to death outside her home in New York City in 1964. Winston Moseley, a Black man from Manhattan, confessed to Genovese's murder and served fifty-two years in prison.[72] In choosing Genovese as its namesake, the project could not help but conjure the view of rape as an interracial crime involving white female victims and Black male assailants. In other cases, women's individual stories of rape reproduced racist stereotypes. For instance, in a 1978 piece in the widely read *Glamour* magazine, Louisa Rogers, a white woman, detailed how a "black man" raped her at "6:20 A.M. in an upper-middle-class, university section of New Orleans." Rogers's description implied that, despite sticking to a presumably white, well-to-do neighborhood, Rogers fell victim to a strange Black man who had entered a community where he did not belong.[73] The myth of the Black rapist hung over these examples, demonstrating how some white feminists, in their desire to highlight sexual oppression above all other forms of oppression, failed to clearly interrogate the widespread conflation of the categories of rapist, stranger, and Black man.[74]

The persistent myth of the stranger rapist, often coded as a man of color, proved problematic for white feminists' discussions of men's intrusive behaviors. While linking men's stranger intrusions with rape helped feminists denaturalize behaviors like catcalling and ogling, the association of rape with "urban strangers" meant this rhetorical turn also perpetuated stereotypes about men of color as some of the likeliest to harass women in public places. White feminists sometimes fed into these stereotypes, while other times they tried to correct the associations between sexual violence and Black and brown men.

Indeed, race was not wholly absent in white feminists' theories of men's stranger intrusions in the early 1970s, but authors sometimes handled racial analysis clumsily or defensively.[75] In an early example, Cate Stadelman, writing for Detroit Women Against Rape in 1971, cautioned women to look out for men who might be following them on the street. Likely self-conscious that she might be accused of encouraging suspicion of men of color, Stadelman insisted, "It isn't racist or anti-humanitarian to FIND OUT if you are being followed."[76] A few years later, Andra Medea and Kathleen Thompson made dubious comparisons between women's fear of rape and Jim Crow social norms that circumscribed Black Americans' freedoms in public space. In *Against Rape*, Medea and Thompson claimed that Black Americans were "no longer expected to 'know your place'" on the street in 1974, and indeed most observers would feel "sick" watching a Black man make himself small to safely navigate a group of hostile whites. Meanwhile, they argued, "women face [the] same kind of badgering and taunting," common under Jim Crow, "and accept it. They have come to think of it as an unavoidable part of life."[77] Here, Medea and Thompson illustrate the classic blind spot of early white feminist work, namely that the universal "woman" was assumed to be white, while the universal African American was assumed to be male. They thus not only suggested that white women experienced worse harassment on the street than Black men but also erased the existence and experiences of Black women.

As in feminist discussions of rape, white feminists who viewed whiteness as the norm sometimes contributed to stereotypes of men of color as more threatening harassers by mentioning race only when a nonwhite man harassed them. For instance, a feminist writer going by the unabashed pseudonym "B. Razen Cunt" described two examples of being harassed on the street, one in which she did not mention the men's race and one in which she did. In the first incident, a "gang of boys about eleven years old" were "terrorizing women" by wrapping their hands around women's necks in the street and then running away in laughter. In the second incident, the writer described a group of "young Puerto Rican men" whom she encountered swinging "stick-ball sticks" on the streets of Manhattan. They were "playfully swatting at women," and the writer "had been frightened."[78] The author's decision to elide the race of the "gang of boys" suggests that their race was invisible to her and thus likely white. Furthermore, while she described the "boys" as "about eleven years old," she failed to clarify the age of the Latino "men." Indeed, the description of the group running down the street "playfully swatting" brings to mind a group of boisterous adolescents rather than a menacing crew of adults, yet the author described them as "Puerto Rican men." While it is impossible to tell what exactly the author saw, her description of each encounter leaves an impression of annoying white youths in contrast to frightening, dangerous men of color. The author thus played into a long-standing white supremacist logic that viewed youths of color as older, more mature, and more dangerous than their white counterparts.[79]

While these early examples show how white feminists might defensively guard themselves against accusations of racism or feed into stereotypes that cast men of color as sexual threats, in other cases white feminists explicitly dismissed race as irrelevant to their analysis of intrusive behaviors. In her essay *Woman and Her Mind*, Meredith Tax maintained that sexual inequality was the most important factor to consider when analyzing intrusions on the street. She insisted that all men had the power to sexualize and objectify all women. "You can say what you like about class and race. Those differences are real," she conceded, continuing, "But in this everyday scenario, any man on earth, no matter what his color or class is, has the power to make the woman who is exposed to him hate herself and her body." She went on, "Any man has this power as man, the dominant sex, to dehumanize woman, even to herself."[80] Tax thus argued that no woman could exert power over a man in everyday interactions in public, ignoring the long history of white women who had done just that. One need only recall Willie Jean Boswell's accusations of "eye rape" against Matt Ingram to shatter this argument, but Tax and many other white feminists struggled to address the way race and class complicated their arguments about sexual violence.

If white feminists had largely forgotten Ingram's case by the 1970s, the memory of the murder of Emmett Till set off the most heated debates of men's intrusive behaviors among feminists. The controversy began with 1975's *Against Our Will*, Susan Brownmiller's groundbreaking monograph on the feminist politics of rape. In the book, Brownmiller dove headfirst into the history of rape accusations against Black men in the United States and devoted a significant section to Emmett Till, the Black teenager who was lynched for supposedly whistling at a white woman, Carolyn Bryant, in Money, Mississippi, in 1955. Brownmiller conceded that "nothing in recent times" could match Till's murder "for sheer outrageousness, for indefensible overkill with community support." A whistle, she insisted, is not a basis for murder. However, she also argued that Till's whistle (which she takes as fact and not merely alleged) was "a deliberate insult just short of physical assault, a last reminder to Carolyn Bryant that this black boy, Till, had in mind to possess her." Till, Brownmiller argued, did not engage in an "innocent flirtation" or a "kid's brash prank" but rather sought to prove to his watching friends that he "could get a white woman." His whistle, in this argument, sent the message that Bryant was an object to be claimed.[81]

Brownmiller went on to describe how the knowledge of Till's murder affected her own reactions to men's stranger intrusions: "At age twenty and for a period of fifteen years after the murder of Emmett Till whenever a black teenager whistled at me on a New York City street or uttered in passing one of several variations on an invitation to congress, I smiled my nicest smile of comradely equality—no supersensitive flower of white womanhood, I—a largess I extended with equal sincerity to white construction workers, truck drivers, street-corner cowboys, indeed, to any and all who let me know from a safe distance their theoretical intent." Brownmiller detailed how she felt it was "white women's" responsibility to "bear the white man's burden of making amends for Southern racism." She thus tried to take every "whistle or a murmured 'May I fuck you?' [as] an innocent compliment." After fifteen years of struggling through these experiences, she explained, she came "to understand the insult implicit in Emmett Till's whistle, the depersonalized challenge of 'I can have you' with or without the racial aspect. Today a sexual remark on the street causes within me a fleeting but murderous rage."[82] Brownmiller plainly articulated here that, for her, the vector of male privilege was the one that mattered in the analysis of Till's murder, that "with or without the racial aspect," a catcall or wolf whistle was a symbol of male power, no matter who wielded it. Brownmiller went so far as to argue that Till and the white men who murdered him "shared something in common. *They both understood* that the whistle was no small tweet of hubba-hubba or melodious approval for a well-turned ankle."[83]

Brownmiller's analysis was one possible extension of the argument that feminists had been making about men's intrusive behaviors. In attempting to both link men's stranger intrusions to more extreme forms of sexual violence and show how they curtailed women's freedoms in public space, feminists indeed argued that small intrusions, like a wolf whistle, had an impact that belied their seemingly trivial nature. However, by failing to analyze how race and class shaped the impact, reception, and response to intrusive behaviors, Brownmiller showed how focusing solely on gender inequality reinforced the same white supremacist logic that led Till's murderers to view his alleged whistle as a dangerous sexual threat.

Indeed, Brownmiller's analysis of Till's murder was the most controversial and denounced portion of *Against Our Will*. Black activist and scholar Angela Davis rebuked Brownmiller for perpetuating racist myths about Black men's lust for white women and for depicting Till as "a guilty sexist—almost as guilty as his white racist murderers." Anne Braden, a white Southern woman and longtime civil rights activist, also admonished Brownmiller for diminishing the impact of racism on claims of rape and sexual assault. She pointed out that white civilians and the state, alike, routinely used claims of interracial rape involving Black men and white women as an excuse for murdering Black men. The rape accusations need not be founded in reality to have devastating consequences for Black men and their families. Braden wrote of Brownmiller that her analysis of sexual violence "ignores the fact that in a society anchored by racism, there can be no liberation for anyone until the race issue is met head on."[84] Davis and Braden clearly articulated the dangers of viewing intrusive behaviors solely through the lens of gender.

Critiques from women of color and antiracist feminists like Davis and Braden shaped later feminist discussions of sexual violence. In 1977, the Kitty Genovese Women's Project appeared to respond to Braden's call to meet "the race issue . . . head on" in feminist analyses of sexual violence. The group published a twenty-page antirape pamphlet that featured a list of every man indicted on sex offender charges in Dallas County between 1960 and 1976, as well as a list of alleged rapists who were yet "unapprehended."[85] Though the project conjured the specter of interracial rape in its choice of namesake, the pamphlet tried to debunk both the ideas that rape happened at the hands of strangers and that Black men were the most likely perpetrators of sexual violence. An unnamed writer for the project noted that the printed list of Dallas County sex offenders included "a disproportionately large percentage of minority and low income males." "In a classist, racist society," the author explained, "the people lowest on the ladder of privilege are first to be punished—and usually overly punished—while white middle and upper class males often have seeming immunity." This disclaimer was intended to caution readers against assuming the sex offender list showed the full breadth of the reality of rape and who was likely to perpetrate it. The author argued that most rapists attacked women of their own race and described how "interracial rape has been used by our racist society to keep white women in fear and Black men in line."[86] Such a critique suggested the ambivalence some feminist antirape groups felt about the impact their awareness-raising tactics might have had on Black men's lives, especially when so many official rape crime statistics reflected the racist society and institutions in which they were produced.

In the face of one-dimensional critiques of stranger intrusions that focused primarily on gender as a category of analysis, Black women and antiracist feminists argued that the experiences of people of color complicated monolithic understandings of sexual violence or intrusive behaviors in the United States. Black feminists and antiviolence activists pointed out that Black women often faced far worse dangers in public space than white women, including racially motivated attacks and murder. They argued that the state intensified these dangers, as predominantly white courts and police officers rarely viewed Black women and other women of color as victims worthy of protection and even perpetrated violence themselves. Women of color feminists also bristled at the way white feminists often depicted street harassers as men of color—or at the very least, as "urban" strangers—while failing to consider how such accusations might endanger Black men and other men of color. Activists in the Black freedom movement had long seen how white women's claims of sexual violence had sent Black men to their deaths for decades. They pointed out that the predominantly white carceral state punished Black men disproportionately and more harshly for sexual violence offenses than it did their white counterparts. Black women and antiracist feminists, while working to center Black women within the Black antiviolence movement, insisted that no feminist analysis of men's stranger intrusions, and sexual violence more broadly, was complete without an understanding of its impact on women *and* men of color.[87]

Catcalling and the "Great White American Hardhat"

As feminists debated how to talk about race in discussions of street harassment, and especially whether their activism was harming men of color, middle-class white men remained all but absent from feminists' attempts to denaturalize and expose street harassment as an omnipresent urban problem. While feminists variously ignored race, adopted stereotypes of sexually predatory men of color, or actively worked against racist stereotyping, the largely middle-class feminists who most concerned themselves with stranger intrusions also struggled to consider the impact of class on their experiences and theories of street harassment. Middle-class white women had a difficult time articulating the subtle sexism they experienced from men of their own racial and class positions. In contrast, many middle-class white feminists felt intrusions from working-class men keenly, so keenly that they developed a shorthand for street harassers that would dominate conversations about stranger intrusions into the twenty-first century: the catcalling construction worker.

Writer Ingrid Bengis exemplified the fixation on construction workers in her 1972 memoir, *Combat in the Erogenous Zone*. In the book—a rumination on love, hate, and sex that was a finalist for the National Book Award—Bengis detailed the anger she felt toward men as a result of her experiences of harassment, rape, and sexual assault. In one essay, Bengis described the "almost daily" intrusive behaviors she experienced from male strangers in public places, from fellow commuters groping her in the subway to the men who "make *psst, psst* noises at me from the sidewalk or from the safety of their cars."[88] A key vignette revolved around a group of construction workers harassing Bengis with what she called "their usual number." Bengis did not feel the need to explain what the construction workers' "usual number" was. It seems she assumed their leers and catcalls were self-evident and implied by their occupation. Bengis went on to call the construction workers' "verbal advances" "extremely crude" and described her violent anger at their catcalls. In her rage, she fantasized about putting her cigarette out in the men's eyes.[89]

In contrast, Bengis self-consciously ruminated on the difficulty she had seeing and denouncing sexism from men she encountered in less "impersonal circumstances." Sexist actions were hard to identify in men she described as "average guy[s]" or men who "at one time or another I had thought might make good platonic friends."[90] Whatever affinities or allegiances Bengis felt toward such "average" men made it difficult for her to articulate their sexism with the same pointedness and anger she reserved for the construction workers who disturbed her walk. Indeed, Bengis had an easier time describing her disappointment with "average" men who did not stand up to construction workers on her behalf than she did describing their own sexist behavior. Bengis explained that she held men like her book editor and "other 'average guys' responsible... for the construction workers." She resented that these middle-class white men "seemed to lack the courage to 'betray their sex' by repudiating the attitudes of construction workers (except in conversations with women, where words are often cheap)."[91] Even more distressing, Bengis knew that the men she saw as potential allies could be as guilty of intrusive behaviors as construction workers. Far worse than ignoring construction workers who whistled and catcalled, Bengis fumed that once a construction worker had chosen a target, "most men . . . will usually join in the ogling . . . except more covertly."[92] Such "respectable men edge[d] up to [her] surreptitiously instead of staring openly" and donned "a veneer of courtly respectability."[93] And yet, the construction worker remained the easiest harasser for Bengis to pinpoint and denounce.

The trope of the catcalling construction worker remained a mainstay of discussions of street harassment long after the publication of Bengis's book. Feminist writers and activists often called out construction workers as especially problematic when it came to street harassment. In Meredith Tax's *Woman and Her Mind*, a pivotal scene revolved around a "walking-down-the-street scenario" in which a young woman had to pass a line of construction workers having lunch "in a line along the pavement." The physical "revulsion" and "terror" she felt were meant to demonstrate the impact of harassment and intimidation that women experienced on the street every day.[94] Popular media picked up on the trope quickly. As early as 1970, *Cosmopolitan* described the "construction site" as the "*classic* milieu" for what the magazine termed "street compliments." The piece tried to convince women they should embrace comments on the street from strangers. Only a stranger could give a truly unbiased compliment, argued author Veronica Geng. But the description of construction workers "on their lunch hour, sitting in a row, forming a kind of gauntlet of inspection to be run by female passersby" more closely resembled how feminists like Tax (or antimashing activists, for that matter) talked about stranger intrusions.[95] When anthropologist Micaela di Leonardo published a political theory of street harassment eleven years later, the trope was still intact. Leonardo cited an acquaintance who "ran an informal test" to determine what kinds of facial expressions and postures drew the most harassment from men on the street. The experimenter chose to run the test at a construction site, betraying an assumption that construction workers were the kind of men who could be counted on to harass a woman on the street.[96]

The anti–construction worker stance of much feminist street harassment literature reflected larger tensions between working-class white men and middle-class American liberal youth. As the 1960s faded into the 1970s, the building trade unions—which, due to decades of racist policies and discrimination against Black workers, were overwhelmingly white—expressed increasingly pro–Vietnam War and pro-Nixon stances in the face of a growing antiwar movement.[97] On May 8, 1970, construction workers and antiwar protesters clashed in the streets of New York City. The so-called Hard Hat Riot was a visible and violent manifestation of the tensions between the student and radical youth movements and Nixon's Silent Majority.[98] Such clashes were not confined to federal policy in Southeast Asia but extended to the sexual culture at home as well. One month after the Hard Hat Riot, in June 1970, the aforementioned "First Official Ladies Floating High Tea, Picnic Lunch, and Ogle" took place at Fifty-Seventh Street and Park Avenue. Perhaps inspired by Karla Jay's Ogle-In of a few months earlier, the event included street theater where women played the parts of both harasser and harassed, catcalling and ogling one another. Unlike Jay's critique of leering Wall Street white-collar workers, however, organizers directed this demonstration at construction workers in an attempt to "give the Great White American Hardhat a taste of his own chauvinism."One woman "pinched the protruding fanny of a construction worker" who was in the vicinity of the performance. In response, the worker hit her.[99]

All of this raises a few questions: Did men of different class positions indeed practice different kinds of intrusive behaviors, or did women's liberationists simply perceive that they did? Were middle-class white men's intrusive behaviors more surreptitious because they were different, quieter behaviors, or did their social position shield them and make the same behaviors harder to identify when practiced by middle-class men rather than by working-class men?

The "Great White American Hardhat" chauvinism was no doubt partly stereotype; however, the stereotype emerged in a cultural and material context that may, in fact, have made construction projects the sites of particularly obtrusive street harassment. As auto factory and assembly-line work declined in the 1960s and 1970s, construction workers became the most visible blue-collar workers and increasingly served as the "archetypical proletarian" in the popular imaginary. Hard-hat culture, notes historian Joshua Freeman, became self-consciously antibourgeois in a way that emphasized a "desire to shock" middle-class sensibilities. This led to a highly (hetero)sexualized work culture that included frequent discussion of sexual matters and sexually explicit slang for common workplace activities (for instance, a very small length of measurement was said to be a "cunt hair"). At the same time, the inherent danger of construction work required workers to establish strong, trusting bonds quickly or else risk bodily harm. The exchange of pornography or a shared experience of whistling at a passing woman became an easy way to build a tight-knit, overtly male community that relied on close bonds for physical safety.[100] Sociologists Cheryl Benard and Edit Schlaffer alluded to the sexual culture of construction sites and the growing resentment between working-class white men and affluent youths in an early study of street harassment, suggesting that working-class men like "construction workers" intentionally harassed "well-dressed, middle-class women" because of the "snobbish privileged class she symbolizes to them."[101]

The physical space of construction sites—closed off to passersby but in full view of streets and sidewalks—may have encouraged the catcalls and ogles that many feminists defined as the construction worker's stock-in-trade. Like men in cars, construction workers could (and still can) leer, whistle, and catcall from "within a zone of psychological and physical safety."[102] The fixed nature of construction sites also made them easy targets for feminists. It was far simpler to critique a confined urban space as a hub of stranger intrusions than to try to give shape and definition to the endless stream of male passersby who ogled or catcalled and then disappeared around a corner. Construction sites were thus a perfect storm of a hypersexualized masculine work culture, bubbling class resentment, and fixed (but protected) physical space that may, indeed, have made them hotbeds of a particularly obnoxious form of stranger intrusions.

While feminists' fixation on the catcalling hard hat may have reflected the peculiar obtrusiveness of construction workers' intrusions, it also suggests the staying power of girl-watching's rules of self-restraint and gentility. Just as working-class men distinguished themselves from middle-class and elite men through sexual boasting and the objectification of women, middle- and upper-class men, according to sociologist Karen D. Pyke, defined themselves in opposition to working-class masculinity by displaying a self-conscious restraint and "civilized demeanor of polite gentility" through to the end of the century.[103] In a practical sense, the "disguise" of furtive girl-watching that middle-class men honed in the 1950s may have made their intrusions more difficult for middle-class white women to see and experience as negative. The shouts and whistles lobbed from construction sites would have been hard to miss by comparison.

While middle-class white women held no love for the more subtle intrusions of middle-class men, some admitted they preferred middle-class subtlety over the louder, more sexually explicit behaviors assumed to be the purview of construction workers and men of color. For example, Ingrid Bengis had described with distaste the "sidling up" of "respectable" middle-class men, but she reserved her fantasies of violent revenge for construction workers. Gwenda Linda Blair explained that she felt less tense and on edge when "hippy-types or middle-class professionals" approached her on the street compared with working-class men and men of color. Of middle-class white men, Blair wrote, "I know that they will be judging me, but they won't take over all the space available—they're not so clearly threatening me.... Their less obnoxious approach may be the more insidious, but at least it allows me to get from one place to another without having to use up all my emotional energy surviving another 'Would I like to fuck you, baby.'" Thus the insidious "judging" from men of Blair's racial and class group was not as destabilizing, or frightening, as the sexually explicit obscenities she implied were common from working-class men and men of color.[104]

As the construction worker became a frequent scapegoat for street harassment, some women with a keen awareness of class inequality spoke out about what they saw as classism in anti–street harassment and antiviolence activism. In 1972, the Rape Crisis Center Collective in Washington, DC, cautioned readers of *Women: A Journal of Liberation* to question sexual violence statistics that implied "that only lower class men rape." In fact, the center insisted, "while middle and upper class men rape, these rapes are infrequently reported and very rarely result in convictions due to the man's increased power and status in society."[105] While the collective's critique was focused on feminists' antirape activism, the way feminists linked stranger intrusions with rape made the critique equally relevant to anti–street harassment activism. A year earlier, Ida Monico-Lemay called out her fellow members in the New York Radical Feminists for "closing in on the wrong target" in their conversations about what was known at the time as the "verbal rapist." At a consciousness-raising discussion of the verbal rapist, Monico-Lemay described how participants "narrow[ed] their attack to the . . . working class." Disheartened, she wrote to the group's newsletter to ask, "Why was the obsequious middle class with its impotent intellectuals, its Madison Avenue creators of the 'beautiful piece of ass' image being ignored?"[106] Indeed, though Monico-Lemay could have participated in Karla Jay's Ogle-In targeting the besuited men of Wall Street just a year earlier, few anti–street harassment actions would explicitly call out white-collar or professional men for the remainder of the decade. By the time Monico-Lemay wrote her letter in September 1971, working-class men, and especially the ubiquitous construction worker, were already dominating conversations of street harassment.

Despite cautions from class-conscious organizations and individuals, the trope of the catcalling construction worker proved resilient, particularly in mainstream media. By the 1980s, major national newspapers often illustrated articles about street harassment with images of construction workers or published pieces that conflated construction workers with all harassers.[107] Even if the construction worker himself was not a target, working-class men remained the most obvious harassers for many. In one telling example, women who wrote to the *Washington Post* to tell their stories of street harassment mentioned harassment only from men in blue-collar or traditionally "unskilled" jobs: a garage attendant, a delivery person, and of course a construction worker.[108] Even as organized responses to street harassment waned, the stereotype of the catcalling construction worker would hold on.

Street Harassment in a Time of Backlash

When Ida Monico-Lemay complained to the New York Radical Feminists that members were too focused on working-class men in discussions of street harassment, she also foreshadowed some of the reasons why anti–street harassment activism waned. While Monico-Lemay recounted how "sexual advances" on the street had made her fearful of going out alone in her youth, she argued that feminists had more important issues to address. Namely, Monico-Lemay urged her fellow feminists to focus their attention on deconstructing the nuclear family, tearing down institutions that sexualized women, and eliminating "marriage," "racism," and "religions." For Monico-Lemay, catcalls were simply one small manifestation of a vast solar system of sexist ideology that permeated society.[109] Over time, the women's liberation movement began to coalesce in agreement with Monico-Lemay's critique that a focus on catcalls and wolf whistles took energy away from bigger fights. They shifted their attention to research and legal reform aimed at combating more extreme forms of sexual violence and abuse, particularly rape and intimate partner violence.[110] Thus, antirape activists, who had argued that men's stranger intrusions kept women in fear of rape, did not, in the end, focus their efforts on eradicating such intrusions. Sexual violence activists likely concluded that if they eliminated the extreme acts on the end of the spectrum of sexual violence, then the acts on the other end of the spectrum, such as street harassment, would fall soon after.

In part because of this shift in priorities, anti–street harassment activists noticed slowing interest in their actions by the mid-1970s. In January 1975, for instance, the New York Radical Feminists' Street Harassment Committee reported it was struggling to recruit new members. Though street harassment remained a "vital and exigent topic, women did not respond by coming to organize." A few months later, the committee announced it was going "underground."[111] Its last hurrah, the Campaign Against Street Harassment (or CASH), encouraged members to inform on businesses where male employees had harassed women. The committee would then send letters to such businesses that read, in part, "Please be advised that a male employee of yours harassed me today on the street.... This behavior is not complimentary to me or any other woman; it is, in fact, contemptuous and insulting." Businesses like the famous Zabar's deli in Manhattan made it onto the feminist blacklist, and the New York Radical Feminists encouraged members to apply pressure via a boycott.[112] By the late 1970s, street harassment was a part of other feminist campaigns but was rarely the primary target of activism. For instance, when Minneapolis women protested the proliferation of pornographic bookstores and theaters on the major thoroughfare of Lake Street in the early 1980s, they pointed to the increase in street harassment as one side effect of so many adult businesses. However, organizing was focused on ousting adult businesses from the area rather than eradicating street harassment per se.[113]

In the 1980s, street harassment activism would have to deal with the larger backlash against feminism that was a feature of the Reagan era. Feminists continued their work, particularly in the realm of antiviolence organizing, but they had to work harder to justify their goals. The mainstream cultural landscape was flooded with an onslaught of messages that suggested feminists had robbed women of the supposed protections of patriarchy, sending them out into the world without the skills or knowledge to succeed or stay safe. Such messages cast women as primarily responsible for their own safety. Law enforcement and rape crisis centers continued to publish self-defense literature but emphasized avoidance over physical strength or confrontation. The right precautions, the logic went, would keep any woman safe from would-be rapists or muggers in public space. In fact, staying home might be the safest option of all. In such a climate, discussions of street harassment turned away from systemic solutions and toward individualized responses.[114] Gone were the calls for antirape squads that would intimidate harassers or for mimeographed anti–street harassment cards that women could hand to catcallers. Women were expected to focus on protecting their own bodies and not channel their frustrations toward organized responses to street harassment.

In the increasingly conservative 1980s, self-proclaimed feminists also began to talk about street harassment in ways that trivialized stranger intrusions. In 1981, for example, when Lindsy Van Gelder published a piece in *Ms.* magazine about her experiences of street harassment while traveling abroad, many women wrote in to describe their own experiences of harassment, but many also suggested that Van Gelder was overstating the problem.[115] One reader was incredulous that intrusive behaviors were worth addressing. As she put it, "The hassler's words (and even grabs) aren't lethal—merely stupid and repulsive," adding, "What *is* the big deal?" She also admitted (or lamented) that she had "never been whistled at, pinched, or grabbed—at home or abroad—even when she wanted to be (yes, there have been such times)."[116] Another reader, who described herself as a forty-eight-year-old psychologist, also explained she was rarely harassed. She wondered whether other women acted in ways that encouraged or discouraged harassment. "Could it be," she asked, "that women who expect to be harassed send out some *unconscious* messages that tell the men around them that they are vulnerable? And could it be that those of us who don't expect to be harassed and/or couldn't care less, just send out the message, don't try it, you don't make an impression anyway?"[117] This critique exemplified the internalizing of 1980s antifeminist discourse that Susan Faludi would target in her 1991 book, *Backlash*. Faludi argued that the counterinsurgency against feminism "is most powerful" when it "lodges inside a woman's mind and turns her vision inward, until she imagines the pressure is all in her head, until she begins to enforce the backlash, too—on herself."[118] In some cases, feminists were already enforcing the backlash against each other in the early 1980s.

The one exception to the diminished interest in street harassment activism was the short-lived "hassle-free zone" movement in Washington, DC. In 1985, Nkenge Touré—at the time the director of community education at the DC Rape Crisis Center—organized a series of events and workshops on street harassment during the city's annual Anti-Rape Week. Touré created DC's Anti-Rape Week in 1979 to raise awareness of sexual violence in the city. As early as 1981, the event culminated with a "Take Back the Night" march that meandered through DuPont Circle, an area notorious for street harassment.[119] By 1985, Anti-Rape Week organizers included a range of programming specifically targeting street harassment. Though the DC Rape Crisis Center explicitly centered the experiences of women of color and intentionally hired women of color on their staff, their conversations with the press tended to elide the antiracist nature of their work. Touré, who had been a member of the Black Panthers in the 1960s, described street harassment as a problem all women face.[120] She told the *Washington Post*, "Women's human rights are being violated when we are denied the right to walk down the street or sit in the park or ride the bus or run in the park or drive our cars without being verbally raped and verbally molested by disrespectful men and boys."[121] The DC Rape Crisis Center director, Cecily M. Robbins, echoed earlier feminist analyses of street harassment when she told the *Post* that men use intrusive behaviors as "tests to see how much they can intimidate a woman or mark her for a potential assault victim."[122]

The following year, the DC Rape Crisis Center and a group of other feminist and antiviolence organizations formed the new Coalition for a Hassle Free Zone to continue the work of combating street harassment.[123] However, like the larger feminist antiviolence movement, the coalition increasingly focused on individualized responses rather than systemic change. In fact sheets and workshops on "confrontation," the coalition encouraged targets of harassment to talk back to harassers. One pamphlet suggested, "Name the behavior of the harasser clearly: 'That's harassment,'" or, "Demand that the behavior stop." Confronting a harasser directly was the best way to combat street harassment, according to the coalition, because it helped the individual woman feel strong and "self-respecting" but also upset the usual power dynamic between men and women on the street. This advice validated women's experiences—"His harassment of you is the problem, not your response," reassured one fact sheet—but the tactic of speaking directly to a harasser was fundamentally an individual, one-on-one response to a widespread social and cultural phenomenon.[124] Perhaps because of the challenge of combating a systemic problem with individual responses, the DC Rape Crisis Center appears to have moved on from its Coalition for a Hassle Free Zone by the end of the 1980s and refocused on serving victims of rape and sexual assault.

THOUGH MEN'S intrusive behaviors ceased to be a major target for sustained feminist organizing in the 1980s, feminists' activism and analyses of street harassment continued to influence how Americans thought about stranger intrusions for decades. While many Americans were still incredulous that something like a catcall or wolf whistle could be harmful, feminists' efforts to denaturalize street harassment introduced a strong counternarrative to the kinds of trivializing rhetoric that had defined girl-watching. Feminist publications, as well as the occasional national women's magazine or newspaper, issued stories about the harmful effects of street harassment into the 1990s.[125] While advice on combating street harassment continued to emphasize avoidance or one-on-one confrontation rather than systemic solutions, the idea that women did not enjoy men's stranger intrusions was no longer beyond the pale.

At the same time, both feminist and mainstream writing on street harassment continued to perpetuate the idea that street harassers were mostly construction workers. Much of the mainstream reporting on street harassment fully embraced the trope of the catcalling construction worker, perhaps the most widespread legacy of 1970s feminist writing on street harassment. Even if an article was not specifically about the problem of "hard hats," newspapers and magazines often illustrated their street harassment pieces with photographs or drawings of construction workers ogling women.[126] In the 1990s, mainstream media often conflated construction workers with catcallers and delighted in pitting white-collar female office workers against blue-collar, wolf-whistling hard hats in a class-tinged battle of the sexes.[127]

Feminists also continued to grapple with the racial politics of street harassment discourses long after Susan Brownmiller sparred with Angela Davis and Anne Braden over the meaning of Emmett Till's murder. In a few notable examples, feminists tried to dispel the myth that men of color were more likely to catcall than white men. When cultural anthropologist Micaela di Leonardo wrote an oft-cited theory of the "political economy of street harassment" in *Aegis* magazine in 1981, she cautioned readers to question the stereotypes they might have heard about street harassment. "We especially need to confront the myth that street harassment occurs only between white women and black men," she wrote. Leonardo suggested that this myth was linked to a similar "fallacy" in the way feminists discussed rape: the "underlying assumption" that "only black men rape, and that black women are never raped." To combat this myth, Leonardo insisted she had been "harassed by men of all races and ages" and had "observed many black women being harassed."[128] The DC Coalition for a Hassle Free Zone similarly tried to spread the message that, while street harassment was "almost exclusively perpetrated by men," those men could be "of all different backgrounds; middle class, working class, young boys through to old men; black, white, latino, asian, single and married."[129] Still, this did not stop the *Washington Post* from illustrating an article on the coalition with a drawing of construction workers, including a Black man, leering at a passing white woman.[130]

Feminists' attempts to denaturalize men's stranger intrusions thus had mixed results. On the one hand, feminists made strong arguments for why street harassment should be viewed as part of a continuum of sexual violence that included rape on its extreme end. Stories of intrusive behaviors making women feel objectified, violated, or endangered shifted the mainstream discourse around street harassment. While trivializing discourses did not disappear, by the 1980s they existed alongside a counternarrative that cast street harassment as harmful behaviors that impinged on women's freedom of mobility. On the other hand, the mostly middle-class white feminists who dominated discussions of street harassment failed to denaturalize stranger intrusions from men of their own racial and class categories. Instead, they reified existing stereotypes of sexually predatory men of color or uncouth, oversexed working-class white men. Feminists' focus on construction workers and "urban strangers" left middle-class white men relatively unscathed in anti–street harassment activism and rhetoric. "Street harassment" as a concept may have helped increase awareness of the effects of men's stranger intrusions, but it left intact the assumption that middle-class white men's looks and comments were surreptitious, unobtrusive, and thus normal or trivial. The normalization of intrusive practices as part of hegemonic masculinity thus remained largely untouched.

EPILOGUE

On October 28, 2014, the anti–street harassment organization Hollaback! published a video on YouTube that was intended to raise awareness of the ubiquity of street harassment. The short film, titled *10 Hours of Walking in NYC as a Woman*, featured actress Shoshana Roberts walking through the streets of New York. The videographer walked ahead of Roberts, a camera on his backpack, capturing all the men who approached her on the street. The film opened with a caption reading, "Ten hours of silent walking through all areas of Manhattan, wearing jeans and a crewneck t-shirt." The caption worked to dispel any suspicion that Roberts was inviting intrusions, implying that her silence and conservative clothing made her an innocent victim. The rest of the video showed men whistling, staring, and propositioning Roberts. One man walked shoulder-to-shoulder alongside Roberts for several minutes without saying a word. The final caption explained that, in the ten hours it took to record the video, Roberts received "100+ instances of verbal harassment" from "people of all backgrounds," not including "countless winks, whistles, etc." The film left a lasting impression of an onslaught of men's stranger intrusions that punctuated Roberts's silent walk through the city.[1]

The video was hugely popular, garnering tens of millions of views and a slew of copycat videos, both serious and comic.[2] Some praised the video for its depiction of what many saw as the ever-present threat of street harassment, including calling for the criminalization of such behaviors.[3] To this day, viewers leave comments on the YouTube video describing their own experiences of street harassment and admonishing the men in the video for bothering Roberts.

However, the video also came under fire for its skewed depiction of street harassment as primarily perpetrated by men of color. The majority of the men featured in the video were Black and Latino, despite the director's protestations that Roberts, a Jewish woman, had been harassed by men of many races and ethnicities. Hanna Rosin, a writer at *Slate*, argued that the video had effectively portrayed the onslaught of harassment women often face in public space but "unintentionally [made] another point: that harassers are mostly Black and

Latino, and hanging out on the streets in midday in clothes that suggest they are not on their lunch break" and thus not gainfully employed. Author Roxane Gay put it more bluntly, posting on Twitter, "The racial politics of the video are fucked up. Like, she didn't walk through any white neighborhoods?" Both the video's director and Hollaback! later issued statements in response to the critiques.[4]

The criticism of the *10 Hours* video brought into sharp relief not only the way men's stranger intrusions remain contested in the twenty-first century but also how middle-class white men continue to fly under the radar when it comes to stranger intrusions and sexual harassment. Dee Lockett, a self-described biracial woman of color and a writer at *Slate*, responded to Rosin's initial critiques by suggesting that, in fact, white men harass and intimidate women in less visible, loud, or easily identifiable ways than men of color. She quoted the film's director, Rob Bliss, who claimed that white men did harass Roberts on the street but "for whatever reason, a lot of what they said was in passing or off camera." The reason, Lockett argued, is that loud, visible forms of street harassment—shouts of "Sexy" or kissing noises, for instance—are a way of asserting power and dominance in public space, something men of color are often trying to do. White men, on the other hand, are already dominant, so "their sexual harassment is less invasive ('in passing,' as Bliss puts it) and harder to recognize." Instead, white men sexualize women in "boardrooms" or on "frat row" or in "other places men of color are never privy to, at least not in positions of power."[5] Just as Ingrid Bengis struggled to articulate the surreptitious, unsettling condescension and sexualization of middle-class white men in the 1970s, Lockett described a culture in 2014 where white men *did* perpetrate stranger intrusions, but their intrusions were quieter and insidious, hidden in plain sight. How much, then, had mainstream discourses of men's stranger intrusions changed since the 1970s and 1980s?

One thing that had changed since the 1970s was the media landscape. The ability to easily view, share, and debate the *10 Hours* YouTube video was a product of the internet age, as was the very existence of the organization Hollaback! The increased accessibility of the internet had fueled a resurgence in anti–street harassment activism in the previous decade. Hollaback! was founded in 2005 by a mixed-gender group of New Yorkers who wanted to use an online blog format to collect stories of street harassment in New York City. Targets of street harassment could log onto the group's website, write and upload their stories, and even pin them to a digital map. Hollaback! chapters soon sprang up across the United States and internationally.[6] Eventually, the organization developed a smartphone app so people could document their experiences while on the street itself.[7] The vast database of stories on the website inspired conversations about anti–street harassment legislation, and academics mined the data for research.[8]

The internet also helped spur more widespread awareness of other forms of normalized gendered harassment and sexual violence. In 2012, British feminist Laura Bates launched the Everyday Sexism Project, a website where people could share "instances of sexism experienced on a day to day basis." Bates explained she hoped to highlight "serious or minor, outrageously offensive or so niggling and normalised" instances of sexism to demonstrate how often women regularly dealt with sexist behaviors of all kinds.[9] Five years later, the revived #MeToo movement exploded onto social media platforms, bringing more focused attention to workplace sexual harassment. #MeToo began as a MySpace post created by activist Tarana Burke in 2006 as part of her work with Black women and girls who had survived sexual violence. It resurfaced with renewed fervor in 2017 in the wake of several high-profile sexual assault allegations against powerful men, including Harvey Weinstein and Donald Trump.[10]

The 2010s revival of anti–street harassment activism came after several decades of relative quiet on the subject within feminist circles. The 1990s had seen a few magazine articles or alternative zines addressing catcalling and street harassment.[11] In 1998, feminist filmmaker Maggie Hadleigh-West produced *War Zone*, a half-hour film about "sex, power and what happens when men—either knowingly or unknowingly—threaten a woman's right to walk undisturbed on the streets." In the film, Hadleigh-West "turns her camera on men in the same way that they turn their aggression on her."[12] By and large, however, the 1980s and 1990s saw feminist activists zero in on rape and intimate partner violence as the most pressing concerns in their fight to end violence against women, and interest in stranger intrusions shifted to the realm of academia.

The 1990s saw a slew of academic studies that focused on the impact of harassment on women's sense of safety or fear in public spaces.[13] Sociologists, anthropologists, and psychologists asked what impact street harassment had on women's lives, how the existence of intrusive behaviors might account for the documented discrepancies in men's and women's fear of crime in public places, and why street harassment remained a relatively understudied phenomenon.[14] Legal scholars debated the best legislation for protecting women from harassment in public, what behaviors counted as harassment under the law, and whether the First Amendment protects behaviors like catcalling. Legal scholars also argued that men's stranger intrusions curtailed women's freedom of movement and thus limited their civil liberties.[15]

In the wake of these studies, scholars turned to interviews and observations to back up the claims in more theoretical or philosophical research. In 1995, sociologist Carol Brooks Gardner published *Passing By*, a study of street harassment in Indianapolis, which drew on almost five hundred interviews with women who experienced street harassment and men who harassed. Gardner's work was hugely influential for the way it showed how scholars could use interviews to understand the nature and impact of street harassment and for its application of theoretical work not previously associated with street harassment. Namely, Gardner drew on Erving Goffman's theory of "civil inattention," the idea that strangers navigating public space tend to afford one another privacy by presuming to ignore one another.[16] Gardner argued that women are not afforded the same right to civil inattention that men enjoy, making them what Goffman calls "open persons," or those whom it is socially acceptable to observe, speak to, or otherwise approach at any point.[17] Gardner's work inspired scholars to seek out more case studies of actual street harassment experiences and to look to existing theories of public space and stranger interactions to bolster their analyses.[18]

With the revived awareness of the prevalence and impact of sexual harassment that came with #MeToo, street harassment activists and researchers took the opportunity to shine a brighter spotlight on men's stranger intrusions, and both activism and research on street harassment have increased in recent years. In part thanks to activists' efforts, France, Portugal, and the United Kingdom all criminalized some form of street harassment after 2017, leading to renewed debate among American activists about the efficacy of such laws.[19] Robust anti–street harassment movements in Mexico and India have received more attention as the general awareness of street harassment has grown.[20] Research on street harassment has also ballooned after #MeToo, particularly in the fields of sociology and psychology.[21] In 2019, for instance, the organization Stop Street Harassment partnered with the University of California San Diego Center on Gender Equity and Health to conduct a study on the prevalence and impact of sexual harassment on the lives of Americans. The study was one of several that emerged in direct response to the #MeToo movement and highlighted public places as the most common locations for sexual harassment.[22]

The normalization and trivialization of sexual harassment has become one of the defining features of recent research, including research that is not necessarily focused on public space. For instance, a groundbreaking 2018 report released by the National Academies of Sciences, Engineering, and Medicine argued that the most common forms of sexual harassment, which the report argues would be better described as "gender harassment," are behaviors that are generally not taken seriously or are dismissed as not true harassment. Gender harassment includes a wide range of verbal and nonverbal behaviors that convey hostility, objectification, exclusion, or second-class status based on someone's gender or gender expression. That can mean anything from demeaning remarks about one's body to the use of sexist slurs or, in a workplace context, sabotaging someone's work or equipment.[23] Importantly, the National Academies study found that most Americans are far less aware of gender harassment than they are of rarer behaviors like sexual coercion or rape, not least because of the media attention on extreme or aberrant crimes committed by perpetrators like Harvey Weinstein. The report's authors described how mainstream discussions of sexual harassment focus on the extreme tip of the "iceberg," leaving hidden the vast depths of gender harassment beneath. Thus, the legal system, the lay public, and even people who experience sexual harassment do not tend to view gender harassment as part of the range of behaviors that count as harassment.[24]

To study men's stranger intrusions is to study this very problem. The masher, the girl-watcher, the catcalling construction worker: They do not live on the tip of this iceberg; they live beneath the surface. The most common forms of street harassment are forms of gender harassment—catcalling, ogling, or staring, perhaps a man standing just a little too close on the subway. Like the Progressive Era reformers who worried that "the masher and the murderer . . . belong to the same species" or the 1970s feminists who warned that street harassment "is one of the ways in which women are *prepared* to be victims" of rape, the 2018 National Academies study found that the acceptance of seemingly lesser forms of harassment makes more severe forms appear normal or acceptable.[25] When institutions fail to address the less extreme and more normalized behaviors that constitute gender harassment, they create an environment where more extreme behaviors like unwanted sexual attention and sexual coercion are more likely to occur.[26]

Despite feminists' best efforts, men's stranger intrusions are still regularly viewed as trivial, as not worthy of serious attention, or even as compliments. A few months before Hollaback! released the *10 Hours* video, for instance, *New York Post* reporter Doree Lewak wrote an opinion piece in which she claimed to enjoy being catcalled and was happy to be "that objectified sex thing for" the "hard hats" she encountered on the street. The article included photographs of Lewak posing with construction workers on the streets of New York.[27] In response to the article, Fox News host Kimberly Guilfoyle defended street harassment, saying, "Let men be men. . . . Look, men are going to be that way. What can you do?" One of Guilfoyle's cohosts explained that she did not like catcalls as a young woman, but now that she was approaching middle age, she was offended if she did not hear them.[28] Two months later, on *CBS This Morning*, Gayle King responded skeptically to the *10 Hours* video, insisting she would not "get upset because somebody said, hey, girl, you look good today" but would instead "twirl and say thank you."[29]

More recently, it remains alarmingly easy to find examples of Americans dismissing men's stranger intrusions as trivial or complimentary, especially on social media and online forums. In 2017, anthropologist and communications scholar Benjamin Bailey found that people who commented on the *10 Hours* YouTube video defended the remarks in the film "as civil talk, highlighting the literal meanings of remarks such as 'Have a nice evening'" rather than interpreting them as uninvited intrusions on a woman's mental and physical autonomy.[30] In college and high school newspapers, where young writers are often confronting for the first time the beliefs with which they grew up, women and LGTBQ+ students frequently express their dismay that friends and family dismiss their experiences of street harassment as harmless.[31] In 2023, comedian Benedict Polizzi had a moment of viral fame with the "polite catcalling" videos he shared on social media. In the films, Polizzi used a megaphone to shout at strangers of all genders as they passed by. However, rather than the predictable sexualized comments, he yelled things like, "You look like you know how to fold a fitted sheet," or, "You look like you clean the stove after you cook." While many found his "polite" intrusions amusing, others questioned whether it was ever appropriate to shout comments at strangers. As one woman told a blogger, men should never yell at strangers, no matter how polite they think they are: "It's a wholly unpleasant experience and really what they actually say to me has no bearings on the feeling of panic and vulnerability the experience causes."[32]

On the other hand, as the mixed reactions to Polizzi's videos suggest, once the women's liberation movement identified "street harassment" as a symptom of a sexist society, this analysis remained a persistent thread in mainstream discussion of men's stranger intrusions. Whereas the antimashing activism of the Progressive Era buckled under the weight of trivializing rhetoric and arguments that "liberated" women did not require protection from the odd ogle, 1970s feminists' analysis of men's stranger intrusions as harmful, embarrassing, and frightening survived a variety of ebbs, flows, and backlashes. Women continued to debate the meaning of these behaviors, and, as Gayle King and Kimberly Guilfoyle can attest, some women still insist they enjoy these behaviors into the present. Yet both the term "street harassment" and the analysis it implies—that intrusive behaviors in public are harmful and not desirable—never disappeared once feminists introduced them in the mid-1970s.

While feminist scholarship and activism have given us a fuller and more nuanced understanding of men's stranger intrusions, there remains surprisingly little research on men who perpetrate stranger intrusions. Most research continues to focus on targets' perceptions of intrusive behaviors and the impact these behaviors have on targets, perhaps in part because of the persistent need to prove that the problem is real and significant in the face of trivializing narratives.[33] There are a few exceptions. Beth Quinn has been widely cited for her analysis of how men use "girl-watching" as a way to "build shared masculine identities."[34] Psychologists Kari A. Walton and Cory L. Pedersen have found that men who "catcall" believe the behavior is a way to "flirt and express sexual interest" and that catcallers often expect women to respond with "friendliness."[35] Several studies have found that targets of street harassment often perceive already marginalized or othered men as more likely to harass or as more dangerous harassers.[36] Still, there remains a dearth of analysis of men's motivations for engaging in stranger intrusions.[37] Thus, while academics, activists, and popular writers have produced ample evidence that men's stranger intrusions harm targets, the role of men in perpetrating intrusive behaviors remains opaque and plagued by racist and classist stereotypes, as the Hollaback! video showed.

The stakes are high when it comes to understanding, denaturalizing, condemning, and eradicating men's stranger intrusions without scapegoating marginalized men. When twenty-two-year-old Elliot Rodger killed six people and injured fourteen in Isla Vista, California, on May 23, 2014, it quickly became clear that Rodger was motivated by a feeling of entitlement over women's bodies that mirrors the entitlement inherent in men's stranger intrusions. In a lengthy manifesto, Rodger claimed his violent rampage was fueled by his hatred of women who would not have sex with him. Feminist writers saw Rodger's actions as a symptom of a wider culture of misogyny and male entitlement that views women as objects who exist purely to fulfill men's needs. They pointed out that Rodger believed women owed him sex and thus, if he did not receive it, they deserved violent punishment.[38] Philosopher Kate Manne linked Rodger's anger at women to men's stranger intrusions. So-called incels, the online subculture of "involuntarily celibate" men (such as Rodger), feel they have been unfairly denied sex that women owe to them. Manne argues this sense of injustice positions women as "human *givers* in moral and social life."[39] If women are perceived as not giving their time, care, attention, and bodies to men who feel entitled to them, Manne warns that "we . . . see symptoms of deprivation mindset" spill out into the public sphere.[40] Rodger's rampage in Isla Vista is one example. Street harassment is another.

Men's stranger intrusions, like all forms of gender harassment, legitimate the widespread feeling that women exist *for* men. When it is seen as normal and natural for men to barrage women with demands for their attention through verbal remarks, staring, and physical touch, the incel's demand for sex is not so out of place. In both cases, men feel entitled to something women can give them, and they exhibit anger and violence when it is denied. Just ask Ruth George, the nineteen-year-old college student who ignored the man catcalling her on the campus of the University of Illinois at Chicago in 2019. Enraged, the man followed her into a parking garage and strangled her to death.[41]

Historically, of course, the story of men's entitlement over women's bodies has been complicated by the uneven embrace of men's stranger intrusions. Neither George's murderer, Donald Thurman, nor Rodger were white. This makes their entitlement no less real, but it does make it less firm, less obvious, less seemingly natural. On some level, Rodger knew this. Before going on his killing spree, Rodger wrote in online forums that he felt socially inferior because he was half Malaysian and suggested his racial identity was partly to blame for his continued celibacy.[42] Just as a culture of misogyny convinced Rodger that women had a duty to give men sex, a culture of white supremacy convinced him that only the most privileged, elite white men could stake their claim to the most socially privileged women. Activists are equally aware of these dynamics and the unlikelihood that white men in positions of power can be held accountable by anti–street harassment legislation. Indeed, in the wake of Black Lives Matter and anti-incarceration movements, many feminist organizations now oppose criminalization as a remedy for street harassment. Hollaback!, which now goes by the name Right to Be, explains on its website that victims of harassment tend to feel unsafe dealing with police after an incident, and criminalization often leads to disproportionate surveillance, arrest, and incarceration of people of color.[43] The continued association of street harassment with men of color and construction workers, while middle-class white men's intrusions are deemed trivial or complimentary, all but ensures that law enforcement would disproportionately target marginalized men were anti–street harassment laws enacted in the United States.

Eradicating men's stranger intrusions is thus not an easy task. The acceptance of middle-class white men's stranger intrusions as normal or mundane legitimates patriarchy and white supremacy. It enshrines entitlement over women's bodies as an aspect of hegemonic masculinity, as something men should aspire to. It is implicated in the incel ideology that has now fueled multiple mass killings. It scapegoats men of color and working-class men for street harassment, ensuring that marginalized men are the most likely to be accused of and punished for intrusive behaviors. Combating men's stranger intrusions requires widespread cultural change, a shift in our "commonsense" beliefs. It requires condemnation of even the seemingly polite, unobtrusive stranger intrusions of middle-class white men, so we can see them for the displays of entitlement over women's time, attention, and bodies that they are. Rape and sexual violence remain rampant and poorly addressed in part because we continue to dismiss and trivialize the everyday violence epitomized in street harassment. Denaturalizing and condemning *all* men's stranger intrusions thus not only helps eradicate other, more extreme forms of sexual and physical violence but is a necessary precursor.

As I write the final sentences of this book, I keep returning to the many calls to action I've encountered from feminists and women's rights activists of the past. I am particularly struck by the words of feminist writer Liz Elling, who, in condemning girl-watching in 1972, suggested that the end of street harassment would require "changing times . . . future generations . . . little boys who know when to grow up."[44] Her prescription, in some ways, matches my own. That is, men's stranger intrusions require long-term cultural shifts. And yet, Elling wrote those words over one hundred years after the first street insults punctuated a woman's foray into public space, and fifty-some more years have now passed. "Changing times" and "future generations" have not brought about an end to men's intrusive behaviors. "Little boys" have not all learned "when to grow up." The ambiguous ellipses in Elling's words suggest that even she was unsure that the onward march of time would be enough to bring about the world she hoped to see. What would she have thought if she had known that women like her had already tried to eradicate street harassment in earlier decades and that their efforts had been largely forgotten by 1972? It is tempting to believe that progress is inevitable, that we need only sit and wait for a safer and more just world to emerge. As I write these words in the year of the United States' 250th anniversary, I know this is a comforting lie. Waiting does not make change happen. Only people can do that, if they resolve to.

ACKNOWLEDGMENTS

I TAKE GREAT PLEASURE in reading an author's acknowledgments and picturing the many communities that make research and writing possible. I hope my own meager contribution makes clear how many people helped bring this book into the world. And I hope they know how grateful I am without having to turn to these pages for confirmation.

So many mentors and cheerleaders have pushed me and challenged me throughout my career. Lynn Hudson started me off with encouragement, wisdom, and chocolate. I am honored to call her my mentor and, now, my friend. She and Jane Rhodes shaped the way I think about both US history and gender history from the start.

The guidance of Jay Cook, Kisha Simmons, Dean Hubbs, and Matt Lassiter has influenced every page of this project, from the earliest concept papers to the first passable manuscript draft. Jay is a generous champion of my work, always ready with thoughtful critiques and a heavy dollop of positive feedback. Kisha challenged me to be a better scholar in more ways than I can count. Dean helped me think about how my roles as an activist, a teacher, and a researcher are deeply intertwined. Matt always brought me back down to earth. From its beginning, Michelle McClellan encouraged me to pursue this project, which I thought might be impossible, and it's thanks to her that I kept going anyway.

I am indebted to the many archivists and librarians who helped me find references to catcalls and ogles in some of the unlikeliest of places. Special thanks go to Mary Biddle at Smith College, Kelly Wooten at the Sallie Bingham Center, and Linnea Anderson at the University of Minnesota. Cari Reynolds at the Jessie Ball duPont Library helped me secure images.

Thanks go to Andreína Fernandez at the University of North Carolina Press for believing in this project from the first moment I brought it to her, years before it was ready for publication. Thanks also go to two anonymous reviewers for their extremely constructive and generous feedback. I could not have asked for more engaged readers. Their efforts have made this book immeasurably stronger.

Sections of chapter 4 and the epilogue first appeared in an article in *Gender & History* in 2025. The anonymous readers who commented on that article inevitably improved the book manuscript, too.

This project would not have been possible without financial support from the University of the South; the Associated Colleges of the South; the University of Michigan's history department, Rackham Graduate School, Institute for Research on Women and Gender, and women's studies department; the Newberry Library Short-Term Fellowship from the Newberry Library in Chicago; the Margaret Storrs Grierson Fellowship from the Sophia Smith Collection at Smith College; and the Mary Lily Research Grant from the Sallie Bingham Center for Women's History and Culture at Duke University.

Many friends and colleagues, all brilliant thinkers, read portions of this work and helped make it stronger, namely Stacey Bishop (offering escapism and wisdom in equal measure), Hayley Bowman, Alex Clayton, John Finkelberg (a great listener and friend), Joseph Ho, D. Lawrence Hutchinson (who lit up a room), Katie Lennard, Rachel Miller (karaoke kween), Daniela Sheinin, Meg Showalter (the warmest Texan in Michigan), Taylor Sims, Jacques Vest, Matt Villeneuve (who still gets roped into reading my drafts), and Dalen Wakeley-Smith (Minnesotans unite).

Academia would be far lonelier and less interesting without the interlocutors we find in workshops and conferences. Thanks go to Nancy Chick, Chelsea Del Rio, Nicole Navarro, Severina Scott, Lucy Smith, and Marie Stango for leading some of the best writing workshops. Jennifer Alzate González, Traci Carson, Anne Clark, Steph Fajardo, Emily Gauld, Chelle Jones, Michelle May-Curry, Kamaria Porter, Zach Schudson, and Victor Mendoza provided revelatory feedback on chapter 3. Andrea Mansker and Kelly Whitmer helped me finally finish chapter 5. Thanks are also due the many incredible historians and feminist scholars who generously interacted with my work at conferences (and beyond), both in formal roles and in the coffee meetups that make conferences hum.

I could not have completed this project without the hard-won salary and health benefits secured by the Graduate Employees' Organization, AFT-MI Local 3550, AFL-CIO. Every worker, academic or otherwise, deserves a union as strong and democratic as GEO.

Baristas at coffee shops around the world—but especially in Ann Arbor, Chattanooga, and Minneapolis and Saint Paul—literally fueled this work. I would never have finished this book without these welcoming local businesses and their oft-underappreciated workers.

No work is worth doing without friends to pull you away from it. During this project's infancy, I fell in love with Michigan because of the friends I made there. In addition to those I've already named, I am continually delighted by my friendships with Luis Flores, Bri Gauger, Austin McCoy, Liz Ratzloff, Brett Smith, and Katie Wataha (the heart to my brain). Many have made my subsequent time in Tennessee beautiful and meaningful, including but not limited to Lisa Burner, Anthony M. Donaldson Jr., Kerry Ginger, Erik Gustafson, Brooks Mendenhall, Kylie Miller, Paige Schneider, and Leslie Todd. These and many other friends never failed to ask me about my work and lift my spirits when the going got tough. To those I have failed to name so I can stay within my word count, the omission is not reflective of how meaningful our friendship is to me. My thanks go to all I have called "friend," in every stage of life.

There are no words to express the decades of love, support, and laughs I've been lucky to share with Kim, Stephen, and Colin, as well as Ringo (RIP), Cody, Matti, and Benito. They have been there for me in all my many lives, and I'm dead chuffed to call them my family.

Gio has sustained me in more ways than I can count for the last seven years. He has helped me stay grounded in the strange world of academia and reminded me of what really matters in this world. Te adoro, Gio. Thank you for going on this, and every, journey with me. And finally, thanks to Sibby, for bringing me such joy in the final moments of completing this project. I can't wait to find out who you become.

NOTES

Abbreviations in the Notes

ASH	Series XXVII: Abram S. Hewitt, 1887–1888, Early Mayor Records, New York City Municipal Archives, New York
CWLUR	Chicago Women's Liberation Union Records, Chicago History Museum, Research Center
NARA	National Archives and Records Administration, College Park, Maryland
SBC	Sallie Bingham Center for Women's History and Culture, Duke University, Durham, NC
SSC	Sophia Smith Collection, Smith College, Northampton, MA

Introduction

1. *Easy Show Tunes Fake Book*, 194–95.
2. Furia and Lasser, *America's Songs*, 224, 251–52.
3. Whitburn, *Billboard Book of Top 40 Hits*, 498; Bronson, *Billboard Book*, 105, 157. Other examples include "Girl Watcher" by the O'Kaysions, "Music to Watch Girls By" by Andy Williams, "Whistle Bait" by Larry Collins, and "Hello Little Girl" written by John Lennon and Paul McCartney and performed by the Fourmost.
4. Feimster, *Southern Horrors*.
5. For more on Ingram's case, see Berry, "'Reckless Eyeballing.'"
6. "Smashing the 'Masher'—A Nation-Wide Crusade," *Atlanta Constitution*, December 31, 1916.
7. Effective September 5, 1905. Houston, Texas, Charter and General Ordinances, ch. 127, § 3 (1910).
8. *Easy Show Tunes Fake Book*, 194–95.
9. The activist organization Right to Be and researchers from Cornell University surveyed 16,607 women worldwide about their experiences of street harassment. Eighty-four percent of respondents had experienced street harassment by the time they were seventeen years old. In the United States, that number was 85 percent, with over a third of respondents reporting they had experienced street harassment before the age of fourteen. "ILR and Hollaback! Release Largest Analysis of Street Harassment to Date," ILR Worker Institute, June 1, 2015, www.ilr.cornell.edu/worker-institute/blog/reports/ilr-and-hollaback-release-largest-analysis-street-harassment-date; "Street Harassment Statistics in the United States (Cornell Survey Project, 2015)," SlideShare, May 15, 2015, www.slideshare.net/slideshow/street-harassment-statistics-in-canada-cornell-survey-project-2015-48200467/48200467.

In 2018, the advocacy group Stop Street Harassment found that 81 percent of women in the United States had experienced some form of sexual harassment or assault in their lifetime, most frequently in public (66 percent of respondents). Holly Kearl et al., *The Facts Behind the #metoo Movement: A National Study on Sexual Harassment and Assault*, Stop Street Harassment, February 2018, www.stopstreetharassment.org/wp-content/uploads/2018/01/Full-Report-2018-National-Study-on-Sexual-Harassment-and-Assault.pdf.

10. Fairchild, "Understanding Street Harassment," 1150.
11. Leskinen et al., "Gender Harassment"; National Academies of Sciences, Engineering, and Medicine, *Sexual Harassment of Women*.
12. Goffman, *Behavior in Public Places*, 83. See also Fileborn and O'Neill, "From 'Ghettoization' to a Field of Its Own," 128; and Gardner, *Passing By*, 93.
13. Benard and Schlaffer, "Man in the Street," 72.
14. Fairchild, "Understanding Street Harassment."
15. Kern, *Feminist City*, 13.
16. Scholz, "Catcalls and Military Strategy," 250–52.
17. Hickey, *Breaking the Gender Code*, 111.
18. Here, I intentionally allude to bell hooks and her identification of an "imperialist white supremacist capitalist patriarchy" as the dominant system in the United States against which anti-oppression movements must fight. hooks, *Writing Beyond Race*, 4.
19. I am inspired here by the revelatory collection of essays historicizing the norms of heterosexuality and heteronormativity in Davis and Mitchell, *Heterosexual Histories*.
20. The earliest use of the term I've found is from a New York feminist newsletter published in 1971. "Street Harassment Statement," *Women's Health and Abortion Project Newsletter*, August 1971, box 1, New York Radical Feminists Records, SBC.
21. For examples of the terminology that did not catch on, see Gwenda Linda Blair, "Standing on the Corner . . . ," *Liberation* 18, no. 9 (1974): 6–8; Jim Sanderson, "Confronting Street Hassling," Liberated Male, *Los Angeles Times*, October 5, 1980; Lindsy Van Gelder, "The International Language of Street Hassling," *Ms.*, May 1981; Geng, "Scorn Not the Street Compliment"; "The Verbal Rapist," *Majority Report*, October 1971, box PW-1 and LW-1, Alix Kates Shulman Papers, SBC; I. Rajeswary, "Anti-Rape Week Will Target Verbal Abuse," *Washington Post*, September 20, 1985, box 5, folder 1, Nkenge Touré Papers, SSC; and Karen De Witt, "The 'Hey, Honey!' Hassle: Intrusive Street Comments on the Increase," *Washington Post*, October 17, 1977.
22. Anita Hill would become the most famous example in the 1990s, but workplace harassment was a significant focus of 1970s and 1980s feminist organizing. Baker, *Women's Movement Against Sexual Harassment*.
23. For a list of popular terminology in scholarly work today, see Fairchild, "Understanding Street Harassment," 1143. A quick internet search will unearth the many popular uses of the term, including by prominent activist organizations like Right to Be (formerly Hollaback!) and RAINN (Rape, Abuse & Incest National Network). "Stand Up Against Street Harassment," Right to Be, January 31, 2022, https://righttobe.org/trainings/stand-up-against-street-harassment/; "Street Harassment," RAINN, accessed May 31, 2024, www.rainn.org/articles/street-harassment.

24. State of North Carolina v. Mack Ingram (Recorder's Court of Caswell County, June 18, 1951), 10, in part 08, series B, NAACP Papers, Library of Congress, ProQuest History Vault, https://www.proquest.com/docview/2623979155?sourcetype=Archival%20Materials.
25. "A 'Fine' Figure Means Just That to Ogling Detroit Males," *Washington Post*, July 24, 1946; Maryon Zylstra, "What Do You Do When a Strange Man Whistles at You?," Inquiring Camera Girl, *Chicago Daily Tribune*, August 18, 1945.
26. See for instance, Anderson, *Cosmopolitan Canopy*.
27. Vera-Gray, *Men's Intrusion*, 11–12.
28. Leonardo, "Political Economy of Street Harassment," 51–52.
29. Herrera and McCarthy, "Street Harassment Interpretations"; Fairchild, "Understanding Street Harassment," 1151–52; Fileborn and O'Neill, "From 'Ghettoization' to a Field of Its Own," 127–28.
30. See Hutson and Krueger, "Harasser's Toolbox," 770; "Identity and Public Harassment," Right to Be, accessed May 31, 2024, https://righttobe.org/guides/identity-and-street-harassment/.
31. Isenberg, *White Trash*, 247–49. For other examples of white people using intrusions like pointed stares or hurled insults as a way to remind Black people of "their place" in the racial hierarchy, see R. Kelley, *Race Rebels*; and Berrey, *Jim Crow Routine*.
32. Armstrong, "'Who's the Slut?'"
33. Alok V. Menon, "On Lying: Street Harassment Is Too High a Price for 'Being Ourselves,'" *ALOK* (blog), August 8, 2015, www.alokvmenon.com/blog/2015/8/11/on-lying-street-harassment-is-too-high-a-price-for-being-ourselves; Kolysh, *Everyday Violence*.
34. M. Fischer, "#Free_CeCe."
35. Hindes and Fileborn, "'Why Did He Do It?,'" 670.
36. The study did not distinguish between cisgender and transgender identities. Stop Street Harassment, *Unsafe and Harassed in Public Spaces: A National Street Harassment Report*, Spring 2014, https://stopstreetharassment.org/our-work/nationalstudy/2014study/.
37. Kolysh, *Everyday Violence*, 27–28.
38. Quinn, "Sexual Harassment and Masculinity," 555–58.
39. This continues a long legacy of men using women as objects with which to build networks between men. As anthropologist Gayle Rubin argues, the exchange of women through rituals such as marriage has historically had more to do with cementing relationships between men than with creating relationships with women. "If it is women who are being transacted" in these rituals, Rubin writes, "then it is the men who give and take them who are linked, the woman being a conduit of a relationship rather than a partner to it." Rubin, "Traffic in Women," 117. See also Sedgwick, *Between Men*.
40. Baptist and Coburn, "Harassment in Public Spaces," 116. See also Hindes and Fileborn, "'Why Did He Do It?,'" 669–70.
41. Hindes and Fileborn, "'Why Did He Do It?,'" 671; Fileborn and O'Neill, "From 'Ghettoization' to a Field of Its Own," 131.
42. Connell, *Gender and Power*.
43. Connell and Messerschmidt, "Hegemonic Masculinity," 832.

44. Messerschmidt, *Hegemonic Masculinity*, 74; Connell and Messerschmidt, "Hegemonic Masculinity," 841.
45. Messerschmidt, *Hegemonic Masculinity*, 133.
46. Griffin, "Hegemonic Masculinity as a Historical Problem," 394. For additional discussion of hegemonic masculinity as a category of historical analysis, see Summers, *Manliness and Its Discontents*, 10–14; Syrett, *Company He Keeps*, 3, 11; and Pascoe and Bridges, "Exploring Masculinities."
47. Scholz, "Catcalls and Military Strategy," 250–51; D. Davis, "Harm That Has No Name"; Donnelly and Calogero, "Role of Stranger Harassment Experiences"; Kissling and Kramarae, "Stranger Compliments."
48. Kelly, *Surviving Sexual Violence*, 77.
49. Kelly, *Surviving Sexual Violence*, 100.
50. Kasson, *Rudeness and Civility*, 128.
51. "Served Out," *Norfolk Advertiser* (Dedham, MA), December 15, 1838.
52. "Youth Strangles Society Woman to Death with Wire," *St. Louis Post-Dispatch*, January 13, 1906; "Youth Owns Brutal Murder of Woman," *Chicago Daily News*, January 13, 1906; Remus, *Shoppers' Paradise*, 180–88.
53. "Terror Due to Murders," *Chicago Daily Tribune*, January 14, 1906.
54. Case 365-012-01, 1978, box 9, Diana Russell Unprocessed Papers, SSC.
55. Vera-Gray, *Men's Intrusion*, 22.
56. Wise and Stanley, *Georgie Porgie*, 114–17. For more recent theorizations of the cumulative effect of intrusions, see Fileborn and Vera-Gray, "'I Want to Be Able to Walk the Street"; Vera-Gray, *Men's Intrusion*.
57. Gardner, *Passing By*, 113; Fileborn, "'I Actually Snapped.'"
58. Deidre Callahan, "Leave Me Alone," *Equal Times*, April 13, 1980, 11, box 53, Jean Kilbourne Papers, SBC.
59. Vera-Gray, *Men's Intrusions*, 145–46.
60. "Catch a Masher and Drill His Ears," *Evening World* (New York), January 2, 1903.
61. Fleming, "On Street Harassment," 239.
62. Manne, *Down Girl*, 176.
63. Ayres et al., "Women's Likelihood of Confronting Sexism"; Hyers, "Resisting Prejudice Every Day"; McCurn, "'I Am Not a Prostitute'"; Tuerkheimer, "Street Harassment as Sexual Subordination."
64. Fleetwood, "Everyday Self-Defence."
65. U.S. Census Bureau, 2010 Census of Population and Housing, *Population and Housing Unit Counts*, CPH-2-1, United States Summary, U.S. Government Printing Office, Washington, DC, 2012, http://census.gov/prod/cen2010/cph-2-1.pdf.
66. Griffin argues hegemonic masculinities are best understood as being created, contested, and reinforced within "communication communities," that is, between people who may have different social positions or physical locations but share the same "mechanisms" for identifying, interpreting, contesting, and being socialized into a shared set of norms. Because of their material, social, and political power, the middle and upper classes are generally members of a "more unified and genuinely national" communication community. Griffin, "Hegemonic Masculinity as a Historical Problem," 385.

67. See, for instance, Halttunen, *Confidence Men and Painted Women*; Radway, *Feeling for Books*; and L. Cohen, *Consumers' Republic*.
68. On how "men's ideas" shape "common-sense" definitions of sexual violence, see L. Kelly, *Surviving Sexual Violence*, 138.
69. Halttunen, *Confidence Men and Painted Women*; Stansell, *City of Women*; Peiss, *Cheap Amusements*; Meyerowitz, *Women Adrift*; Enstad, *Ladies of Labor*; Kasson, *Rudeness and Civility*; Ryan, *Women in Public*; Wood, *Freedom of the Streets*; Garland-Thomson, *Staring*; Remus, *Shoppers' Paradise*.
70. Vera-Gray has beautifully described how women "trade freedom for safety" when they curtail their own mobility and adjust their physical presentation to avoid men's stranger intrusions in public space. Vera-Gray, *Right Amount of Panic*.
71. Bowman, "Street Harassment," 520–21.

Chapter One

1. Streetcars never ran on Fifth Avenue because wealthy residents opposed the laying of the necessary rails. Roess and Sansone, *Wheels That Drove New York*, 265–66.
2. A Young Lady, "Outrages on Ladies in Street Cars: Testimony of a Young Lady," *New York Times*, October 23, 1869.
3. A Young Lady, "Outrages on Ladies in Street Cars."
4. For examples of entertainment venues, see "Outrages on Ladies in Cars and Stages," *New York Times*, October 17, 1869; Baldwin, *In the Watches of the Night*, 83; and Kasson, *Rudeness and Civility*, 127.
5. In 1840, the populations of Boston and New York City were 93,383 and 312,710, respectively. US Census Bureau, "Facts by Decade: 1840," Census.gov, accessed June 20, 2025, www.census.gov/about/history/historical-censuses-and-surveys/decade-facts.html.
6. Halttunen, *Confidence Men and Painted Women*, 34–39.
7. Wilson, *Sphinx in the City*, 5–7.
8. Flanagan, *Constructing the Patriarchal City*, 1–7.
9. Wilson, *Sphinx in the City*, 9.
10. Kern, *Feminist City*, 6.
11. Kern, *Feminist City*, 3; Hill, *Their Sisters' Keepers*, 115.
12. For more on sex work in the nineteenth-century city, see Baldwin, *In the Watches of the Night*; C. Blair, *I've Got to Make My Livin'*; Stansell, *City of Women*; Gilfoyle, *City of Eros*; and Walkowitz, *City of Dreadful Delight*.
13. "The Corner Loafer Nuisance," *New York Herald*, May 26, 1872; W. E. Waller, letter to the editor, *Trenton State Gazette*, October 20, 1874.
14. Gray, "Mixed Company," 142–47.
15. *Independent Mechanic*, May 11, 18, 25, 1811, as quoted in Stansell, *City of Women*, 27.
16. Flanagan, *Constructing the Patriarchal City*.
17. See, for instance, Baldwin, *In the Watches of the Night*; Deutsch, *Women and the City*; Halttunen, *Confidence Men and Painted Women*; Hill, *Their Sisters' Keepers*; Kasson, *Rudeness and Civility*; Ryan, *Women in Public*; and Stansell, *City of Women*.

18. Feminist theorists have describe the flaneur as the "embodiment of the 'male gaze.'" Wilson, *Contradictions of Culture*, 78–79.
19. Whitman, *Leaves of Grass*; Dickens, *Night Walks*.
20. Wilson, *Sphinx in the City*, 16.
21. For more on Holmes and "The Autocrat of the Breakfast-Table" column, see Dowling, *Oliver Wendell Holmes in Paris*.
22. Oliver Wendell Holmes Sr., "The Autocrat of the Breakfast-Table," *Atlantic Monthly*, June 1858, 109. Emphasis in original.
23. Sewell, *Women and the Everyday City*.
24. Kasson, *Rudeness and Civility*, 128–32.
25. J. N. Hyde, "Running the Gauntlet—A Scene in Front of a Popular Hotel in New York City at Five O'Clock P.M.," *Frank Leslie's Illustrated Newspaper*, May 16, 1874.
26. *OED Online*, "Gauntlet, n.2," accessed June 19, 2018, www.oed.com/view/Entry/77149.
27. Buntline, *Mysteries and Miseries of New York*; Waller, letter to the editor; "Mashers Lining Monroe Avenue Annoy Women Without Escorts When Police Relax Espionage," *Detroit Free Press*, July 5, 1914.
28. Wilson, *Contradictions of Culture*, 74.
29. See Hill, *Their Sisters' Keepers*, 2. For other treatments of nineteenth-century sex work and its intersections with working-class culture, see Deutsch, *Women and the City*; Gilfoyle, *City of Eros*; Stansell, *City of Women*; Srebnick, *Mysterious Death of Mary Rogers*, 49; and Allen, *Horrible Prettiness*, 139.
30. McCabe, *Lights and Shadows*, 52.
31. Deutsch, *Women and the City*, 12; Welter, "Cult of True Womanhood"; Wilson, *Contradictions of Culture*.
32. People v. Blanch, June 16, 1826, New York County District Attorney Indictment Records, New York City Municipal Archives. For more on similar complaints, see Gilfoyle, *City of Eros*.
33. People v. Bernard Murthe, October 12, 1841, New York County District Attorney Indictment Records, New York City Municipal Archives.
34. "Roughs in a Street Car," *Times-Picayune* (New Orleans), January 31, 1876; "Street Car and Police," *Times-Picayune*, June 16, 1875.
35. "Street Car and Police."
36. "An Ingenious Method of Obtaining an Introduction," *Wisconsin Democrat* (Madison), June 9, 1849.
37. "Served Out," *Norfolk Advertiser*, December 15, 1838. See also "Another Street Insult," *Sun* (Baltimore), May 9, 1840.
38. A Young Lady, "Outrages on Ladies in Street Cars."
39. "A Cowhiding Affair," *Cincinnati Daily Enquirer*, August 1, 1870.
40. Garland-Thomson, *Staring*, 69.
41. Bill Lounger, "Gossip with the Editor, About Men and Things in Town and Country," *Cleveland Daily Herald*, January 6, 1841; "Ingenious Method of Obtaining an Introduction"; "Street Car and Police."
42. A Young Lady, "Outrages on Ladies in Street Cars."
43. "Outrages on Ladies in Cars and Stages."

44. Kasson, *Rudeness and Civility*, 126; Deutsch, *Women and the City*; Garland-Thomson, *Staring*, 66.
45. De Valcourt, *Illustrated Manners Book*, 268, 73.
46. De Valcourt, *Illustrated Manners Book*, 267.
47. De Valcourt, *Illustrated Manners Books*, 73.
48. C. Hartley, *Gentlemen's Book of Etiquette*, 66.
49. See Ruth, *Decorum*, 117–19; C. Hartley, *Gentlemen's Book of Etiquette*, 66–68; and S. Wells, *How to Behave*, 101.
50. De Valcourt, *Illustrated Manners Book*, 103. See also Longstreet, *Social Etiquette of New York*, 21–23.
51. A Young Lady, "Outrages on Ladies in Street Cars." For more examples, see "Served Out"; and "Corner Loafer Nuisance."
52. "Depraved Humanity," *Minneapolis Tribune*, December 22, 1876; "Street Car and Police."
53. "Corner Loafer Nuisance"; Waller, letter to the editor.
54. "Outrages on Ladies in Cars and Stages."
55. A. Brother, letter to the editor, *Sun* (Baltimore), April 28, 1838; response to A. Brother, letter to the editor, *Sun* (Baltimore), April 28, 1838.
56. "Corner Loafer Nuisance"; response to A. Brother.
57. "Ingenious Method of Obtaining an Introduction"; "Another Street Insult"; "Corner Loafer Nuisance."
58. I. Brown, "Racism and Sexism," 128. See also Lemire, *"Miscegenation,"* 88; and Cobb, *Picture Freedom*, 124–25.
59. D'Emilio and Freedman, *Intimate Matters*, 37, 217–19; R. Davis, *Fierce Desires*, 139–40. See also Hodes, *White Women, Black Men*; Sommerville, *Rape and Race in the Nineteenth-Century South*; Feimster, *Southern Horrors*; and Eaves, *Sexual Violence and American Slavery*.
60. "Another Street Insult."
61. Baldwin, *In the Watches of the Night*, 41; Sewell, *Women and the Everyday City*, 6.
62. Domosh and Seager, *Putting Women in Place*, 88.
63. Baldwin, *In the Watches of the Night*, 151; Hill, *Their Sisters' Keepers*, 214.
64. "A Trip in the Street Cars," *Godey's Lady's Book*, June 1865.
65. "Miscellany," *Constitution* (Middletown, CT), March 22, 1865; "Cowhiding Affair"; "The Police and the Street-Cars," *New York Times*, May 25, 1871; "Street Car and Police"; "Roughs in a Street Car"; "A Naughty Boy," *St. Louis Dispatch*, January 10, 1877. For more details of the larger debate over travel in streetcars, see Baldwin, *In the Watches of the Night*, 138–78.
66. "Outrage in a Street Car," *New York Times*, October 2, 1869.
67. Hamilton held a position as secretary of the Central American Transit Company, a company that held shipping interests in Panama. See, for instance, "Nicaragua: The Central-American Transit Company," *New York Times*, July 31, 1868.
68. "A Detective on Trial," *New York Herald*, October 2, 1869.
69. "Outrages on Ladies in Cars and Stages."
70. Deutsch, *Women and the City*, 63–76.

71. "The Treatment of Ladies in Stages and Cars," *New York Times*, October 31, 1869.
72. "Treatment of Ladies in Stages and Cars."
73. Untitled, *New York Times*, October 25, 1869.
74. Untitled, *New York Times*, October 21, 1869.
75. "Outrages on Ladies in Cars and Stages."
76. Untitled, *New York Times*, October 21, 1869.
77. A Young Lady, "Outrages on Ladies in Street Cars."
78. "Outrages on Ladies in Cars and Stages."
79. Farrar, *Young Lady's Friend*, 333.
80. Kasson, *Rudeness and Civility*, 128; Garland-Thomson, *Staring*, 70.
81. F. Hartley, *Ladies' Book of Etiquette*, 109.
82. Untitled, *New York Times*, October 25, 1869.
83. "Treatment of Ladies in Stages and Cars."
84. Untitled, *New York Times*, October 25, 1869.
85. "Treatment of Ladies in Stages and Cars." Question mark omitted in the original.
86. Untitled, *New York Times*, October 25, 1869.
87. Untitled, *New York Times*, October 25, 1869.
88. "Treatment of Ladies in Stages and Cars."
89. "Treatment of Ladies in Stages and Cars."
90. "Treatment of Ladies in Stages and Cars."
91. "Treatment of Ladies in Stages and Cars."
92. Untitled, *New York Times*, October 25, 1869.
93. A Young Lady, "Outrages on Ladies in Street Cars."
94. Buntline, *Mysteries and Miseries of New York*, 10–11. For more on how city guides bolstered antivice campaigns and linked victimhood with whiteness, see Hill, *Their Sisters' Keepers*, 69; and Hodes, *White Women, Black Men*, 153–62.
95. Letter to the editor, *Sun* (Baltimore), April 28, 1838; Lounger, "Gossip with the Editor."
96. "Street Insults," *Sun* (Baltimore), December 28, 1840.
97. Morgan, *Laboring Women*; Rosen, *Terror in the Heart of Freedom*.
98. Cobb, *Picture Freedom*, 74, 114–45.
99. Foner, "Battle to End Discrimination," 262; B. Kelley, *Right to Ride*, 15.
100. Pryor, *Colored Travelers*, 1.
101. As quoted in Lemire, *"Miscegenation,"* 118.
102. B. Kelley, *Right to Ride*, 11.
103. "Shameful," *Christian Recorder* (Philadelphia), September 23, 1865.
104. Quoted in B. Kelley, *Right to Ride*, 18.
105. "Legal Rights Vindicated," *Frederick Douglass' Paper*, March 2, 1855.
106. "Outrage upon Colored Persons," *Frederick Douglass' Paper*, July 28, 1854, quoted in B. Kelley, *Right to Ride*, 19.
107. For more on the Jennings case and the antidiscrimination cases it inspired, see B. Kelley, *Right to Ride*, 15–32.
108. Laura S. Haviland, "The Assault on Sojourner Truth," *National Anti-Slavery Standard*, October 14, 1865; Truth and Gilbert, *Narrative of Sojourner Truth*.
109. I. Wells, *Crusade for Justice*, 18–19; Coleman, "Black Women and Segregated Public Transportation"; Silkey, *Black Woman Reformer*, 49.
110. S. S. H., "The Riot in Detroit," *Liberator*, March 20, 1863.

111. H. Davis, *"We Will Be Satisfied with Nothing Less,"* 30.
112. Dunbar, *Fragile Freedom*, 50.
113. Simmons, *Crescent City Girls*, 56–59.
114. Letter to the editor, *Sun* (Baltimore), April 28, 1838; "Street Insults"; "Outrages on Ladies in Cars and Stages"; "Naughty Boy"; "The Street-Car Murder," *Harper's Weekly*, May 20, 1871.
115. "Served Out." See also "Cowhiding Affair."
116. "Roughs in a Street Car."
117. "Street Insults." Emphasis in original.
118. Block, *Rape and Sexual Power*, 29–30.
119. A. Brother, letter to the editor.
120. Srebnick, *Mysterious Death of Mary Rogers*, 95–97. For more on the history of the New York City police, see Guariglia, *Police and the Empire City*.
121. Waller, letter to the editor.
122. "Police and the Street-Cars."
123. "Depraved Humanity."
124. "Street Car and Police."
125. "Served Him Right," *New York Times*, December 15, 1870.
126. "Corner Loafer Nuisance."
127. "Street-Car Murder." See also Baldwin, *In the Watches of the Night*, 138–41.
128. "Ruffianism in Street-Cars," *New York Times*, April 28, 1871.
129. "Street-Car Murder."
130. Depictions of dangerous urban spaces and threatening strangers were not confined to reporting on street insults. Fictional accounts and melodramas sold as city guides or exposés on urban life often featured stories of interactions between strangers, including street insults, that precipitated tragic ends. Smith, *Sunshine and Shadow in New York*; H. Morgan, *Boston Inside Out!*; Martin, *Secrets of the Great City*.
131. See, for instance, Kasson, *Rudeness and Civility*, 128.
132. "Corner Loafer Nuisance."
133. "Outrages on Ladies in Cars and Stages."
134. Thornwell, *Lady's Guide to Perfect Gentility*, 78; Martine, *Martine's Book of Etiquette*, 131; Louis, *Decorum*, 119; R. Wells, *Manners, Culture and Dress*, 129. See also Remus, *Shoppers' Paradise*, 50.
135. Morris, *Life on the Stage*, 88–90. Morris's rules may ring a bell for some readers. They are similar to advice women still receive from parents, schools, popular media, and law enforcement about how to avoid attack and rape in public spaces.
136. Potter, *Hairdresser's Experience in High Life*, 135.
137. Domosh and Seager, *Putting Woman in Place*, 93, 100.

Chapter Two

1. "What Can Be Done to Rid the Palmer House Block of Mashers," *Chicago Daily Tribune*, February 4, 1906.
2. Most of these women were quoted using their husband's names. I found full names in Leonard, *Woman's Who's Who*; and in *Sixteenth Annual Report of the Illinois Farmers' Institute*.

3. "What Can Be Done to Rid the Palmer House Block of Mashers."
4. Articles that use the term "crusade" to describe antimashing organizing include "The Police Crusade to Rid the City of Thieves, Thugs and Burglars," *St. Louis Post-Dispatch*, February 25, 1888; John T. McCutcheon, *An Incident in the Anti-Mashers Crusade*, June 4, 1903, box 1, folder 11, John T. McCutcheon Papers, Newberry Library, Chicago; Esther Andrews, "New York Women Start 'Smash the Masher' Crusade," *Tacoma Times*, September 19, 1916; and "Smashing the 'Masher': Nation-Wide Crusade Cities of America Unite to Protect Women," *Duluth News-Tribune*, October 8, 1916.
5. Of the 568 newspaper articles I consulted, 42 were published in the 1880s, 31 in the 1890s, 139 in the first decade of the 1900s, 232 in the 1910s, 94 in the 1920s, and 29 in the 1930s. These numbers are derived from newspaper reports that explicitly mention mashers, male flirts, etc. and from reporting that linked men's stranger intrusions to other kinds of vice or crime.
6. "Masher Nearly Killed," *Boston Globe*, April 15, 1901; "Two Little Fists Subdue Masher," *Morning Oregonian* (Portland), October 16, 1908; "Smash the Street Masher," *St. Paul (MN) Daily Globe*, August 9, 1885; "Urges Workhouse Sentences to Drive out Masher Evils," *Dallas Morning News*, October 27, 1912.
7. "The Masher," *Green Bay Semi-Weekly Gazette*, September 23, 1908.
8. "Planning Rule Against Mashers," *Ottumwa Tri-Weekly Courier*, July 23, 1914; "Total Population for Iowa's Incorporated Places: 1850–2000," Iowa Data Center, accessed August 19, 2025, www.iowadatacenter.org/datatables/PlacesAll/plpopulation18502000.pdf.
9. "Vile-Tongued Mashers Nightly Insult Women on Downtown Street, Untouched by Police," *Detroit Free Press*, June 18, 1914; "Girls Lured to City Face Unforeseen Dangers," *Chicago Daily Tribune*, April 8, 1906; "Now Jitney Flirt Bobs Up to Scare Poor, Timid Girls," *Detroit Free Press*, September 15, 1921; Nixola Greeley-Smith, "New York Mashers, Their Insulting Tricks and the Different Brands of the Pests," *Evening World* (New York), July 13, 1912.
10. Mitchell, *Righteous Propagation*; Cooper, *Beyond Respectability*.
11. Bederman, *Manliness and Civilization*; Hoganson, *Fighting for American Manhood*; Syrett, *Company He Keeps*, 140; Murphy, *Political Manhood*.
12. For more on the links between women's rights, suffrage, and antimashing activism, see Freedman, *Redefining Rape*, 191–209.
13. Before 1910, most of these women were US-born white women, though many were also foreign-born or the first-generation children of immigrants. After 1900, thousands of African American women migrated alone or with their families to cities in the North and the West, escaping racial violence in the South. Meyerowitz, *Women Adrift*, 5–7; Odem, *Delinquent Daughters*, 2–3.
14. See, for instance, Enstad, *Ladies of Labor*; Peiss, *Cheap Amusements*; Wood, *Freedom of the Streets*; Wolcott, *Remaking Respectability*; Hicks, *Talk with You Like a Woman*; Bunch-Lyons, *Contested Terrain*; and Ervin, *Gateway to Equality*.
15. Evans, *Born for Liberty*, 150–52. See also K. Blair, *Clubwoman as Feminist*; Flanagan, "Gender and Urban Political Reform"; Gere, *Intimate Practices*; and Morris-Crowther, *Political Activities of Detroit Clubwomen*.

16. Louise de Koven Bowen, "Some Legislative Needs in Illinois" (Juvenile Protective Association of Chicago, 1912), box 10, folder 133, Juvenile Protective Association Records, University of Illinois Chicago, Special Collections and University Archives.
17. "Travelers Aid: The Badge That Marks the Trusted Friend from Journey's Start to Journey's End," box 1, Travelers Aid Association of America Records, Social Welfare History Archives, University of Minnesota.
18. Odem, *Delinquent Daughters*, 8–37; Freedman, *Redefining Rape*, 125–46.
19. Freedman, *Redefining Rape*, 196.
20. Odem, *Delinquent Daughters*, 4–5.
21. "Masher Will Be Clubbed," *St. Louis Post-Dispatch*, April 4, 1895; S. S. M., "Mashing a Masher," *Day Book* (Chicago), August 9, 1915; "Have You Met a Nervy Flirt?," *Chicago Daily Tribune*, May 7, 1916; Anna Carroll, "Invalids, Old Men with Whiskers, and Policemen—All Males Flirtatious," *Day Book*, August 12, 1916.
22. Countess Annie de Montaigu, "Mashers," *Los Angeles Times*, September 15, 1889.
23. Dreiser, *Sister Carrie*; Freedman, *Redefining Rape*, 195–96.
24. Alice M. Johnson, "The Truth About Mashing!," *Chicago Daily Tribune*, January 18, 1914.
25. "Why Girls Go Wrong," *New York Times*, March 15, 1913.
26. Carby, "Policing the Black Woman's Body."
27. Pliley, *Policing Sexuality*; Carby, "Policing the Black Woman's Body," 739; C. Blair, *I've Got to Make My Livin'*.
28. Knupfer, *Toward a Tenderer Humanity*; Jones, *All Bound Up Together*; Dunbar, *Fragile Freedom*; Cooper, *Beyond Respectability*.
29. Mitchell, *Righteous Propagation*.
30. For examples of mashers on public transit, see "Cold Doesn't Save 'Flirt,'" *Chicago Daily Tribune*, December 1, 1914; S. S. M., "Mashing a Masher"; "Another Masher Mashed," *Day Book*, September 11, 1916; and "A Smile for a Ride," Voice of the People, *Chicago Daily Tribune*, June 25, 1921.

For examples of uninvited touching in movie theaters, see "Woman's Fists Land on Masher," *Evening World* (New York), December 3, 1903; "Gay Film Flirt Flirts Himself into Flirt Cell," *Chicago Daily Tribune*, September 7, 1916; and "It's Dangerous to Flirt in a Movie Theater," *Chicago Defender*, January 30, 1926.
31. For examples of speaking, see "Indignant Girls," *New Haven Register*, June 5, 1895; "Give Him to a Policeman," *New Haven Register*, July 6, 1895; "Masher's Slang Cause of Faint," *Detroit Free Press*, February 28, 1910; and "Drunken Men Insult Women on the Street," *Morning Olympian* (WA), May 18, 1911.

For examples of men following women, see Solomon Shingle, "The Owl Papers: The Doo-de-Duden Dude," *Beadle's Weekly*, September 8, 1883; "Smash the Street Masher"; "One Masher Scared," *St. Louis Post-Dispatch*, April 6, 1895; "Slashed Masher's Ear, She Says," *Sun* (New York), January 1, 1903; "'Masher' Laid Out by Woman," *San Francisco Chronicle*, June 27, 1905; "Professor Held as Masher," *Washington Post*, May 24, 1909; "Rout State Street Mashers," *Chicago Daily Tribune*, June 3, 1909; "Girl Stenographer Uses Glove on Masher," *Bisbee (AZ) Daily Review*, June 17, 1909; "Finds Chicago Men Do Flirt," *Chicago Daily Tribune*, September 2, 1911; "Three Months for Masher,"

Boston Globe, October 28, 1915; "Mashers to Have Hard Sledding," *Ottumwa Tri-Weekly Courier*, April 25, 1916; "Masher Put to Flight by Girl's Hatpin," *Milwaukee Journal*, October 10, 1921; and "Flirt Is Fined $25," *New York Times*, March 30, 1926.

For examples of men who shouted from cars or offered women rides, see "Our Dirty Automobile Mashers!," *Chicago Defender*, August 10, 1912; "Is an Auto a License to Flirt?," *Chicago Daily Tribune*, July 8, 1921; "Mashers and Auto Cruisers Infect City Streets, Is Claim," *Afro-American* (Baltimore), August 1, 1925; and "Police Drive on Auto Mashers; 17 Boys Seized," *Chicago Daily Tribune*, July 12, 1928.

32. "Insulted White Women," *Arizona Republican*, June 11, 1895. See also Margaret Barnley to Abram S. Hewitt, March 21, 1888, box 1365, folder 239, ASH.

33. Rouse, *Her Own Hero*, 78.

34. Just under half of mashing accounts that mention intrusive looking used the term "ogling." The following are representative examples of reports using the various terms for intrusive looking.

Stare: "The Matinee Masher," *Daily Inter Ocean* (Chicago), September 23, 1880; "Attempt to Kidnap Washington Woman from an Express Train," *Washington Post*, July 1, 1906; "Have You Met a Nervy Flirt?," *Chicago Daily Tribune*, May 14, 1916.

Glance: "The 'Mashers' Mashed," *Daily Inter Ocean*, May 5, 1881; "From the State's Capital," *Cleveland Gazette*, August 7, 1886.

Goo-goo eyes: "Goo-Goo Eyes," *Dallas Morning News*, September 8, 1905; "Watch Out for the Goo Goo Man," *Oregonian* (Portland), December 1, 1906; "Goo Goo Gnat," *Flint Journal*, August 2, 1911.

Smile: "A Healthy Ordinance," *Sedalia (MO) Weekly Bazoo*, May 17, 1881; "The Masher," *Evening Bulletin* (Maysville, KY), November 24, 1882; "Death Penalty for Mashing," *Wichita Daily Eagle*, March 17, 1903; Lillian Collins, "The Girl or the Dress," *Los Angeles Times*, September 4, 1912.

Making eyes: "Poses as Masher," *Los Angeles Herald*, July 30, 1905; "The Masher Was Game," *Albuquerque Morning Journal*, February 27, 1906; "Cold Doesn't Save 'Flirt.'"

Lustful gaze: "Vile-Tongued Mashers Nightly Insult Women on Downtown Street."

Ogling: "Man About Town: He Watches the Toughs as They Ogle the Girls," *Trenton Evening Times*, January 19, 1893; "Mashers Must Move; Complaints of Ogling," *Fort Worth Star-Telegram*, May 6, 1911; "Detroit Club Women to Hear of Mashing Evil and How to Curb Ogling Sidewalk Youths," *Detroit Free Press*, December 7, 1914; "Ogling by Mashers on Public Streets Banned in New City Ordinance," *Flint Journal*, June 7, 1921.

35. For examples of "masher" and "ogler" used interchangeably, see "Bargain Counter Oglers Must Go," *Evening Statesman* (Walla Walla, WA), March 2, 1907; "Nashville Streets Free from 'Oglers,'" *Nashville Tennessean*, May 24, 1907; "Victim Calls Masher Fool," *Los Angeles Times*, June 2, 1911; "Mashing Don't Go, Not in Phoenix Says Moore," *Arizona Republican*, March 29, 1912; and "Woodward and Beavers Join in a Crusade Against Vice," *Atlanta Constitution*, January 12, 1913.

36. Anna Carroll, "'He-Flirt' More Deadly Than 'She,'" *Day Book*, August 11, 1916.

37. Of the 568 mashing reports consulted for this project, 180 mentioned some form of intrusive looking. In comparison, 199 mentioned intrusive greetings or verbal remarks,

89 described men following women, 85 mentioned uninvited physical contact, 59 mentioned some kind of violent attack or assault, 3 mentioned whistling, and 1 described an incident of indecent exposure. Many reports also used euphemisms or vague language, such as "accost" or "insult," to describe a masher's intrusion, and 134 articles mentioned no specific intrusion or behavior, opting for vague language or simply mentioning a masher had been fined, berated, fought off, or the like.

38. "'Mashers' on the Postoffice Steps Annoy Women Nightly," *Detroit Free Press*, August 7, 1910.
39. A. Johnson, "Truth About Mashing!"
40. "Oglers in the Subway," *New York Times*, January 26, 1912.
41. Enstad, *Ladies of Labor*, 180–83; Remus, *Shoppers' Paradise*, 199–202.
42. See, for instance, "The Most Beautiful Woman in Chicago," *Chicago Daily Tribune*, February 4, 1906; and Scobey, "Nymphs and Satyrs."
43. *I Am Seeing Great Things*, ca. 1915, X2011.34.106, Museum of the City of New York.
44. Nevius and Nevius, *Inside the Apple*, 184–85.
45. "Masher's Mecca," *San Francisco Chronicle*, September 15, 1912.
46. "A Flatiron Soliloquy," *New York Times*, April 19, 1903.
47. Brinkley, *Woman's Thoughts About Men*, 4, 10, 62–66.
48. "The Masher," *Daily Inter Ocean*, December 23, 1880.
49. "The Masher," *Evening Bulletin*; "Masher Will Be Clubbed"; "What Can Be Done to Rid the Palmer House Block of Mashers"; "Texas Reformer Is in Portland," *Oregonian*, November 28, 1906; Ethel Intrapodi, "Smashing Cures Mashing—Get Busy, Girls!," *Day Book*, August 26, 1912.
50. "A Curious Creature at Coney Island," *Puck*, July 19, 1882. For more on xenophobic depictions of immigrants in this period, see Jacobson, *Whiteness of a Different Color*; Guglielmo, *White on Arrival*; and Marinari, *Unwanted*.
51. "What to Do with the Masher," *Detroit Free Press*, October 15, 1911.
52. For complaints about old mashers, see de Montaigu, "Mashers"; "Police Aim to Check Mashers," *Chicago Daily Tribune*, May 7, 1901; W. L. Bodine, "How the Board of Education Is Trying to Protect School Girls from the Pest," *Chicago Daily Tribune*, January 27, 1907; and "'Official Flirt' Finds No Masher," *Chicago Daily Tribune*, September 1, 1911.
53. "Urges Workhouse Sentences to Drive out Masher Evils." For more examples of articles that label mashers as foreigners, see Clarence L. Cullen, "The Judge and the Mashers," *Hawaiian Star*, July 8, 1911; "Seek Woman Who Accused Flirt Shot by Police," *Chicago Daily Tribune*, January 18, 1915; "City-Wide Hunt for Masher Slayer of Policeman," *Day Book*, December 19, 1916; Nixola Greeley-Smith, "Flirtation Squad of Girl Detectives Will Clear All the Peacock Alleys of the Hotel Mashers of Both Sexes," *Evening World*, January 2, 1917; and "Chinese Flirt Fined $25," *New York Times*, February 8, 1923.
54. Untitled, *Washington Standard*, December 4, 1908.
55. Joe to Abram S. Hewitt, May 25, 1887, box 1357, folder 173; A. Citizen to Abram S. Hewitt, July 12, 1888, box 1366, folder 240; A Taxpayer of the 7th Ward to Abram S. Hewitt, July 21, 1888, box 1359, folder 188; Tenants to Abram S. Hewitt, August 7, 1888, box 1366, folder 241; John McCullagh to William Murray, October 8, 1888, box 1366, folder 241, all in ASH.

56. A Taxpayer of the 7th Ward to Hewitt, July 21, 1888, ASH; Tenants to Hewitt, August 7, 1888, ASH.
57. Freedman, *Redefining Rape*, 192. See also Remus, *Shoppers' Paradise.*
58. "Inman Park," *New Georgia Encyclopedia* (blog), accessed July 8, 2025, www.georgiaencyclopedia.org/articles/counties-cities-neighborhoods/inman-park/.
59. "A Colored Masher," *Atlanta Constitution*, April 26, 1895.
60. "Girl Tells of Negro Masher Hugging Her," *St. Louis Post-Dispatch*, February 16, 1906; "Negro Seized a White Woman on Street," *Evening News* (San Jose), August 22, 1906; "Negro Masher with Revolver," *Courier-Journal* (Louisville), March 19, 1916.
61. Some mashing accounts in Black newspapers were actually identical to, or very similar to, reports published in white papers. See "Official Flirt in Chicago," *Cleveland Gazette*, October 7, 1911; and "Girls, Don't Flirt," *Broad Ax* (Chicago), November 10, 1923.
62. "Joe Bunkers Budget," *Washington Bee*, January 28, 1888.
63. "On Indiana Avenue," *Freeman* (Indianapolis), April 25, 1903.
64. For more, see Rouse, *Her Own Hero*, 86.
65. An early example of a Black woman who had a white man arrested for mashing can be found in "News of Interest," *Washington Bee*, January 24, 1891.
66. "Stenographer Battles White Flirt on Car," *Chicago Defender*, July 21, 1928.
67. Wells-Barnett, *Red Record*, 127.
68. "Slays Masher," *Chicago Defender*, June 3, 1916.
69. "White Sailor Masher Cut Fifteen Times," *Chicago Defender*, April 28, 1928.
70. On the presumption of Black women's sexual promiscuity, see Carby, "Policing the Black Woman's Body"; and Mumford, *Interzones*, 112–13.
71. A. Fischer, *Streets Belong to Us*, 27, 31. See also Heap, *Slumming.*
72. Letter from anonymous to William E. Dever, October 1, 1926, box 4, folder 29, William E. Dever Papers, Chicago History Museum Research Center. I am indebted to Nora Krinitsky for highlighting this letter for me. Krinitsky, "Politics of Crime Control."
73. "Girls Whip White Mashers," *Pittsburgh Courier*, October 27, 1928; "White Mashers Whipped by Two Girls," *Afro-American*, October 27, 1928. For more on Central Avenue and the surrounding neighborhood, see Chapple, "From Central Avenue to Leimert Park."
74. Five years before the incident with Howell and Garth, the *Los Angeles Times* had declared "No Masher Problem in Los Angeles." Mary E. Walter, "No Masher Problem in Los Angeles," *Los Angeles Times*, November 4, 1923.
75. For instance, Simmons has documented intraracial street harassment within the New Orleans Black community in the 1930s and 1940s, just a few years after the mashers' heyday. Simmons, *Crescent City Girls*, 76–78.
76. Freedman, *Redefining Rape*, 208; Rouse, *Her Own Hero*, 84. See Darlene Clark Hine's groundbreaking work on the protective silence Black women placed around their personal lives that allowed them to publicly emphasize their virtuousness and dignity, even at the expense of calling out sexual violence. Hine, "Rape and the Inner Lives of Black Women."
77. Greeley-Smith, "New York Mashers."

78. "Thrashing a Masher," *Huntsville (AL) Gazette*, September 4, 1886; "Policeman Dismissed for Flirting," *Chicago Daily Tribune*, April 7, 1895; "'Masher' Must Go, Says Kiely," *St. Louis Post-Dispatch*, December 11, 1901; Greeley-Smith, "New York Mashers"; "Urges Workhouse Sentences to Drive out Masher Evils"; "Professor Held as Masher"; "Two Arrested as 'Mashers,'" *Chicago Daily Tribune*, April 7, 1914; "Immunity to Endearing Young Charms Alone Will Qualify for 'Masher' Jury," *Washington Post*, November 20, 1914; "'Flirt-Proof' Jury Fails to Convict," *San Francisco Chronicle*, November 21, 1914; "Women Police Grapple with the Masher Evil," *New York Times*, March 23, 1924.
79. "A Variety of Things," *Plaindealer* (Detroit), December 27, 1889.
80. "The Masher," *Huntsville Gazette*, July 22, 1882; "The Masher," *Evening Bulletin*; "Matinee Masher."
81. "Matinee Masher."
82. "The Masher," *Daily Inter Ocean*.
83. "Girls Be Careful," *New Iberia (LA) Enterprise and Independent Observer*, July 2, 1921.
84. Untitled, *Las Vegas Daily Gazette*, January 28, 1883; "Flirting Is Forbidden," *Washington Post*, October 5, 1894.
85. "Urges Workhouse Sentences to Drive out Masher Evils."
86. "Police Aim to Check Mashers."
87. Untitled, *Daily Inter Ocean*, May 7, 1881.
88. "Cure for a Masher," *Washington Bee*, September 1, 1900.
89. Peiss, *Cheap Amusements*; Rabinovitz, *For the Love of Pleasure*; Clement, *Love for Sale*; D'Emilio and Freedman, *Intimate Matters*, 194–201; R. Davis, *Fierce Desires*, 175–77.
90. Constance Weinberger and S. D. Alinsky, "The Public Dance Hall," 1928, box 126, folder 10, Ernest W. Burgess Papers, University of Chicago Library, Department of Special Collections.
91. "Woman's Fists Land on Masher"; "Have You Met a Nervy Flirt? Finally Drove Him Off," *Chicago Daily Tribune*, February 20, 1916; "Women Police Grapple with the Masher Evil"; "Mashers and Auto Cruisers Infect City Streets"; "Fined $50 for Annoying Young Girl at Belle Isle," *Detroit News*, July 18, 1927, *Detroit News* Clipping Files, Archives of Michigan, Lansing; "Alleged New York Elk Flirt Is Forced to Leave Capital," *Afro-American*, September 14, 1935.
92. "An Atlanta Girl Thrashes Masher," *Augusta Chronicle*, November 22, 1913; "Gay Film Flirt Flirts Himself into Flirt Cell"; "It's Dangerous to Flirt in a Movie Theater."
93. "At the Movies," *Daily Gate City* (Keokuk, IA), November 11, 1914; "To Isolate Movie Mashers," *Star-Independent* (Harrisburg, PA), November 12, 1914; "Favor Segregation," *Evening Public Ledger* (Philadelphia), November 14, 1914.
94. I found thirty-seven examples of mashing on trains and sixty-four on streetcars. For an example of a woman accosted on a streetcar platform, see "A Trounced Scoundrel," *Daily Inter Ocean*, September 5, 1881.
95. "To Drive the Mashers Out of Chicago," *Chicago Daily Tribune*, January 27, 1907.
96. Donald Allen, "A Mole and a Scar," *Boston Globe*, January 12, 1913.
97. "The Pre-Adolescent Girl," February 1917, box 7, folder 4, Lea Taylor Papers, Chicago History Museum Research Center.

98. As Mary Odem has argued, social workers and female reformers also increasingly saw working-class women as sexually deviant in the early twentieth century, in a shift from earlier calls to protect innocent working women from seducers and white slavers. Odem, *Delinquent Daughters.*
99. Theodore Roosevelt was known for lauding the benefits of a "strenuous life." Bederman, *Manliness and Civilization*; Hoganson, *Fighting for American Manhood*; Syrett, *Company He Keeps*, 140; Murphy, *Political Manhood.*
100. "Discovering the Causes of Prostitution," *Dallas Morning News*, March 16, 1913.
101. "Masher Will Be Clubbed." For more on the intersection between dress and middle-class and elite masculinity, see Breward, *Suit.*
102. S. L. Sprout, "The Weak Sex," *Day Book*, December 6, 1916.
103. "Masher," *Day Book*, July 1, 1913.
104. Doris Blake, "The Word 'Flirt' Reeks of Mothballs; It's Out of Use, Now," *Chicago Daily Tribune*, December 6, 1929.
105. "Smashing the Mashers," *Los Angeles Times*, July 19, 1911.
106. "What Can Be Done to Rid the Palmer House Block of Mashers"; "To Drive the Mashers Out of Chicago"; Greeley-Smith, "New York Mashers."
107. "On Indiana Avenue"; "What Can Be Done to Rid the Palmer House Block of Mashers."
108. "Bargain Counter Oglers Must Go"; Carroll, "Invalids, Old Men with Whiskers, and Policemen."
109. See, for instance, "The Season of Flirting Is Now at Its Dizziest Height," *Washington Times*, July 13, 1902; "Girl Tells of Negro Masher Hugging Her"; "Smashing the Mashers Newest Aim of Police," *Washington Times*, July 10, 1910; and "Drunken Men Insult Women on the Street."
110. "The Pre-Adolescent Girl in Her Home," Lea Taylor Papers; "What Can Be Done to Rid the Palmer House Block of Mashers."
111. Rose Cecil O'Neill, "Could Man Stand Comment Which Assails Woman?," *Day Book*, September 8, 1916; O'Neill, *Story of Rose O'Neill.*
112. "'Masher' Laid Out by Woman."
113. Intrapodi, "Smashing Cures Mashing."
114. For more on the mashing crisis as a focal point in the history of the women's self-defense movement, see Rouse, *Her Own Hero.*
115. "Urge War on 'Mashers,'" *Chicago Daily Tribune*, April 17, 1903.
116. Remus, *Shoppers' Paradise*, 147–90.
117. "Doom of 'Mashers,'" *Chicago Daily Tribune*, November 8, 1903.
118. "What Can Be Done to Rid the Palmer House Block of Mashers."
119. "Healthy Ordinance"; untitled, *Las Vegas Daily Gazette*, January 28, 1883.
120. Effective September 5, 1905. Houston, Texas, Charter and General Ordinances, ch. 127, § 3 (1910).
121. "Texas Reformer Is in Portland."
122. Those locations were Albany and Portland in Oregon; Houston and Fort Worth in Texas; Detroit, Michigan; Atlantic City, New Jersey; Milwaukee, Wisconsin; Lewistown, Montana; Omaha, Nebraska; Mount Vernon, Council Bluffs, and Denison

in Iowa; Fort Wayne, Indiana; Raleigh, North Carolina; and New York City. "The Round-Up," *Daily Capital Journal* (Salem, OR), May 21, 1913; "Watch Out for the Goo Goo Man"; "Goo-Goo Eyes"; "Mashers Must Move; Complaints of Ogling"; "Place Ban on Men Flirts," *Washington Post*, September 8, 1911; "Will Squeeze the Huggers," *Fergus County (MT) Democrat*, August 13, 1912; "Milwaukee's 'Masher' Law Pending," *Detroit Free Press*, January 16, 1910; "Girl Fined for Flirting," *Rock Island Argus*, February 16, 1910; "Omaha Judge Smashes the Masher," *Wilkes-Barre (PA) Times-Leader*, May 12, 1913; "Planning Rule Against Mashers"; "Mashers to Have Hard Sledding"; "Pass 'Masher's' Ordinance," *Denison (IA) Review*, August 21, 1918; "Street Corner Loafers Due for Rude Shake-Up," *Fort Wayne News and Sentinel*, May 24, 1918; "Work or Fight," *Charlotte Observer*, May 24, 1918; "Ogling by Mashers on Public Streets Banned in New City Ordinance."

123. "Trouble Brewing for Masher," *Detroit Free Press*, January 19, 1910.
124. Bowen, "Some Legislative Needs in Illinois."
125. Bodine, "How the Board of Education Is Trying to Protect School Girls."
126. "Social Legislation," *Survey* 34, no. 6 (1915): 143. See also "Need New Ordinance," *Fort Worth Telegram*, August 24, 1906; "Law Aimed at Loafers," *Morning Oregonian*, October 25, 1910; "Wants 'Move-on' Ordinance," *Dallas Morning News*, August 5, 1915; "Street Corner Loafers Due for Rude Shake-Up"; and "Work or Fight." For more on vagrancy laws and so-called ugly laws that targeted transients, the unemployed, and disabled people, see Schweik, *Ugly Laws*; and Goluboff, *Vagrant Nation*.
127. "No Law for the 'Masher,'" *Brooklyn Daily Eagle*, January 10, 1900.
128. Andrew J. White to Abram S. Hewitt, June 9, 1887, box 1339, folder 27, ASH.
129. S. H. Vial to Abram S. Hewitt, June 5, 1887, box 1357, folder 172, ASH.
130. Captain Phil Cassidy to Inspector George W. Dilks, June 14, 1887, box 1357, folder 172, ASH.
131. A. Citizen to Abram S. Hewitt, June 4, 1887, box 1365, folder 236, ASH.
132. Captain Alexander S. Williams to Superintendent William Murray, June 11, 1887, box 1365, folder 236, ASH.
133. See, for instance, Odem, *Delinquent Daughters*, 28–30.
134. "Police Aim to Check Mashers."
135. Bodine, "How the Board of Education Is Trying to Protect School Girls." See also Herman Schuettler, "Police Are Handicapped by Unwillingness of Women to Appear in Court Against Mashers," *Chicago Daily Tribune*, January 27, 1907.
136. "Urges Workhouse Sentences to Drive out Masher Evils." See also "Judge Blames Girls," *Washington Post*, October 15, 1915.
137. Clarence L. Cullen, "Special Cop Squads," *Evening Star* (Washington, DC), March 2, 1907.
138. "Man Accused as Flirt Freed," *New York Times*, January 26, 1922.
139. Rouse, *Her Own Hero*, 84; Freedman, *Redefining Rape*, 208.
140. "Not Always the Men," *Los Angeles Herald*, November 20, 1892; Martin Green, "The Man Higher Up," *Evening World*, October 8, 1904; Schuettler, "Police Are Handicapped by Unwillingness of Women"; Doris Blake, "The 'Ogled,' Rather Than the 'Ogler,' Is to Blame," *Chicago Daily Tribune*, May 10, 1914.

141. "Bold Flirt Is Taken to Jail," *Chicago Defender*, April 12, 1924.
142. "'Official Flirt' Finds No Masher"; "Finds Chicago Men Do Flirt"; "The Flirt-Catcher," *Irish Times* (Dublin); Richard Henry Little, "The Official Flirt in 1950," *Chicago Daily Tribune*, September 4, 1911; "Official Flirt in Chicago"; "Smiles Are Lure to Trap Masher," *Detroit Free Press*, July 25, 1910; "Chief Brushes Away the Web," *Los Angeles Times*, August 30, 1911.
143. Bowen, *Safeguards for City Youth*, 49; "Heiresses Join Ranks of Policewomen," *Ogden Standard*, July 24, 1915. For more on policewomen, see Freedman, *Redefining Rape*, 202–5, 209; Rouse, *Her Own Hero*, 86–87, 88; and Odem, *Delinquent Daughters*, 128–56.
144. "Policewomen Badly Needed," *Chicago Defender*, June 13, 1914.
145. "Ten New Policewomen Appointed by Enright," *New-York Tribune*, May 28, 1919; "Death on Mashers," *Chicago Defender*, January 29, 1927; "D.C. Policewoman Nabs White Masher," *Afro-American*, November 16, 1929.
146. Rouse, *Her Own Hero*, 114.
147. "Plucky Phone Girl Fights a Masher," *Seattle Star*, June 22, 1912.
148. "Hatpins for Defense," *Washington Post*, June 27, 1909; "Masher Put to Flight by Girl's Hatpin"; "Fifty Girls of Spokane Train to Whip Mashers," *Washington Post*, December 26, 1914; "She Smashed Masher with Her White Fists," *Albuquerque Evening Citizen*, August 29, 1905; "Four Girls, Using Fists, Put 3 Mashers to Flight," *St. Louis Post-Dispatch*, June 21, 1908; "Two Little Fists Subdue Masher"; "Mashers and Thugs Beware! Girls Plan Jiu Jitsu Club," *Los Angeles Herald*, April 29, 1906; "Girl's Wit and Jiu Jitsu Land Masher on Back," *Chicago Daily Tribune*, April 4, 1909.
149. From the *Day Book*: Esther Andrews, "Smash the Masher!," September 8, 1916; Intrapodi, "Smashing Cures Mashing"; S. S. M., "Girl Fights a Masher," June 25, 1912; "Miss Nellie Hight," December 3, 1912; "Local Doings in Tabloid Form," December 11, 1912; "She Battered a Man Up for Flirting with Her," August 11, 1913; "Girls Punish Masher," November 23, 1914.
150. "Plucky Phone Girl Fights a Masher." For another example, see Laura Jean Libbey, "False Modesty of Women, and the Would-Be Masher," *Los Angeles Times*, January 12, 1914.
151. "Stenographer Battles White Flirt on Car."
152. Gendzel, "What the Progressives Had in Common."

Chapter Three

1. For historical weather data, see "Climate," NOAA's National Weather Service, accessed July 16, 2025, www.weather.gov/wrh/climate.
2. Canfield was a prosperous neighborhood in the late nineteenth century but fell into decline in the 1930s. "West Canfield Historic District," *Encyclopedia of Detroit*, Detroit Historical Society, accessed November 29, 2018, https://detroithistorical.org/learn/encyclopedia-of-detroit/west-canfield-historic-district.
3. For Jansen's race and occupation, see 1940 US Federal Census, MyHeritage.com, accessed December 10, 2018, https://records.myheritagelibraryedition.com/research/record-10053-775908862/william-jansen-in-1940-united-states-federal-census.

4. Lochbiler, "Sheep's Eyes to Get Wolves in Trouble," *Detroit News*, July 23, 1946, Library of Michigan, Lansing.
5. Lochbiler, "Sheep's Eyes to Get Wolves in Trouble."
6. "Fined $50 for Annoying Young Girl at Belle Isle," *Detroit News*, July 18, 1927, Library of Michigan; "Two Girls Complain and 'Mashers' Are Held," *Detroit News*, August 31, 1928; "40 Movie Mashers Caught," *Detroit News*, February 10, 1929; "Masher Talks Way to Jail for 90 Days," *Detroit Free Press*, July 10, 1946.
7. Lochbiler, "Sheep's Eyes to Get Wolves in Trouble."
8. Witherite was white. Charles Witherite, 1940 US Federal Census, MyHeritage.com, accessed December 10, 2018, https://records.myheritagelibraryedition.com/research/record-10053-736804788/charles-witherite-in-1940-united-states-federal-census.
9. Lochbiler, "Sheep's Eyes to Get Wolves in Trouble."
10. "$25 Per Ogle Is Detroit Rate," *Palm Beach Post*, July 24, 1946; "A 'Fine' Figure Means Just That to Ogling Detroit Males," *Washington Post*, July 24, 1946; "Detroit's Oglers May Be Ogling Jail Cell Bars If They Disobey an Old Law Frowning on Ogling," *Lewiston (ME) Daily Sun*, July 24, 1946; "Ogling Detroit Girls Is to Flirt with Jail Term!," *Chicago Daily Tribune*, July 24, 1946; "Old Law Bans 'Ogling' Girls, but Pinup Favorite Likes It," *Los Angeles Times*, July 24, 1946.

    Ads for Belmont's shows appeared in the *Detroit Free Press* in July and October of that year. "'Centennial' Premier Brings Film Stars to Fox," *Detroit Free Press*, July 17, 1946; ad for Dale Belmont at Penobscot Club, *Detroit Free Press*, October 21, 1946.
11. Lochbiler, "Sheep's Eyes to Get Wolves in Trouble"; "War on Ogling (What Is It?) Opens," *Detroit Free Press*, July 24, 1946.
12. Bederman, *Manliness and Civilization*; Freedman, *Redefining Rape*; Silkey, *Black Woman Reformer.*
13. M. S. Johnson, "Gender, Race, and Rumours."
14. White and Marshall, *What Caused the Detroit Riot?*; Langlois, "The Belle Isle Bridge Incident"; M. S. Johnson, "Gender, Race, and Rumours"; Wolcott, "Gendered Perspectives on Detroit History"; Shantz, "'They Think Their Fannies Are as Good as Ours.'"
15. On the formation of a national media in the United States, see Starr, *Creation of the Media*; and Ohmann, *Selling Culture.*
16. Jones, *Vanguard.*
17. D'Emilio and Freedman, *Intimate Matters*, 239–42; Littauer, *Bad Girls.*
18. Doris Blake, "The Word 'Flirt' Reeks of Mothballs; It's Out of Use, Now," *Chicago Daily Tribune*, December 6, 1929.
19. Hillis, *Live Alone and Like It*, 94, 97–98; Scutts, *Extra Woman*, 111.
20. Hillis, *Live Alone and Like It*, 149.
21. Berebitsky, *Sex and the Office*, 7.
22. Littauer, *Bad Girls*, 7.
23. D'Emilio and Freedman, *Intimate Matters*, 262.
24. Marquis Alderman, "Life History: Albert Caputo" (1931), Ernest W. Burgess Papers, box 126, folder 10, University of Chicago Library, Department of Special Collections.
25. Case record notes, 1924, part 1, folder 10, Mary McDowell Settlement Records, Chicago History Museum Research Center.

26. "Case #3721: Adams, Muriel," August 1944, box 26, folder 3721, Travelers Aid Association of America Records, Social Welfare History Archives, University of Minnesota.
27. See also Odem, *Delinquent Daughters*, 95–127.
28. "Alcock Revives Old Custom of Jailing Flirts," *Chicago Daily Tribune*, August 9, 1931.
29. "Police Drive on Auto Mashers; 17 Boys Seized," *Chicago Daily Tribune*, July 12, 1928. The *Tribune* also reported that 225 men had been arrested on similar charges in 1927.
30. "Alcock Revives Old Custom of Jailing Flirts."
31. Starr, *Creation of the Media*.
32. J. B. Kennedy, "Model Maids," *Collier's*, February 8, 1930, 61; Brown, *Work!*, 7, 5.
33. Mulvey, "Visual Pleasure and Narrative Cinema," 57–68.
34. For more examples, see R. Davis, *Fierce Desires*, 177–78.
35. See, for instance, *Mildred Pierce* (Warner Bros., 1945); *It's a Wonderful Life* (RKO Radio Pictures, 1946); or *Easter Parade* (Metro-Goldwyn-Mayer, 1948).
36. *On the Town* (Metro-Goldwyn-Mayer, 1949); *The Stranger* (RKO Radio Pictures, 1946).
37. Smoodin, *Animating Culture*, 7–43.
38. Benjaminson, *Life and Times of Betty Boop*, xiii, 11–12, 26.
39. J. Greene, "Proper Dash of Spice."
40. Smoodin, *Animating Culture*, 37.
41. *Little Red Walking Hood* (Warner Bros., 1937); *Red Hot Riding Hood* (Metro-Goldwyn-Mayer, 1943). As of this writing, these short films are available to stream on HBO Max and Amazon Prime, respectively.
42. Avery released at least two additional retellings of fairy tales, including *Swing Shift Cinderella* (Metro-Goldwyn-Mayer, 1945) and *Little Rural Riding Hood* (Metro-Goldwyn-Mayer, 1949).
43. For analyses of the sexual undertones in Little Red Riding Hood, see Brownmiller, *Against Our Will*, 309–10; and Zipes, *Little Red Riding Hood*.
44. Chauncey, *Gay New York*, 65–98.
45. "'Wolf' Finds Self in the Dog House over Ogling Law," *Chicago Daily Tribune*, October 22, 1946; Associated Press, "Wolf-Call Protester Told to Go Whistle," *Detroit News*, July 19, 1947, *Detroit News* Clipping Files, Whistlers and Whistling, Archives of Michigan; Sheila John Daly, "He Cries 'Wolf' over Feminine Eager Beavers," *Chicago Daily Tribune*, April 9, 1949.
46. Quite literally. At one point, her shoulder drips with ice and snow.
47. West was a legendary sex symbol of the 1930s. A flashing neon sign above Grandma's penthouse reads, "Come up and see me some time," Mae West's most famous one-liner.
48. Beck, *50 Greatest Cartoons*. The 1994 film *The Mask* (New Line Cinema, 1994) spoofed the nightclub scene from *Red Hot Riding Hood*, using special effects to turn Jim Carrey into the Wolf. A similar nightclub scene also appears in *Who Framed Roger Rabbit?* (Buena Vista Pictures, 1988). For more examples of Avery's influence on American film and popular culture, see Place-Verghnes, *Tex Avery*, 179–83.
49. Quoted in Alex Marshall, "The Surprising History of the Wolf-Whistle," BBC, March 23, 2018, www.bbc.com/culture/story/20180322-the-surprising-history-of-the-wolf-whistle.

50. Smoodin, *Animating Culture*, 28.
51. Smoodin, *Animating Culture*, 27; K. Cohen, *Forbidden Animation*, 37–38.
52. R. Davis, *Fierce Desires*, 220–23.
53. D'Emilio and Freedman, *Intimate Matters*, 289.
54. D'Emilio, *Sexual Politics*, 24.
55. Bérubé, *Coming Out Under Fire*; Canaday, *Straight State*, 138–39.
56. Hegarty, *Victory Girls*, 7.
57. Hegarty, *Victory Girls*; Winchell, *Good Girls*.
58. Hegarty, *Victory Girls*, 86.
59. Hiltner, *Taking Leave*, 4.
60. *Ashore in San Diego* (Welfare Department of the Naval Training Station, 1942), entry 44, box 1, Records of the Office of Community War Services, RG 215, NARA.
61. *Ashore in San Diego*, 20.
62. Christine Cook of the US Army War College advised me of the distinction between expectations for enlisted men's sexual behaviors compared with expectations for officers. She is currently researching how officers' manuals differed from literature geared toward enlisted men, particularly in presenting distinct masculine norms.
63. Hegarty, *Victory Girls*, 85.
64. Statement of Joseph Earle Moore, MD, Chairman, Subcommittee on Venereal Diseases, National Research Council Before the Joint Army and Navy Committee on Welfare and Recreation, Washington, DC, February 28, 1941, box 10, Records of the Bureau of Medicine and Surgery, RG 52, NARA. See also Hegarty, *Victory Girls*, 87–88.
65. Quoted in Terkel, *"Good War,"* 124.
66. Hiltner, *Taking Leave*, 206–7, 82, 78.
67. D'Emilio and Freedman, *Intimate Matters*, 261.
68. Eliot Ness, *What About Girls?*, November 1943, p. 17, entry 44, box 5, RG 215, NARA.
69. Richard H. Anthony, "The Girl and the Man in Uniform" (Massachusetts Society for Social Hygiene, 1942), 5, entry 44, box 4, RG 215, NARA.
70. Ness, *What About Girls?*, 21.
71. *So You've Got Furlough?*, 1944, entry 44, box 1, RG 215, NARA.
72. Hegarty, *Victory Girls*; Winchell, *Good Girls*.
73. Ness, *What About Girls?*, 22.
74. Canaday, *Straight State*.
75. "Victory Celebrations," *Life*, August 27, 1945, 27.
76. "Victory Celebrations," 21–27.
77. "Victory Celebrations," 21–27.
78. See, for instance, one of the first feminist critiques to be cited widely by news sources, "The Kissing Sailor, or 'The Selective Blindness of Rape Culture,'" *Crates and Ribbons* (blog), September 30, 2012, https://cratesandribbons.com/2012/09/30/the-kissing-sailor-or-the-selective-blindness-of-rape-culture-vj-day-times-square/.
79. Eisenstaedt and Goldsmith, *Eye of Eisenstaedt*, 56.
80. Greta Zimmer Friedman, interview by Patricia Redmond, transcript, August 23, 2005, Veterans History Project, Library of Congress, Washington, DC, http://memory.loc.gov/diglib/vhp/story/loc.natlib.afc2001001.42863/transcript?ID=sr0001.

81. Brooke L. Blower, "WWII's Most Iconic Kiss Wasn't Romantic—It Was Terrifying," *Washington Post*, February 22, 2019.
82. Associated Press Wirephoto, "Phone Calls Can Wait When There's Ogling to Do," *Chicago Daily Tribune*, October 26, 1945.
83. Canaday, *Straight State*, 142.
84. Canaday, *Straight State*, 143; E. May, *Homeward Bound*, 9.
85. Blower, "V-J Day," 73–75.
86. Associated Press, "Soldiers May Ogle in Beauty Contest," *Spokesman-Review* (Spokane), July 26, 1946.
87. "Oglers Get the 'Aye,'" *New York Times*, July 29, 1946.
88. Quoted in Malcolm W. Bingay, "What Is an Ogle?," Good Morning, *Detroit Free Press*, July 31, 1946.
89. Bingay, "What Is an Ogle?," July 31, 1946; Jack Freeman, reader letter, Voice of the People, *Detroit Free Press*, August 19, 1946.
90. Bingay, "What Is an Ogle?," July 31, 1946.
91. "You Can Ogle, but Ask First," *Detroit Free Press*, August 10, 1946.
92. Robert Sturgiss, "Women Rush to Defense of City's Outlaw Oglers," *Detroit Free Press*, August 22, 1946.
93. Ogler 1/C, "Ghost Town Ogling," Voice of the People, *Detroit Free Press*, September 4, 1946.
94. Quoted in Bingay, "What Is an Ogle?," July 31, 1946.
95. Malcolm W. Bingay, "The Experts," Good Morning, *Detroit Free Press*, August 6, 1946.
96. Bingay, "What Is an Ogle?," July 31, 1946.
97. Ogler 1/C, "Ghost Town Ogling."
98. Arvo Wain, "What Price Beauty," Voice of the People, *Detroit Free Press*, August 9, 1946.
99. "Detroit's Oglers May Be Ogling Jail Cell Bars If They Disobey an Old Law Frowning on Ogling."
100. Sturgiss, "Women Rush to Defense of City's Outlaw Oglers."
101. For more on how women associate themselves with "emphasized femininity," see Connell, *Gender and Power*, 183; and Messerschmidt, *Hegemonic Masculinity*, 29, 51.
102. The women's names suggest a variety of ethnic identities, including Jewish, Hispanic, and Polish.
103. Maryon Zylstra, "What Do You Do When a Strange Man Whistles at You?," Inquiring Camera Girl, *Chicago Daily Tribune*, August 18, 1945.
104. Maryon Zylstra, "Does Being Beautiful Have Any Disadvantages?," Inquiring Camera Girl, *Chicago Daily Tribune*, July 14, 1944.
105. Henry and Curry, *Aaron Henry*, 28.
106. A. Fischer, *Streets Belong to Us*.
107. "Ofay Masher, Accused by Young Woman, Is Fined $5 and Costs," *Afro-American*, April 18, 1936.
108. "White Masher Gets Only a Reprimand," *Afro-American*, August 6, 1938.
109. "Gangsters Insult and Kick Two Women," *Boston Chronicle*, May 7, 1932.
110. "To Parents of Girls," *Boston Chronicle*, May 7, 1932. See also Deutsch, *Women and the City*, 265.

111. "Arrests White Man; Negro Cop on Spot," *Chicago Defender*, January 17, 1948.
112. McGuire, "'It Was Like All of Us Had Been Raped,'" 909; Simmons, *Crescent City Girls*, 91.
113. Simmons, *Crescent City Girls*, 23, 57, 67, 93–107.
114. Simmons, *Crescent City Girls*, 91.
115. Presstman Street was in a neighborhood of Baltimore that was over 92 percent Black in 1940. Percentage of Black Residents in Baltimore, 1940, Social Explorer, www.socialexplorer.com/ac8d7116d5/view (based on data from the US Census Bureau, accessed May 12, 2020).
116. "Ofay Flirt Escapes Being Lynched," *Afro-American*, July 8, 1933.
117. Albert Jefferson, "Remember Way Back in 1945?," *Afro-American*, January 12, 1946.
118. Jefferson, "Remember Way Back in 1945?"
119. "Obscene Letter Traps Masher," *Afro-American*, September 7, 1940; "Subway Masher Gets Penitentiary Sentence," *Afro-American*, August 30, 1941; "White Masher Cries 'Holdup'; 5 Arrested," *Afro-American*, September 18, 1943; "Movie Masher Gets 60 Days," *Michigan Chronicle* (Detroit), March 24, 1951; "Masher Gets 90 Day Term for Molesting Girl," *Michigan Chronicle*, November 3, 1956; "Shot by Masher," *Chicago Daily Defender*, January 15, 1957; "Coed, 18, Shoots Masher in Car," *Chicago Daily Defender*, February 13, 1958; "Husband Shot Defend Wife from Masher," *Chicago Defender*, June 30, 1958; "Order Woman Held in Fatal Auto Assault on 'Masher,'" *Chicago Daily Defender*, October 29, 1958; "Masher Dies from Blow on Head with Glass," *Chicago Daily Defender*, May 18, 1960.
120. "What Method Do You Use to Get Rid of a 'Wolf'?," *Afro-American*, April 28, 1956.
121. Alvin White, "Danger Lurks for Unescorted Women in N.Y. Subways," *Afro-American*, November 30, 1946.
122. "Rape-Deaths Puzzle Police," *Michigan Chronicle*, August 17, 1946.
123. "Holds Girl in Car, Man Faces Kidnap Charges," *Michigan Chronicle*, August 17, 1946.
124. Bingay may have confused Holmes Jr. with his father, Oliver Wendell Holmes Sr., whose writing on the pretty faces that make up the "picture gallery" of the city street appeared in chapter 1.
125. Malcolm W. Bingay, "What Is an Ogle?," Good Morning, *Detroit Free Press*, July 27, 1946.

Chapter Four

1. "Negro Jailed Because White Woman Saw Him," *Daily Worker*, July 9, 1951.
2. "Convict Man for Assault 75 Ft. Away," *New York Amsterdam News*, July 14, 1951.
3. A. M. Rivera Jr., "Gets 2 Years for 'Looking' at Girl!," *Pittsburgh Courier*, July 21, 1951.
4. For more examples, see "Assault at Fifty Feet," *Arkansas State Press*, July 27, 1951; "Will Appeal Mental Rape Conviction," *Michigan Chronicle*, July 28, 1951; "Farmer Convicted On 'Assault Charge,'" *Atlanta Daily World*, August 2, 1951.
5. State of North Carolina v. Mack Ingram (Recorder's Court of Caswell County, June 18, 1951), 2, in part 08, series B, NAACP Papers, Library of Congress, ProQuest History Vault, https://www.proquest.com/docview/2623979155?sourcetype=Archival%20Materials.

6. "November 1951," Claude A. Barnett Papers: The Associated Negro Press, 1918–1967, part 1, series B, Chicago Historical Society, ProQuest History Vault, https://congressional.proquest.com/histvault?q=001584–047–0160.
7. Hine, "Rape and the Inner Lives of Black Women"; McGuire, *Dark End of the Street*.
8. "Houston Lawyer Admits Goo-Goo Eyes Violation," *Washington Post*, January 4, 1951; "'Goo-Goo Eyes' Charge Costs Texas Man $50," *Washington Post*, March 6, 1951; Bob Carpenter, "Eye Troubles of the Houston Swains," *Atlanta Journal and Constitution*, May 6, 1951.
9. "What Happened to Matt Ingram," *Ebony*, September 1953, 38–44; Berry, "'Reckless Eyeballing.'"
10. "Books Published Today," *New York Times*, November 3, 1954; Sauers, *Girl Watcher's Guide*.
11. Myron Kandel, "Pageant to Hail 'Girl Watching,'" *New York Times*, July 27, 1962; Phyllis Battelle, "Rules for Girl-Watching," *Detroit News*, March 27, 1962.
12. Jack Smith, "Girl Watcher Forms Club to Watch Form," *Los Angeles Times*, October 13, 1963; "Girl Watching," *Chicago Tribune*, October 20, 1963.
13. *Girl Watcher*, March 1959, http://archive.org/details/girl_watcher_no1_bonanza_1959-03.
14. The O'Kaysions' hit peaked at number 5 on the Billboard Hot 100. "Billboard Hot 100," *Billboard*, October 5, 1968, 59. Bob Crewe and Andy Williams both had hits with versions of "Music to Watch Girls By." "Billboard Hot 100," *Billboard*, February 11, 1967, 24; "Billboard Hot 100," *Billboard*, April 29, 1967, 20.
15. Cecil Smith, "Time Is Ripe for Girl-Watching," *Los Angeles Times*, August 8, 1962; Larry Townsend, "Girl-Watching Champ Views Beauty Contest," *Chicago Tribune*, May 21, 1972.
16. Wallace, "Girl Watching at Expo 67."
17. Daniel Shulman, "Girl-Watching," *Seventeen*, June 1963, 92–93, 143; Haupt, *"Seventeen" Guide*, 54.
18. Sauers, *Girl Watcher's Guide*, 9.
19. Kandel, "Pageant to Hail 'Girl Watching'"; Linda Kramer, "American Society of Girl Watchers Has 50,000 Card Carrying Members," *Sarasota Herald-Tribune*, October 15, 1970; "Girl-Watching Guide Catalogs Specimens," *Los Angeles Times*, December 9, 1970.
20. W. L. Boswell had taken Ingram to the gas station to buy petrol a few days after Ingram had first moved to the area. "State of North Carolina v. Ingram Rape Case," 1951–1953, part 08, series B, NAACP Papers, Library of Congress, ProQuest History Vault, https://congressional.proquest.com/histvault?q=001532-027-0372.
21. "State of North Carolina v. Ingram Rape Case."
22. State of North Carolina v. Mack Ingram (Recorder's Court of Caswell County, June 18, 1951), 10.
23. Rivera, "Gets 2 Years for 'Looking' at Girl!"; "State of North Carolina v. Ingram Rape Case." For more on the NAACP's initial offer of help, see "Convict Man for Assault 75 Ft. Away."
24. "Convict Negro of Assault for Leering at Girl," *Chicago Daily Tribune*, November 12, 1952; "Guilty of 'Assault by Look,'" *Manchester Guardian*, November 12, 1952; "Jury Find Mack Ingram Guilty in 'Reckless Eye-Balling' Case," *Atlanta Daily World*,

November 12, 1952; "Negro in North Carolina Convicted of Assault by 'Leer' at White Girl," *New York Times*, November 12, 1952; "'Leerer' to Appeal Assault Conviction," *Detroit Free Press*, November 13, 1952; "Negro Escapes Jail in Assault by Leer," *New York Times*, November 13, 1952; "Assault by Leering," *South China Morning Post*, November 14, 1952; Rufus Wells, "'Look' Attacker on Trial 3rd Time," *Afro-American*, November 15, 1952.

25. "'Leering' Conviction Appealed," *New York Times*, December 11, 1952; "Jury Discrimination Charged in 'Look Attack,'" *Afro-American*, December 20, 1952.

26. On the attorney general's agreement with Ingram's lawyers: "New Turn in Race Case," *New York Times*, January 29, 1953; "N.C. Attorney General Joins NAACP in Ingram Case Plea," *Atlanta Daily World*, February 1, 1953; "N.C.'s Attorney General Joins NAACP in Asking Review of Ingram Case," *Afro-American*, February 7, 1953.

On the voided conviction: "'Assault by Leer' Verdict Voided in North Carolina," *Christian Science Monitor*, February 25, 1953; "'Leer Attack' Conviction Thrown Out," *Atlanta Constitution*, February 26, 1953; "Leering at Girl Held Not Assault," *Globe and Mail* (Toronto), February 26, 1953; "Negro's Conviction Quashed," *Manchester Guardian*, February 26, 1953; "North Carolina High Court Reverses 'Assault by Leer' Conviction of Mack Ingram," *Atlanta Daily World*, February 26, 1953; "N.C. High Court Overrules 'Leer' Case Conviction," *Pittsburgh Courier*, February 28, 1953; "Carolina Hi Court Frees Ingram," *Arkansas State Press*, March 6, 1953; "North Carolina Supreme Court 'Frees' Mack Ingram," *Plain Dealer* (Kansas City, KS), March 6, 1953; "Free Mack Ingram in Look Assault Case," *Chicago Defender*, March 7, 1953; "North Carolina Supreme Court Free Mack Ingram," *Jackson (MS) Advocate*, March 7, 1953; "Sharecropper Freed as Court Voids Old Law," *Cleveland Call and Post*, March 7, 1953.

27. "Assault at Fifty Feet"; "November 1951," Claude A. Barnett Papers. A reporter for London's *Daily Mirror* covered the superior court retrial. A. M. Rivera, "N.C. 'Eye-Balling' Case Ends Mistrial," *Pittsburgh Courier*, November 24, 1951.

28. See, for instance, these headlines: "'Rape by Look' Case Fizzles as Jury Locks," *Cleveland Call and Post*, November 24, 1951; "Ingram Put on Probation For 'Eye-Ball Rape,'" *Atlanta Daily World*, November 13, 1952; "Appeal Guilty Verdict in N.C. Eye-Rape Case," *Chicago Defender*, November 22, 1952.

29. "State of North Carolina v. Ingram Rape Case"; Cliff Mackay, "Stalin Just Loves N.C.," *Afro-American*, February 2, 1952; "'Look' Case Verdict Brings Varied Editorial Comment," *Afro-American*, November 22, 1952.

30. State of North Carolina v. Mack Ingram (Recorder's Court of Caswell County, June 18, 1951), 5.

31. Rivera, "N.C. 'Eye-Balling' Case Ends Mistrial."

32. "State of North Carolina v. Ingram Rape Case"; "Legal Department Monthly Report," November 1951, part 01, NAACP Papers, Library of Congress, ProQuest History Vault, https://congressional.proquest.com/histvault?q=001410-002-0184.

33. "Calls Mistrial in Leering Case, Hits Hung Jury," *Chicago Daily Tribune*, November 17, 1951; "2 Jurors Halt Attempt to Jail 'Looking' Dad," *Afro-American*, November 24, 1951; "'Rape by Look' Case Fizzles as Jury Locks"; "Mistrial Declared in Case of 'Assault at 75 Feet,'" *Negro Star*, November 30, 1951.

34. "Man Wins Mistrial in Assault on Girl Who Wasn't Touched," *Evening Star*, November 16, 1951; "November 1951," Claude A. Barnett Papers.

35. "State of North Carolina v. Ingram Rape Case."
36. Jacquet, *Injustices of Rape*, 15–26.
37. Freedman, *Redefining Rape*, 253–70. See also Goodman, *Stories of Scottsboro.*
38. "'Evil Eye' Ingram to Appeal 'Leering' Conviction," *Jet*, November 27, 1952.
39. Dorr, *White Women*, 2–3.
40. Dorr, *White Women*, 213.
41. "2 Jurors Halt Attempt to Jail 'Looking' Dad"; "'Rape by Look' Case Fizzles as Jury Locks." White locals and reporters usually referred to Ingram as Mack rather than Matt. Berry, "'Reckless Eyeballing,'" 233.
42. Mackay, "Stalin Just Loves N.C."
43. For more on Emmett Till, see Anderson, *Emmett Till*; Whitfield, *Death in the Delta*; and Tyson, *Blood of Emmett Till.*
44. "State of North Carolina v. Ingram Rape Case."
45. The *New York Post*'s editorial was reprinted in "'Look' Case Verdict Brings Varied Editorial Comment."
46. Berry argues that the Ingram case shows how African Americans have long been denied the "right to sexual expression." That is, even if Ingram did look at Boswell and derived pleasure from that look, he was simply exercising the "fundamental human right" of "sexual freedom." Berry, "'Reckless Eyeballing,'" 232–33.
47. "Robert Ruark," American Society of Authors and Writers, accessed May 26, 2020, http://amsaw.org/amsaw-ithappenedinhistory-122903-ruark.html.
48. Robert Ruark, "Scientific Appraisal of Ogles and Oglers," *Oshkosh Daily Northwestern*, December 1, 1952.
49. Ruark, "Scientific Appraisal of Ogles and Oglers"; Robert Ruark, "Watch That Eyebrow, Buster," *Detroit Free Press*, December 1, 1952; Robert C. Ruark, "Europeans Far Ahead in Art of Ogling," *Victoria (TX) Advocate*, December 2, 1952.
50. Ruark, "Europeans Far Ahead in Art of Ogling."
51. Ruark, "Scientific Appraisal of Ogles and Oglers."
52. Hickey, *Breaking the Gender Code*, 89.
53. Fraterrigo, *"Playboy" and the Making of the Good Life*, 10–11; Beth Bailey, *From Front Porch to Back Seat*, 103–8; Cuordileone, *Manhood and American Political Culture.*
54. D. Johnson, *Lavender Scare*; Hubbs, *Queer Composition*; Sherry, *Gay Artists.*
55. Fraterrigo, *"Playboy" and the Making of the Good Life*, 5.
56. Examples of young people embracing girl-watching include the aforementioned *Seventeen* publications and the hit pop single "I'm a Girl Watcher." Shulman, "Girl-Watching"; Haupt, *"Seventeen" Guide*. On the acceptability of girl-watching for married men, see "He Guides Girl-Watchers," *Times Pictorial* (Dublin), January 15, 1955; and Gillian Frank and Lauren Gutterman, "How the 'Girl Watching' Fad of the 1960s Taught Men to Harass Women," *Jezebel* (blog), October 8, 2020, https://jezebel.com/how-the-girl-watching-fad-of-the-1960s-taught-men-to-ha-1844916738.
57. "Wife of Expert Not Upset over Husband's Hobby," *Boston Globe*, April 10, 1955. On occasion, wives also reportedly attended girl-watching club meetings or bought their husbands memberships to such clubs. Joe Radoff, "1500 Male 'Vigilantes' Are Busy Putting Gals Under Scrutiny for Good Tastes in Fashions," *Women's Wear Daily*, October 27, 1965.

58. William M. Freeman, "Advertising: People," *New York Times*, August 10, 1960; "Obituary of Donald J. Sauers," *LancasterOnline*, September 13, 2013, https://lancasteronline.com/obituaries/donald-j-sauers/article_1ee34b92-b438-5bec-b003-76ff96e5eeef.html.
59. Kandel, "Pageant to Hail 'Girl Watching.'"
60. Sauers, *Girl Watcher's Guide*.
61. Spelling and styling as in the original. Radoff, "1500 Male 'Vigilantes' Are Busy Putting Gals Under Scrutiny for Good Tastes in Fashions." See also Marjory Smith, "Smoked Glasses Badge of Girl Watcher Cult," *Atlanta Constitution*, April 26, 1956.
62. Sauers, *Girl Watcher's Guide*, 31, 26.
63. For a contemporary example, see Quinn, "Sexual Harassment and Masculinity," 555.
64. *Girl Watcher*, March 1959.
65. Sauers, *Girl Watcher's Guide*, 32; J. Smith, "Girl Watcher Forms Club to Watch Form."
66. Sauers, *Girl Watcher's Guide*, 12.
67. Richard Joseph, "On Crocodile Wrestling, Girl Watching in Jamaica," *Chicago Tribune*, October 13, 1963.
68. Brawley and Dixon, "Searching for Dorothy Lamour," 5.
69. S. May, *Michener's South Pacific*.
70. Battelle, "Rules for Girl-Watching."
71. Sauers, *Girl Watcher's Guide*, 29, 43–63.
72. Robert C. Harvey, "Dedini, Eldon Lawrence," *American National Biography Online*, 2008, www.anb.org/articles/17/17-01703.html.
73. Associated Press, "International Girl Watcher Tells What Techniques Are Best to Use," *Florence (AL) Times–Tri-Cities Daily*, September 26, 1972; Bruce West, "Girl-Watching," *Globe and Mail*, November 11, 1970; Shulman, "Girl-Watching"; Marjory Smith, "Smoked Glasses Badge of Girl Watcher Cult."
74. Sauers, *Girl Watcher's Guide*, 33. Ray-Bans took advantage of this advice for an ad campaign that promised to equip both men and women with sunglasses they could use to watch each other. Ray-Bans advertisement, *Playboy*, June 1968, 25.
75. Quoted in Patricia McCormack, "It's Swell for Girl Watchers," *Atlanta Constitution*, July 2, 1965.
76. "Montreal Said Girl Watchers Paradise," *Toronto Daily Star*, August 17, 1967.
77. Sauers, *Girl Watcher's Guide*, 33.
78. "Girl Watching Week Is Once-a-Year Happening," *Los Angeles Times*, November 9, 1972.
79. "Girl-Watchers' Rules," *Jerusalem Post*, April 21, 1967.
80. Sauers, *Girl Watcher's Guide*, 32.
81. Quoted in Battelle, "Rules for Girl-Watching."
82. Sauers, *Girl Watcher's Guide*, 8–9, 29–33.
83. Radoff, "1500 Male 'Vigilantes' Are Busy Putting Gals Under Scrutiny for Good Tastes in Fashions"; Phyllis Battelle, "Too Much Girl Repels True-Blue Watchers," *Detroit News*, February 10, 1969.
84. Sauers, *Girl Watcher's Guide*, 22.
85. Lyle W. Price, "On the Art of Girl Watching—Or, Phooey on the Guys: In Los Angeles," *Ann Arbor News*, October 2, 1972.
86. Jane Lee, "Girl Watchers Sprout in Summer . . . Annoy," *Detroit News*, August 7, 1974.

Indeed, some women professed to enjoying "man-watching," but the concept never took off or gained near the popularity of girl-watching. See, for instance, "Two-Way Street," Your Letters, *Seventeen*, August 1963; Frances Cawthon, "Try Boy-Watching in Eskimo Sunglasses," *Atlanta Journal and Constitution*, February 28, 1965; Joyce Carter, "Man-Watching," *Globe and Mail*, February 10, 1972; "Boy-Watching," *Atlanta Constitution*, June 16, 1974; "Men-Watchers Society Opens for Membership," *Los Angeles Sentinel*, October 11, 1973; and "Morning Briefing: O. J. Simpson Among Men the Man Watchers Watch," *Los Angeles Times*, December 30, 1976.

87. "He Guides Girl-Watchers"; "The Dangers of Girl-Watching," *Jerusalem Post*, July 18, 1973; "Girl-Watchers' Rules."
88. "Strike May Cut into Airliner Girl-Watching," *Los Angeles Times*, February 26, 1965; Ron Bailey, "Girl Watching: Always a Chicago Spectacular," *Chicago Tribune*, July 29, 1962; "Girl Watcher Forgets Meters," *Los Angeles Times*, April 12, 1961; "Girl-Watching Week," *Los Angeles Times*, July 30, 1970; Jeff Prugh, "Girl Watching, Si! Football? Well . . . ," *Los Angeles Times*, October 13, 1971; "Girl Watching Week Is Mall Coming Attraction," *Los Angeles Times*, July 6, 1972.

    Aurora Wallace has shown that girl-watching reporting often depicted women as an integral part of the cityscape who, like birds, were some of the native species that enthusiastic watchers could catalog. Wallace, "Geography of Girl Watching."
89. L. Cohen, *Consumers' Republic*, 11, 8, 19.
90. D'Emilio and Freedman, *Intimate Matters*, 305, 278, 302; Brumberg, *Body Project*.
91. Fraterrigo, *"Playboy" and the Making of the Good Life*, 3.
92. Fraterrigo, *"Playboy" and the Making of the Good Life*, 7.
93. Garland-Thomson, *Staring*, 29.
94. Denning, *Cover Stories*, 109. For more on the voyeurism of early to mid-twentieth-century popular media, see Mulvey, "Visual Pleasure and Narrative Cinema."
95. Kuhn, *Women's Pictures*, 112.
96. Kandel, "Pageant to Hail 'Girl Watching.'" Examples of these ads can be found with a quick search of large university dailies, such as the *Michigan Daily*.
97. Lester Gaba, "Ideas for Sweater Windows," *Women's Wear Daily*, May 3, 1955.
98. Radoff, "1500 Male 'Vigilantes' Are Busy Putting Gals Under Scrutiny for Good Tastes in Fashions."
99. Patricia McCormack, "Chief Girl-Watcher May Found Society to Prevent Longer Skirts," *Flint Journal*, July 18, 1967.
100. Battelle, "Too Much Girl Repels True-Blue Watchers."
101. Bob Talbert, "Seeing Through the Quarry Takes Sport Out of Girl-Watching," *Detroit Free Press*, July 8, 1969.
102. Radoff, "1500 Male 'Vigilantes' Are Busy Putting Gals Under Scrutiny for Good Tastes in Fashions."
103. Advertisement for Revlon lipstick, *Vogue*, April 1, 1970, 14–15; "Fall Foundations: Stand-Up for Stripes," *Women's Wear Daily*, May 19, 1966; Marji Kunz, "Girl Watcher," *Detroit Free Press*, February 4, 1966.
104. Advertisement for Finesse stockings by J. P. Stevens & Co., *Vogue*, October 15, 1968, 44.
105. "Nude Look to Dress Up Bra Business," *Women's Wear Daily*, September 5, 1968, 24.

106. RetroGoop, *DIET PEPSI girl-watching Tv Commercial 1965*, accessed March 14, 2016, www.youtube.com/watch?v=G1RXYEr4O_g (site discontinued).
107. PepsiCo, Incorporated, "Annual Report, 1968," March 1969, ProQuest Annual Reports, www.proquest.com/docview/88198959/citation/26DB27C011614286PQ/3; PepsiCo, Incorporated, "Annual Report, 1967," March 1968, ProQuest Annual Reports, www.proquest.com/docview/88198312/citation/26DB27C011614286PQ/4. See also Love, *Soda Goes Pop*, 43–44.
108. Don Sauers, *The Girl Watcher's Guide*, 2nd ed. (American Society of Girl Watchers, 1967).
109. Kandel, "Pageant to Hail 'Girl Watching'"; "History," Miss Rheingold, accessed November 11, 2019, http://missrheingold.com/history/.
110. Radoff, "1500 Male 'Vigilantes' Are Busy Putting Gals Under Scrutiny for Good Tastes in Fashions"; Bruce W. Farcau, "Girl Watching," *Los Angeles Times*, September 22, 1971; "Girl Watching Week Is Mall Coming Attraction"; Associated Press, "International Girl Watcher Tells What Techniques Are Best to Use"; Price, "On the Art of Girl Watching"; "Girl Watching Week Is Once-a-Year Happening"; Skip Ferderber, "It's Girl-Watching Time Again in Century City," *Los Angeles Times*, September 20, 1973; "Girl Watching Week Slated," *Los Angeles Times*, September 1, 1974; "Girl Watching Judging Slated," *Los Angeles Times*, September 5, 1974.
111. Townsend, "Girl-Watching Champ Views Beauty Contest."
112. "Radio Station Grabs Zany Promotion for 'Yum Yum,' a Girl Watchers Club," *Boxoffice*, January 13, 1964.
113. Cawthon, "Try Boy-Watching in Eskimo Sunglasses."
114. Girl-watchers often remind me of the famous Monty Python sketch in which Eric Idle's smarmy, cheeky bar patron sidles up to Terry Jones's stuffy office worker and tries to talk to him about sex using only euphemisms and a suggestive "wink wink, nudge nudge."
115. For a feminist analysis of how rape jokes normalize sexual violence, see Lockyer and Savigny, "Rape Jokes Aren't Funny."
116. Gerbner, *Dynamics of Cultural Resistance*, 48.
117. Hickey, *Breaking the Gender Code*, 87.
118. Brian Bell, "Girl-Watching Fine Sport In Breezy Buenos Aires," *Globe and Mail*, May 21, 1960; Kandel, "Pageant to Hail 'Girl Watching'"; Joseph, "On Crocodile Wrestling, Girl Watching in Jamaica"; J. Smith, "Girl Watcher Forms Club to Watch Form"; Ken Lubas, "Furtive Leer Comes Out in Open," *Los Angeles Times*, August 7, 1969. For other examples, see Bob Talbert, "Girl-Watching Readers Irate at Suggestion of 'Lost' Challenge," *Detroit Free Press*, July 31, 1969; David Fortney, "On Girl Watching: Do the Sexes See Eye to Eye? The Watchers," *Chicago Tribune*, June 30, 1973; Gay Pauley, "When Heat's on Women Play Old Skin Game," *Flint Journal*, August 12, 1973; and Cheryl Pilate, "Unhand Us, Ya Perverts," *Michigan Daily*, May 23, 1974, Bentley Historical Library, University of Michigan.
119. "Standin' on the Corner," *Los Angeles Tribune*, August 14, 1959. Griffith worked briefly as a comedic monologist and host for CBS Radio before joining CBS television for *The Andy Griffith Show* in 1960. Don Page, "CBS to Dish Out Laugh Fare Daily," *Los Angeles Times*, July 12, 1959.

120. Sauers, *Girl Watcher's Guide*, 9. Emphasis in the original.
121. Rotundo, *American Manhood*, 239–44.
122. For more on the connections between masculinity and sport, see Bundgaard, *Muscle and Manliness*.
123. "Girl Watching Week Is Once-a-Year Happening"; "He Guides Girl-Watchers"; "Highly Popular Pastime Demands a Technique Which Is Attained Only thru Long Practice," *Chicago Daily Tribune*, January 16, 1955; "Girl-Watchers' Rules."
124. Lubas, "Furtive Leer Comes Out in Open"; Linda Kramer, "Girl Watching Is—Wait, There Goes One Now!," *Flint Journal*, September 17, 1970.
125. Kandel, "Pageant to Hail 'Girl Watching'"; Kramer, "American Society of Girl Watchers Has 50,000 Card Carrying Members."
126. Radoff, "1500 Male 'Vigilantes' Are Busy Putting Gals Under Scrutiny for Good Tastes in Fashions"; J. Smith, "Girl Watcher Forms Club to Watch Form."
127. Radoff, "1500 Male 'Vigilantes' Are Busy Putting Gals Under Scrutiny for Good Tastes in Fashions."
128. See, for instance, Rubin, "Traffic in Women."
129. Battelle, "Too Much Girl Repels True-Blue Watchers."
130. PepsiCo, Incorporated, "Annual Report, 1970," March 1971, ProQuest Annual Reports, www.proquest.com/docview/88200676/citation/DAD004EB28C64B45PQ/1. The girl-watcher campaign is not mentioned in Pepsi's 1970 annual report after several years of prominent placement.
131. A quick online search will reveal numerous iterations of this design.
132. "Girl-Watching Week."
133. "Girl Watching Week Is Mall Coming Attraction"; United Press International, "Annual Girl Watching Week Begins in LA," *Sarasota Journal*, September 25, 1972; Associated Press, "International Girl Watcher Tells What Techniques Are Best to Use"; Liz Elling, "On the Art of Girl Watching—Or, Phooey on the Guys," *Ann Arbor News*, October 2, 1972; "Girl Watching Week Is Once-a-Year Happening"; Ferderber, "It's Girl-Watching Time Again in Century City"; "Girl Watching Week Slated"; "Girl Watching Judging Slated."
134. "Girl Watching Week Is Mall Coming Attraction." The mall opened in October 1964. "Area Growth Highlights '64," *Los Angeles Times*, December 27, 1964.
135. "Girl Watching Week Is Mall Coming Attraction"; Ferderber, "It's Girl-Watching Time Again in Century City."
136. Farcau, "Girl Watching."
137. Associated Press, "International Girl Watcher Tells What Techniques Are Best to Use." Note here the almost verbatim similarities to antimasher rhetoric that scorned the "scrutinizing attention" of mashers and warned that such leering looks forced women to change their routes through the city. For example, see "'Mashers' on the Postoffice Steps Annoy Women Nightly," *Detroit Free Press*, August 7, 1910.
138. Ferderber, "It's Girl-Watching Time Again in Century City." This article also dubiously claimed that feminists had tried to sabotage the event in previous years by submitting "ugly girls" to compete in the girl-watching contest.
139. Price, "On the Art of Girl Watching."
140. Elling, "On the Art of Girl Watching."

141. Ferderber, "It's Girl-Watching Time Again in Century City." Emphasis in original.

142. See, for example, Ingrid Bengis, "On Getting Angry," *Ms.*, July 1972, 66–71, 124–28; Fortney, "On Girl Watching"; and Pilate, "Unhand Us, Ya Perverts."

Women by no means universally condemned girl-watching. In fact, in the wake of attacks on girl-watching from women's liberationists, newspaper reporters increasingly turned to women to confirm or refute the feminist analysis of girl-watching in the late 1960s and early 1970s. See Fortney, "On Girl Watching"; and Lee, "Girl Watchers Sprout in Summer . . . Annoy."

143. For post-1970s examples of "girl-watching" as a more generic term, see Dick Mayer, "'The Lady Stroh's Open': Great Days for Golf and Girl Watching," *Detroit Free Press*, August 13, 1978; "Watching All the Persons Go By," *New York Times*, September 13, 1980; "Paris Has Decided on Girl Watching," *Globe and Mail*, November 26, 1985; Jim Sanderson, "Galled by Her Girl-Watching Fiance," *Los Angeles Times*, April 8, 1987; Abigail Van Buren, "Girl Watching Upsets Girlfriend: Dear Abby," *Chicago Tribune*, April 28, 1989; "Girl Watching: An Inevitable Outcome of Living in New York Where Someone Is Always Taller," *New York Times*, August, 28 2005; and Jennifer Medina, "Girl-Watching, Tanning and (of Course) Lifesaving," *New York Times*, September 4, 2005.

144. I am reminded here of many white people's cries of "All Lives Matter" in their response to the Black Lives Matter movement. For more on this idea, see Judith Butler and George Yancy, "What's Wrong With 'All Lives Matter'?," *Stone* (blog), January 12, 2015, https://archive.nytimes.com/opinionator.blogs.nytimes.com/2015/01/12/whats-wrong-with-all-lives-matter/.

145. Patricia McCormack, "Girl-Watching Can Be Pleasing and Profitable to Engineers," *Chicago Daily Defender*, July 26, 1965; Patricia McCormack, "Hunt for the Male Is Exhilarating Sport," *Afro-American*, January 1, 1966; Phyllis Battelle, "The New, and Ever Old, Art of Girl Watching," *New Journal and Guide* (Norfolk, VA), January 29, 1955; Robert Musel, "Hemlines: What Goes Up Eventually Comes Down," *New Journal and Guide*, January 6, 1968.

146. An exception is the photograph of a young white boy watching a grown white woman in a bikini on a beach that the *Chicago Daily Defender* reprinted from United Press International in 1964. "Tiny Tot's Double-Take," *Chicago Daily Defender*, June 18, 1964.

147. "On the Beach at A.C.," *Afro-American*, July 29, 1967. Spelling as in the original.

148. "On the Beach at A.C." A similar piece published in a Black Milwaukee newspaper included a photo essay of beachgoers enjoying Lake Michigan on the first hot day of the year and mused on the excellent girl-watching that could be had there. "Heat: Common Denominator Equals Love on the Lake," *Milwaukee Star*, June 12, 1968.

149. "Girl Watcher Fall Fashions," *Milwaukee Star*, October 19, 1968.

150. "For Girl Watchers Only," *Afro-American*, May 3, 1969.

151. "Fancy Fox: Kenneth Coulter, Jr.," *Milwaukee Star*, January 4, 1969.

152. United Press International, "Champ," *Los Angeles Sentinel*, March 25, 1971.

153. For a few other examples of the use of girl-watching in the Black press, see George F. Brown, "No Cover Charge: Answer to Kinsey Report and Theatrical Tattle," *Pittsburgh Courier*, November 6, 1954; The Duffer, "Girl Watching Puts New Dimension in His Golf," *Afro-American*, August 20, 1966; "Now Hear This!," *Los Angeles Sentinel*, May 25,

1972; and Reverend James A. Pollard Sr., "Can Christians Be Girl Watchers?," *Philadelphia Tribune*, May 28, 1977.

154. Estes, *I Am a Man!*, 132.

155. These demands would only intensify as some Black activists argued for greater militancy in their fight for liberation. See Estes, *I Am a Man!*, 153–77.

156. Box 5, Project Girl Records, Social Welfare History Archives, University of Minnesota.

157. Estes, *I Am a Man!*, 6.

Chapter Five

1. For examples, see "Girl on Wall St. Turns Bull and Bear into Wolf," *New York Times*, September 20, 1968; United Press International, "Wall St. Waits in Vain for Francine," *Boston Globe*, September 21, 1968; "10,000 Wait in Vain for Reappearance of Wall Street's Sweater Girl," *New York Times*, September 21, 1968; "'Bulls' and 'Bears' Become 'Wolves,'" *Washington Post*, September 21, 1968; "Prominent Figure on Wall St.," *Globe and Mail*, September 21, 1968; "Wall Street's New Statistics: 43–25–37," *Los Angeles Times*, September 21, 1968; "Wall Street Traffic Jam Waiting for Francine," *Jerusalem Post*, September 25, 1968; Kenneth J. Fanucchi, "She Out-Figures Wall St.'s Francine," *Los Angeles Times*, October 3, 1968; Associated Press, "Bust Boom Brings Police," *Kentucky New Era* (Hopkinsville), October 5, 1968; Associated Press, "It's Boom or Bust Day for Wall Street," *Tuscaloosa News*, October 5, 1968; Associated Press, "Real Battle 'Busts' Out," *Montreal Gazette*, October 5, 1968; Arthur Everett, "Wall St.'s Day of Boom, Bust," *Boston Globe*, October 5, 1968; Betty Flynn, "Francine Brought 'Sunshine,'" *Washington Post*, February 23, 1969; "43–25–37 Still Able to Attract Dividends," *Los Angeles Times*, April 4, 1969.
2. *Dr Karla Jay at HOLLARev 2014*, righttobeorg, 2014, 11:48, www.youtube.com/watch?v=kJBQ_xs35oU.
3. "Now: 'Women's Liberation,'" 1970, Marlene Sanders Papers, Wisconsin Historical Society Archives, Madison; "Women's Liberation," videotape, *Now*, May 25, 1970, Marlene Sanders Papers.
4. *Dr Karla Jay at HOLLARev 2014*.
5. R. Morgan, *Sisterhood Is Powerful*, xv–xvi.
6. Ann Sheldon, "Rape: A Solution," *Women: A Journal of Liberation*, 1972, 22, box 10, folder 9, *Women: A Journal of Liberation* Records, SSC.
7. B. Thompson, "Multiracial Feminism"; Roth, *Separate Roads to Feminism*; R. Davis, *Fierce Desires*, 264.
8. Farrell, *Yours in Sisterhood*, 34; see also D'Emilio and Freedman, *Intimate Matters*, 310–14.
9. B. Thompson, "Multiracial Feminism," 346–47.
10. Jacquet, *Injustices of Rape*, 78.
11. Selection of NYRF Member Activities 1972–1984, box 1, New York Radical Feminists Records, SBC; Brown, "Effects of Consciousness-Raising Group Participation."
12. Nanette Rainone, "Men and Violence," 1970, box 15, CWLUR.
13. Susi Kaplow, "Getting Angry," 1971, box 15, CWLUR.

14. Georgina Hickey describes this strategy in the larger feminist movement, arguing, "In making this connection to rape, the movement to end violence against women named the source of harassment and violence as a society that tolerated and even encouraged the subjugation of women, what today we call rape culture." Hickey, *Breaking the Gender Code*, 111.
15. "The Verbal Rapist," *Majority Report*, October 1971, box PW-1 and LW-1, Alix Kates Shulman Papers, SBC; Ida Monico-Lemay, "Speaking Out: A Case of the Wrong Target," *New York Radical Feminists Newsletter*, December 1971, box 1, New York Radical Feminists Records, SBC; Sheldon, "Rape: A Solution," SSC; Andra Medea and Kathleen Thompson, "Little Rapes," *Kitty Genovese Women's Project*, March 8, 1977, box 6, folder 2, Violence Against Women Collection, SSC.
16. Duncan Chappell, "Forcible Rape and the Criminal Justice System: Surveying Present Practices and Projecting Future Trends," paper presented at 6th Alabama Symposium on Justice and the Behavioral Sciences, University of Alabama, Tuscaloosa, January 20–22, 1975. The FBI dropped the term "forcible" beginning in 2013. "Forcible Rape," *FBI: Uniform Crime Reporting*, 2012, https://ucr.fbi.gov/crime-in-the-u.s/2012/crime-in-the-u.s.-2012/violent-crime/rape/rapemain; "Rape," *FBI: Uniform Crime Reporting*, 2018, https://ucr.fbi.gov/crime-in-the-u.s/2018/crime-in-the-u.s.-2018/topic-pages/rape.
17. Case 533–031–02, 1978, box 11, Diana Russell Unprocessed Papers, SSC.
18. Meredith Tax, *Woman and Her Mind: The Story of Daily Life* (Bread and Roses, 1970), 2, Labadie Pamphlet Collection, University of Michigan, Special Collections.
19. Sheldon, "Rape: A Solution," 22, SSC. Sheldon's article appears on a reading list for a course in the Chicago Women's Liberation Union School. "Course Outline" (Chicago Women's Liberation Union, c. 1972), box 15, CWLUR.
20. Case 278–001–01, 1978, box 6, Diana Russell Unprocessed Papers, SSC.
21. Sheldon, "Rape: A Solution," SSC.
22. "Women Will Stop Rape," in *Stop Rape* (Women Against Rape, 1971), 43, box 27, CWLUR. For more on antirape squads, see Jacquet, "Fighting Back, Claiming Power," 73–74; and Jacquet, *Injustices of Rape*, 90–91.
23. "Women Against Pornography," c. 1981, box 1, folder 5, Edith Van Horn Papers, Walter P. Reuther Library, Wayne State University. Emphasis in original. See also Helen Katopoulos, "Women Speak Out Against Rape," *Woman's World*, April 15, 1971, box PW-1 and LW-1, Alix Kates Shulman Papers, SBC.
24. Quoted in Rainone, "Men and Violence," 43.
25. Bengis, *Combat in the Erogenous Zone*, 25.
26. Tax, *Woman and Her Mind*, 5, University of Michigan, Special Collections.
27. Bengis, *Combat in the Erogenous Zone*, 24.
28. "Street Harassment Statement," SBC.
29. Letter in response to "How Much Do You Really Know About Rapists?," June 1974, carton 1, folder 13, Letters to *Ms.*, 1972–1980, Schlesinger Library, Radcliffe Institute, Harvard University.
30. Gwenda Linda Blair, "Standing on the Corner . . . ," *Liberation* 18, no. 9 (1974): 6–8.
31. See, for instance, Judith Pasternak, "Me and My Flasher: A Feminist's Dilemma," *New York Radical Feminists Newsletter*, May 1976, box 1, New York Radical Feminists

Records, SBC. Georgina Hickey tracks the development of this kind of "sixth sense" throughout the twentieth century. Hickey, *Breaking the Gender Code*.

32. Boxes 1, 3–9, and 11–13 in Diana Russell Unprocessed Papers, SSC. In places, I have cleaned up the interviewer's notes, for example substituting "you" for "u," etc.
33. G. Blair, "Standing on the Corner," 8.
34. Sheldon, "Rape: A Solution," 22, SSC.
35. Boxes 1 and 3–9, Diana Russell Unprocessed Papers, SSC.
36. Tax, *Woman and Her Mind*, 5, University of Michigan, Special Collections.
37. Today, sexual violence researchers call this mental and physical girding the "safety work" women must do to navigate public space. Vera-Gray and Kelly, "Contested Gendered Space."
38. Medea and Thompson, *Against Rape*, 49–50. Emphasis in original.
39. Medea and Thompson, *Against Rape*, 47.
40. Medea and Thompson, *Against Rape*, 50.
41. Medea and Thompson, *Against Rape*, 51–52.
42. Christine Noschese, *Rape and Welfare Discussion*, 1974, National Congress of Neighborhood Women Records, SSC, https://media.smith.edu/departments/ssc/ncnw/ncnw_playlist.html.
43. Catherine Henry, "How to Eliminate Rape (and Other Crimes Against Women)," *Woman's World*, April 15, 1971, 5, box PW-1 and LW-1, Alix Kates Shulman Papers, SBC. This essay, which is otherwise riddled with homophobic and transphobic attacks, would be worth examining as an early example of the way feminist critiques of gendered violence sometimes led to the demonization of gay men and trans women.
44. Sharon Kass, "Dealing with Street Harassment" (Coalition for a Hassle Free Zone, 1986), box 5, folder 1, Nkenge Touré Papers, SSC. See also Crindi Loschinkohl, "Street Harassment: Based on a Workshop," *Aegis: Magazine on Ending Violence Against Women*, 1985, 35.
45. *White Riot*, box 27, CWLUR.
46. Georgina Hickey calls this the "crowd-level response" that feminists employed in anti–street harassment activism. Hickey, *Breaking the Gender Code*, 111.
47. *She's Beautiful When She's Angry* (Music Box Films, 2014).
48. Brown, *Plain Brown Rapper*, 43. Thank you to Lynn Hudson for directing me to this source.
49. Robin Reisig, "Biting the Hand That Feels You: Bitches Ogle Hardhats," *Village Voice*, June 18, 1970, box 112, Meredith Tax Papers, SBC.
50. "Street Harassment Statement," SBC.
51. Joan Goldman, "The Street Harassment Workshop: A Progress Report," *New York Radical Feminists Newsletter*, January 1975, box 1, New York Radical Feminists Records, SBC; liz quinn, "Learning to Confront Harassment," *Off Our Backs*, January 1984, http://www.jstor.org/stable/25794222; Loschinkohl, "Street Harassment"; "Evaluation for Sexual Harassment Workshop," c. 1986, box 5, folder 1, Nkenge Touré Papers, SSC; C. Lamson, "Off Women's Backs: Making Washington, DC, a Hassle Free Zone," *Off Our Backs*, April 1986, box 5, folder 1, Nkenge Touré Papers, SSC.
52. "Verbal Rapist," SBC.

53. Judy Sullivan, "Prostitution Conference: Workshop Report," *New York Radical Feminists Newsletter*, February 1972, box 1, New York Radical Feminists Records, SBC.
54. Hickey, *Breaking the Gender Code*, 112.
55. G. Blair, "Standing on the Corner," 6.
56. Hickey, *Breaking the Gender Code*, 96. See also Sugrue, *Origins of the Urban Crisis*; Muhammad, *Condemnation of Blackness*; Hinton, *From the War on Poverty*; and Hernández, *City of Inmates*. For more on the development of "stranger danger" mentality in the 1980s, see Renfro, *Stranger Danger*.
57. Bronstein, *Battling Pornography*; Hickey, "Geography of Pornography"; Delegard, "Contested Geography."
58. K. S. Kerpen, "Inside a Rape Crisis Center," *Majority Report*, May 1973, 8, box 5, folder 12, Violence Against Women Collection, SSC.
59. Marion Cutler, *Rape: The Crime Against Women* (Dallas Women Against Rape), box 53, Jean Kilbourne Papers, SBC.
60. Debbie Margolin, "Rape: The Facts," *Women: A Journal of Liberation*, 1972, 20, box 10, folder 9, *Women: A Journal of Liberation* Records, SSC. Other feminist publications reported that about half of rapes occurred at the hands of a stranger. Pat Miller and Joanne Parrent, "Some Factual Information," in *Stop Rape* (Women Against Rape, 1971), 1–5, box 27, CWLUR.
61. Louis Harris & Associates, Louis Harris & Associates Poll: September 1977, Question 49, USHARRIS.102477.R2A (Cornell University, Roper Center for Public Opinion Research, 1977), survey question, DOI: 10.25940/ROPER-31103250.
62. In fact, the United States didn't begin to criminalize marital rape until the mid-1970s. Freedman, *Redefining Rape*, 282.
63. This style of avoidance advice is widespread in the period 1970–90, though feminist publications tended to be somewhat more likely to include self-defense techniques as well. "What You Need to Know About Rape" (Citizens Committee for Victim Assistance, 1975), box 27, CWLUR; *What Every Woman Should Know About Rape* (Channing L. Bete Co., 1976), box 53, Jean Kilbourne Papers, SBC; Bobbi Snyder, *Feminist Karate Union: Student Manual Beginning Level*, 10th ed. (Pittsburgh, 1977), SBC; Harrisburg Area Rape Crisis Center, *Training Manual: Harrisburg Area Rape Crisis Center*, 1977, SBC; Elizabeth Dobell, "Self-Defense," *Seventeen*, April 1977, 194–95, 216–17; "Center Against Sexual Assault," box 205, folder 6, Gloria Steinem Papers, SSC; Chicago Women Against Rape pamphlets, box 27, CWLUR; Cutler, *Rape*, SBC; "Help for Victims of Sexual Assault" (Rape Crisis Center of Binghamton, NY), box 5, folder 15, Violence Against Women Collection, SSC; Wanda Horn, "Self-Defense Art for Women Aired," *Advocate*, box 5, folder 12, Violence Against Women Collection, SSC; "How to Avoid Rape Situations," (WBBM-TV/Chicago), box 113, Meredith Tax Papers, SBC; "Protective Measures to Prevent Rape" (Police Department of the City of New York), box 132, folder 9, National Congress of Neighborhood Women Records, SSC; "Rape: A Reference for Women in DC" (DC Rape Crisis Center), box 5, folder 4, Nkenge Touré Papers, SSC; "Rape: How to Keep it From Happening to You" (Mayor's Task Force on Rape, The City of New York), box 132, folder 9, National Congress of Neighborhood Women Records, SSC; "Rape Prevention: Campus and Community"

(Campus Security, Buffalo State University College), box 4, folder 15, Nkenge Touré Papers, SSC; "Rape Prevention Tactics" (DC Rape Crisis Center), box 5, folder 15, Violence Against Women Collection, SSC; "Sexual Assault Is Everyone's Problem" (DC Rape Crisis Center), box 5, folder 4, Nkenge Touré Papers, SSC; Nadia Telsey, "Some Facts on Self-Defense," box 4, folder 15, Nkenge Touré Papers, SSC; training materials, box 4, folder 15, Nkenge Touré Papers, SSC.

64. Hickey, *Breaking the Gender Code*, 96.

65. Jacquet, *Injustices of Rape*, 146–59. Antiracist activists agreed with some feminist critiques of the state, adding that law enforcement disproportionately targeted minority defendants for sexual violence crimes.

66. Sheldon, "Rape: A Solution," SSC.

67. Mary Ann Manhart, Joan Mathews, and Florence Rush, "Speaking Out: Rape Is . . . ," *New York Radical Feminists Newsletter*, October 1971, box 1, New York Radical Feminists Records, SBC.

68. Kathleen Barry, "The Vagina on Trial," in *Stop Rape* (Women Against Rape, 1971), 7, box 27, CWLUR.

69. Andra Medea and Kathleen Thompson, "How Much Do You Really Know About Rapists?," *Ms.*, July 1974, 114; "Speak-Outs, Conferences, and Other Activities Around Sexual Abuse of Women and Children, 1971–1976," box 1, folder 4, New York Radical Feminists Records, SBC; *What Every Woman Should Know About Rape*, SBC; Snyder, *Feminist Karate Union*, SBC; Pauline Bart, "Avoiding Rape," box 80, Pauline Bart Papers, SBC.

70. "Rape Data," box 57, Pauline Bart Papers, SBC. The survey is discussed in Karen A. Holmes and Joyce E. Williams, *Problems and Pitfalls of Rape Victim Research: An Analysis of Selected Methodological, Ethical and Pragmatic Concerns* (Trinity University, 1978), 2, www.ojp.gov/ncjrs/virtual-library/abstracts/problems-and-pitfalls-rape-victim-research-analysis-selected; and Jennifer Romolini, "Phallus in Wonderland," *Stiffed*, accessed June 5, 2024, https://crooked.com/podcast/phallus-in-wonderland/.

Viva was a short-lived experiment in creating a pornographic magazine for women readers. The sister publication of *Penthouse*, it ran from about 1973 to 1980 and was led by Kathy Keeton, the longtime girlfriend of *Penthouse* founder Bob Guccione. Anna Wintour briefly worked there in the late 1970s. Oppenheimer, *Front Row*, 116–50.

71. Laura A. Kiernan, "Rape Crisis Center Described," *Washington Post*, October 12, 1972, box 5, folder 12, Violence Against Women Collection, SSC.

72. Rosenthal, *Thirty-Eight Witnesses*; Cook, *Kitty Genovese*; Gallo, *"No One Helped."*

73. Louisa Rogers, "Four Years Ago I Was Raped," *Glamour*, September 1978, box 5, folder 12, Violence Against Women Collection, SSC.

74. Some white antiracist feminists also fought against these stereotypes. In addition to examples in this manuscript, see Jacquet, *Injustices of Rape*, 131–46.

75. Some of this defensiveness likely arose from high profile interracial rape cases where defense lawyers discredited white female accusers, describing them as fantasists or liars or perpetuating rape myths, in order to exonerate Black male defendants. Jacquet, *Injustices of Rape*, 131–46.

76. Cate Stadelman, "Fighting Back," in *Stop Rape* (Women Against Rape, 1971), 15, box 27, CWLUR.

77. Medea and Thompson, *Against Rape*, 51.
78. B. Razen Cunt, "Experiments in Hostility: 1," *Off Our Backs*, January 1973, 10.
79. For more on the history of white people describing youths of color as adults—not to mention trying and convicting them as adults in courts of law—when they are perceived as dangerous to white people, see Suddler, *Presumed Criminal*; Agyepong, *Criminalization of Black Children*; and Bush, *Who Gets a Childhood?*
80. Tax, *Woman and Her Mind*, 5, University of Michigan, Special Collections.
81. Brownmiller, *Against Our Will*, 245–47.
82. Brownmiller, *Against Our Will*, 245–48.
83. Brownmiller, *Against Our WIll*, 247. Emphasis in the original.
84. Quoted in Jacquet, *Injustices of Rape*, 144–45.
85. *Kitty Genovese Women's Project*, March 8, 1977, box 6, folder 2, Violence Against Women Collection, SSC.
86. "Racism and Rape," *Kitty Genovese Women's Project*, March 8, 1977, 4, box 6, folder 2, Violence Against Women Collection, SSC.
87. Valk, *Radical Sisters*; Jacquet, *Injustices of Rape*; A. Fischer, *Streets Belong to Us*; C. Greene, *Free Joan Little*.
88. Bengis, *Combat in the Erogenous Zone*, 24, 18. Portions of this essay first appeared in *Ms.* magazine four months before the book's publication; see Ingrid Bengis, "On Getting Angry," *Ms.*, July 1972.
89. Bengis, *Combat in the Erogenous Zone*, 39.
90. Bengis, *Combat in the Erogenous Zone*, 36–39.
91. Bengis, *Combat in the Erogenous Zone*, 43.
92. Bengis, *Combat in the Erogenous Zone*, 48. Second ellipsis in the original text.
93. Bengis, *Combat in the Erogenous Zone*, 49.
94. Tax, *Woman and Her Mind*, 5, University of Michigan, Special Collections.
95. Geng, "Scorn Not the Street Compliment," 75–79. The book's front matter indicates this article was first published in *Cosmopolitan* in 1970.
96. Leonardo, "Political Economy of Street Harassment," 53.
97. Goldberg and Griffey, *Black Power at Work*; Sugrue, "Affirmative Action from Below"; Freeman, "Hardhats."
98. Foner, *U.S. Labor and the Vietnam War*; Freeman, "Hardhats." The protesters, mostly high school and college students, were marching against President Nixon's invasion of Cambodia and the police shooting of student demonstrators at Kent State University. Members of the local building trades unions violently confronted protesters in New York's financial district. The following evening, local television stations filmed the three hundred or so construction workers who made their way through downtown New York, attacking students and antiwar demonstrators with lead pipes and crowbars.
99. Reisig, "Biting the Hand That Feels You," SBC.
100. Freeman, "Hardhats," 725–33.
101. Cheryl Benard and Edit Schlaffer, "The Man in the Street: Why He Harasses," *Ms.*, May 1981, 19.
102. Freeman, "Hardhats," 730.
103. Pyke, "Class-Based Masculinities," 531–32.
104. G. Blair, "Standing on the Corner," 6–8.

105. Rape Crisis Center Collective, "Rape: The Response," *Women: A Journal of Liberation*, 1972, 68, box 11, folder 1, *Women: A Journal of Liberation* Records, SSC. For more on the DC Rape Crisis Center, see Jacquet, *Injustices of Rape*, 88–89, 95–97.
106. Monico-Lemay, "Speaking Out," SBC. Monico-Lemay's letter is dated September 1971.
107. Jim Sanderson, "Confronting Street Hassling," Liberated Male, *Los Angeles Times*, October 5, 1980; Jim Sanderson, "Speak Up, Ladies; Men Do Listen," Liberated Male, *Los Angeles Times*, December 28, 1980; Courtland Milloy, "Give Women a Break," *Washington Post*, September 26, 1985; Carol Dana, "Talking Back to Street Harassers," *Washington Post*, August 19, 1986, box 5, folder 1, Nkenge Touré Papers, SSC; Michael McLeod, "Boors Should Realize Smiles Pay Better Compliments Than Catcalls Calls," *Orlando Sentinel*, October 27, 1988; Mike McLeod, "OK, Fellas, Cool It with the Catcalls," *Sun Sentinel* (Fort Lauderdale, FL), November 1, 1988; Ann Marie Lipinski, "Blues in White Collar World: Miracle Mile Construction Crews Get Little Respect," *Chicago Tribune*, August 15, 1989.
108. "Letters to the Editor: Strategies for Street Harassment," *Washington Post*, August 30, 1986.
109. Monico-Lemay, "Speaking Out," SBC.
110. Fileborn and Vera-Gray, "'I Want to Be Able to Walk the Street,'" 204.
111. Goldman, "Street Harassment Workshop," SBC; Flora, "Announcements," *New York Radical Feminists Newsletter*, July 1975, box 1, New York Radical Feminists Records, SBC; Joan Goldman, "Street Harassment Goes Underground," *New York Radical Feminists Newsletter*, August 1975, box 1, New York Radical Feminists Records, SBC.
112. "Campaign Against Street Harassment Letter," *New York Radical Feminists Newsletter*, November 1975, box 1, New York Radical Feminists Records, SBC; "Women in the Law Courts: A Victory," *New York Radical Feminists Newsletter*, November 1975, box 1, New York Radical Feminists Records, SBC; "Ms. Ellaneous," *Women's Press*, December 1975.

The campaign was inspired by a suit from customer Charlotte Sheedy, who claimed a Spanish-speaking male employee of Zabar's "thrust up against [her] backside" several times with his erect penis. The deli's manager, George Torres, reportedly did nothing in response to Sheedy's complaint. The customer was likely the prominent literary agent Charlotte Sheedy, described at the time as a "writer." Morris Kaplan, "Judge Rules Woman Has Right to Sue Zabar's in Assault Case," *New York Times*, August 1, 1975.
113. Hickey, *Breaking the Gender Code*, 136–41; Delegard, "Contested Geography."
114. Hickey, *Breaking the Gender Code*, 121–25.
115. Lindsy Van Gelder, "The International Language of Street Hassling," *Ms.*, May 1981.
116. Letter in response to "The International Language of Street Hassling," c. May 1981, carton 10, folder 8, Letters to *Ms.*, 1970–1998, Schlesinger Library, Radcliffe Institute, Harvard University. Emphasis in original.
117. Letter in response to "The International Language of Street Hassling," May 18, 1981, carton 10, folder 8, Letters to *Ms.*, 1970–1998, Schlesinger Library, Radcliffe Institute, Harvard University. Emphasis in original. This logic would lead many, including self-described feminists, to blame victims of sexual harassment and violence for their own victimization. Hickey, *Breaking the Gender Code*, 125.

118. Faludi, *Backlash*, xxii.
119. Reynolds, "Never Silent," 31–32. For more on the Take Back the Night movement, see Valk, "Take Back the Night," 126–32.
120. Levy, *Great Uprising*, 210.
121. I. Rajeswary, "Anti-Rape Week Will Target Verbal Abuse," *Washington Post*, September 20, 1985, box 5, folder 1, Nkenge Touré Papers, SSC.
122. Milloy, "Give Women a Break."
123. Juanita Thompson, "A Hassle Free Zone? Groups Seeks to Make Sexual Street Harassment Illegal," *Afro-American*, March 8, 1986.
124. Coalition for a Hassle Free Zone, "Fact Sheet on Street Harassment," c. 1986, box 5, folder 1, Nkenge Touré Papers, SSC; Sharon Kass, "Dealing with Street Harassment" (Coalition for a Hassle Free Zone, 1986), box 5, folder 1, Nkenge Touré Papers, SSC; Dana, "Talking Back to Street Harassers," SSC; "Community Events July 17–23," *Washington Post*, July 17, 1986; "Confrontation Workshops," *Washington Post*, August 19, 1986.
125. See, for instance, Elizabeth Kuster, "Don't 'Hey Baby' Me," *Glamour*, September 1992; "The Many Faces of Feminism," *Ms.*, July 1994; "Random Acts of Violence," *Off Our Backs*, July 1996; Teresa Yunker, "When Street Harassment Gets Nasty . . . Should You Mouth Off or Bite Your Tongue?," *On the Issues*, July 31, 1996, 29; and Andi Zeisler, "Baby Tease," *Bitch*, July 31, 1997.
126. Sanderson, "Confronting Street Hassling"; Leonardo, "Political Economy of Street Harassment"; Van Gelder, "International Language of Street Hassling"; "Verbal Abuse on the Street: How to Talk Back," *Glamour*, February 1984; Coalition for a Hassle Free Zone, "Fact Sheet on Street Harassment," SSC; Kass, "Dealing with Street Harassment," SSC; Lamson, "Off Women's Backs"; Dana, "Talking Back to Street Harassers," SSC.
127. "Street Harassment of Women," *Washington Post*, March 26, 1990; "Worker Centers Split Californians," *Christian Science Monitor*, May 14, 1990; Kim Y. Edmonds, "'Ugly Sounds of Summer,'" *Washington Post*, June 10, 1990; Steven Pratt, "At Least These Wolves Are Caged," *Chicago Tribune*, June 20, 1990; Cheryl Lavin, "Falling for the World's Only Shy Construction Worker," *Chicago Tribune*, June 21, 1992; Joan Beck, "Catcalls and Wolf Whistles Hassle Women, but Are They Criminal?," *Orlando Sentinel*, March 12, 1993; Joann Byrd, "Obvious Only to the Editors," *Washington Post*, August 15, 1993; Jason Vest, "Oglers Get the Evil Eye," *Washington Post*, August 17, 1993; John Leo, "PC Rule: Stand on Corner but Don't Watch the Girls," *Orlando Sentinel*, August 24, 1993; Robin Abcarian, "Despite Giggles and Leers, It's Sexism Stripped Bare," *Los Angeles Times*, March 16, 1994; "Construction Company Agrees to Stop Workers' Wolf Whistles," *Sun* (Baltimore), September 20, 1994.
128. Leonardo, "Political Economy of Street Harassment," 55. Leonardo's essay was the earliest explicitly academic theory of street harassment I could find. Scholars have cited it widely in subsequent research on the phenomenon.
129. Coalition for a Hassle Free Zone, "Fact Sheet on Street Harassment," SSC.
130. Dana, "Talking Back to Street Harassers," SSC.

Epilogue

1. Rob Bliss Creative, *10 Hours of Walking in NYC as a Woman*, 2014, www.youtube.com/watch?v=b1XGPvbWnoA.
2. *10 Hours Walking in NYC as a Goth*, 2014, www.youtube.com/watch?v=TTRkoEHUrFk; *10 Hours of Walking but This Time She Talks Back (BEST CATCALL Parody)*, 2014, www.youtube.com/watch?v=35KqGNa1FGA; *10 Hours of Walking in NYC as a Woman in Hijab*, 2014, www.youtube.com/watch?v=mgw6y3cH7tA; *10 Hours of Walking in NYC as a Man*, 2014, www.youtube.com/watch?v=EC21NF5rbSk.
3. Cavan Sieczkowski, "Watch This Woman Receive 100 Catcalls While Walking Around for a Day," *HuffPost*, October 28, 2014, www.huffpost.com/entry/walking-in-nyc-as-a-woman_n_6063054; Norah O'Donnell and Vinita Nair, "The Public Service Announcement Which Was in Part Shot Here in Times Square Is Meant to Give Viewers a Third Party Idea of What It's Like to See Street Harassment," *CBS This Morning*, October 29, 2014, www.proquest.com/other-sources/public-service-announcement-which-was-part-shot/docview/1795833876/se-2?accountid=14751; Deepti Hajela, "Viral Video Documents New York Street Harassment," AP News, October 30, 2014, https://apnews.com/general-news-arts-and-entertainment-8a14cf9039814de5ad502f0b75916698; Emily Badger, "Harassing Women on the Street Isn't Just Offensive. It's Also Often Illegal," *Washington Post*, October 29, 2014.
4. Hanna Rosin, "The Problem with That Catcalling Video," *Slate*, October 29, 2014, http://www.slate.com/blogs/xx_factor/2014/10/29/catcalling_video_hollaback_s_look_at_street_harassment_in_nyc_edited_out.html; Alicia Lu, "The Catcalling Video Edited Out White Men, Undermining the Video's Entire Purpose," *Bustle*, October 30, 2014, www.bustle.com/articles/46801-the-catcalling-video-edited-out-white-men-undermining-the-videos-entire-purpose; Dave Schilling, "Is That Viral Catcalling Video Racist?," *Vice*, October 31, 2014, www.vice.com/en_us/article/av4qjk/catcalling-viral-video-racist-twir-131; "Statement: Hollaback! On Rob Bliss' Viral Street Harassment PSA," Hollaback! Together We Have the Power to End Harassment, October 30, 2014, www.ihollaback.org/blog/2014/10/30/statement-about-recent-street harassment-psa/; Bethonie Butler, "Hollaback Responds to Criticism of Racial Bias in Street Harassment Video," *Washington Post,* October 30, 2014; Kat Chow, "Video Calls Out Catcallers, but Cuts Out White Men," NPR, November 1, 2014, www.npr.org/sections/codeswitch/2014/11/01/360422087/hollaback-video-calls-out-catcallers-but-cuts-out-white-men. Roxane Gay's Twitter post is quoted in Rosin, "Problem."

   The actress featured in the video reported a deluge of rape and death threats after it went viral and later sued the video's director for additional compensation for her work. Hermione Hoby, "The Woman in 10 Hours Walking in NYC: 'I Got People Wanting to Slit My Throat,'" *Guardian* (UK), December 17, 2014; Ben Mathis-Lilley, "Star of Viral Catcalling Video Sues Director, YouTube, T.G.I. Friday's," *Slate*, July 14, 2015, https://slate.com/news-and-politics/2015/07/street-harassment-video-lawsuit-actress-shoshana-roberts-sues-director-others.html.
5. Dee Lockett, "White Men Don't Catcall. They Harass in Other Ways," *Slate*, October 31, 2014, https://slate.com/human-interest/2014/10/catcalling-what-hollabacks-viral-video-reveals-about-white-men-and-street-harassment.html.

6. Sarah Feightner, "Beware, Street Harassers," *Chicago Tribune*, November 29, 2006; Karen Zraick, "Helping Women Fight Back Against Street Harassment, Seconds After It Occurs," *New York Times*, November 8, 2010; Melissa Ruggieri, "Tech Student Helps Create Street Harassment App: Doctoral Candidate Builds Tool to Allow Incident Reporting," *Atlanta Journal-Constitution*, December 13, 2010; Nicole Finkbiner, "Hollaback Girls," *Philadelphia Weekly*, June 22, 2011; Tabitha Clark, "Hollaback! To End Street Harassment," *Daily News* (Jacksonville, NC), December 26, 2012; Joe Sharkey, "A Worldwide Fight Against Street Harassment," *New York Times*, October 22, 2013; Rebecca Nuttall, "Sticks and Stones," *Pittsburgh City Paper*, January 8, 2014; Tessa Miller, "Apps and Online Programs Offer New Ways to Report Street Harassment," *Daily Beast*, April 2, 2014, www.thedailybeast.com/apps-and-online-programs-offer-new-ways-to-report-street-harassment.
7. Carmen Rios, "Hollaback! Launches New App to Report Street Harassment to NYC Officials in Real Time," *Feminist Majority Foundation* (blog), August 20, 2013, https://feminist.org/news/hollaback-launches-new-app-to-report-street-harassment-to-nyc-officials-in-real-time/.
8. Fleetwood, "Everyday Self-Defence"; Hutson and Krueger, "Harasser's Toolbox"; Baptist and Coburn, "Harassment in Public Spaces"; Herrera and McCarthy, "Street Harassment Interpretations."
9. Laura Bates, Everyday Sexism Project, September 23, 2024, https://everydaysexism.com/; Laura Bates, "The Everyday Sexism Project: A Year of Shouting Back," *Guardian*, April 16, 2013.
10. Linda Burstyn, "The Weinstein Effect," *Ms.*, January 4, 2018, https://msmagazine.com/2018/01/04/the-weinstein-effect/; Burke, *Unbound*.
11. BE, "Comfortable and Free to Walk Down the Street," *Riot Grrrl*, no. 5, 1991; Elizabeth Kuster, "Don't 'Hey Baby' Me," *Glamour*, September 1992; Teresa Yunker, "When Street Harassment Gets Nasty . . . Should You Mouth Off or Bite Your Tongue?," *On the Issues*, July 31, 1996.
12. Maggie Hadleigh-West, "War Zone," *YoMaggie* (blog), accessed June 12, 2025, http://www.yomaggie.com/war-zone-2/; *War Zone*, directed by Maggie Hadleigh-West (Film Fatale Inc., 1998); "War Zone," *Ms.*, October 1998.
13. For recent literature reviews of street harassment from the 1980s to today, see Fairchild, "Understanding Street Harassment"; and Fileborn and O'Neill, "From 'Ghettoization' to a Field of Its Own."
14. Kissling and Kramarae, "Stranger Compliments," 75; Larkin, "Sexual Terrorism on the Street"; Cooke, "Street Remarks"; Lenton et al., "Sexual Harassment in Public Places"; Scholz, "Catcalls and Military Strategy"; Crouch, "Sexual Harassment in Public Places."
15. Bowman, "Street Harassment"; D. Davis, "Harm That Has No Name"; D. Thompson, "Woman in the Street"; Tuerkheimer, "Street Harassment as Sexual Subordination." For later examples, see Laniya, "Street Smut"; Nielsen, "Situating Legal Consciousness"; Nielsen, "Power of 'Place'"; Chhun, "Catcalls"; McCurn, "'I Am Not a Prostitute'"; and Fileborn and Vera-Gray, "'I Want to Be Able to Walk the Street.'"
16. Goffman, *Behavior in Public Places*, 83.
17. Gardner, *Passing By*, 93; Goffman, *Presentation of Self*.
18. See Walkowitz, "Going Public"; Cooke, "Street Remarks"; Fairchild and Rudman,

"Everyday Stranger Harassment"; Horgan, "Urban Interaction Ritual"; Logan, "Street Harassment."

19. On France: Colin Dwyer, "France Bans Street Harassment, Approving Hefty Fines for Catcallers," NPR, August 2, 2018, www.npr.org/2018/08/02/634866222/france-bans-street-harassment-approving-hefty-fines-for-cat-callers; Emma Batha, "France Fines More Than 700 in First Year of 'Cat-Call' Law," Reuters, August 6, 2019, www.reuters.com/article/world/france-fines-more-than-700-in-first-year-of-cat-call-law-idUSKCN1UW1NW/; Stéphanie Fillion, "2 Years Later, What We Can Learn from France's Anti-Catcalling Law," *Forbes*, accessed June 19, 2024, www.forbes.com/sites/stephaniefillion/2021/01/26/2-years-later-what-we-can-learn-from-frances-anti-catcalling-law/.

    On Portugal: Laura Bates, "Portugal Has Made Street Harassment a Crime—Why Hasn't the UK?," *Guardian*, February 25, 2016.

    On the United Kingdom: Lewis, "'We Call It Getting Your Eye In'"; Emily Reynolds, "Criminalising Street Harassment Works. Britain Must Follow France's Lead," *Guardian*, May 2, 2019; Maya Tutton, "Street Harassment of Young Girls Should Not Be 'Normal.' I Won't Rest Until It Is Illegal," *Guardian*, October 10, 2019; Naomi Pike, "These Sisters Were Sick of Being Catcalled. Now They're Fighting to Make Street Harassment a Crime," *British Vogue*, September 8, 2020; Sophie Gallagher, "Staring on Public Transport: 'His Eyes Were Glued on Me,'" *BBC News*, April 29, 2022, www.bbc.com/news/uk-61263393; Sam Francis, "MPs Approve Plans to Make Street Sexual Harassment a Crime," *BBC News*, March 24, 2023, www.bbc.com/news/uk-politics-65065154; Hannah Walsh, "Street Harassment: Doubts New Law Will Change Behaviour," *BBC News*, July 22, 2023, www.bbc.com/news/uk-england-hampshire-65986394.

    On the United States: Christina Cauterucci, "Laws Banning Catcalling Won't Stop Street Harassment in France, the U.S., or Anywhere Else," *Slate*, August 3, 2018, https://slate.com/news-and-politics/2018/08/marie-laguerre-catcalling-video-laws-banning-street-harassment-wont-stop-the-practice-in-france-or-the-u-s.html; Mores, "When a Stranger Catcalls"; "Artist Tatyana Fazlalizadeh Wants You to Stop Telling Women to Smile," *1A*, National Public Radio, February 19, 2020, www.npr.org/2020/02/19/807407891/artist-tatyana-fazlalizadeh-wants-you-to-stop-telling-women-to-smile.

20. On Mexico: Rigoberto Hernandez, "'Stop Telling Women to Smile': Denouncing 'Jackals' and Catcalling in Mexico," NPR, February 10, 2015, www.npr.org/sections/codeswitch/2015/02/10/384994475/stop-telling-women-to-smile-denouncing-jackals-and-catcalling-in-mexico; Lauren Ferreira Cardoso, "Street Harassment Is a Public Health Problem: The Case of Mexico City," *The Conversation*, March 20, 2017, http://theconversation.com/street-harassment-is-a-public-health-problem-the-case-of-mexico-city-73962.

    On India: Bharucha and Khatri, "Sexual Street Harassment Battle"; Michael Safi, "India's Female Students Say 'To Hell with It, We Won't Stand for Molesting and Eve-Teasing,'" *Guardian*, October 7, 2017; Alisha Rahaman Sarkar, "Indian Court Says Calling Unknown Woman 'Darling' Is Sexual Harassment," *Independent* (UK), March 5, 2024.

21. Examples include Fileborn and Hardley, "'I'd Be in My School Uniform'"; Mills, *Street Harassment*; Iqbal, "Speaking Up"; McDonald, "Cat-Calls, Compliments and Coercion"; Kolysh, *Everyday Violence*; DelGreco and Christensen, "Effects of Street

Harassment"; Fazlalizadeh, *Stop Telling Women to Smile*; Mellgren et al., "'It Happens All the Time'"; Donnelly and Calogero, "Role of Stranger Harassment Experiences"; Flores, "Tweeting the Gendered City."

22. University of California San Diego Center on Gender Equity and Health and Stop Street Harassment, *Measuring #MeToo*. Hollaback! conducted a similar but less comprehensive study in 2015 with Cornell University. "ILR and Hollaback! Release Largest Analysis of Street Harassment to Date," ILR Worker Institute, June 1, 2015, www.ilr.cornell.edu/worker-institute/blog/reports/ilr-and-hollaback-release-largest-analysis-street-harassment-date.
23. National Academies of Sciences, Engineering, and Medicine, *Sexual Harassment of Women*, 25–29, 42–43.
24. National Academies of Sciences, Engineering, and Medicine, *Sexual Harassment of Women*, 32, 38.
25. "What Can Be Done to Rid the Palmer House Block of Mashers," *Chicago Daily Tribune*, February 4, 1906; Medea and Thompson, *Against Rape*, 49–50.
26. National Academies of Sciences, Engineering, and Medicine, *Sexual Harassment of Women*, 47.
27. Doree Lewak, "Hey, Ladies—Catcalls Are Flattering! Deal with It," *New York Post*, August 18, 2014.
28. The segment was met with protestations from anti–street harassment organizations, feminist publications, and other mainstream news outlets. Colin Campbell, "Fox News Hosts Defend Catcalling Women," *Business Insider*, August 28, 2014, www.businessinsider.com/fox-news-outnumbered-defend-catcalling-women-2014-8; Holly Kearl, "FOX News Is Wrong about Street Harassment," Stop Street Harassment, August 28, 2014, http://www.stopstreetharassment.org/2014/08/foxnews/.

    When the *10 Hours* video was released, a male host at Fox News reported on the video by "adding" his own catcall to the barrage hurled at Shohana Roberts. Kelsey McKinney, "Fox News Covered Street Harassment by Catcalling a Victim on the Air," *Vox*, October 30, 2014, www.vox.com/xpress/2014/10/30/7131613/fox-news-covered-street-harassment-and-it-was-exactly-as-awful-as.
29. "The Public Service Announcement Which Was in Part Shot Here in Times Square Is Meant to Give Viewers a Third Party Idea of What It's Like to See Street Harassment," *CBS This Morning*, produced by Norah O'Donnell and Vinita Nair, CBS, October 29, 2014, www.proquest.com/other-sources/public-service-announcement-which-was-part-shot/docview/1795833876/se-2?accountid=14751.
30. Benjamin Bailey, "Greetings and Compliments."
31. For recent examples, see Kate McQuarrie, "Stop Telling Me to Take the Compliment," *Daily Trojan*, January 9, 2024, https://dailytrojan.com/2024/01/09/stop-telling-me-to-take-the-compliment/; Madelyn Walthall, "Catcalling on Campus," Lomabeat.com, October 26, 2022, https://lomabeat.com/catcalling-on-campus/; Rebecca Meluch, "Catcalls Are Not Compliments," *The DePaulia*, December 22, 2019, https://depauliaonline.com/44982/opinions/opinion-catcalls-are-not-compliments/; and Brittany Soto, "Catcalling Is Not a Compliment, It's Harassment," UMKC Women's Center, May 2, 2019, https://info.umkc.edu/womenc/2019/05/02/catcalling-is-not-a-compliment-its-harassment/.

32. *I Catcalled Girls . . . Politely*, 2022, www.youtube.com/watch?v=V7cZPrEQHoo; Abby Connolly, "He's Been Out on the Street Doing What He Calls 'Polite Catcalling,' and His Compliments Are Kind and Hilarious," *Chip Chick*, May 12, 2023, www.chipchick.com/2023/05/hes-been-out-on-the-street-doing-what-he-calls-polite-catcalling-and-his-compliments-are-kind-and-hilarious.html; Georgia Aspinall, "Can 'Polite Catcalling' Ever Be a Thing?," *Grazia*, October 2, 2023, https://graziadaily.co.uk/life/tv-and-film/what-is-polite-catcalling-benedict-polizzi/.
33. This is beginning to change. See, for instance, Zahn et al., "Did Your Mum Not Hug You Enough?"; and Shoukat and Zaman, "Exploring Social Dimensions of Compulsive Staring."
34. Quinn, "Sexual Harassment and Masculinity."
35. Walton and Pedersen, "Motivations Behind Catcalling." A similar study used only victims' accounts to understand perpetrators' motivations for engaging in stranger intrusions. Hindes and Fileborn, "'Why Did He Do It?"
36. Fileborn and O'Neill, "From 'Ghettoization' to a Field of Its Own," 131. This remains true regardless of location and what constitutes marginalization or otherness in specific contexts.
37. This lack was identified as long ago as 2015 in Laura Logan's state of the field article. Logan, "Street Harassment."
38. Jessica Valenti, "Elliot Rodger's California Shooting Spree: Further Proof That Misogyny Kills," *Guardian,* May 25, 2014; Laurie Penny, "Let's Call the Isla Vista Killings What They Were: Misogynist Extremism," *New Statesman*, May 25, 2014; Katie McDonough, "Elliot Rodger's Fatal Menace: How Toxic Male Entitlement Devalues Women's and Men's Lives," *Salon*, May 25, 2014, www.salon.com/2014/05/25/elliot_rodgers_fatal_menace_how_toxic_male_entitlement_devalues_womens_and_mens_lives/.
39. Emphasis in original. Manne, *Down Girl*, 175.
40. Manne, *Down Girl*, 176.
41. Julie Bosman, "A College Student Was Killed by a Man Whose Catcalls She Tried to Ignore, Prosecutors Say," *New York Times*, November 27, 2019.

    As I was completing this book, news broke of another catcalling-related murder. In June 2024, James Bernard Johnson shot and killed forty-two-year-old Nikki Loffredo in Des Moines, Iowa. Johnson had shouted at Loffredo from his car and she told him to "fuck off." He told a Polk County jury he had fired at Loffredo because he felt disrespected. Johnson is Black and Loffredo was white. "Des Moines Man Convicted of First-Degree Murder in Shooting of Loffredo," PolkCountyIowa.gov, April 9, 2025, www.polkcountyiowa.gov/county-attorney/news/des-moines-man-convicted-of-first-degree-murder-in-shooting-of-loffredo/.
42. Srinivasan, *Right to Sex*.
43. "Policy Recommendations," Right to Be, accessed June 19, 2024, https://righttobe.org/guides/policy-recommendations/. See also Lizzie Crocker, "Street Harassment Shouldn't Be a Crime," *Daily Beast*, October 29, 2014, www.proquest.com/blogs-podcasts-websites/street-harassment-shouldnt-be-crime/docview/1649044377/se-2?accountid=14751.
44. Ellipses in original. Liz Elling, "On the Art of Girl Watching—Or, Phooey on the Guys," *Ann Arbor News*, October 2, 1972.

BIBLIOGRAPHY

Primary Sources

MANUSCRIPT COLLECTIONS

Archives of Michigan, Lansing, MI
    Detroit News Clipping Files
Bentley Historical Library, University of Michigan, Ann Arbor, MI
Chicago History Museum Research Center, Chicago, IL
    Chicago Women's Liberation Union Records
    Lea Taylor Papers
    Mary McDowell Settlement Records
    William E. Dever Papers
Library of Congress, Washington, DC
    National Association for the Advancement of Colored People (NAACP) Papers
    Veterans History Project
National Archives and Records Administration, College Park, MD
    Records of the Bureau of Medicine and Surgery, RG 52
    Records of the Office of Community War Services, RG 215
Newberry Library, Chicago, IL
    John T. McCutcheon Papers
New York City Municipal Archives, New York, NY
    Early Mayor Records
    New York County District Attorney Indictment Records
Sallie Bingham Center for Women's History and Culture, Duke University, Durham, NC
    Alix Kates Shulman Papers
    Jean Kilbourne Papers
    Meredith Tax Papers
    New York Radical Feminists Records
    Pauline Bart Papers
Schlesinger Library, Radcliffe Institute, Harvard University, Cambridge, MA
    Letters to *Ms.*, 1970–1998
    Letters to *Ms.*, 1972–1980
Social Welfare History Archives, University of Minnesota, Minneapolis, MN
    Project Girl Records
    Travelers Aid Association of America Records

Sophia Smith Collection, Smith College, Northampton, MA
Diana Russell Unprocessed Papers
Gloria Steinem Papers
National Congress of Neighborhood Women Records
Nkenge Touré Papers
Violence Against Women Collection
Women: A Journal of Liberation Records
University of Chicago, Department of Special Collections, Chicago, IL
Ernest W. Burgess Papers
University of Illinois Chicago, Special Collections and University Archives, Chicago, IL
Juvenile Protective Association Records
University of Michigan, Special Collections, Ann Arbor, MI
Labadie Pamphlet Collection
Walter P. Reuther Library, Wayne State University, Detroit, MI
Edith Van Horn Papers
Wisconsin Historical Society Archives, Madison, WI
Marlene Sanders Papers

NEWSPAPERS AND PERIODICALS

Aegis: Magazine on Ending Violence Against Women
Afro-American (Baltimore)
Albuquerque Evening Citizen
Albuquerque Morning Journal
Ann Arbor News
Arizona Republican
Arizona Sun
Arkansas State Press
Atlanta Constitution
Atlanta Daily World
Atlanta Journal and Constitution
Atlanta Journal-Constitution
Atlantic Monthly
Augusta Chronicle
Beadle's Weekly
Billboard
Bisbee (AZ) Daily Review
Bitch
Boston Chronicle
Boston Globe
Boxoffice
British Vogue
Broad Ax (Chicago)
Brooklyn Daily Eagle
Charlotte Observer
Chicago Daily News
Chicago Daily Tribune
Chicago Defender
Chicago Tribune
Christian Recorder (Philadelphia)
Christian Science Monitor
Cincinnati Daily Enquirer
Cleveland Call and Post
Cleveland Daily Herald
Cleveland Gazette
Collier's
Constitution (Middletown, CT)
Courier-Journal (Louisville)
Daily Capital Journal (Salem, OR)
Daily Gate City (Keokuk, IA)
Daily Inter Ocean (Chicago)
Daily News (Jacksonville, NC)
Daily Worker
Dallas Morning News
Day Book (Chicago)
Denison (IA) Review
Detroit Free Press

Detroit News
Duluth News-Tribune
Ebony
Evening Bulletin (Maysville, KY)
Evening News (San Jose)
Evening Public Ledger (Philadelphia, PA)
Evening Star (Washington, DC)
Evening Statesman (Walla Walla, WA)
Evening World (New York)
Fergus County (MT) Democrat
Flint Journal
Florence (AL) Times–Tri-Cities Daily
Fort Wayne News and Sentinel
Fort Worth Star-Telegram
Fort Worth Telegram
Frank Leslie's Illustrated Newspaper
Frederick Douglass' Paper
Freeman (Indianapolis)
Girl Watcher
Glamour
Globe and Mail (Toronto)
Godey's Lady's Book
Green Bay Semi-Weekly Gazette
Guardian (UK)
Harper's Weekly
Hawaiian Star
Huntsville (AL) Gazette
Independent (UK)
Independent Mechanic
Irish Times (Dublin)
Jackson (MS) Advocate
Jerusalem Post
Jet
Kentucky New Era (Hopkinsville)
Las Vegas Daily Gazette
Lewiston (ME) Daily Sun
Liberation
Liberator
Life
Los Angeles Herald
Los Angeles Sentinel
Los Angeles Times
Los Angeles Tribune
Majority Report
Manchester Guardian
Michigan Chronicle (Detroit)
Michigan Daily
Milwaukee Journal
Milwaukee Star
Minneapolis Tribune
Montreal Gazette
Morning Olympian (WA)
Morning Oregonian (Portland)
Ms.
Nashville Tennessean
National Anti-Slavery Standard
Negro Star
New Haven Register
New Iberia (LA) Enterprise and Independent Observer
New Journal and Guide (Norfolk, VA)
New Statesman
New York Amsterdam News
New York Herald
New York Post
New York Times
New-York Tribune
Norfolk Advertiser (Dedham, MA)
Off Our Backs
Ogden Standard
On the Issues
Oregonian (Portland)
Orlando Sentinel
Oshkosh Daily Northwestern
Ottumwa Tri-Weekly Courier
Palm Beach Post
People's Advocate
Philadelphia Tribune
Philadelphia Weekly
Pittsburgh City Paper
Pittsburgh Courier
Plain Dealer (Kansas City, KS)
Plaindealer (Detroit)
Puck
Rock Island Argus
San Francisco Chronicle
Sarasota Herald-Tribune
Sarasota Journal

Seattle Star
Sedalia (MO) Weekly Bazoo
Seventeen
South China Morning Post
Spokesman-Review (Spokane)
Star-Independent (Harrisburg, PA)
St. Louis Dispatch
St. Louis Post-Dispatch
St. Paul (MN) Daily Globe
Sun (Baltimore)
Sun (New York)
Sun Sentinel (Fort Lauderdale, FL)
Survey
Tacoma Times
Times-Picayune (New Orleans)
Times Pictorial (Dublin)
Toronto Daily Star
Trenton Evening Times
Trenton State Gazette
Tuscaloosa News
Vice
Victoria (TX) Advocate
Village Voice
Vogue
Washington Bee
Washington Post
Washington Standard
Washington Times
Wichita Daily Eagle
Wilkes-Barre (PA) Times-Leader
Wisconsin Democrat (Madison)
Woman's World
Women: A Journal of Liberation
Women's Health and Abortion Project Newsletter
Women's Press
Women's Wear Daily

PUBLISHED MATERIAL

Bengis, Ingrid. *Combat in the Erogenous Zone*. Alfred A. Knopf, 1972. Reprint, Harper-Perennial, 1991.

Bowen, Louise Hadduck Koven. *Safeguards for City Youth at Work and at Play*. Macmillan, 1914.

Brinkley, Mrs. Hugh L. *A Woman's Thoughts About Men*. New York: Derby Brothers, 1879.

Brown, Barbara May. "The Effects of Consciousness-Raising Group Participation on Stereotypic Interests, Behaviors, Self-Perceptions and Self-Actualization." PhD diss., Hofstra University, 1975.

Brown, Rita Mae. *A Plain Brown Rapper*. Diana Press, 1976.

Brownmiller, Susan. *Against Our Will: Men, Women, and Rape*. Simon and Schuster, 1975.

Buntline, Ned. *The Mysteries and Miseries of New York: A Story of Real Life*. New York: Bedford, 1848.

De Valcourt, Robert. *The Illustrated Manners Book: A Manual of Good Behavior and Polite Accomplishments*. New York: Leland Clay and Company, 1855.

Dickens, Charles. *Night Walks*. Penguin, 2010.

Dreiser, Theodore. *Sister Carrie*. Doubleday, Page, 1900.

The Easy Show Tunes Fake Book: 100 Songs in the Key of "C." Hal Leonard Corporation, 2007.

Eisenstaedt, Alfred, and Arthur Goldsmith. *The Eye of Eisenstaedt*. Viking, 1969.

Farrar, Mrs. John. *The Young Lady's Friend*. Boston, MA: American Stationers' Company, 1836.

Geng, Veronica. "Scorn Not the Street Compliment." In *The Cosmo Girl's Guide to the New Etiquette*. Wilshire Book Company, 1979.

Hartley, Cecil B. *The Gentlemen's Book of Etiquette and Manual of Politeness.* Boston: DeWolfe, Fiske & Co., 1875.

Hartley, Florence. *The Ladies' Book of Etiquette and Manual of Politeness.* Boston: J. S. Locke, 1876.

Haupt, Enid A. *The "Seventeen" Guide to Your Widening World.* Macmillan, 1965.

Henry, Aaron, and Constance Curry. *Aaron Henry: The Fire Ever Burning.* University Press of Mississippi, 2000.

Hillis, Marjorie. *Live Alone and Like It: A Guide for the Extra Woman.* Bobbs-Merrill, 1936.

Leonard, John William. *Woman's Who's Who of America: A Biographical Dictionary of Contemporary Women of the United States and Canada.* American Commonwealth, 1914.

Leonardo, Micaela di. "Political Economy of Street Harassment." *Aegis: Magazine on Ending Violence Against Women*, Summer 1981, 51–57.

Longstreet, Abby Buchanan. *Social Etiquette of New York.* New York: D. Appleton, 1879.

Louis, S. L. *Decorum: A Practical Treatise on Etiquette and Dress of the Best American Society.* New York: Union, 1882.

Martin, Edward Winslow. *The Secrets of the Great City: A Work Descriptive of the Virtues and the Vices, the Mysteries, Miseries and Crimes of New York City.* Philadelphia: Jones Brothers, 1868.

Martine, Arthur. *Martine's Book of Etiquette and Guide to True Politeness.* New York: Dick & Fitzgerald, 1866.

McCabe, James Dabney. *Lights and Shadows of New York Life: Or, the Sights and Sensations of a Great City.* Philadelphia: National Publishing, 1872.

Medea, Andra, and Kathleen Thompson. *Against Rape.* Farrar, Straus and Giroux, 1974.

Morgan, Henry. *Boston Inside Out! Sins of a Great City!* Boston: Shawmut, 1883.

Morgan, Robin, ed. *Sisterhood Is Powerful: An Anthology of Writings from the Women's Liberation Movement.* Vintage Books, 1970.

Morris, Clara. *Life on the Stage: My Personal Experiences and Recollections.* Phillips, 1901.

Moser, Gustav von. *On Change.* New York: Samuel French, 1885.

O'Neill, Rose. *The Story of Rose O'Neill: An Autobiography.* Edited by Miriam Forman-Brunell. University of Missouri Press, 2022.

Potter, Eliza. *A Hairdresser's Experience in High Life.* Edited by Xiomara Santamarina. Cincinnati: Ricky and Mallory, 1859. Reprint, University of North Carolina Press, 2009.

Ruth, John A. *Decorum: A Practical Treatise on Etiquette and Dress of the Best American Society.* Chicago: J. A. Ruth, 1878.

Sauers, Donald J. *The Girl Watcher's Guide.* Harper, 1954.

The Sixteenth Annual Report of the Illinois Farmers' Institute. Illinois Farmers' Institute, 1911.

Smith, Matthew Hale. *Sunshine and Shadow in New York.* Hartford: J. B. Burr, 1868.

Terkel, Studs. *"The Good War": An American Oral History of World War II.* Phoenix, 2001.

Thornwell, Emily. *The Lady's Guide to Perfect Gentility.* New York: Derby & Jackson, 1856.

Truth, Sojourner, and Olive Gilbert. *Narrative of Sojourner Truth.* Boston, 1875.

Wells, Ida B. *Crusade for Justice: The Autobiography of Ida B. Wells.* Edited by Alfreda M. Duster. University of Chicago Press, 2013.

Wells, Richard A. *Manners, Culture and Dress of the Best American Society*. Omaha: Clark Publishing, 1891.

Wells, Samuel R. *How to Behave: A Pocket Manual of Republican Etiquette, and Guide to Correct Personal Habits*. New York: Fowler and Wells, 1856.

Wells-Barnett, Ida B. *A Red Record: Tabulated Statistics and Alleged Causes of Lynchings in the United States*. Chicago: Donohue & Henneberry, 1895.

White, Walter Francis, and Thurgood Marshall. *What Caused the Detroit Riot? An Analysis*. National Association for the Advancement of Colored People, 1943.

Whitman, Walt. *Leaves of Grass*. New York: W. E. Chapin, 1867.

Secondary Sources

Agyepong, Tera Eva. *The Criminalization of Black Children: Race, Gender, and Delinquency in Chicago's Juvenile Justice System, 1899–1945*. University of North Carolina Press, 2018.

Allen, Robert Clyde. *Horrible Prettiness: Burlesque and American Culture*. University of North Carolina Press, 1991.

Anderson, Devery S. *Emmett Till: The Murder That Shocked the World and Propelled the Civil Rights Movement*. University Press of Mississippi, 2015.

Anderson, Elijah. *The Cosmopolitan Canopy: Race and Civility in Everyday Life*. W. W. Norton, 2011.

Armstrong, Lynzi. "'Who's the Slut, Who's the Whore?': Street Harassment in the Workplace Among Female Sex Workers in New Zealand." *Feminist Criminology* 11, no. 3 (2016): 285–303.

Autry, Robyn, and Daniel J. Walkowitz. "Editors' Introduction: Undoing the Flaneur." *Radical History Review*, no. 114 (Fall 2012): 1–5.

Ayres, Melanie M., Carly K. Friedman, and Campbell Leaper. "Individual and Situational Factors Related to Young Women's Likelihood of Confronting Sexism in Their Everyday Lives." *Sex Roles* 61, no. 7 (2009): 449–60.

Bailey, Benjamin. "Greetings and Compliments or Street Harassment? Competing Evaluations of Street Remarks in a Recorded Collection." *Discourse & Society* 28, no. 4 (2017): 353–73.

Bailey, Beth L. *From Front Porch to Back Seat: Courtship in Twentieth-Century America*. Johns Hopkins University Press, 1988.

Baker, Carrie N. *The Women's Movement Against Sexual Harassment*. Cambridge University Press, 2008.

Baldwin, Peter C. *In the Watches of the Night: Life in the Nocturnal City, 1820–1930*. University of Chicago Press, 2012.

Baptist, Joyce, and Katelyn Coburn. "Harassment in Public Spaces: The Intrusion on Personal Space." *Journal of Feminist Family Therapy* 31, no. 2–3 (2019): 114–28.

Beck, Jerry. *The 50 Greatest Cartoons: As Selected by 1,000 Animation Professionals*. JG Press, 1998.

Bederman, Gail. *Manliness and Civilization: A Cultural History of Gender and Race in the United States, 1880–1917*. University of Chicago Press, 1995.

Benard, Cheryl, and Edit Schlaffer. "The Man in the Street: Why He Harasses." In *Feminist*

Frameworks: Alternative Theoretical Accounts of the Relations Between Women and Men, edited by Alison M. Jaggar and Paula S. Rothenberg. McGraw-Hill, 1984.

Benjaminson, Peter. *The Life and Times of Betty Boop: The 100-Year History of an Animated Icon*. Applause Theatre and Cinema Books, 2023.

Berebitsky, Julie. *Sex and the Office: A History of Gender, Power, and Desire*. Yale University Press, 2012.

Berrey, Stephen A. *The Jim Crow Routine: Everyday Performances of Race, Civil Rights, and Segregation in Mississippi*. University of North Carolina Press, 2015.

Berry, Mary Frances. "'Reckless Eyeballing': The Matt Ingram Case and the Denial of African American Sexual Freedom." *Journal of African American History* 93, no. 2 (2008): 223–34.

Bérubé, Allan. *Coming Out Under Fire: The History of Gay Men and Women in World War Two*. Free Press, 1990.

Bharucha, Jehangir, and Rita Khatri. "The Sexual Street Harassment Battle: Perceptions of Women in Urban India." *Journal of Adult Protection* 20, no. 2 (2018): 101–9.

Blair, Cynthia M. *I've Got to Make My Livin': Black Women's Sex Work in Turn-of-the-Century Chicago*. University of Chicago Press, 2010.

Blair, Karen J. *The Clubwoman as Feminist: True Womanhood Redefined, 1868–1914*. Holmes & Meier, 1980.

Block, Sharon. *Rape and Sexual Power in Early America*. University of North Carolina Press, 2006.

Blower, Brooke L. "V-J Day, 1945, Times Square." In *The Familiar Made Strange: American Icons and Artifacts After the Transnational Turn*, edited by Brooke L. Blower and Mark Philip Bradley. Cornell University Press, 2015.

Bowman, Cynthia Grant. "Street Harassment and the Informal Ghettoization of Women." *Harvard Law Review* 106, no. 3 (1993): 517–80.

Brawley, Sean, and Chris Dixon. "Searching for Dorothy Lamour: War and Sex in the South Pacific, 1941–45." *Australasian Journal of American Studies* 18, no. 1 (1999): 3–18.

Breward, Christopher. *The Suit: Form, Function and Style*. Reaktion Books, 2016.

Bronson, Fred. *The Billboard Book of Number One Hits*. Billboard Books, 2003.

Bronstein, Carolyn. *Battling Pornography: The American Feminist Anti-Pornography Movement, 1976–1986*. Cambridge University Press, 2011.

Brown, Elspeth H. *Work! A Queer History of Modeling*. Duke University Press, 2019.

Brown, Ira V. "Racism and Sexism: The Case of Pennsylvania Hall." *Phylon* 37, no. 2 (1976): 126–36.

Brumberg, Joan Jacobs. *The Body Project: An Intimate History of American Girls*. Vintage, 1998.

Bunch-Lyons, Beverly A. *Contested Terrain: African American Women Migrate from the South to Cincinnati, 1900–1950*. Routledge, 2014.

Bundgaard, Axel. *Muscle and Manliness: The Rise of Sport in American Boarding Schools*. Syracuse University Press, 2005.

Burke, Tarana. *Unbound: My Story of Liberation and the Birth of the Me Too Movement*. Flatiron Books, 2021.

Bush, William S. *Who Gets a Childhood? Race and Juvenile Justice in Twentieth-Century Texas*. University of Georgia Press, 2010.

Canaday, Margot. *The Straight State: Sexuality and Citizenship in Twentieth-Century America*. Princeton University Press, 2009.

Carby, Hazel V. "Policing the Black Woman's Body in an Urban Context." *Critical Inquiry* 18, no. 4 (1992): 738–55.

Chapple, Reginald. "From Central Avenue to Leimert Park: The Shifting Center of Black Los Angeles." In *Black Los Angeles: American Dreams and Racial Realities*, edited by Darnell Hunt and Ana-Christina Ramón. New York University Press, 2010.

Chauncey, George. *Gay New York: Gender, Urban Culture, and the Making of the Gay Male World, 1890–1940*. Basic Books, 1995.

Chhun, Bunkosal. "Catcalls: Protected Speech or Fighting Words?" *Thomas Jefferson Law Review* 33, no. 2 (2011): 273–95.

Clement, Elizabeth Alice. *Love for Sale: Courting, Treating, and Prostitution in New York City, 1900–1945*. University of North Carolina Press, 2006.

Cobb, Jasmine Nichole. *Picture Freedom: Remaking Black Visuality in the Early Nineteenth Century*. New York University Press, 2015.

Cohen, Karl F. *Forbidden Animation: Censored Cartoons and Blacklisted Animators in America*. McFarland, 2004.

Cohen, Lizabeth. *A Consumers' Republic: The Politics of Mass Consumption in Postwar America*. Knopf, 2003.

Coleman, Willie. "Black Women and Segregated Public Transportation: Ninety Years of Resistance." *Negro History Bulletin* 63, no. 1–4 (2000): 17–22.

Connell, Raewyn. *Gender and Power: Society, the Person and Sexual Politics*. Stanford University Press, 1987.

Connell, R. W., and James W. Messerschmidt. "Hegemonic Masculinity: Rethinking the Concept." *Gender and Society* 19, no. 6 (2005): 829–59.

Cook, Kevin. *Kitty Genovese: The Murder, the Bystanders, the Crime That Changed America*. W. W. Norton, 2014.

Cooke, Sheryl. "Street Remarks: A Cross Cultural Study." *Language Matters* 30, no. 1 (1999): 171–96.

Cooper, Brittney C. *Beyond Respectability: The Intellectual Thought of Race Women*. University of Illinois Press, 2017.

Crouch, Margaret. "Sexual Harassment in Public Places." *Social Philosophy Today* 25 (2009): 137–48.

Cuordileone, K. A. *Manhood and American Political Culture in the Cold War*. Routledge, 2005.

Dabel, Jane E. *A Respectable Woman: The Public Roles of African American Women in 19th-Century New York*. New York University Press, 2008.

Davis, Deirdre. "Harm That Has No Name: Street Harassment, Embodiment, and African American Women." *UCLA Women's Law Journal* 4, no. 2 (1994): 133–78.

Davis, Hugh. *"We Will Be Satisfied with Nothing Less": The African American Struggle for Equal Rights in the North During Reconstruction*. Cornell University Press, 2011.

Davis, Rebecca L. *Fierce Desires: A New History of Sex and Sexuality in America*. W. W. Norton, 2024.

Davis, Rebecca L., and Michele Mitchell, eds. *Heterosexual Histories*. New York University Press, 2021.

Delegard, Kirsten. "Contested Geography: The Campaign Against Pornography and the Battle for Urban Space in Minneapolis." In *U.S. Women's History: Untangling the Threads of Sisterhood*, edited by Leslie Brown, Jacqueline Castledine, and Anne Valk. Rutgers University Press, 2017.

DelGreco, Maria, and John Christensen. "Effects of Street Harassment on Anxiety, Depression, and Sleep Quality of College Women." *Sex Roles* 82 (April 2020): 473–81.

D'Emilio, John. *Sexual Politics, Sexual Communities: The Making of a Homosexual Minority in the United States, 1940–1970*. 2nd ed. University of Chicago Press, 1998.

D'Emilio, John, and Estelle B. Freedman. *Intimate Matters: A History of Sexuality in America*. 3rd ed. University of Chicago Press, 2012.

Denning, Michael. *Cover Stories: Narrative and Ideology in the British Spy Thriller*. Routledge and Kegan Paul, 1987.

Deutsch, Sarah. *Women and the City: Gender, Space, and Power in Boston, 1870–1940*. Oxford University Press, 2000.

Domosh, Mona, and Joni Seager. *Putting Women in Place: Feminist Geographers Make Sense of the World*. Guilford Press, 2001.

Donnelly, Lois C., and Rachel M. Calogero. "The Role of Stranger Harassment Experiences in College Women's Perceived Possibility of Gender Crimes Happening to Them." *Journal of Applied Social Psychology* 48, no. 3 (2018): 165–73.

Dorr, Lisa Lindquist. *White Women, Rape, and the Power of Race in Virginia, 1900–1960*. University of North Carolina Press, 2004.

Dowling, William C. *Oliver Wendell Holmes in Paris: Medicine, Theology, and the Autocrat of the Breakfast Table*. University of New Hampshire Press, 2006.

Dunbar, Erica Armstrong. *A Fragile Freedom: African American Women and Emancipation in the Antebellum City*. Yale University Press, 2008.

Eaves, Shannon. *Sexual Violence and American Slavery: The Making of a Rape Culture in the Antebellum South*. University of North Carolina Press, 2024.

Enstad, Nan. *Ladies of Labor, Girls of Adventure: Working Women, Popular Culture, and Labor Politics at the Turn of the Twentieth Century*. Columbia University Press, 1999.

Ervin, Keona K. *Gateway to Equality: Black Women and the Struggle for Economic Justice in St. Louis*. University Press of Kentucky, 2017.

Estes, Steve. *I Am a Man! Race, Manhood, and the Civil Rights Movement*. University of North Carolina Press, 2005.

Evans, Sara M. *Born for Liberty: A History of Women in America*. Simon and Schuster, 1997.

Fairchild, Kimberly. "Understanding Street Harassment as Gendered Violence: Past, Present, and Future." *Sexuality & Culture* 27, no. 3 (2023): 1140–59.

Fairchild, Kimberly, and Laurie A. Rudman. "Everyday Stranger Harassment and Women's Objectification." *Social Justice Research* 21, no. 3 (2008): 338–57.

Faludi, Susan. *Backlash: The Undeclared War Against American Women*. Crown, 1991.

Farrell, Amy Erdman. *Yours in Sisterhood: "Ms." Magazine and the Promise of Popular Feminism*. University of North Carolina Press, 1998.

Fazlalizadeh, Tatyana. *Stop Telling Women to Smile: Stories of Street Harassment and How We're Taking Back Our Power*. Seal Press, 2019.

Feimster, Crystal Nicole. *Southern Horrors: Women and the Politics of Rape and Lynching*. Harvard University Press, 2011.

Fileborn, Bianca. "'I Actually Snapped': Conceptualizing Resistance to Street Harassment as Feminist Snap and Erosion." *Gender & Society* 39, no. 4 (2025): 535–60.

Fileborn, Bianca, and Jess Hardley. "'I'd Be in My School Uniform': The Informal Curriculum of Street Harassment." *Gender and Education* 35, no. 4 (2023): 330–47.

Fileborn, Bianca, and Tully O'Neill. "From 'Ghettoization' to a Field of Its Own: A Comprehensive Review of Street Harassment Research." *Trauma, Violence, & Abuse* 24, no. 1 (2023): 125–38.

Fileborn, Bianca, and F. Vera-Gray. "'I Want to Be Able to Walk the Street Without Fear': Transforming Justice for Street Harassment." *Feminist Legal Studies* 25, no. 2 (2017): 203–27.

Fischer, Anne Gray. *The Streets Belong to Us: Sex, Race, and Police Power from Segregation to Gentrification*. University of North Carolina Press, 2022.

Fischer, Mia. "#Free_CeCe: The Material Convergence of Social Media Activism." *Feminist Media Studies* 16, no. 5 (2016): 755–71.

Flanagan, Maureen. *Constructing the Patriarchal City: Gender and the Built Environments of London, Dublin, Toronto, and Chicago, 1870s into the 1940s*. Temple University Press, 2018.

Flanagan, Maureen. "Gender and Urban Political Reform: The City Club and the Woman's City Club of Chicago in the Progressive Era." *American Historical Review* 95, no. 4 (1990): 1032–50.

Fleetwood, Jennifer. "Everyday Self-Defence: Hollaback Narratives, Habitus and Resisting Street Harassment." *British Journal of Sociology* 70, no. 5 (2019): 1709–29.

Fleming, Patrick. "On Street Harassment (or Why It Can Be Wrong to Be Friendly to Strangers)." *International Journal of Applied Philosophy* 32, no. 2 (2018): 231–41.

Flores, Nina. "Tweeting the Gendered City: Analysis of Harassment, Reflections on Justice." *Journal of Critical Thought and Praxis* 6, no. 3 (2017): 115–27.

Foner, Philip S. "The Battle to End Discrimination Against Negroes on Philadelphia Streetcars: (Part I) Background and Beginning of the Battle." *Pennsylvania History: A Journal of Mid-Atlantic Studies* 40, no. 3 (1973): 260–90.

Foner, Philip S. *U.S. Labor and the Vietnam War*. International Publishers, 1989.

Fraterrigo, Elizabeth. *"Playboy" and the Making of the Good Life in Modern America*. Oxford University Press, 2009.

Freedman, Estelle B. *Redefining Rape: Sexual Violence in the Era of Suffrage and Segregation*. Harvard University Press, 2013.

Freeman, Joshua B. "Hardhats: Construction Workers, Manliness, and the 1970 Pro-War Demonstrations." *Journal of Social History* 26, no. 4 (1993): 725–44.

Furia, Philip, and Michael L. Lasser. *America's Songs: The Stories Behind the Songs of Broadway, Hollywood, and Tin Pan Alley*. Taylor & Francis, 2006.

Gallo, Marcia M. *"No One Helped": Kitty Genovese, New York City, and the Myth of Urban Apathy*. Cornell University Press, 2015.

Gardner, Carol Brooks. *Passing By: Gender and Public Harassment*. University of California Press, 1995.

Garland-Thomson, Rosemarie. *Staring: How We Look*. Oxford University Press, 2009.

Gendzel, Glen. "What the Progressives Had in Common." *Journal of the Gilded Age and Progressive Era* 10, no. 3 (2011): 331–39.

Gerbner, George. *The Dynamics of Cultural Resistance*. Oxford University Press, 1978.
Gere, Anne Ruggles. *Intimate Practices: Literacy and Cultural Work in U.S. Women's Clubs, 1880–1920*. University of Illinois Press, 1997.
Gilfoyle, Timothy J. *City of Eros: New York City, Prostitution, and the Commercialization of Sex, 1790–1920*. W. W. Norton, 1992.
Goffman, Erving. *Behavior in Public Places: Notes on the Social Organization of Gatherings*. Free Press, 1966.
Goffman, Erving. *The Presentation of Self in Everyday Life*. Doubleday, 1959.
Goldberg, David A., and Trevor Griffey. *Black Power at Work: Community Control, Affirmative Action, and the Construction Industry*. Cornell University Press, 2011.
Goluboff, Risa Lauren. *Vagrant Nation: Police Power, Constitutional Change, and the Making of the 1960s*. Oxford University Press, 2016.
Goodman, James. *Stories of Scottsboro*. Vintage Books, 1995.
Gray, Katherine Jorgensen. "Mixed Company: Elite Youth and Heterosociability in Philadelphia, 1750–1815." PhD diss., Johns Hopkins University, 2011.
Greene, Christina. *Free Joan Little: The Politics of Race, Sexual Violence, and Imprisonment*. University of North Carolina Press, 2022.
Greene, Jane M. "A Proper Dash of Spice: Screwball Comedy and the Production Code." *Journal of Film and Video* 63, no. 3 (2011): 45–63.
Griffin, Ben. "Hegemonic Masculinity as a Historical Problem." *Gender & History* 30, no. 2 (2018): 377–400.
Guariglia, Matthew. *Police and the Empire City: Race and the Origins of Modern Policing in New York*. Duke University Press, 2023.
Guglielmo, Thomas A. *White on Arrival: Italians, Race, Color, and Power in Chicago, 1890–1945*. Oxford University Press, 2004.
Halttunen, Karen. *Confidence Men and Painted Women: A Study of Middle-Class Culture in America, 1830–1870*. Yale University Press, 1982.
Heap, Chad C. *Slumming: Sexual and Racial Encounters in American Nightlife, 1885–1940*. University of Chicago Press, 2009.
Hegarty, Marilyn E. *Victory Girls, Khaki-Wackies, and Patriotutes: The Regulation of Female Sexuality During World War II*. New York University Press, 2008.
Hernández, Kelly Lytle. *City of Inmates: Conquest, Rebellion, and the Rise of Human Caging in Los Angeles, 1771–1965*. University of North Carolina Press, 2017.
Herrera, Jennifer, and Bill McCarthy. "Street Harassment Interpretations: An Exploration of the Intersection of Gender and Race/Ethnicity, and Mediator Variables." *Violence Against Women* 29, no. 3–4 (2023): 453–74.
Hickey, Georgina. *Breaking the Gender Code: Women and Urban Public Space in the Twentieth Century United States*. University of Texas Press, 2023.
Hickey, Georgina. "The Geography of Pornography: Neighborhood Feminism and the Battle against 'Dirty Bookstores' in Minneapolis." *Frontiers: A Journal of Women Studies* 32, no. 1 (2011): 125–51.
Hicks, Cheryl D. *Talk with You Like a Woman: African American Women, Justice, and Reform in New York, 1890–1935*. University of North Carolina Press, 2010.
Hill, Marilynn Wood. *Their Sisters' Keepers: Prostitution in New York City, 1830–1870*. University of California Press, 1993.

Hiltner, Aaron. *Taking Leave, Taking Liberties: American Troops on the World War II Home Front*. University of Chicago Press, 2020.

Hindes, Sophie, and Bianca Fileborn. "'Why Did He Do It? Because He's a Fucking Bloke': Victim Insights into the Perpetration of Street Harassment." *British Journal of Criminology* 63, no. 3 (2023): 668–86.

Hine, Darlene Clark. "Rape and the Inner Lives of Black Women in the Middle West: Preliminary Thoughts on the Culture of Dissemblance." *Signs* 14, no. 4 (1989): 912–20.

Hinton, Elizabeth. *From the War on Poverty to the War on Crime: The Making of Mass Incarceration in America*. Harvard University Press, 2016.

Hodes, Martha Elizabeth. *White Women, Black Men: Illicit Sex in the Nineteenth-Century South*. Yale University Press, 1997.

Hoganson, Kristin L. *Fighting for American Manhood: How Gender Politics Provoked the Spanish-American and Philippine-American Wars*. Yale University Press, 1998.

hooks, bell. *Writing Beyond Race: Living Theory and Practice*. Routledge, 2013.

Horgan, Mervyn. "Urban Interaction Ritual: Strangership, Civil Inattention and Everyday Incivilities in Public Space." *Pragmatics* 30, no. 1 (2019): 116–41.

Hubbs, Nadine. *The Queer Composition of America's Sound: Gay Modernists, American Music, and National Identity*. University of California Press, 2004.

Hutson, Ashley Colleen Feely, and Julie Christine Krueger. "The Harasser's Toolbox: Investigating the Role of Mobility in Street Harassment." *Violence Against Women* 25, no. 7 (2019): 767–91.

Hyers, Lauri L. "Resisting Prejudice Every Day: Exploring Women's Assertive Responses to Anti-Black Racism, Anti-Semitism, Heterosexism, and Sexism." *Sex Roles* 56, no. 1 (2007): 1–12.

Iqbal, Yeshim. "Speaking Up Versus Standing One's Ground: The Role of Women's Social Networks in Confronting Street Harassment." *Journal of Community & Applied Social Psychology* 33, no. 2 (2023): 469–82.

Isenberg, Nancy. *White Trash: The 400-Year Untold History of Class in America*. Penguin, 2016.

Jacobson, Matthew Frye. *Whiteness of a Different Color: European Immigrants and the Alchemy of Race*. Harvard University Press, 1999.

Jacquet, Catherine O. "Fighting Back, Claiming Power: Feminist Rhetoric and Resistance to Rape in the 1970s." *Radical History Review*, no. 126 (October 2016): 71–83.

Jacquet, Catherine O. *The Injustices of Rape: How Activists Responded to Sexual Violence, 1950–1980*. University of North Carolina Press, 2019.

Johnson, David K. *The Lavender Scare: The Cold War Persecution of Gays and Lesbians in the Federal Government*. University of Chicago Press, 2004.

Johnson, Marilynn S. "Gender, Race, and Rumours: Re-Examining the 1943 Race Riots." *Gender & History* 10, no. 2 (1998): 252–77.

Jones, Martha S. *All Bound Up Together: The Woman Question in African American Public Culture, 1830–1900*. University of North Carolina Press, 2007.

Jones, Martha S. *Vanguard: How Black Women Broke Barriers, Won the Vote, and Insisted on Equality for All*. Basic Books, 2020.

Kasson, John F. *Rudeness and Civility: Manners in Nineteenth-Century Urban America*. Hill & Wang, 1990.
Kelley, Blair L. M. *Right to Ride: Streetcar Boycotts and African American Citizenship in the Era of Plessy v. Ferguson*. University of North Carolina Press, 2010.
Kelley, Robin D. G. *Race Rebels: Culture, Politics, and the Black Working Class*. Free Press, 1994.
Kelly, Liz. *Surviving Sexual Violence*. University of Minnesota Press, 1988.
Kern, Leslie. *Feminist City: A Field Guide*. Between the Lines, 2019.
Kissling, Elizabeth Arveda, and Cheris Kramarae. "Stranger Compliments: The Interpretation of Street Remarks." *Women's Studies in Communication* 14, no. 1 (1991): 75–93.
Knupfer, Anne Meis. *Toward a Tenderer Humanity and a Nobler Womanhood: African American Women's Clubs in Turn-of-the-Century Chicago*. New York University Press, 1996.
Kolysh, Simone. *Everyday Violence: The Public Harassment of Women and LGBTQ People*. Rutgers University Press, 2021.
Krinitsky, Nora C. "The Politics of Crime Control: Race, Policing, and Reform in Twentieth-Century Chicago." PhD diss., University of Michigan, 2017.
Kuhn, Annette. *Women's Pictures: Feminism and Cinema*. Verso, 1994.
Langlois, Janet L. "The Belle Isle Bridge Incident: Legend Dialectic and Semiotic System in the 1943 Detroit Race Riots." *Journal of American Folklore* 96, no. 380 (1983): 183–99.
Laniya, Olatokunbo Olukemi. "Street Smut: Gender, Media, and the Legal Power Dynamics of Street Harassment, to 'Hey Sexy' and Other Verbal Ejaculations." *Columbia Journal of Gender and the Law* 14, no. 1 (2005): 91–130.
Larkin, June. "Sexual Terrorism on the Street: The Moulding of Young Women into Subordination." In *Sexual Harassment: Contemporary Feminist Perspectives*, edited by Alison M. Thomas and Celia Kitzinger. Open University Press, 1997.
Lemire, Elise Virginia. *"Miscegenation": Making Race in America*. University of Pennsylvania Press, 2002.
Lenton, Rhonda, Michael D. Smith, John Fox, and Norman Morra. "Sexual Harassment in Public Places: Experiences of Canadian Women." *Canadian Review of Sociology and Anthropology* 36, no. 4 (1999): 517–40.
Leskinen, Emily A., Lilia M. Cortina, and Dana B. Kabat. "Gender Harassment: Broadening Our Understanding of Sex-Based Harassment at Work." *Law and Human Behavior* 35, no. 1 (2011): 25–39.
Levy, Peter B. *The Great Uprising: Race Riots in Urban America During the 1960s*. Cambridge University Press, 2018.
Lewis, Sian. "'We Call It Getting Your Eye In': Policing Sexual Harassment on the London Underground Through the Lens of Haraway's Situated Knowledges and Cyborgs." *British Journal of Criminology* 63, no. 5 (2023): 1129–45.
Littauer, Amanda H. *Bad Girls: Young Women, Sex, and Rebellion Before the Sixties*. University of North Carolina Press, 2015.
Lockyer, Sharon, and Heather Savigny. "Rape Jokes Aren't Funny: The Mainstreaming of Rape Jokes in Contemporary Newspaper Discourse." *Feminist Media Studies* 20, no. 3 (2020): 434–49.

Logan, Laura S. "Street Harassment: Current and Promising Avenues for Researchers and Activists." *Sociology Compass* 9, no. 3 (2015): 196–211.

Love, Joanna. *Soda Goes Pop: Pepsi-Cola Advertising and Popular Music.* University of Michigan Press, 2019.

Manne, Kate. *Down Girl: The Logic of Misogyny.* Oxford University Press, 2018.

Marinari, Maddalena. *Unwanted: Italian and Jewish Mobilization Against Restrictive Immigration Laws, 1882–1965.* University of North Carolina Press, 2019.

May, Elaine Tyler. *Homeward Bound: American Families in the Cold War Era.* Basic Books, 1988.

May, Stephen J. *Michener's South Pacific.* University Press of Florida, 2011.

McCurn, Alexis S. "'I Am Not a Prostitute': How Young Black Women Challenge Street-Based Micro-Interactional Assaults." *Sociological Focus* 50, no. 1 (2017): 52–65.

McDonald, Lucy. "Cat-Calls, Compliments and Coercion." *Pacific Philosophical Quarterly* 103, no. 1 (2022): 208–30.

McGuire, Danielle L. *At the Dark End of the Street: Black Women, Rape, and Resistance—a New History of the Civil Rights Movement from Rosa Parks to the Rise of Black Power.* Alfred A. Knopf, 2010.

McGuire, Danielle L. "'It Was Like All of Us Had Been Raped': Sexual Violence, Community Mobilization, and the African American Freedom Struggle." *Journal of American History* 91, no. 3 (2004): 906–31.

Mellgren, Caroline, Mika Andersson, and Anna-Karin Ivert. "'It Happens All the Time': Women's Experiences and Normalization of Sexual Harassment in Public Space." *Women & Criminal Justice* 28, no. 4 (2018): 262–81.

Messerschmidt, James W. *Hegemonic Masculinity: Formulation, Reformulation, and Amplification.* Rowman & Littlefield, 2018.

Meyerowitz, Joanne J. *Women Adrift: Independent Wage Earners in Chicago, 1880–1930.* University of Chicago Press, 1988.

Mills, Melinda A. *Street Harassment as Everyday Violence.* Lexington Books, 2022.

Mitchell, Michele. *Righteous Propagation: African Americans and the Politics of Racial Destiny After Reconstruction.* University of North Carolina Press, 2004.

Mores, Chandler L. "When a Stranger Catcalls: The Need for Street Harassment Remedies in Iowa." *Iowa Law Review* 106, no. 2 (2021): 971–1006.

Morgan, Jennifer L. *Laboring Women: Reproduction and Gender in New World Slavery.* University of Pennsylvania Press, 2004.

Morris-Crowther, Jayne. *The Political Activities of Detroit Clubwomen in the 1920s: A Challenge and a Promise.* Wayne State University Press, 2013.

Muhammad, Khalil Gibran. *The Condemnation of Blackness: Race, Crime, and the Making of Modern Urban America.* Harvard University Press, 2010.

Mulvey, Laura. "Visual Pleasure and Narrative Cinema." In *Feminism and Film Theory,* edited by Constance Penley. Routledge, 1988.

Mumford, Kevin J. *Interzones: Black/White Sex Districts in Chicago and New York in the Early Twentieth Century.* Columbia University Press, 1997.

Murphy, Kevin P. *Political Manhood: Red Bloods, Mollycoddles, and the Politics of Progressive Era Reform.* Columbia University Press, 2010.

National Academies of Sciences, Engineering, and Medicine. *Sexual Harassment of Women: Climate, Culture, and Consequences in Academic Sciences, Engineering, and Medicine.* National Academies Press, 2018.

Nevius, Michelle, and James Nevius. *Inside the Apple: A Streetwise History of New York City.* Simon and Schuster, 2009.

Nielsen, Laura Beth. "The Power of 'Place': Public Space and Rights Consciousness." In *The New Civil Rights Research: A Constitutive Approach*, edited by Benjamin Fleury-Steiner and Laura Beth Nielsen. Ashgate, 2006.

Nielsen, Laura Beth. "Situating Legal Consciousness: Experiences and Attitudes of Ordinary Citizens About Law and Street Harassment." *Law & Society Review* 34, no. 4 (2000): 1055–90.

Odem, Mary E. *Delinquent Daughters: Protecting and Policing Adolescent Female Sexuality in the United States, 1885–1920.* University of North Carolina Press, 1995.

Ohmann, Richard M. *Selling Culture: Magazines, Markets, and Class at the Turn of the Century.* Verso, 1996.

Oppenheimer, Jerry. *Front Row: Anna Wintour: The Cool Life and Hot Times of "Vogue"'s Editor-in-Chief.* Macmillan, 2005.

Pascoe, C. J., and Tristan Bridges. "Exploring Masculinities: History, Reproduction, Hegemony, and Dislocation." In *Exploring Masculinities: Identity, Inequality, Continuity, and Change.* Oxford University Press, 2016.

Peiss, Kathy Lee. *Cheap Amusements: Working Women and Leisure in New York City, 1880 to 1920.* Temple University Press, 1986.

Place-Verghnes, Floriane. *Tex Avery: A Unique Legacy.* Indiana University Press, 2006.

Pliley, Jessica R. *Policing Sexuality: The Mann Act and the Making of the FBI.* Harvard University Press, 2014.

Pryor, Elizabeth Stordeur. *Colored Travelers: Mobility and the Fight for Citizenship Before the Civil War.* University of North Carolina Press, 2016.

Pyke, Karen D. "Class-Based Masculinities: The Interdependence of Gender, Class, and Interpersonal Power." *Gender and Society* 10, no. 5 (1996): 527–49.

Quinn, Beth. "Sexual Harassment and Masculinity: The Power and Meaning of 'Girl Watching.'" In *The Gendered Society Reader*, edited by Michael S. Kimmel and Amy Aronson. Oxford University Press, 2008.

Rabinovitz, Lauren. *For the Love of Pleasure: Women, Movies, and Culture in Turn-of-the-Century Chicago.* Rutgers University Press, 1998.

Radway, Janice A. *A Feeling for Books: The Book-of-the-Month Club, Literary Taste, and Middle-Class Desire.* University of North Carolina Press, 1997.

Remus, Emily. *A Shoppers' Paradise: How the Ladies of Chicago Claimed Power and Pleasure in the New Downtown.* Harvard University Press, 2019.

Renfro, Paul M. *Stranger Danger: Family Values, Childhood, and the American Carceral State.* Oxford University Press, 2020.

Reynolds, Keisa. "Never Silent: Evolution of Black Women's Anti-Rape Organizing, 1965–1985." MA thesis, Loyola University Chicago, 2018.

Roess, Roger P., and Gene Sansone. *The Wheels That Drove New York: A History of the New York City Transit System.* Springer Science & Business Media, 2012.

Rosen, Hannah. *Terror in the Heart of Freedom: Citizenship, Sexual Violence, and the Meaning of Race in the Postemancipation South*. University of North Carolina Press, 2009.

Rosenthal, A. M. *Thirty-Eight Witnesses: The Kitty Genovese Case*. University of California Press, 1999.

Roth, Benita. *Separate Roads to Feminism: Black, Chicana, and White Feminist Movements in America's Second Wave*. Cambridge University Press, 2004.

Rotundo, E. Anthony. *American Manhood: Transformations in Masculinity from the Revolution to the Modern Era*. Basic Books, 1993.

Rouse, Wendy L. *Her Own Hero: The Origins of the Women's Self-Defense Movement*. New York University Press, 2017.

Rubin, Gayle. "The Traffic in Women: Notes on the 'Political Economy' of Sex." In *Feminism and History*, edited by Joan Wallach Scott. Oxford University Press, 1996.

Ryan, Mary P. *Women in Public: Between Banners and Ballots, 1825–1880*. Johns Hopkins University Press, 1990.

Scholz, Sally J. "Catcalls and Military Strategy." In *Peacemaking: Lessons from the Past, Visions for the Future*, edited by Sally J. Scholz and Judith Presler. Rodopi, 2000.

Schweik, Susan M. *The Ugly Laws: Disability in Public*. New York University Press, 2010.

Scobey, David. "Nymphs and Satyrs: Sex and the Bourgeois Public Sphere in Victorian New York." *Winterthur Portfolio* 37, no. 1 (2002): 43–66.

Scutts, Joanna. *The Extra Woman: How Marjorie Hillis Led a Generation of Women to Live Alone and Like It*. Liveright, 2018.

Sedgwick, Eve Kosofsky. *Between Men: English Literature and Male Homosocial Desire*. Columbia University Press, 2015.

Sewell, Jessica Ellen. *Women and the Everyday City: Public Space in San Francisco, 1890–1915*. University of Minnesota Press, 2011.

Shantz, J. "'They Think Their Fannies Are as Good as Ours': The 1943 Detroit Riot." *Studies in the Literary Imagination* 40, no. 2 (2007): 75–92.

Sherry, Michael S. *Gay Artists in Modern American Culture: An Imagined Conspiracy*. University of North Carolina Press, 2007.

Shoukat, Hajra, and Sahira Zaman. "Exploring Social Dimensions of Compulsive Staring Behavior Among Men in the Light of Gender Schema Theory." *Human Nature Journal of Social Sciences* 6, no. 2 (2025): 95–104.

Silkey, Sarah. *Black Woman Reformer: Ida B. Wells, Lynching, and Transatlantic Activism*. University of Georgia Press, 2015.

Simmons, LaKisha Michelle. *Crescent City Girls: The Lives of Young Black Women in Segregated New Orleans*. University of North Carolina Press, 2015.

Smoodin, Eric. *Animating Culture: Hollywood Cartoons from the Sound Era*. Rutgers University Press, 1993.

Sommerville, Diane Miller. *Rape and Race in the Nineteenth-Century South*. University of North Carolina Press, 2005.

Srebnick, Amy Gilman. *The Mysterious Death of Mary Rogers: Sex and Culture in Nineteenth-Century New York*. Oxford University Press, 1995.

Srinivasan, Amia. *The Right to Sex: Feminism in the Twenty-First Century*. Farrar, Straus and Giroux, 2021.

Stansell, Christine. *City of Women: Sex and Class in New York, 1789–1860*. Knopf, 1986.

Starr, Paul. *The Creation of the Media: Political Origins of Modern Communications.* Basic Books, 2004.

Suddler, Carl. *Presumed Criminal: Black Youth and the Justice System in Postwar New York.* New York University Press, 2019.

Sugrue, Thomas J. "Affirmative Action from Below: Civil Rights, the Building Trades, and the Politics of Racial Equality in the Urban North, 1945–1969." *Journal of American History* 91, no. 1 (2004): 145–73.

Sugrue, Thomas J. *The Origins of the Urban Crisis: Race and Inequality in Postwar Detroit.* Princeton University Press, 2014.

Summers, Martin Anthony. *Manliness and Its Discontents: The Black Middle Class and the Transformation of Masculinity, 1900–1930.* University of North Carolina Press, 2004.

Syrett, Nicholas L. *The Company He Keeps: A History of White College Fraternities.* University of North Carolina Press, 2009.

Thompson, Becky. "Multiracial Feminism: Recasting the Chronology of Second Wave Feminism." *Feminist Studies* 28, no. 2 (2002): 337–60.

Thompson, Deborah M. "Woman in the Street: Reclaiming the Public Space from Sexual Harassment." *Yale Journal of Law and Feminism* 6, no. 2 (1994): 313–48.

Tuerkheimer, Deborah. "Street Harassment as Sexual Subordination: The Phenomenology of Gender-Specific Harm." *Wisconsin Women's Law Journal* 12, no. 2 (1997): 167–206.

Tyson, Timothy B. *The Blood of Emmett Till.* Simon and Schuster, 2017.

University of California San Diego Center on Gender Equity and Health and Stop Street Harassment. *Measuring #MeToo: A National Study on Sexual Harassment and Sexual Assault.* April 2019. https://drive.google.com/file/d/14U6Ik54id5DSEREX-dKLA0BfxeHDN3c2/view.

Valk, Anne M. *Radical Sisters: Second-Wave Feminism and Black Liberation in Washington, D.C.* University of Illinois Press, 2010.

Valk, Anne M. "Take Back the Night and the Public Memory of Feminism." In *U.S. Women's History: Untangling the Threads of Sisterhood*, edited by Leslie Brown, Jacqueline Castledine, and Anne Valk. Rutgers University Press, 2017.

Vera-Gray, Fiona. *Men's Intrusion, Women's Embodiment: A Critical Analysis of Street Harassment.* Routledge, 2017.

Vera-Gray, Fiona. *The Right Amount of Panic: How Women Trade Freedom for Safety in Public Space.* Policy Press, 2018.

Vera-Gray, Fiona, and Liz Kelly. "Contested Gendered Space: Public Sexual Harassment and Women's Safety Work." *International Journal of Comparative and Applied Criminal Justice* 44, no. 4 (2020): 265–75.

Walkowitz, Judith R. *City of Dreadful Delight: Narratives of Sexual Danger in Late-Victorian London.* University of Chicago Press, 1992.

Walkowitz, Judith R. "Going Public: Shopping, Street Harassment, and Streetwalking in Late Victorian London." *Representations* 62 (Spring 1998): 1–30.

Wallace, Aurora. "The Geography of Girl Watching in Postwar Montreal." *Space and Culture* 10, no. 3 (2007): 349–68.

Wallace, Aurora. "Girl Watching at Expo 67." In *Expo 67: Not Just a Souvenir*, edited by Rhona Richman Kenneally and Johanne Sloan. University of Toronto Press, 2010.

Walton, Kari A., and Cory L. Pedersen. "Motivations Behind Catcalling: Exploring Men's

Engagement in Street Harassment Behavior." *Psychology & Sexuality* 13, no. 3 (2022): 689–703.

Welter, Barbara. "The Cult of True Womanhood: 1820–1860." *American Quarterly* 18, no. 2 (1966): 151–74.

Whitburn, Joel. *The Billboard Book of Top 40 Hits*. Billboard Publications, 1985.

Whitfield, Stephen J. *A Death in the Delta: The Story of Emmett Till*. Johns Hopkins University Press, 1991.

Wilson, Elizabeth. *Contradictions of Culture: Cities, Culture, Women*. Sage, 2000.

Wilson, Elizabeth. *The Sphinx in the City: Urban Life, the Control of Disorder, and Women*. University of California Press, 1992.

Winchell, Meghan K. *Good Girls, Good Food, Good Fun: The Story of USO Hostesses During World War II*. University of North Carolina Press, 2008.

Wise, Sue, and Liz Stanley. *Georgie Porgie: Sexual Harassment in Everyday Life*. Pandora, 1987.

Wolcott, Victoria W. "Gendered Perspectives on Detroit History." *Michigan Historical Review* 27, no. 1 (2001): 75–91.

Wolcott, Victoria W. *Remaking Respectability: African American Women in Interwar Detroit*. University of North Carolina Press, 2001.

Wood, Sharon E. *The Freedom of the Streets: Work, Citizenship, and Sexuality in a Gilded Age City*. University of North Carolina Press, 2005.

Zahn, Alina, Florian Hutzler, and Sarah Schuster. "Did Your Mum Not Hug You Enough? The Effects of Attachment Experience and Callous-Unemotional Traits on Catcalling Behavior in Men." *Violence Against Women*, July 28, 2025. doi: 10.1177/10778012251362216.

Zipes, Jack. *The Trials and Tribulations of Little Red Riding Hood*. Routledge, 2017.

INDEX

Please note that page numbers in italics indicate illustrations.